Why Do You Need This New Edition?

If you're wondering why you should buy this new edition of *Connections: Writing, Reading, and Critical Thinking,* here are 10 good reasons!

❶ The third edition introduces the **paragraph writing process** in Chapter 1, providing you with a solid foundation at the start of your college term.

❷ **New readings** on contemporary issues will challenge your critical reading skills and will lead to lively class discussions. Media multitasking, the USA Patriot Act, and the hands-free cell phone debate are among the issues you'll explore.

❸ **New writing assignments** on topics such as surveillance technology and electronic badges/IDs for children will fuel debate, foster critical thinking, and lead to analytical writing.

❹ An **enhanced study skills section** includes information on taking notes, managing time effectively, understanding your learning style, selecting a good tutor, and writing and revising on the computer.

❺ New to this edition—Style Tips! A section on style appears at the end of Chapters 3 through 9, providing techniques for moving beyond grammar rules toward writing clearer, more concise, and varied sentences.

❻ Poetry, song lyrics, and fiction excerpts are integrated into the body of the chapters and provide alternate approaches and varied interpretations to contemporary topics.

❼ A **timed writing chapter** presents assignments to sharpen existing writing skills and techniques for writing under pressure.

❽ **Expanded sentence work** provides more opportunities for practice and practical application in your writing.

❾ And now—use *Connections* alongside Pearson's unique **MyWritingLab** (www.mywritinglab.com) and find a world of resources developed specifically for you!

❿ *Connections* will assist you in achieving your collegiate and workplace goals by providing you with the tools and practice needed to take your **reading, writing, and critical thinking skills** to the next level.

PEARSON
Longman

Connections

Writing, Reading, and Critical Thinking

Third Edition

Tammy Montgomery
Folsom Lake College

Megan C. Rainey
Cosumnes River College

PEARSON
Longman

New York • San Francisco • Boston
London • Toronto • Sydney • Tokyo • Singapore • Madrid
Mexico City • Munich • Paris • Cape Town • Hong Kong • Montreal

Acquisitions Editor: Matthew Wright
Marketing Manager: Thomas DeMarco
Senior Supplements Editor: Donna Campion
Development Editor: Janice Wiggins-Clarke
Production Manager: Stacey Kulig
Project Coordination, Text Design, and Electronic Page Makeup: Nesbitt Graphics, Inc.
Cover Design Manager: John Callahan
Cover Image: Matthias Kulka/Masterfile
Photo Researcher: Rebecca Karamehmedovic
Senior Manufacturing Buyer: Roy Pickering
Printer and Binder: Edwards Brothers, Inc.
Cover Printer: Phoenix Color Graphics

For permission to use copyrighted material, grateful acknowledgment is made to the copyright holders on pp. 546–548, which are hereby made part of this copyright page.

Library of Congress Cataloging-in-Publication Data

Boeck, Tammy.
  Connections : writing, reading, and critical thinking / Tammy Montgomery,
Megan C. Rainey. -- 3rd ed.
      p. cm.
  Includes bibliographical references and index.
  ISBN-13: 978-0-205-60733-4
  ISBN-10: 0-205-60733-0
  1. English language--Rhetoric. 2. Critical thinking--Problems, exercises,
etc. 3. Report writing--Problems, exercises, etc. 4. College readers. I.
Rainey, Megan. II. Title.
  PE1408.B573 2008
  808'.0427--dc22
                              2008020800

Please visit us at www.ablongman.com

ISBN 13: 978-0-205-60733-4
ISBN 10: 0-205-60733-0

2 3 4 5 6 7 8 9 10—EB—11 10 09

Contents

Readings by Theme

Television and the Media

Surveillance Technology

Contemplation

Preface for Instructors

Welcome to the third edition of *Connections!* Whether new to the text or a veteran of an earlier edition, you'll find *Connections* packed with a number of exciting features—all designed to provoke student thought and empower student writing.

A few years have passed since the release of the second edition of *Connections.* During this period, we've reexamined our approach to basic skills development in light of our experiences with student writers. These experiences have led us to rethink and revise portions of the text. We've also added several new features, some in response to our experiences with students and others in response to requests by instructors using the text. But please don't worry if you're used to an earlier edition. We've maintained the essential structural elements and features of the earlier editions. At the same time, you'll find that many of the chapters in the third edition have been reworked. Where appropriate, we've added new readings and writing assignments, updated sentence work, and created more opportunities for students to exercise their writing, reading, and critical thinking skills.

So what's new to the third edition of *Connections?*

- *Students dig into the writing process sooner.* In Chapter 1, students engage the writing, reading, and critical thinking processes immediately as they preview the elements of these processes and practice writing the academic paragraph.

- *Reading and writing assignments have been enhanced.* Assignments from earlier editions have been evaluated and updated, deleted, or replaced. A number of new assignments focusing on contemporary issues such as media multitasking replace assignments in earlier editions.

- *All readings are fully integrated into the chapters* of the text (as opposed to some being relegated to a "supplemental readings" section) to stimulate discussion and idea generation.

- *"Writing the in-class essay" is now featured in a chapter.*

- *Poetry, song lyrics, and fiction excerpts have been woven into the body chapters* to attract interest, provoke discussion, and challenge student thought.

- *Style Tips in Chapters 3 through 9 teach students techniques for writing clearer, more concise, and varied sentences.*

- *Enhanced skills sections focus on mastery learning.*

The third edition of *Connections* continues to promote writing, reading, and critical thinking as interrelated skills. Because proficiency in these skills is expected of college students, *Connections* introduces students to effective processes for developing their skills and achieving collegiate-level proficiency in reading and writing. Although more traditional writing texts often separate writing, reading, and critical thinking tasks and ask students to practice them in isolation, our experience continues to reinforce the theory that real progress in student writing occurs only when these processes are *connected*.

Instructors who use this text will find the support they require to engage student interest and guide students through chapters that integrate critical reading and thinking skills, writing skills, and sentence work. Section I of *Connections* covers the processes and skills essential to success in college. In Chapter 1, students engage in the writing, reading, and critical thinking processes and apply them in a set of paragraph assignments. In Chapters 2 through 4, students learn and practice effective processes for critical reading, summary writing, and essay writing. Then in Section II, students practice their reading and writing processes as they complete progressively more challenging reading and essay writing assignments. Paragraphs are taught in the context of essay preparation. Sentence work is taught within the context of the paragraph. Thus, no time is wasted trying to get students to apply to their writing what they learned in drill and exercise work. With *Connections,* students engage in authentic essay assignments while learning about paragraphs, focus, development, organization, analysis, and sentence clarity.

The result: Developmental writers too often marginalized in the college classroom join the ranks of their fellow students, wrestling meaning out of challenging texts, providing support for their opinions, and constructing well-developed essays that respond to the issues raised.

GOALS OF THIS TEXT

Because basic writing students are often enrolled in courses requiring essays and reports, they are anxious to understand the structure of and the processes for producing effective academic writing. In other words, they seek an authentic college-level approach to improving their writing skills. *Connections* provides such an approach.

Sharpen Study Skills   For students to succeed in college, they must take notes, organize their work, seek tutorial help, use computers, understand the features of their textbooks, and use dictionaries. The third edition of *Connections* provides a review of these basic study skills in the section "Mastering Your Study Skills."

Engage Students as Participants in College   The thematic approach to each chapter in *Connections*—along with journal assignments, discussion questions, activities, readings, critical thinking questions, and writing assignments—fosters an empowering learning environment. Through the repeated reading and writing processes used in *Connections,* students learn to approach a subject critically and from an academic perspective. They also learn the value of others' points of view. As a result, students find themselves participants in a collective learning process.

Cultivate Critical Reading and Thinking Skills   Although *Connections* is a writing text with a writing emphasis, critical reading and thinking are major components. Better readers and thinkers are also better writers. Students who use *Connections* will learn how to approach their readings (through an effective *process* in which they preview, anticipate, read and reread, think about, and summarize their readings) in order to wrestle meaning out of difficult texts. They will also analyze audience, purpose, development, focus, organization, and effective sentence structure in their readings, and then apply newly discovered strategies to their own writing.

Develop Writing Skills   *Connections* emphasizes the writing process as key to generating meaningful text. Researchers such as Mina Shaughnessy (see "Beyond the Sentence" in *Errors and Expectations*) have shown that as inexperienced writers learn an effective process for completing writing assignments, they are able to create essays with improved focus, development, organization, and clarity. Individual elements (e.g., topic sentences) and skills (e.g., focus) must be taught and studied, but all the practicing and studying should be done within authentic writing tasks.

In working toward these goals, students will develop a clear sense of the process writers follow to achieve coherence and clarity. Even the sentence work is woven into the writing process. The grammar exercises connect in topic to the themes of the chapters, and the exercises prepare students for the unique sentence challenges each writing assignment brings.

CONTENT OVERVIEW

A resource for student writers, the third edition of *Connections* provides tools and support in five sections of instruction. While promoting a progression of skill development, the text is designed to be flexible. Instructors can select from chapters or segments of chapters that address their students' particular needs. In the *Instructor's Manual,* sample syllabi provide detailed plans for the chapters and assignments.

Section I Establishes the Writing-Reading-Critical Thinking Connection
Chapter 1 introduces the writing-reading-critical thinking connection and reviews the academic paragraph. A set of assignments focused on writing in the workplace offers students the opportunity to practice their paragraph writing skills.

Because students will encounter a variety of texts in college, Chapter 2 introduces the unique characteristics of academic and journalistic writing and teaches students how to summarize both types of text. Chapter 3 explores the PARTS of the reading process: **Preview, Anticipate, Read and Reread, Think Critically About,** and **Summarize.** Developing an effective essay writing process is the focus of Chapter 4, which takes students through the recursive process that leads from discovery to drafting, revising, and editing.

Sentence work (appearing at the end of each chapter) encourages students to develop sentence skills within the context of their own writing and reinforces each chapter's focus and theme. In Chapters 1 through 4, students will review sentence basics: verbs, subjects, clauses and phrases. Beginning in Chapter 3, a segment called Style Tips appears at the end of each chapter as a supplement to sentence work. While learning to construct grammatically correct sentences, students will also practice writing clearer, more concise, varied sentences.

Section II Develops the Writing-Reading-Critical Thinking Connection

Emphasizing a discrete writing skill per chapter—focus, development, organization, and analysis—Chapters 5 through 9 teach students how to construct coherent, unified paragraphs and essays. In each chapter, students engage in discussions, activities, and readings that lead directly to writing assignments. They investigate heroes in Chapter 5, then examine *focus* in their writing as they select particular heroes and *focus* on their heroic qualities in their essays. They weigh the pros and cons of television and the media in Chapter 6 and focus on *development* in their writing. In Chapter 7, students explore the effects of new forms of surveillance technology while developing their *organizational* skills. In Chapter 8, they *analyze* and write about music lyrics and poetry. Finally, in Chapter 9, students apply all they have learned to writing the in-class essay.

Sentence work continues to appear at the end of each chapter and to connect to thematic content. In these chapters, however, the sentence work moves beyond the basics, focusing sometimes on the unique rhetorical challenges that come with each writing assignment and at other times focusing more generally on complex sentence patterns. In Chapter 5, for example, students review pronouns and parallelism, for the assignment on heroes calls for students to rely on pronouns and create descriptions. Since Chapter 6 offers students a challenging argumentative essay, the sentence work helps students learn to use subordinators, concessions, and transitions effectively. Chapters 7 through 8 offer the most challenging reading and writing assignments in *Connections* and, similarly, the sentence work challenges students to create complex sentences by embedding phrases and joining clauses.

Style Tips continues to support sentence work. Extending through Chapter 9, the tips focus on achieving sentence variety, enhancing sentences through detail and description, and avoiding common errors.

Section III Offers Instruction on Mastering Study Skills
Designed to supplement reading and writing instruction, this section contains chapters on cultivating study skills, enhancing basic skills, and using outside sources. The chapters can be assigned to individuals needing extra help or to the entire class. Students learn how to take notes and organize a notebook, find and work with a tutor, and write and revise on the computer. In "Discovering Your Learning Style," students find out how they learn best and how to use

study skills that complement their own styles. Mini-chapters—"Using the Dictionary," "Building Your Vocabulary," "Spelling Matters," and "Reading Aloud"—offer instruction and reinforcement activities that lead to increased vocabulary as well as stronger reading and writing skills. In "Using Outside Sources," students learn how to integrate quotations and cite sources in their essays as they write.

Section IV Addresses the Most Common Sentence Errors and Teaches Students How to Correct and Then Avoid Them   Students will follow a process for understanding and correcting common sentence errors. Through completing the exercises in this section, students will learn to recognize, correct, and avoid verb form, verb tense, and subject-verb agreement errors. In addition, they will learn to recognize, correct, and avoid fragments, run-ons, and comma splices.

Section V Contains Easy Reference Charts for Review   At a glance, students have access to a list of right-word choices, capitalization rules, punctuation rules, and Style Tips.

FEATURES

The following features of *Connections* support students' development as writers and contribute to their writing success in college and the workplace:

Academic Focus   Students engage in the kinds of critical reading and writing activities—summarizing, discussing, and analyzing—they'll encounter in other college classes and at work.

Flexibility   Five distinct sections and nine distinct chapters allow instructors to select writing instruction according to skill level and subject matter.

Chapter Preview Pages   Main topics for each chapter appear highlighted on each opening page of Chapters 1 through 9, providing an instant overview of the chapter and preparing students to engage with the chapter.

Writing Skills Support   Students engage in a step-by-step writing process. Journal assignments, prereading questions, readings, questions for critical thought, and workshop activities assist students in moving from the discovery phase through the brainstorming, drafting, revising, and editing phases of this process. Students are encouraged throughout the text to take advantage of tutorial assistance and their school's computer or writing lab.

Reading Skills Support   Students are taught effective reading strategies through the PARTS of the reading process—Preview, Anticipate, Read and

Reread, Think Critically About, and Summarize. Prereading activities appear at the beginning of most readings, with questions for critical thought following the readings. Also, glossed vocabulary words appear at the beginning of readings in Chapters 1 and 2 as students develop their dictionary skills.

Writing Assignments Linked to Readings   Students read, analyze, and summarize articles from magazines and newspapers, textbook excerpts, song lyrics, poems, and essays as they consider and develop their own perspectives on the issues presented.

Level-Appropriate, High-Interest Multicultural Readings   Readings from academic and other sources reflect contemporary issues and diverse opinions on issues such as writing in the workplace, the characteristics of a hero, the effects of television and the media, the impact of new surveillance technologies on citizens' privacy, and more. Representing a variety of styles and sources, these pieces vary in length and difficulty.

Integrated Sentence Skills Support   Sentence work connects to each chapter's theme and readings. In "Your Own Writing," students create new sentences and apply instruction to current writing assignments.

Opportunities for Collaboration   Activities, journal assignments, discussion questions, and draft workshops provide ample opportunities for group discussion and collaboration and help students recognize the value of establishing a writing community.

Student Writing Samples   Examples of successful student writing appear throughout the text.

In-Class Writing Support   A chapter on writing in class teaches students how to read a prompt, budget time, outline, draft, revise, and edit under pressure. Writing the argumentative essay in class is emphasized.

Style Tips   Promoting sentence clarity, conciseness, and variety, Style Tips appears at the end of Chapters 3 through 9 as a supplement to sentence work. These tips help students become more aware of the functions of grammar and the relationships between sentence parts. Practice exercises encourage students to use this knowledge in creating clearer sentences.

Coverage of Study Skills   Section III offers instruction in taking notes, keeping a notebook, working with a tutor, and using computers. In addition, it includes instruction in using the dictionary, building vocabulary, spelling, reading aloud, and using outside sources.

Learning Styles   In "Discovering Your Learning Style," also in Section III, students find out how they learn best and how to use study skills that complement their individual styles. The activities throughout *Connections* actively engage visual, auditory, tactile, and kinesthetic learners.

"Using Outside Sources"   This unique chapter gives students basic instruction in integrating sources, using quotations, and citing source information in their writing.

Easy Reference Rules and Style Tips   Easy-to-read charts help students check punctuation rules, capitalization rules, right-word choices, and Style Tips.

Glossary   Definitions for terms appearing in bold throughout the text are listed for easy reference in the Glossary.

THE OTHER TEXTS IN THIS SERIES

Connections is the second text in a three-book developmental writing series.

Book One, *Expressions*, is for students three levels below freshman composition. Books at this level are traditionally created as sentence-to-paragraph books. *Expressions*, however, is built on the same premise as *Connections*: Developmental writers learn best when reading, writing, and critical thinking tasks are woven together. *Expressions* initiates the developmental writer into the world of college by offering a survey of different types of written expression (diaries, letters, academic paragraphs, autobiographies, fairy tales, and academic essays). As students study the readings, they build their awareness of purpose, audience, and style. The writing assignments, then, offer students opportunities to write academic paragraphs in response to the readings or to practice the genres themselves. Because *Expressions* is meant to prepare students for the kind of work found in *Connections*, *Expressions* devotes significant time to study skills, vocabulary building, and sentence work. Unique features include Skill Spotlights (on subjects such as brainstorming and making your writing interesting with detail), Sentence Style activities that draw sentences from the readings, and Computer Notes.

Book Three in this series, *Interpretations*, is for the advanced developmental writer. This essay-level writing text challenges students to read, write, and think critically as it prepares them for entry into freshman composition. Students will spend significant time studying, summarizing, and interpreting current controversial issues in their reading and writing assignments. In addition, they will gain experience in writing in the humanities as they interpret literature and film. Finally, reading, writing, and critical thinking work relates to corresponding sentence-level work. Not only will students practice traditional punctuation and usage in their writing, but they will also develop the ability to integrate a variety of sentence structures to make their writing more interesting and effective.

TEACHING AND LEARNING PACKAGE

The Instructor's Manual

The *Instructor's Manual* offers an updated discussion of the underlying pedagogy and an overview of features in *Connections*. The manual also offers diagnostic materials, sample syllabi, in-class writing assignments, sentence work answers, and chapter-by-chapter support materials: chapter previews, preparation suggestions, overhead transparencies for class discussion activities, brainstorming and support activities, and a detailed, day-to-day lesson plan for one or two major assignments per chapter. For ordering, the ISBN is 0-205-61645-3.

In addition to the *Instructor's Manual,* many other skills-based supplements are available for both instructors and students. For more information about additional supplements, please contact your local Pearson sales representative.

Electronic and Online Offerings

MyWritingLab, Where Better Practice Makes Better Writers   MyWriting-Lab is an online writing practice system that offers better practice to make better writers for college and life. The mastery-based format allows multiple attempts so students can learn from mistakes and build a solid foundation of writing principles. MyWritingLab offers:

- *Progressive Learning Exercises.* The exercises move from literal comprehension to critical application to demonstrating concepts in actual writing. This progressive learning process helps to transfer the skills into writing.
- *Easy Planning.* Based on the book chosen for the course and the work done in MyWritingLab, the system will generate an easy-to-use Study Plan to guide writing success.
- *A Comprehensive Exercises Program.* The 9,000 exercises include grammar, paragraph development, essay development, and research.
- *Diagnostic Testing.* A comprehensive diagnostic assesses students' understanding of grammar and reflects the areas where help is needed most.
- *Easy Progress Tracking.* My Gradebook enables students to monitor and track work done in MyWritingLab.
- *Valuable Additional Resources.* Other resources for students in MyWritingLab include access to our English Tutor Center, the interactive Study Skills Website, and *Research Navigator.*

Visit www.mywritinglab.com for more information and a video walkthrough.

MyWritingLab and Your Course: Integration

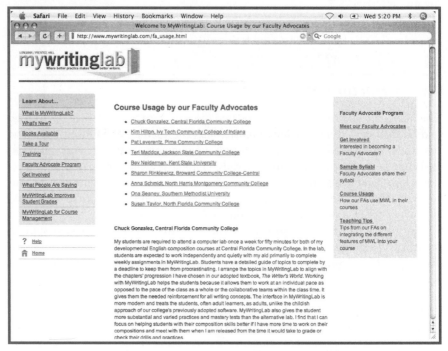

MyWritingLab is incredibly flexible and can be used in several useful ways in your classroom. Students can use it to focus on their individual areas of weakness, or the instructor can choose the MWL course that matches the table of contents of the Pearson textbook used in the course.

To find out how other instructors have integrated MyWritingLab into their course, visit our Faculty Advocate page on our website at **www.mywritinglab .com/facultyadvocates.html**. There you will find teaching tips, their syllabi with MyWritingLab integrated, and more!

Here is what some of the Faculty Advocates themselves have to say . . .

In order to avoid slowing the whole class down, I have found it very useful to assign elements of MWL to those students who are having particular ESL difficulties other students are not experiencing. MWL has also helped in reinforcing comments I make on students' papers.

—Ona Seaney, Southern Methodist University

We use the Watch feature in class as we study select areas of grammar and editing and engage in discussion to clarify with examples and verbal explanations. Some practices are then assigned to the whole class, but much of the value of MyWritingLab is its accessibility to students for individualized grammar and editing exercises. After each final paper is graded, I assign each student a MyWritingLab topic to practice based on needs assessed from the graded paper.

—Pat Leverentz, Pima Community College

MyWritingLab and Your Course: Assessment

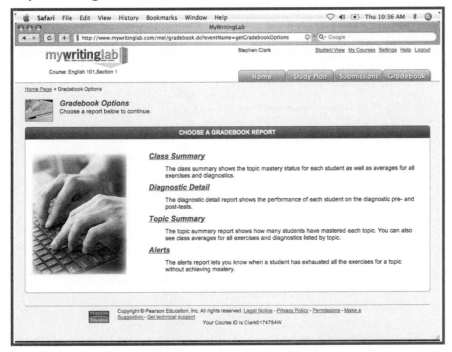

Comprehensive, detailed reporting provides both instructors and students with progress tracking for the skill work in MyWritingLab. At a glance, an instructor can see details such as student mastery, individual progress, time on task, topic averages, diagnostic details, alerts to indicate students who are struggling, and more!

Pearson Tutor Services:
With MyWritingLab, students receive complimentary access to Pearson Tutor Services, powered by SMARTTHINKING, Inc. Students can submit a specified number of papers or essays each semester to Smartthinking's highly qualified e-structors,™ who provide detailed feedback on how to improve the essay. Feedback is usually returned within 24 hours.

MyWritingLab and Your Course: Students Find It Useful

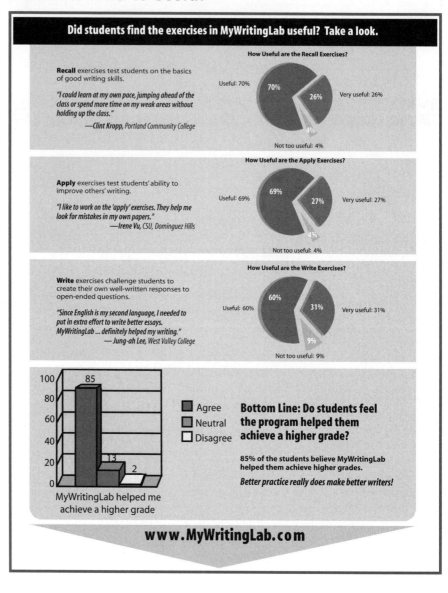

Did students find the exercises in MyWritingLab useful? Take a look.

Recall exercises test students on the basics of good writing skills.

"I could learn at my own pace, jumping ahead of the class or spend more time on my weak areas without holding up the class."

—*Clint Kropp, Portland Community College*

How Useful are the Recall Exercises?
Useful: 70% — 70%
Very useful: 26% — 26%
Not too useful: 4% — 4%

Apply exercises test students' ability to improve others' writing.

"I like to work on the 'apply' exercises. They help me look for mistakes in my own papers."

—*Irene Vu, CSU, Dominguez Hills*

How Useful are the Apply Exercises?
Useful: 69% — 69%
Very useful: 27% — 27%
Not too useful: 4% — 4%

Write exercises challenge students to create their own well-written responses to open-ended questions.

"Since English is my second language, I needed to put in extra effort to write better essays. MyWritingLab ... definitely helped my writing."

—*Jung-ah Lee, West Valley College*

How Useful are the Write Exercises?
Useful: 60% — 60%
Very useful: 31% — 31%
Not too useful: 9% — 9%

MyWritingLab helped me achieve a higher grade
- 85 Agree
- 13 Neutral
- 2 Disagree

Bottom Line: Do students feel the program helped them achieve a higher grade?

85% of the students believe MyWritingLab helped them achieve higher grades.

Better practice really does make better writers!

www.MyWritingLab.com

MyWritingLab and Your Course: The Basics

LONGMAN / PRENTICE HALL
mywritinglab ™
Where better practice makes better writers.

Results Show that Students Overwhelmingly Support MyWritingLab

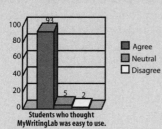

■ Agree
■ Neutral
□ Disagree

Students who thought MyWritingLab was easy to use.

What do students think of MyWritingLab?

A recent survey of 531 students who used MyWritingLab for at least one semester (3/2007) revealed extremely positive results. The graph at left shows how easy students found the system to use.

What is MyWritingLab?

MyWritingLab from Pearson Education is the first online learning system built from the ground up to help low-literacy learners improve their writing skills. MyWritingLab combines established pedagogy with an easy-to-use online platform.

The Pedagogy

- **Diagnostics:** MyWritingLab first diagnoses students on their writing strengths and weaknesses.

- **Study Plan:** The diagnostics lead to a Study Plan that is unique to each student. The Study Plan provides access to the exercises students need to work on to improve their skills.

- **Step-by-Step Exercises:** A team of educators created exercises — Recall, Apply, and Write — to challenge students at the Knowledge, Application, and Synthesis levels of the cognitive domain. More than ten thousand questions help your students move beyond the recall of grammatical facts to the ability to express themselves in written form.

The Platform

The best pedagogy in the world is worthless if hidden behind confusing web pages. A team of instructional designers, writing teachers and students worked together tirelessly to put all this pedagogy behind an intuitive, easy-to-use platform. Our guiding principles:

- **The "3 Tab Rule":** Devoid of confusing drop down menus, busy pages, or unnecessary images, the pages include 3 simple tabs at the top to guide students.

- **Most Important Information Up Front:** The content in the four panels on the homepage changes depending on what the student needs to do next.

- **Use the Simplest Language at All Times:** Every word of instruction has been carefully scrutinized for reading comprehension.

ACKNOWLEDGMENTS

We appreciate the continued support of Longman Publishers and Matthew Wright, acquisitions editor for Basic English and Developmental Writing, who has guided us through the third edition. We wish to thank Janice Wiggins-Clarke, our development editor, who has provided sound advice. Likewise, we want to thank Haley Pero for editorial assistance, Thomas DeMarco for marketing, Wesley Hall for text permissions, and Rebecca Karamehmedovic for photo research. Credit goes to Stacey Kulig, production manager, for overseeing the publication of the third edition. And we're thankful for Donna Campion's support on the *Instructor's Manual*. In addition, we're grateful for the support of Susan McIntyre, senior project manager, and the staff at Nesbitt Graphics, Inc., who have helped produce a quality text.

We also wish to acknowledge and thank those who served as prerevision reviewers for the third edition. We've implemented many of their suggestions in the revision of the text.

Margaret Burnett, Metropolitan Community College

Lesley Gale, Cosumnes River College

Eileen Hermann-Miller, Dominican University of California

Amy S. Lerman, Mesa Community College

Jason P. Mitchell, Ph.D., Gulf Coast Community College

Anne Marie Prendergast, Bergen Community College

Emmanuel Sigauke, Cosumnes River College

Sharisse Turner, Tallahassee Community College

And we want to thank our colleagues who reviewed earlier editions of the text.

Alice Adams, Glendale Community College

Alan Ainsworth, Houston Community College

Dennis Chowenhill, Chabot College

Robert Fuhrel, Community College of Southern Nevada

Sugie Goen, San Francisco State University

Susanmarie Harrington, Indiana University–Purdue University at Indianapolis

Linda Houston, The Ohio State University Agricultural Technical Institute

Peggy Karsten, Ridgewater College

Laura Knight, Mercer County Community College

Mary Ann Lee, Longview Community College

Randall Popken, Tarleton State University

Harvey Rubenstein, Hudson County Community College

Valerie Russell, Valencia Community College

Athene Sallee, Forsyth Technical Community College

Mary Sauer, Indiana University–Purdue University at Indianapolis

Nancy Taylor, California State University, Northridge

Ben Thomserson, Crafton Hills College

Others who contributed to earlier editions include Mollie Burroughs who generously compiled the index, Milenko Vlaisavljevic who contributed his talents in photography and design, and colleagues, friends, and family members whose continued support has sustained us through the development of three editions of the text.

Special thanks to Dr. Stephanie Tucker of California State University, Sacramento, whose inspirational teaching and insight into the needs of developmental writers fueled our desire to create this text.

Finally, we'd like to thank our students at Cosumnes River College, Folsom Lake College, West Valley College, and California State University, Sacramento, for being open to new materials and a new approach. We especially wish to acknowledge those students who've contributed essays, paragraphs, or sentences to the text: Jennifer Arch, Allison Baxter, Melody Bruley, Diony Fernandez, Maria Gonzales, Paul Gregorio, Keisha Harris, Ruth Hathaway, Yvonne Liu-Fong, Doris Maysonet, Stacy Michel, Aura Northy, Parris Ray, Rector Sajor, and Miguel Viera. Your willingness to share your work with others makes this a better, more collaborative text.

Tammy Montgomery
Megan C. Rainey

A Note to Students

Dear Student,

Welcome to a challenging and dynamic textbook that will help you further develop your academic writing skills. If you are used to doing drill work and fill-in-the blank exercises in your English courses, you will be surprised by what you find here. We hope to engage you in interesting, challenging topics that encourage discussion and lead to discovery. Our goal is to guide you through the realistic and productive reading and writing processes that help you write thoughtful paragraphs and essays.

The title of the text is *Connections* because all the links of the communication chain are connected here so that each piece of work you do makes sense and leads to honest, meaningful communication. You'll learn strategies for approaching and responding to writing topics and for stating, explaining, and proving your claims in your essays. In other words, you'll learn what experienced writers know—that to write well, you must engage in an effective writing process, a process that also involves critical reading and thinking.

The Premise of This Book

Connections is built on the premise that developing good writing skills requires you to connect three key elements:

Writing—The First Link

It is obvious that developing strong writing skills requires you to write. But what if you don't have much confidence in your ability to write? What if you aren't sure what to write about? What if you're in the class to learn how to write essays, reports, summaries, or other work required in college and on the job? Just where should you begin?

For many years, students were asked to fill in blanks and do many, many sentence drills. However, research shows that such approaches only slightly improve a person's writing skill and may, in fact, discourage the writer who may not see the value of the drills or be able to apply the concepts in the exercises to his or her own writing. That's why fill-in-the-blank work is used only as an occasional method of warming up in *Connections*.

Instead, you will focus on writing activities designed to stimulate thought and help you develop opinions about the issues raised in the text. Rather than just writing *about* an issue you may be unfamiliar with, you'll actively *engage* that issue in journal assignments, summaries, and paragraph and essay assignments. Even the sentence work connects to the issues and requires you to write out whole sentences or paragraphs. This combination of writing activities provides a productive approach to developing writing skills. Yet these types of assignments aren't enough by themselves.

Reading—The Second Link

Writing assignments are linked to reading assignments in this text. Working on both reading and writing skills at the same time will speed up your progress in developing stronger language skills. The reading work you do in this book will help you build your vocabulary, become more familiar with the forms of academic and journalistic writing, understand writing styles and techniques, and learn how to summarize and synthesize information you can use in your paragraphs and essays.

Critical Thinking—The Third Link

The final link, critical thinking, connects to both reading and writing. Critical thinking work helps you analyze the issues and make sense of the readings so that you can develop ideas worth communicating in your essays. Critical thinking also helps you make important choices about what to include in or exclude from your writing.

Connecting the Links

Of course, simply having each link present between the front and back covers of this book is not enough. The links must actually be joined. In Chapters 1 through 4, you'll learn more about each link and how they should connect when you are working on your reading and writing skills. In these chapters, you'll also learn about the reading and writing processes—the necessary steps for approaching and completing your reading and writing work successfully. Then the links are dynamically connected in Chapters 5 through 8 as each chapter focuses on a theme: heroes, television and media, surveillance technology, and poetry and music. All the discussion activities, questions for critical thought, journal responses, readings, writing assignments, and sentence exercises stay focused on the theme of each chapter. Finally, Chapter 9 helps you make these connections in timed-writing situations. Each piece of work you do as you complete an assignment will connect to the next, and you'll be able to watch your own writing process develop as you construct your paragraphs and essays.

Goals

As you work on effectively connecting these links, you'll be working toward these specific goals:

Writing Goals

- Cultivate an effective writing process.
- Write focused paragraphs.
- Write concise summaries.
- Write thoughtful, well-developed essays.
- Construct clear and varied sentences.

Reading Goals

- Develop an effective reading process.
- Recognize the shape of essays and other types of texts.
- Improve your vocabulary and your approach to vocabulary.
- Increase your knowledge of writing styles and techniques.

Critical Thinking Goals

- Sharpen your questioning and thinking skills so that you better understand readings.
- Learn strategies for analyzing complex topics.
- Improve your ability to make good choices when writing your own essays.

Connecting the links and working toward these goals will be challenging, but this text offers you the tools and the guided steps to lead you to success. Let's take a look at the types of assignments you can expect in *Connections*.

Understanding the Assignments in Connections

You'll encounter several types of assignments in this text: journal responses, activities, readings, paragraphs and essays. Each type of assignment has been created to teach you something about the relationship between reading, writing, and critical thinking, and each offers you practice in applying what you've learned.

Journal Assignments   Usually consisting of a series of questions, **journal assignments** are designed to get you thinking critically about a topic or issue. These are "freewriting zones." In other words, journal assignments provide you the opportunity to explore your ideas on paper. They're much like a diary in that you're allowed to write honestly without fear of judgment. Your instructor may write back in response to your journal but will not judge your ideas or point out grammatical errors.

Activities   Within the text, **activities** help you put into practice new writing concepts or ideas. Chapters include activities such as writing summaries, organizing ideas with cue cards, and sharing rough drafts of your writing with classmates. As you'll discover, this text offers a variety of individual and group activities designed to help you practice new concepts, share ideas, or offer feedback to classmates.

Reading Assignments   **Reading Assignments** will help you practice the steps of the reading process that you'll learn about in this text. Carefully selected readings complement writing assignments and chapter themes. For instance, Chapter 5 focuses on heroes, so in that chapter you'll discover a selection of readings on heroes. Although readings are tied directly to the writing assignments, as you complete them, you'll be developing your reading skills also.

Questions for Critical Thought   Following the readings in the text, Questions for Critical Thought help you understand and analyze what you've read. They help you think critically about the writer's message as well as the strategies used to convey the message to the reader. They also serve as springboards to class discussion. When responding to these questions, you may discover ideas to use in your writing assignments. Such questions also bolster reading comprehension and strengthen critical thinking and discussion skills.

Writing Assignments   You'll practice several forms of writing in Chapters 1 through 3: journal assignments, activities, paragraphs, and summaries. Then in Chapter 4 you'll encounter a more formal form of **writing assignment,** the essay. Each writing assignment will take you through a series of stages that will help you develop and improve your writing. And you'll write on a wide range of contemporary issues and topics: advertisements, heroes, television and media, surveillance technology, music, and poetry.

Sentence Work   Throughout this text, sentence exercises will help you learn to develop and refine your sentence structure. You may find the work here different from the grammar exercises you've done before. For one thing, you'll be creating many of your own sentences as you practice what you've learned. Also, the practice segments are closely connected to the readings and issues discussed in the chapters. These grammar segments, which appear at the end of Chapters 1 through 8, are designed to help you continue developing your writing, reading, and critical thinking skills.

Get Involved!   As supplements to learning, *Get Involved!* activities send you outside the text for more information. You may be asked to visit a Web site, watch a film, or conduct an interview and then return to class to share what you've learned. Such activities enrich class discussion and provide additional information to help you complete your writing assignments.

Each type of assignment in *Connections* provides you with an opportunity to strengthen your writing, reading, and critical thinking skills. Because these skills are linked, chances are you'll experience significant improvement in all three areas and begin to realize your writing goals.

Best Wishes,
Tammy Montgomery
Megan C. Rainey

Establishing the Connections

In this section of Connections, *you'll explore the writing-reading-critical thinking connection. You'll study the shapes of academic and journalistic writing and learn how to summarize texts. In addition, you'll review and practice the reading and writing processes as you complete a number of reading and writing assignments in Chapters 1–4.*

The Writing-Reading-Critical Thinking Connection

Main Topics

- Making the writing-reading-critical thinking connection

- Considering audience and purpose in effective communication

- Reviewing your history as a writer, reader, and critical thinker

- Writing the paragraph

- Establishing reading, writing, and critical thinking goals for the semester

- Identifying, describing, and defining verbs

Calvin and Hobbes   by Bill Watterson

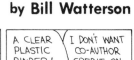

CALVIN AND HOBBES © 1989 Watterson. Dist. by UNIVERSAL PRESS SYNDICATE.
Reprinted with permission. All rights reserved.

Notes

Y ou may believe that the ability to write well is something that you're either born with or not. However, the fact is that successful writers develop their writing skills in much the same way as sculptors develop their artistic skills. Just as the sculptor begins with a lump of clay and then kneads, massages, and molds it into a vase or other object, so the writer begins with a cluster of ideas to explore, develop, and shape into a paragraph or an essay.

Of course, with practice the sculptor becomes skilled at shaping the clay. In the same way, the writer becomes skilled at writing through practicing the craft. Like anyone learning a craft, the writer needs the right tools and techniques to fashion the work. This text will provide you with both the tools and techniques. While you read this chapter and those that follow, think in terms of sculptor and clay, writer and words, as you shape thoughts and ideas into expression.

INTRODUCING THE CONNECTIONS

This textbook may have surprised you. You may have expected it to begin with a discussion of the parts of speech or a series of grammar exercises. Although most writing textbooks start with sentence work, this text is different. *Connections* was designed with the conviction that writing skills are developed through linking reading, writing, and critical thinking. Perhaps you've heard the saying "A chain is only as strong as its weakest link." It's a reminder that each link must be strong enough to hold its share of the weight.

What does this comparison suggest in terms of your writing skills? To become an effective writer, you must strengthen not only your writing, but also your reading and critical thinking skills. In this section, you'll examine and practice the **writing-reading-critical thinking connection.**

As you read this chapter and those that follow, you'll need to keep a dictionary, loose-leaf notebook, pen, and highlighter ready. Throughout the text, blank space in the margins gives you room to write down any thoughts, questions, or notes as you read.

The Writing Link

Writing serves many functions. In your personal life, it may help you reflect on your experiences or explore and discover ideas. It's also a form of communication. From office memos to e-mail, from term papers to love letters, we often communicate our thoughts in writing. You've probably already discovered the need for strong writing skills. In fact, you may have discovered that writing well is one key to your future success.

Notes

> ### *Journal Assignment*
>
> The journal assignments in this text are opportunities for you to express yourself thoughtfully and freely. Concentrate on exploring ideas and don't worry about spelling, punctuation, grammar, or style.
>
> ### A Writer Today
>
> Think of some ways in which writing is a part of your life. How many things, personal or professional, have you had to write in the past few days or weeks? What might you have to write in the future? Respond to these questions in your notebook.

Your History as a Writer   Although strong writing skills are required of both students and employees, many people lack confidence in their writing. If you don't enjoy writing, a look at your own history as a writer may show when, why, and how your apprehensions about writing developed. Or, if you're one of the lucky people who finds writing fun and easy, your history may reveal how you developed a more positive view toward writing.

> ### *Journal Assignment*
> ### *Your History as a Writer*
>
> In your notebook, trace your development as a writer. How far back can you remember writing? Try to remember what it was like to write in grade school for a teacher, parent, or friend. Explain what you were writing about and whom it was for. How did you feel about your writing at that time? What kind of feedback (if any) did you receive?
>
> Now answer the same set of questions for your writing in your middle school years and your high school years. Finally, describe your writing experiences since high school. Overall, would you say your experiences have been positive or negative? Explain.

The Reading Link

Now let's take a look at the second link in our chain of connections: *reading*. Like writing, reading is a part of our daily lives. Even the most basic street sign is impossible to understand when you don't know how to read it (unless it's accompanied by a picture). If you've ever traveled to a country where you didn't speak the language, then you've probably discovered how much we rely on our reading skills.

We read all the time, often without thinking about it. At the grocery store, for instance, we may stop to read a label to make sure a product doesn't contain too much fat. Or we may browse through a newspaper or magazine while waiting for a doctor's or dentist's appointment. If you've had the opportunity to surf the Web, then you may be reading e-mail or other documents from all over the world.

Journal Assignment

A Reader Today

Think of some ways in which reading is a part of your daily life. How many things, personal or professional, have you read in the past few days or weeks? How important are strong reading skills for success in today's world?

Your History as a Reader   As you did earlier with "Your History as a Writer," take time now to consider your history as a reader. If you have always enjoyed reading, your history should show what you like to read and how you gained your love for reading. If you haven't enjoyed reading in the past, your history may show when, why, and how your concerns about reading developed.

Journal Assignment

Your History as a Reader

Think about your own history as a reader. Did anyone (a parent, teacher, friend, or sibling) read to you as a child? How old were you when you first began to read on your own? Did you enjoy reading as a young person? Why, or why not? If you didn't read much, what activities took the place of reading in your life? Can you recall any book that you especially appreciated? (If you don't remember the title, tell what happened in the book.)

Get Involved!
Go to the Reading and Writing Center and/or computer lab on your campus and inquire about services and days and hours of operation. Sign up for tutoring or to use a computer this semester as you take this class. Return to class with evidence that you've inquired about the services and prepare to discuss the tutorial and computer options available at your college.

Making the Writing-Reading Connection

To be a good writer, you must be a good reader. Reading helps you understand concepts and ideas while providing information to use in your writing. Reading also helps you learn the techniques of good writing. This joining of skills is what we call the writing-reading connection.

- **We often respond to reading through writing.**

    At work: You might be asked to read a report and write a summary of it for your supervisor.

At school: Many exams require you to read a short article and then write an essay in response.

At home: After reading an e-mail you've received, you might respond by writing and sending your own e-mail.

- **We read to gather ideas we might want to write about.**

A slash (/) between words such as maternity/paternity usually means "or."

At work: Perhaps as a personnel manager, you need to write a memo explaining new laws concerning maternity/paternity leave. You would first need to read government information about these new laws.

At school: If your history instructor wants a research paper on an American hero, you would need to read books, essays, and articles to gather the necessary information.

At home: Perhaps you want your medical insurance provider to pay for your X-rays. You would need to read your insurance plan materials before writing a letter to the company.

- **When we write, we expect to be read.**

At work: If you write a proposal suggesting that the company pay the tuition costs for employees who take college courses, you expect someone to read your ideas.

At school: After you've diligently worked on your English essay about music lyrics, you expect your instructor to read it.

At home: When you leave a note reminding your roommate that rent was due two days ago, you expect her to read it (and also pay the rent).

Activity

Activities in the text are designed to help you practice new concepts. In this activity, you'll practice making the writing-reading connection.

Making the Writing-Reading Connection

Follow these steps as you read and discuss "Writing in a Knowledge Economy," which follows.

1. Before reading "Writing in a Knowledge Economy":

   - Review your journal entry, "A Writer Today," from page 4, and think about the kinds of writing you do on a daily basis.

- Discuss with classmates what the title "Writing in a Knowledge Economy" might mean.

- Review the "terms and definitions" before you begin reading.

- Read the two sentences just below the title and the author's name and discuss who the target audience might be.

2. Read "Writing in a Knowledge Economy."

3. Answer the questions and complete the Journal Assignment following the reading.

In this chapter, words you may not be familiar with are listed before the readings by paragraph (par.) with their definitions.

Terms and definitions:

Par. 5 *inscribed:* engraved

Par. 6 *shekel:* silver coin; *caravan:* a group of merchants traveling across the desert on business

Par. 9 *indexed:* organized, usually written as a list (see Index at the back of this book for an example); *meta-information:* additional information

Par. 10 *globalization:* worldwide expansion

Par. 11 *Poynter Institute:* an institution dedicated to training journalists and maintaining ethics in journalism

Par. 12 *stakeholders:* the group of people who share a common interest or investment in a company

Writing in a Knowledge Economy*
by Kenneth W. Davis, Ph.D.

A business consultant, Dr. Davis has authored and coauthored a number of books about business communication and writing. This selection is from his book, *The McGraw-Hill 36-Hour Course in Business Writing and Communication.*

1   . . . Many messages that a hundred years ago would have been put into writing are now transmitted orally by telephone wire and satellite

---

*From Kenneth W. Davis, *The McGraw-Hill 36-Hour Course in Business Writing and Communication,* pp. 6–8. Copyright © 2005 by Kenneth W. Davis. Reproduced with permission of the McGraw-Hill Companies.

relay. "Why write a letter," I've been asked, "when you can pick up a telephone?"

2   This question is an important one. To be sure, oral communication has great advantages:

- First, it can be instantaneous; the moment you decide to say something, you can say it.
- Moreover, oral communication, especially when it is face to face, can carry far more information than mere words can express. A rising pitch or a raised eyebrow can convey shades of meaning not possible on the written page.
- Perhaps most important, oral messages can be answered with immediate feedback, even during the message. You can constantly adjust your communication based on your listener's response.

Speaking, in short, is fast, easy, and efficient.

3   Writing, in contrast, is almost always slower and more difficult. This is partly because we have much less practice at it. And in a business, writing is expensive, requiring equipment and materials. In addition, the written word, for most of the history of business, has been slow to move, taking hours and days to get from one office, one city, or one nation to another. For all these reasons, the telephone was a godsend to business. Thus, during the late nineteenth century and most of the twentieth century, the proportion of business communication put in writing almost surely decreased.

4   But oral communication has its disadvantages, too:

- The main one is impermanence. Speech vanishes as soon as it's uttered; this is why an oral contract is "not worth the paper it's written on." Speech can, of course, be recorded, but much of its important content doesn't survive the recording process.
- And even if speech is recorded on tape or disc, its content is extraordinarily difficult to search and retrieve. Try finding every mention of Microsoft in an audio or video recording of a two-day meeting.

5   Writing, on the other hand, is forever. A written communication can last as long as the material on which it is inscribed, and it is always available for rechecking. This is, in fact, why writing was invented—and for "business" purposes at that. When humanity experienced . . . moving from hunting and gathering to agriculture, the first writing began to appear, in the form of warehouse inventories and other business documents, on clay tablets. These ancient pieces of business writing are still being found throughout the Middle East.

6   In her book, *Doing Business,* Olivia Vlahos quotes from one of these documents, a clay tablet sent from creditors in the city of Assur, in

modern Iraq, to a debtor at the end of a caravan route in modern Turkey: "Thirty years ago you left the city of Assur. You have never made a deposit since, and we have not recovered one shekel of silver from you, but we have never made you feel bad about this. Our tablets have been going to you with caravan after caravan, but no report from you has ever come here. . . . Please do come back right away or deposit the silver for us. If not, we will send you a notice from the local ruler and the police, and thus put you to shame in the assembly of merchants. You will also cease to be one of us."

7   As Vlahos says, "the modern debt collector would be hard put to better that communication."

8   The relative permanence of writing also lets it be used to "freeze" oral discussion. Lee Wood, who worked as a writer at Resort Condominiums International, tells of the use of writing there "to give closure, to record agreement." And Terry Pearce, in his acclaimed book *Leading Out Loud,* points out the importance of writing as a way of "disciplining your voice" in preparation for oral communication. "Writing," he says, "reveals fuzzy thinking, exposes slurred distinctions: it clarifies."

9   In addition to its permanence, written communication has the advantage of being easily skimmed or indexed so that a reader can find exactly that part of the message that she needs. For this reason, many digital audio and video recordings are now accompanied by "written" meta-information: the index of tracks on an audio CD or "chapters" on a DVD, for example. Some CD-ROM products index, in writing, audio or video material down to the level of individual words so that you can, in fact, find every time the word *Microsoft* was spoken during a two-day meeting.

10   Moreover, the old gap between speech and writing in speed and cost has essentially closed. Computers, networks, and satellite data transmission have made a written message as cheap and fast as a phone call while retaining all the advantages of written words. In addition, the globalization of business, requiring communication across many time zones, has made phone conversations exceedingly inconvenient.

11   As a result, the century-long trend toward spoken communication has reversed. More and more business communication is being conducted in writing. E-mail and Web pages are, after all, written documents produced to be read. A 2000 study by the Poynter Institute found that readers of online news sites look first at the text—a very different way of reading than in print media, where readers tend to look first at graphics. On the Web, only 22 percent of users look at graphics first.

> 12   . . . The latest use of writing in business is in the form of *blogs,* Web logs of links and other information that can provide crucial just-in-time information to a company's employees or wider stakeholders. *Fast Company* magazine has reported the use of blogs by (predictably) Microsoft and Verizon, as well as (perhaps less predictably) DaimlerChrysler, Hartford Financial Services Group, and IBM.

Questions for Critical Thought

Questions for Critical Thought, which follow most readings in the text, have been developed to help you better understand and analyze what you've read. They help you think critically about the writer's message as well as the strategies the writer uses to convey the message to the reader.

"Writing in a Knowledge Economy"

Get Involved!

Go online and read the article, "Tomorrow's Jobs," http://www.bls .gov/oco/oco2003.htm, from the *Occupational Outlook Handbook,* by the U.S. Department of Labor, Bureau of Labor Statistics. Review the twenty fastest-growing occupations from 2004–2014. In your notebook, list the types of communication skills that may be required of workers in these fields.

1. Author Kenneth W. Davis lists three advantages of oral communication or speaking in this reading. **Paraphrase** (put into your own words) each of these advantages on a page in your notebook. What other advantages do you believe oral communication has? Write these in your notebook, being careful to explain why you believe each might be considered an advantage.

2. Davis also lists two disadvantages of oral communication. Paraphrase these disadvantages in your notebook. What other disadvantages to speaking might there be? Add these to your notebook with an explanation for each.

3. Now paraphrase the advantages of the written communication Davis describes in the reading. Are there other advantages to writing that you can see? Add these, with explanations, to your notebook.

4. In your opinion, what might be some of the disadvantages of written communication? List these in your notebook along with the reasons why you see them as possible disadvantages.

5. According to Davis, what kinds of writing are people doing in the modern world? Which of these newer forms of communication do you prefer? Why? If you haven't used any of these newer forms, then explain how you prefer to communicate and why.

> ### *Journal Assignment*
>
> ### *Considering the Impact of Technology on Communication*
>
> Think about what you've learned from "Writing in a Knowledge Economy." Think about the ways you use writing in your own life. Think about how new forms of technology are changing the way we communicate. Then respond in your notebook to the following questions: *How has technology changed the way we communicate today? Do you believe these changes are positive or negative? Why? Do you agree with Davis and other experts who claim that good writing skills are more important today than twenty or thirty years ago? Why, or why not?*

The Critical Thinking Link

While strong writing and reading skills are important to your success, your ability to **think critically** about issues or ideas is equally important. When you use your critical thinking skills, you look beyond the surface of an issue or action and examine the purpose or motivation behind it.

As you read Kenneth W. Davis's "Writing in the Knowledge Economy," for example, you used your critical thinking skills in a variety of ways. You thought critically as you examined the title and basic information about the author and considered what these clues suggested the reading might be about. You used your critical thinking skills as you read and anticipated what was coming next in the reading. You used these skills again as you thought about and answered the questions following the reading. And you used your critical thinking skills as you prepared to write about the communication skills necessary to be successful in today's job market. The fact is that every time you examine an issue and take the time to consider the available information, including the viewpoints of others, you are thinking critically.

Critical Thinkers

- consider different views and possibilities when looking at an issue or problem;
- consider the possible reasons or motivations behind issues or actions;
- question the ideas presented before agreeing, disagreeing, or seeking an alternative; and

- question ideas and seek new ideas.

Critical thinkers use their ability to reason—questioning, evaluating, and judging every issue or idea they read, discuss, and write about.

Don't Believe Everything You Read or Hear   It would be a scary and confusing world *if we believed everything we read or heard*. Sometimes even reliable sources have to be questioned.

- After reading only a few advertisements, we might believe that the only road to happiness, power, and beauty is to buy new cars, jewelry, and clothing.
- If we read one essay in favor of the death penalty and believed it, and then read another essay against the death penalty and believed it, we would be very confused.
- If we believed everything we heard, we might panic, as some 1.7 million people did on Halloween in 1938 during a radio presentation of H. G. Wells's *War of the Worlds*. (They believed Martians were invading Earth because they mistook a dramatic reading of fiction for an emergency radio broadcast.)

Think Before You Write   Consider how difficult or even embarrassing it would be to write without carefully thinking through ideas first.

- A writer who dives into an essay on the death penalty without careful thinking (critical thinking) might waste significant time by writing things he doesn't believe or that don't make sense.
- A writer who reads about the death penalty, thinks about it, discusses it, and then takes a side on the issue is prepared to write what he believes.

Consider Audience and Purpose   With a few exceptions, most of your writing is directed at a specific audience for a specific purpose.

- Your **audience** includes anyone you intend to communicate to.
- Your **purpose** is your reason for writing and should be the driving force behind your writing.

Whether you are composing a letter to a loved one or writing a report for your employer, you use your critical thinking skills and consider your audience and purpose. Doing so ensures that you convey your ideas to your audience in a way that allows you to be heard.

Activity

Helping Calvin Connect Reading and Thinking to Writing

As you've read in this chapter, writers must use their reading and critical thinking skills when they write. They should have a clear purpose and keep the needs of their audience in mind.

Reread the *Calvin and Hobbes* cartoon on page 2 and then answer the questions below on a separate piece of paper.

1. From Calvin's point of view, who is his audience for his report?

2. From Calvin's point of view, what is his purpose in writing? (*Why* did he write his report?)

3. What do you think Calvin's purpose should be when he writes a report? How could reading and critical thinking help his writing?

There's a simple message behind the *Calvin and Hobbes* strip that can help you with your writing: Think critically about audience and purpose to communicate effectively.

Journal Assignment

Your History as a Critical Thinker

Reflect on times when you've used your critical thinking skills. Were any of them connected to reading and/or writing? Did any instructors or employers encourage critical thinking? How did they encourage you? What has been your response to activities requiring critical thinking? Write about your experiences as a critical thinker.

THE WRITING PROCESS: MAKING THE CONNECTIONS

Now it's time to use the writing-reading-critical thinking chain we've constructed. This chain can give you the power to learn new ideas and to say new things. Although the links can be separated and used individually, when connected they make your communication more interesting and powerful. In this section, you'll use the writing-reading-critical thinking chain to write a formal paragraph.

Notes

The Writing Process

The **writing process** is a term used throughout the text to refer to the steps a writer takes when completing a writing assignment. You'll use a modified version of the writing process in this chapter (the full process is covered in Chapter 4) as you complete your first writing assignment.

In this chapter, you'll find the writing process organized into four stages: predrafting, drafting, revising, and editing.

- **Predrafting** activities will prepare you to write your paper. Discussing an issue, reading about it, and thinking critically about it are considered predrafting activities. Predrafting also includes planning and organizing ideas to use in your paper.
- **Drafting** means writing your paper (by hand or on computer). Your first draft, called a **rough draft** is usually pretty basic, so you'll probably want to improve it.
- **Revising** is the act of improving each draft of your paper until you're satisfied that it communicates your ideas accurately and completely.
- **Editing** involves correcting sentence structure, punctuation, and spelling.

While defined separately here, the stages of the writing process usually overlap. For example, you might discover as you're drafting your paper that you need more information. In this case, you would return to your reading (a predrafting activity) to find information to add to your draft. With these essential stages in mind, you're ready to begin writing a formal paragraph.

Writing the Paragraph

In this chapter, you'll practice the writing process as you write a paragraph. The **paragraph** is a single unit of writing that makes a specific point. Most paragraphs begin with an introductory sentence called a **topic sentence** that describes what the paragraph will be about. The topic sentence is usually followed by several sentences of support in the form of examples, explanations, descriptions, and/or details. Sometimes the paragraph contains a final statement that draws the paragraph to a close.

Let's examine paragraph 9 from Davis's "Writing in a Knowledge Economy." In paragraph 8, Davis discusses the permanence of writing. In paragraph 9, Davis shifts his focus to discuss the importance of the written word as reference material. Notice how Davis makes the paragraph point clear in the topic sentence of the paragraph. Following the topic sentence, Davis offers examples that help explain why written information often accompanies audio and video products.

Notes

> 9   In addition to its permanence, <u>written communication has the advantage of being easily skimmed or indexed so that a reader can find exactly that part of the message that she needs</u>. For this reason, many digital audio and video recordings are now accompanied by "written" meta-information: the index of tracks on an audio CD or "chapters" on a DVD, for example. Some CD-ROM products index, in writing, audio or video material down to the level of individual words so that you can, in fact, find every time the word *Microsoft* was spoken during a two-day meeting.

The topic sentence explains what the paragraph is about.

Explanation and examples support the topic sentence.

While relatively short, this paragraph makes an important point about the advantage written material has over audio or video material. It may be "skimmed or indexed so that a reader can find exactly that part of the message that she needs." Notice the paragraph includes a topic sentence and examples that support the topic sentence. In this case, there is no **wrap-up** sentence (a final sentence summing up the paragraph). You'll continue to examine the parts of the paragraph in the next activity.

Activities

Examining a Paragraph

Follow these steps as you examine the paragraph below:

1. Read the paragraph.

2. Underline the topic sentence.

3. On a sheet of paper, paraphrase (put into your own words) what the topic sentence says the paragraph will be about.

4. In the margin, identify the parts of the paragraph: topic sentence, support (in the form of examples, explanations, and details), and wrap-up statement (if there is one).

5. Prepare to discuss how well the writer supported the paragraph topic.

> A computer is a luxury that today's students often take for granted. Having access to e-mail, for example, allows students to

Notes

correspond with their instructors. If a student has a question about a math problem, she can e-mail the instructor and ask for help. In the past, the student would have needed to stop by the instructor's office during office hours for such help. If the instructor's office hours weren't convenient for the student, then the student would have had to wait for class to see how the problem could be worked out. Today there are also math labs online where a student can go for a virtual tutorial session. This is a luxury that students of the past did not have. In fact, some online labs are open twenty-four hours a day, which means if a student is working late into the night, help is still available online. Twenty years ago, such instantaneous help was not available. The computer, via the Internet, also makes library and research materials available twenty-four hours a day, seven days a week. Students in the past had to plan to visit the library within its hours of operation, which certainly didn't include holidays or twenty-four hour service. Finally, the computer is a word processor for today's students, making revision and editing much easier. Students of the past had to use typewriters to type their papers. A small mistake usually meant dabbing gooey Wite-Out™ on the page to "blot out" the error. A larger mistake meant retyping the entire page. Today's students sometimes get frustrated when the Internet is down or when they have to wait online to be helped by the next available online tutor. However, they might want to reconsider their impatience. Compared to precomputer days, today's students have it pretty good.

Supporting the Main Idea

You've learned that the topic sentence or introductory sentence(s) of the paragraph explains to the reader what the entire paragraph will be about. And you've learned that the topic sentence is typically followed by many kinds of support such as examples, explanations, descriptions, and details. For this activity, you'll practice supporting topic sentences that have been created for you.

1. Here are some sample topic sentences you might use to begin a paragraph:

   a. The written word has more advantages than the spoken word.

   b. The spoken word has more advantages than the written word.

   c. Writing skills are even more important today than in the past.

   d. To compete in today's job market, you must have good writing skills.

2. Select one of the sample topic sentences and list examples and ideas you could use to support it. (Return to "Writing in a Knowledge Economy," pages 7–10, for additional ideas.)

3. In a small group, share the topic sentence you chose and your list of supporting examples and ideas. If classmates suggest other ideas, consider adding them to your list.

Writing the Topic Sentence

In the last activity, you practiced supporting one of several topic sentences that had been created for you. In this activity, you'll practice creating your own topic sentences. (Remember, the topic sentence tells the reader what the paragraph will be about.)

1. Read each of the topics (in italics) and the possible supporting ideas that follow:

   a. *Living in a college dorm:* computer and printer, bed and bedding (sheets, blankets, comforter), towels and toiletries (personal care items)

   b. *Attending a ballgame:* tickets, hot dogs, baseball caps

   c. *Spending the day at the beach:* blanket, cooler, sunblock, sunglasses

   d. *Throwing a party:* balloons, cake, games, kids, invitations

2. Create topic sentences for *a–d* that would prepare you to write about each situation. Let's use *c* as an example:

   Spending the day at the beach: blanket, cooler, sunblock, sunglasses

   Here is a potential topic sentence for a paragraph about the beach:

   A day at the beach can be fun and relaxing, but only if you're prepared.

3. After creating topic sentences for *a–d,* select the topic sentence you like best and list examples and ideas you could use to support it. Prepare to share it with classmates in a small group.

4. In a small group, share your topic sentence and your list of supporting examples and ideas. If classmates offer other ideas, consider adding them to your list.

Notes

Writing Assignment: "Be Your Own Communication Department"

Earlier in the chapter you explored the importance of writing skills in a knowledge economy. In this assignment, you'll consider the broader area of communication skills and the reasons why communicating effectively is essential to competing successfully in today's job market. Here is the writing assignment you are preparing for.

Write a paragraph in which you answer this question: What are one or two of the most important things you have learned in this chapter that will help you to be a successful communicator in the modern work world?

Before writing your paragraph, you'll complete a set of predrafting activities. First, you'll read "Be Your Own Communication Department," also from Kenneth W. Davis's *The McGraw-Hill 36-Hour Course in Business Writing and Communication*. Second, you'll answer a series of critical thinking questions that should fuel class discussion and provide you with some information you can use as support in your paragraph. Third, you'll complete a journal response to generate even more ideas for your paragraph.

Predrafting Activities

Reading About Communication Skills

1. Before reading the selection that follows:

   - Discuss with classmates what the title "Be Your Own Communication Department" might mean.

   - Discuss who the author's intended audience might be.

   - Review the "terms and definitions" before you begin reading.

2. Read "Be Your Own Communication Department."

3. Make a list of the most important points made by the author in the reading.

4. Discuss the questions that follow the reading.

Terms and definitions:

Par. 1 *New Post-Industrial Information Society:* a reference to modern society in which the economy is driven by information as opposed to the industrial society of the past in which the economy was driven by manufacturing

Par. 2 *abstraction:* concept or idea

Par. 3 *entrepreneurs:* people who organize and develop businesses; *intrapreneurs:* people who organize and develop projects within a company

Par. 6 *compilation:* collection

Par. 11 *homogeneous:* all the same

Be Your Own Communication Department*
by Kenneth W. Davis, Ph.D.

A business consultant, Dr. Davis has authored and coauthored a number of books about business communication and writing. This selection is from his book, *The McGraw-Hill 36-Hour Course in Business Writing and Communication.*

1   A *New Yorker* cartoon shows a tiny newsstand with a big sign. "Fred's Newsstand—," it reads, "Forefront of the New Post-Industrial Information Society."

2   We're all Fred, of course. The information society is a fact, and it affects the work every one of us does, from building cars to selling newspapers. As John Naisbitt has written, "The information society is an economic reality, not an intellectual abstraction." Yet most of us haven't learned the skills we need to survive and thrive in this new knowledge economy.

3   This fact is particularly important given that more and more of us are entrepreneurs—and "intrapreneurs." For the small business owner—or for the owner of "You, Inc.," within a large business—the upside of the knowledge economy is the fact that the creation or communication of knowledge does not require a large organization; the lone David can compete effectively with the Goliath. For example, some of the computer programming for a London cab company has been done by a lone entrepreneur working from his Indiana farmhouse. The downside, however, is that the same standards of communication excellence are expected from a one- or two-person operation as a giant corporation with its own communication department.

4   So how do you compete? By being your own communication department.

5   Begin by understanding the times we live in. One of the most perceptive commentators on the knowledge economy is Alvin Toffler. His book *The Third Wave* outlines three times of major change in human activity:

1. The first of these "waves," says Toffler, came several thousand years ago when hunting and fishing were replaced by farming as humanity's main work. In the resulting agricultural economy, wealth consisted chiefly of the ownership of land.

2. The second wave happened only about 150 to 200 years ago when farming was replaced by manufacturing as our major economic activity. (That revolution—the industrial revolution—was not a bloodless one: the U.S. Civil War was, to some extent, a conflict between a largely agricultural South and an increasingly industrialized North.) In the resulting industrial economy, wealth consisted chiefly of the ownership of factories.

3. Now, says, Toffler, a third wave is sweeping over us. Manufacturing has been giving way rapidly to the processing of information as humanity's major economic activity. As we have entered the information or knowledge economy, wealth has come to consist of the ownership of information—or rather, the ability to collect and communicate information. James Champy is right when he says, in his book *Reengineering Management*, "Knowledge is power, as the cliché has it. But knowledge is not easy to come by. You earn it by thinking. And all we have to think about is information. So make sure that the information 'gets around.'"

6   As early as the late 1980s, Tom Peters was finding striking examples of the wealth that lies in communicating information. Peters reported that the little publication called *The Official Airline Guide*—a for-sale compilation of schedule information that the airlines gave away free—sold in 1988 for $750 million, three times the selling price of Ozark Airlines the same year.

7   In other words, the right formula for collecting and communicating free airline information was worth more than all the planes, equipment, and other assets of an airline itself.

8   If collecting and communicating information is our main work for today and tomorrow, we'd better get good at it. In a knowledge economy, our personal success and the success of our organizations depend on this "knowledge work." Management guru Peter Drucker, writing in *Managing in the Next Century*, puts it this way: "Physical resources no longer provide much of an advantage, nor does skill. Only the productivity of knowledge workers makes a measurable difference."

9   Unfortunately, however, most of us are not very good at communicating our knowledge, and the results can be disastrous. W. Edwards

Deming estimated that "85 percent of failures in quality are failures in communication." A big part of the problem is the way we think about communication. Too often we make third-wave communication decisions as if we were still living in a first- or second-wave society.

10   In first- and second-wave societies, communication often was one-way, top-down. Information was held at the very top of organizational pyramids and passed down to workers only as needed. Most of the time, most people—whether they worked in a field or in a factory—needed to be only passive receivers of communication.

11   Moreover, in the first- and second-wave societies, communication communities were small and homogeneous. A first-wave farmer may have communicated with only a few hundred people in a lifetime, all people very much like himself. A second-wave plant manager communicated with more people, but that manager probably saw them as interchangeable.

12   In their book *Thinking for a Living,* Ray Marshal and Marc Tucker point out that our educational system has not yet caught up with the communication needs of a knowledge economy. "Schools' curriculum and methods," they write, "are matched to the needs of a half-century ago, rather than to today's requirements. Fifty years ago, relatively few students needed sophisticated communications skills, so students were not required to write much and teachers were not asked to spend much time working with them to improve what they wrote. Students are still not required to write much and teachers are given very little time to help them improve their writing."

13   In third-wave organizations, pyramids have been flattened or dissolved, and valuable knowledge resides everywhere. All members of the organization have to be not only consumers of communication but also producers of it. Everyone in a third-wave organization has to be a skilled communicator. As marketing wizard Harry Beckwith writes in *The Invisible Touch,* "Communication is not a skill. It is *the* skill." And "perhaps the most important lesson from the Iraq war," write David Newkirk and Stuart Crainer, "is that managing real-time communications is as important as managing real-time processes. Communication is moving from being a peripheral, specialist responsibility to being an essential and integral element of corporate leadership." Similarly, central to all five recommendations of the 9/11 Commission was the need for improved communication.

14   Moreover, a third-wave knowledge worker may well communicate with tens of thousands of people from diverse backgrounds around the world. This diverse audience makes communication much more complex, demanding greater flexibility and sensitivity.

Notes

15   In the knowledge economy, the benefits of improved communication are many. In the insurance industry, for example, the cover letter from the agent, the "producer," to the underwriter is crucial. As Robert Goldstone, vice president and medical director at Pacific Mutual Life, has written, "A good cover letter may save your case." *Forbes* magazine has reported that "at AMEC Offshore, the big British engineering and construction firm, the cost of piping offshore oil platforms dropped 15 percent after intensive work on communication skills." The Families and Work Institute found that "the number one factor employees say will convince them to accept a job offer" is "open communication." And a Watson Wyatt study comparing financially high-performing companies with their lower-performing competitors found that

- "Communications professionals in high-performing organizations play a strategic role."
- "High-performing organizations do a better job of explaining change."
- "High-performing organizations focus on communicating with and educating their employees."
- "High-performing organizations provide channels for upward communication."
- "Employees in high-performing organizations have a better understanding of organizational goals and their part in achieving them."

Questions for Critical Thought

"Be Your Own Communication Department"

1. What does Davis mean when he claims that we live in a "New Post-Industrial Information Society"?

2. Davis sums up "three times of major change in human activity" from Alvin Toffler's book *The Third Wave*. Paraphrase (put into your own words) these times of change. Then describe how the new information society differs from societies of the past.

3. Davis claims that money can be made from communicating information. What example(s) does he use to support this claim?

4. According to Davis and other experts, why aren't some organizations good at communicating their knowledge? What can organizations do to improve their communication of information?

5. How well is our educational system preparing young people to compete in the knowledge economy? What might schools do differently to better prepare students to succeed in this economy?

6. Why is it essential for all members of the organization to be able to communicate in an information economy?

7. According to experts in the reading, what are some of the benefits of improved communication in an information economy?

8. Davis uses a number of **quotations** (word-for-word statements) from industry experts to help support his paragraph ideas. Select two specific quotations from different paragraphs. Explain how each quotation helps support the paragraph in which it appears.

Journal Assignment

Considering How Changes in the Economy Affect Communication

Think about what you've learned from "Be Your Own Communication Department." Consider how changes in the economy have resulted in the need for stronger communication skills. Then respond in your notebook to the following question: *Given that strong communication skills are important in today's workforce, what might you do to improve your own communication skills?*

Predrafting

After reading and discussing "Be Your Own Communication Department," you should have a fairly good idea about why communication skills are considered important in today's job market. You should also be able to explain why companies that employ good communicators have an advantage over companies that do not. Now it's time to return to the writing assignment and begin to plan your paragraph.

Here, again, is the assignment:

> *Write a paragraph in which you answer this question: What are one or two of the most important things you have learned in this chapter that will help you to be a successful communicator in the modern work world?*

Paraphrase the Assignment   In your own words, write down what you're being asked to explain in your paragraph.

Write Down Ideas Related to the Assignment   Write down any ideas that might be used in your paragraph. These ideas may have come from the readings, questions for critical thought, or class discussion. Review your list of ideas. Discuss this list with classmates. Add to the list. The goal is to get as many ideas down as possible so that you can select the best ideas from your list to use in your paragraph. Highlight or underline your best ideas.

Drafting

Once you've identified some ideas you would like to include in your paragraph, you're ready to begin drafting your paragraph. First, you'll create a topic sentence. Then, once you have a topic sentence in place, you can begin to write your paragraph.

Create Your Topic Sentence   Review the assignment and your list of highlighted ideas, and then write a topic sentence for your paragraph. Remember, your topic sentence should tell your reader what you intend to show or prove in your paragraph. (You may need to change or improve your topic sentence as you write the rest of the paragraph. It's fine to revise your topic sentence throughout the writing process.)

Plan Your Paragraph   Returning to your highlighted list of ideas, select those you believe will best support your topic sentence. Decide the order in which you plan to present these ideas.

Draft Your Paragraph   Using your paragraph plan, begin writing your paragraph. Keep in mind that your goal is to support your topic sentence. As you write, feel free to refer back to your list of ideas, the readings, and your class notes to find examples, explanations, and details to add to your paragraph. At this point, your paragraph may seem pretty rough. That's okay for now. The goal is to complete a first draft of your paragraph. It needn't be perfect.

Revising

At this stage of the writing process, it's time to take a closer look at your rough draft.

Revise Your Paragraph   Begin by rereading what you've written. Consider these questions:

- Does your paragraph respond to the writing assignment?
- Does your paragraph have a strong topic sentence that addresses the assignment and tells the reader what you plan to show or prove?
- Are there enough examples or explanations in your paragraph to prove your topic sentence?
- Is there room for more support? If so, what kinds of support might make your paragraph stronger?
- Have you included a final statement to wrap up your discussion? If not, consider adding one.
- Could any of your examples be stronger? If so, how can you strengthen them?
- Is there an example that just doesn't seem to belong? If so, remove it.

Read Each Other's Work Apply the same questions to your classmates' paragraphs and allow them to do the same to yours. Keep your classmates' suggestions in mind as you revise your paragraph again. (Remember, though, your classmates are only making suggestions. It's up to you to decide which of the suggestions you believe will improve your paragraph.)

Get Involved!

Take your paragraph to your college's Reading and Writing Center and ask a tutor to read your paragraph and make suggestions for improvement.

Editing

At this point, your paragraph should have a strong topic sentence addressing the assignment. It should also have plenty of support (examples, explanations, descriptions, and details) that proves the topic sentence. Now it's time to edit your paragraph.

Edit Your Paragraph Although you might not feel equipped to correct sentence errors this early in the term, you can still *listen for possible errors* when someone reads your paragraph aloud. Ask a friend or one of your classmates to read your paragraph aloud to you. If your reader struggles with a word or sentence, then you need to look at that word or sentence carefully to determine if there is an error. Correct the errors you can. If there are errors you aren't sure how to fix, then ask your instructor or a tutor at your college's Reading and Writing Center to explain how you can fix them.

Notes

Wrapping Up the Assignment

There are a number of ways to share the final draft of your work. If your class has an online bulletin board, you could post your work for all your classmates to read. Some instructors ask students to exchange final drafts and read them to themselves. Others ask for volunteers to read their own papers out loud. Take advantage of the postwriting opportunities with which you're most comfortable. Simply sharing your final work privately with a trusted friend or family member (in addition to your instructor) is a good idea. You might be surprised at how sharing your writing can bolster confidence and inspire future writing projects.

Journal Assignment

Your Goals as a Writer, Reader, and Critical Thinker

Take time to *reread* interesting sections of this first chapter, your journals, and your class notes. *Think* about the skills you want to gain in this class and how you might use them. Consider what some of your classmates have said. Consider what your instructor has said. Consider, honestly, your strengths and weaknesses. *Write* down your goals as a writer, reader, and critical thinker.

SUMMARY OF CHAPTER 1

In Chapter 1 you've learned about the writing-reading-critical thinking connection. In particular, you've

- examined the importance of each connection as you've explored your history as a writer, reader, and critical thinker;
- reviewed the paragraph and its parts;
- practiced the writing process as you wrote your first paragraph of the term; and
- set your writing goals for the term.

SENTENCE WORK

Throughout this text, sentence practice material (also called **sentence work**) will help you learn to develop and refine your sentences. You may find the work here different from the grammar exercises you've done before. For one thing, you'll be creating many of your own sentences as you practice what you've learned. Also, the practice segments are closely connected to the readings and issues discussed in the chapters. These grammar segments, which appear at the end of each chapter, are designed to help you continue developing your writing, reading, and critical thinking skills.

The Hows and Whys   When you learn how to drive a car, you don't have to know the names of all the parts of the car or how the car was assembled. You do, however, need to know a few key terms: emergency brake, hazard lights, high beams. You also need to know how to use these items. As you become a more experienced driver, you easily pick up more knowledge. For example, you learn how to check the fluids and change the oil. Many people who love cars and driving continue to learn even more about the technical aspects of cars: What is a flange gasket? How do you replace a flange gasket?

How does all of this apply to you as a writer? First, remember that you are a writer because you already know some important basics about writing. For example, you know thousands of words, and you've written these words in various forms—letters, essays, reports—over the years.

The exercises in this text will help you learn or get a better handle on *key writing terms* that will help you shape clear and effective sentences. You don't need to recite definitions of *all* the parts of speech, but knowing these terms will help you develop more control over your writing. That way, when you turn in essays to your instructor (or reports to your boss), you won't feel like you just turned over your prized car to a mechanic who knows everything when you know too little.

Completing the Sentence Exercises   You'll find that the exercises in this text call for you to read and research material, create and discuss ideas, and practice your reading-writing-critical thinking skills. These are the most effective methods for learning about sentences. You'll be exploring, and the more energy you put into your explorations, the better the results you will see.

Notes   As you complete the exercises, you'll discover that writing good sentences will become second nature for you, and you'll gain the ability to discuss your writing with others. Throughout this book, you'll continue to pick up more terminology and more ways of shaping sentences. In the end, you'll leave your class knowing that you have better control over your sentences and, consequently, the thoughts you choose to communicate.

INTRODUCTION TO VERBS

The Complete Sentence
Identifying and Supplying Verbs

The sentence work in this book begins with verbs because verbs are one of the key ingredients of sentences. You might even call the verb the heart of the sentence because understanding and identifying verbs will help you understand and identify all the other elements in a sentence. In this chapter, you'll first consider the sentence as a whole. Then you'll zero in on the verb and how it functions in a sentence.

The Complete Sentence

To understand the sentence, you'll need to be familiar with a few key terms:

- A **complete sentence** will have a subject and a verb and will express a complete idea.
- A **subject** is a person, place, thing, or idea that is performing an action or that is being described.
- A **verb** expresses the action in the sentence or links the subject to descriptive information.
- The **predicate** is the verb and everything that comes after the verb.

In these complete sentences, verbs are underlined twice, and subjects are underlined once.

<u>Savannah</u> <u>read</u> the help wanted ads.

<u>Three jobs</u> <u>looked</u> promising.

<u>She</u> <u>plans</u> to apply for all three.

In the next set of sentences, predicates are underlined twice, and subjects are underlined once.

Jorge <u>attended</u> a job placement seminar.
He <u>learned</u> how to write a good résumé.
The <u>seminar</u> <u>was</u> helpful.

Notes

Identifying and Supplying Verbs

Identifying and understanding verbs will help you talk about and gain better control over your sentences. The exercises that follow will give you practice identifying and supplying verbs.

Practice #1   Supplying Verbs, Part One

Rewrite sentences 1–10 by adding verbs that make sense. (Try not to add the same verb to more than one sentence.) The first one is done for you.

1. Joss *enrolled* in college.
2. He _____ that college _____ just like high school.
3. But it _____ not.
4. The instructors _____ twice as much reading.
5. They also _____ more writing.
6. Joss _____ the extra homework at first.
7. Then he _____ his attitude.
8. College _____ his new job.
9. This new job _____ him busy.
10. It also _____ him for the future.

Practice #2   Supplying Verbs, Part Two

- Copy all the sentences in the following exercise (even the sentences that aren't missing any words).
- Add the missing verbs.
- Because there is more than one way to complete some of these sentences, experiment to find verbs that fit the best.
- Your finished product should be three paragraphs long. (Be sure to *indent* your paragraphs. This means that the beginning of each paragraph should be "pushed in" five spaces so that your reader will know that a new paragraph is starting. You can use your *tab* key on your computer keyboard to indent.)

Notes

- Some verbs consist of more than one part. If part of a verb has been provided for you, it has already been underlined. And when complete verbs have been supplied, they have been underlined as well.

Applying for a Job:
Resumes and Application Forms

Resumes and application forms <u>are</u> two ways to provide employers with written evidence of your qualifications and skills. Generally, the same information <u>appears</u> on both the resume and the application form, but the way in which it <u>is presented</u> differs. Some employers _____ a resume and others _____ an application form.

There _____ many ways of organizing a resume; <u>choose</u> the format that best _____ your skills and experience. It <u>may</u> _____ helpful to look for examples on the Internet or in books at your local library or bookstore. Typically, an employer _____ a very limited amount of time to review your resume. It _____ important to make sure it <u>is</u> clear and concise and _____ your skills and experiences effectively through the use of formatting, ordering, and headings.

Many employers <u>scan</u> resumes into databases, which they then <u>search</u> for specific keywords or phrases. The keywords _____ usually nouns referring to experience, education, personal characteristics, or industry buzz words. _____ keywords by reading the job description and qualifications; <u>use</u> the same words in your resume that _____ in the job ad. For example, if the job description _____ customer service tasks, <u>use</u> the words "customer service" on your resume. Scanners sometimes <u>misread</u> paper resumes, which <u>could</u>

_____ some of your keywords <u>don't get</u> into the database. So, if you _____

that your resume <u>will be scanned</u>, and you _____ the option, <u>e-mail</u> an elec-

tronic version. If you <u>must</u> _____ a paper resume, <u>make</u> it scannable by using

a simple font and avoiding underlines, italics, and graphics. It _____ also a

good idea to send a traditionally formatted resume along with your scannable

resume, with a note on each <u>marking</u> its purpose.

These paragraphs are adapted from "Tomorrow's Jobs," from *The Occupational Outlook Handbook, 2006–07 Edition*, a publication of the U.S. Department of Labor, Bureau of Labor Statistics. The document in its entirety may be found at www.bls.gov/oco/print/oco20043.htm.

Practice #3   Quick Verb Quiz

Be sure to look at your paragraphs in the section "Identifying and Supplying Verbs" when you are looking for the answers to this quiz.

1. Can a verb be made up of more than one word?
2. Can a sentence have more than one verb?

IDENTIFYING SPECIFIC KINDS OF VERBS

Action Verbs
Linking Verbs
Helping Verbs

So far, you have practiced identifying verbs, and you have gotten a sense of what a verb is and how it works within the sentence. Now you're ready to look at several specific types of verbs: action, linking, and helping.

Action Verbs

One type of verb is called the *action verb*. An **action verb** expresses activity or movement.

Practice #4   Traditional Roles

Copy and complete sentences 1–8, and you'll begin to see how action verbs work. Be sure to underline the verbs twice.

Notes

> *Traditionally, people believed that men and women should have clear, defined roles in the household and the workplace.*
>
> 1. Women <u>make</u> the food.
> 2. Men _____ the lawns.
> 3. Daughters _____ the dirty clothes.
> 4. Sons _____ the oil in the car.
> 5. Women _____ school.
> 6. Men _____ fires.
> 7. Girls _____ to sew.
> 8. Boys _____ newspapers.

Linking Verbs

The words you supplied in Practice #1 and Practice #4 are *action verbs:* They represent movement, work, or someone doing something. Another kind of verb is called a *linking verb*. A linking verb, as you'll see, doesn't show action. A **linking verb** connects (or links) the subject to information in the sentence.

See the chart of linking verbs on page 33.

Practice #5   Role Reversal

Rewrite and complete sentences 1–8 using a different linking verb for each sentence. (The first one is done for you.) Be sure all the linking verbs you choose would make sense if the eight sentences were written as one paragraph. (You may want to refer to the chart that follows when searching for the best linking verb.)

Traditional roles <u>are</u> important to some people, but not all.

1. He <u>is</u> happy in the kitchen.
2. He thinks that the kitchen _____ wonderful when bread is baking.
3. She _____ eager to work in the yard.
4. She _____ anxious if she must stay in the house all day.
5. The young woman _____ exhilarated working as a stockbroker.
6. The young father _____ happy caring for the children all day.
7. He _____ content to be a house husband.
8. She _____ fulfilled to be the breadwinner.

All forms of "to be"
    is
    am
    are
    was
    were

Words associated with the five senses
    look
    sound
    smell
    feel
    taste

A few others
    appear
    seem
    become
    grow
    turn
    prove
    remain

These verbs must be followed by descriptive information or a noun that renames a subject when they are acting as linking verbs.

Identifying Specific Kinds of Verbs

As you can see from Practice #5, linking verbs often help you express feelings or describe things. They don't show action. They link the subject to a description or feeling.

Linking verbs work well when you are describing a feeling or appearance. However, sometimes when you are revising your writing, you'll want to look for places where you can use an action verb instead of a linking verb. This is especially important when you are writing about an action or event and want to add energy to your description and information.

Practice #6   On Vacation: Ocean Scene
In the following exercise, revise the sentences by replacing the linking verb that is underlined twice with an action verb. Besides changing the verb, you may also change and add other words too. Be creative and have fun making the sentences more lively and vivid.

Notes

When changing the verb, try to use single-word verbs. For example use *sat* instead of *was sitting*.

Example: I <u>was</u> on the roof.

• I sat cross-legged on the roof.

1. The splintery brown shingles <u>were</u> scratchy on my legs.
2. The house <u>was</u> on a cliff by the coast.
3. The seagulls <u>were</u> loud.
4. The sandpipers <u>were</u> at the water's edge.
5. A small white sailboat <u>was</u> out near the edge of the world.
6. A group of children <u>were</u> on the beach.
7. A dog <u>was</u> in the water.
8. A kite <u>was</u> in the sky.
9. A couple <u>was</u> near the pier.
10. The fog <u>was</u> in the distance.

Practice #7   Using Action Verbs

Write five sentences of your own that use *only* action verbs. Be sure to underline these verbs twice and check your work with a classmate.

Hint: Try to describe activities. It's okay to write about five unrelated activities.

Practice #8   Using Linking Verbs

Now write five sentences of your own that use *only* linking verbs. Be sure to underline these verbs twice and check your work with a classmate.

Hint: You may want to write about feelings or descriptions. The sentences don't need to connect to one another.

Practice #9   Creating an Action Paragraph

Now, here's your chance to flex your verb muscles: Write a paragraph that uses only action verbs. (All sentences should relate to one another and flow together.) This will probably be easier if you write about some sort of activity, such as picnicking at the park or playing basketball. Any activity will do. To be successful at this, follow these directions carefully:

a. List at least three *specific* topics you might write about. Then circle the one that seems most promising.

b. Draft a paragraph using mainly action verbs. Write at least five sentences that fit together. Then underline all verbs. (Don't try to use only action verbs at this point. For now, focus on getting your ideas written down.)

c. Go back and check all your verbs. Circle any linking verbs you may have used.

d. Change the sentences with linking verbs and use action verbs instead.

e. Rewrite your paragraph. The final version of your paragraph should be neatly written with no spelling errors.

f. Underline all verbs twice.

Helping Verbs

A **helping verb** is a verb that works with another verb to create a complete verb. Here is a list of some helping verbs:

am	*do*	*must*	*will*
are	*does*	*shall*	*would*
can	*is*	*should*	
could	*may*	*was*	
did	*might*	*were*	

Some of these verbs can work alone as regular verbs, or they can work with others as helping verbs. (*Note: Is, am, are, was,* and *were* can be linking verbs or helping verbs, depending on how they are used in a sentence.) In the following sentences, each complete verb (made of a helping verb and another verb) is underlined twice:

She <u>is working</u> on her English homework.

He <u>did discuss</u> his ideas with his classmates.

He <u>might finish</u> his essay tonight.

The instructor <u>has canceled</u> class.

The students <u>had been hoping</u> for a break.
[Sometimes a complete verb consists of two helping verbs *plus* another verb.]

They <u>do</u> not <u>mind</u> missing one class.
["Not" and "never" sometimes come between the parts of a verb.]

<u>Will</u> we <u>meet</u> next week?
[In a question, the parts of a verb are often separated, with the subject in between.]

Notes

Practice #10   A Day at the Beach

In the paragraph that follows, identify the verbs by underlining them twice. After you have checked your work with a classmate and feel that you have identified all the verbs, highlight the complete verbs that are made up of a helping verb *plus* another verb. The first two sentences are done for you.

A day at the beach <u>can be</u> fun and relaxing, but only if you <u>are</u> prepared. Too often we <u>have made</u> the spontaneous decision to head to the beach. Then we have discovered someone has forgotten something such as his or her swimsuit or towel. So now I plan ahead. First, I check the weather forecast. If it appears favorable, the kids and I begin loading up the car with beach essentials: towels, beach chairs, sunglasses, and sunblock. If we are going to a particularly sunny beach with no shady spots, I bring our beach umbrella. Next, I plan the cooler items such as sodas, bottled water, juice boxes, carrot and celery sticks, and a variety of sandwiches. In addition to cooler items, I bring other snacks. Apples or raisins travel especially well and offer a between-meal energy boost to tired kids. Also, I might pack up our volleyball or badminton set. At the very least I bring the Frisbee and beach ball with us. Before leaving home, I check for swimsuits, flip-flops, and beach toys. We do not want to forget the essentials. On our way out of town we stop to fill up the car with gas and buy a twenty-pound bag of ice for the cooler. Some people enjoy spontaneity. But I would rather be prepared. For this reason, I plan carefully for a day at the beach.

Practice #11   Using Helping Verbs

Create ten original sentences in which you use a helping verb with another verb. Underline your complete verbs twice.

Your Own Writing: Identifying Specific Kinds of Verbs

Copy two paragraphs from one of the journal responses you wrote for this chapter and underline the verbs twice.

- Mark action verbs with an "A."

- Mark linking verbs with an "L."

- Highlight verbs that are made up of a helping verb plus another verb.

- If you see places where changing a linking verb to an action verb would make your writing clearer and more lively, make the necessary revisions.

Using Connections *Online with* mywritinglab

For more practice with using verbs in sentences, log onto www .mywritinglab.com to access the online resources for *Connections,* Third Edition.

Identifying Specific Kinds of Verbs

2

The Structure of Writing and How to Summarize Texts

Main Topics

- Examining the structure of writing

- Building summary skills

- Reading, writing, and thinking about gender roles, stereotypes, and relationships

- Manipulating verb tense

- Identifying verb imposters and prepositional phrases

© United Feature Syndicate Inc.

Your reading and writing assignments will become easier as you begin to understand the structure of writing and how to summarize. Let's begin by studying how the structure of an item reveals its function.

First, imagine a skyscraper and a sports stadium. Although both hold many people, these buildings have been designed for different reasons and to serve different functions. The skyscraper may have a small base since it must fit within a city block, but lack of ground space is made up for in the number of stories. Inside are offices and cubicles, allowing many people to work on individual jobs. The sports stadium, however, may take up several acres of land. With its stadium seating, it's designed to give the most people the best possible view of a game.

Just as the structures of these buildings suggest their functions, so the structure of a piece of writing tells you about its function. In the first part of this chapter, you'll examine several types of writing—essays, textbook excerpts, and journalistic writing—and discover how their structures reveal their functions.

Once you've analyzed several forms of writing, you'll learn how to summarize them. When you summarize, you retell the main points and important supporting points of essays, textbook excerpts, or articles. As you learn to summarize, you'll produce condensed versions of documents that express the author's meaning. In your classes, if you get into the habit of summarizing chapters as you complete them, you'll have a summary from each chapter to study when it's time for a test. In the workplace, if you have developed strong summary skills, you'll be able to summarize documents and present them in condensed form to your boss or colleagues. In the second portion of this chapter, you'll develop the techniques for writing effective summaries.

UNDERSTANDING THE STRUCTURE OF ACADEMIC WRITING

Academic writing, such as an essay or textbook chapter, usually appears as a group of paragraphs working together to prove a point, explain an issue, describe a process, or relate an incident. Normally this group of paragraphs follows a specific organizational structure and may be broken into three basic parts: the introduction, the body, and the conclusion.

The **introduction** (the opening paragraph or two) explains what the essay or chapter will be about and suggests the order and direction of the paragraphs that will follow. The **body** (usually made up of several paragraphs) supports whatever claim has been established in the introduction. The **conclusion** (the final paragraph) summarizes the most important points made in the body or restates the writer's claim from the introduction, while at the same time drawing the essay or chapter to a close. Many textbook chapters and most of the essays you'll read and write in college follow this basic format.

It may help you to think of an essay or textbook chapter as a passenger train. In the same way that an engine pulls the various cars of the train toward a specific destination, an introduction powers the body paragraphs and conclusion toward a specific point the writer is trying to make. And although a train's cars are different (there could be a sleeper car, a dining car, and a baggage car), they are all being pulled in the same direction along the same track.

Each body paragraph, too, though proving different points and containing different kinds of evidence, is guided by the introduction. Finally, as the caboose signals the end of the train, the conclusion signals the end of the essay or chapter.

EXAMINING AN ESSAY

Consider the structure of an essay and how it works as you read the following selection. In "Women Play the Roles Men Want to See," author Maggie Bandur challenges women to defy female stereotypes. As you read, pay close attention to the essay's parts—introduction, body, and conclusion—which are labeled.

In this chapter, words you may not be familiar with are listed before the readings by paragraph (par.) with their definitions.

Terms and definitions:

Par. 1 *Victoria's Secret catalog:* a mail order catalog specializing in women's undergarments and lingerie; *objectification of women:* the treatment of women as objects; *scantily clad:* barely clothed

Par. 2 *antiquated:* outdated; *stereotypes of women:* oversimplified patterns of belief about women

Par. 3 *ogling:* staring; *not synonymous with:* not the same as; *fared:* done

Par. 4 *defy:* go against

Par. 5 *credence:* validity

Women Play the Roles Men Want to See
by Maggie Bandur

This column appeared in the *Daily Northwestern*, Northwestern University, January 23, 1996.

1   A favorite assignment of media courses is to have students analyze advertisements. Without fail, some boy will bring in a picture from the Victoria's Secret catalog as an example of the objectification of women. Does it objectify women? Considering how many sex-starved, male dorm residents steal the mailroom's copies to check out the scantily clad women wearing submissive, come-hither looks, I would have to say "yes." The male-dominated society's lack of respect for women is alive and well!

2   What is not always pointed out, but should be, is that the catalog is marketed to women. And this type of marketing apparently works. The women are just as excited as the men on the day it arrives. Many antiquated attitudes and stereotypes of women persist because men still have a lot of power. But what makes it hard to destroy the stereotypes is that some women still go along with them.

3   Sometimes, I'm one of those women. As much as I hate the fact that men think women are stupid, I have on occasion played dumb to get male assistance. As much as I am offended by male ogling, there have been times when I have worn tight clothing and endured the agony of heels so that men would pay attention to me. (Keep in mind, of course, that attention is not synonymous with being touched.) As saddened as I am at how many women will let men treat them horribly, I haven't fared much better. As much as I try not to give in to all the stereotypes and societal expectations, I sometimes do, but I don't think I am alone.

4   In high school, when my friends and I would go out to dinner, none of the girls would want the guys to see us actually eating. Ordering anything more than a salad and a Diet Coke would supposedly insure that all the boys would think you were a cow. Every once in a while, the other girls and I would agree that this was ridiculous, that we were hungry, and that we would order whatever we darn well pleased. We'd get to the table and I, like a fool, would order first. "Hamburger and chocolate milk shake, please." And then those traitors would all order salads and Diet Cokes. If four or five girls can't work together on a trip to a restaurant, can all womankind join together to defy male expectations? If everyone dressed comfortably, let themselves reach the weight their bodies wanted, and stubbornly refused to give men the time of day until they treated women with the respect they deserved, men would

Notes

The *introduction* of an essay appears first. Here the writer introduces the subject and explains what the essay will be about.

Note: This author introduces the subject of her essay in the first *two* paragraphs.

The *body* paragraphs of the essay appear next. In each body paragraph, the author makes a specific point that helps to support the main idea of the essay.

The *conclusion* appears at the end of the essay. In it, the writer may summarize the main points of the essay or explain what he or she has learned. Its main job is to draw the essay to a close.

come around a whole helluva lot faster. But there is always someone who is going to order that Diet Coke.

5   Sometimes it's easier to play along, and some people will; but in the long run it's better for all women if you don't. Every woman who embraces a stereotype—even if it is as a tool to get ahead in the world that men have made harder for women—is giving that stereotype more credence.

6   It may take a while before I have the strength to resist every dictate of male society, but I am trying. I have almost accepted the fact that I will always be forty to fifty pounds heavier than supermodels my height, and I can almost get through a large meal with a man without apologizing for eating. Small victories, I will admit, but at least it's a start.

A CLOSER LOOK AT THE PARTS

Now that you've read "Women Play the Roles Men Want to See" and have identified the three basic parts of the essay, you're ready to examine these parts more closely.

The Introduction Powers the Essay

As we mentioned, most academic writing (such as essays and textbook chapters) starts with an introduction, one or two paragraphs that establish the subject of the essay and the essay's route or direction—much like an engine powers the cars of a train along a track. Here you can tell your reader what to expect in your essay. Typically the introduction begins with general information and becomes more specific toward the end.

Look back at the introduction of Bandur's essay (the first two paragraphs of the essay). In paragraph 1, Bandur leads us to believe that her paper will focus on how men buy into the stereotyping of women. However, in paragraph 2, Bandur points out that women may also feed this stereotyping and reveals the true focus of her essay.

The Thesis Guides the Essay

At the very end of an introduction, you'll often find a specific statement or two that convey the author's main idea for the entire essay or chapter. This is called the **thesis statement,** and its job is to keep an essay on track as it heads toward its destination.

Notes

Activity

Identifying the Thesis

Underline the thesis statement in "Women Play the Roles Men Want to See." In your own words, write in your notebook what the author intends to talk about in her essay. Share your ideas with a classmate.

The Body Paragraphs Carry the Evidence

The middle paragraphs of an essay (which follow the introduction and precede the conclusion) are called **body paragraphs.** Body paragraphs, like the cars of a train, carry cargo in the form of evidence and support.

Body paragraphs have a particular structure, too. They usually start with a general statement—called a topic sentence—that introduces the main idea of the paragraph. (Sometimes it takes more than one sentence to tell what the paragraph will be about, so a paragraph topic may be introduced in one or more sentences.) The rest of the paragraph supplies more specific pieces of information or examples that support the topic sentence. Often the paragraph includes a final sentence that wraps up the paragraph idea.

Activity

Identifying Topic Sentences

Review the body paragraphs in "Women Play the Roles Men Want to See" and then complete the following tasks.

1. After reviewing, go back and highlight the topic sentences—the general statements that begin the body paragraphs. In your notebook, write down the body paragraph numbers (3–5), and next to each number write down *in your own words* what the author says each paragraph will be about. Compare your ideas to a classmate's to see if you agree. Discuss any differences.

2. Farther down on your sheet of paper, make a separate list called "specific support." Then list any examples or details you find in the body paragraphs. How many specific pieces of support did you find? Which paragraph contains the most support? Compare your findings with a classmate's.

The Conclusion Signals Completion

Finally, at the end of the essay or chapter, there is often a concluding paragraph or section that sums up what has been said earlier and that helps the reader "make sense" of the entire piece. Here, the writer may tell the reader what she's learned from her experiences or what she wants the reader to learn from her essay. Sometimes the writer opts to summarize main ideas as she draws her essay to a close. In other words, the conclusion's job is to signal the end of the essay.

Get Involved!

With a partner or two, create a picture or diagram of an essay. Consider the structure of an essay. Besides drawing a train, how else might you illustrate an essay? You may want to use different colors and shapes to show where the general statements are and where specific information appears. Share your diagrams with classmates.

Activity

Examining the Conclusion

Look back at the conclusion of "Women Play the Roles Men Want to See." In your notebook, list the main points that appear in the conclusion. Did Bandur repeat all of the main points at the end of the essay? What does Bandur want you to learn from her essay?

Journal Assignment

Making the Pieces Fit

Now that you've read about the structure of academic writing and studied Maggie Bandur's essay, you're ready to take another look at the *Peanuts* cartoon on page 38. In a few sentences, explain what is happening in the cartoon and how successful you think Linus and Snoopy will be and why. Now, imagine that Linus and Snoopy are actually working on an academic essay. What are the pieces of an essay that they would be working with? Explain why they wouldn't be able to create a clear essay using their energetic method of making things fit.

THE WRITER'S PURPOSE AND AUDIENCE

So far, you've considered the structure of an essay and how it works. But an essay's message is important as well. For instance, Maggie Bandur uses the essay form to explain to her audience (her readers) how women sometimes practice the stereotypical behaviors they claim to despise. Like Bandur, every writer has a purpose for writing, as well as a message to convey to a chosen audience. The essay form that we've examined in this chapter is one of the possible ways for writers to communicate their messages.

Questions for Critical Thought

Questions for Critical Thought help you examine the writer's message as well as the strategies used to convey that message to the reader.

"Women Play the Roles Men Want to See"

1. According to Bandur, what do men expect women to look like?

2. Does Bandur believe that men are the only ones who try to make women match this stereotype? Explain why Bandur believes it's so hard to get rid of stereotypical views of women.

3. Bandur admits to having played into some of these stereotypes herself. Do you believe that women in society today defy or follow the expectations encouraged by images such as the stereotypical supermodel? Explain.

4. What is the main message of Bandur's column? Mark parts of the text that point to this message.

5. Describe the readers in Bandur's audience. Consider these questions as you describe the readers: Where was this column published? Who would relate best to her examples? What specific words from Bandur's column give us clues about her audience? Your answers to these questions should help you make some thoughtful guesses about the ages and interests of her readers.

Journal Assignment

Making the Writing-Reading-Critical Thinking Connection

Explain what Bandur means when she says that it's "easier to play along" but "better for all women if you don't." Would you say this is useful advice for women? Respond honestly to the article.

EXAMINING A TEXTBOOK CHAPTER

Academic writing in the form of textbook chapters or sections often follows the same basic format as an essay. This is especially true in textbooks for courses such as history, sociology, anthropology, and

Get Involved!

Rent and watch the film *The Family Man* (2000) starring Nicolas Cage and Téa Leoni and directed by Brett Ratner. In your next class meeting, share your reactions to the film and discuss what it has to say about the American family and family values.

psychology. These texts must include a range of important information in a form that is easy for students to follow.

In each segment of a textbook chapter, there should be an introductory paragraph or two, supporting body paragraphs, and a conclusion (or end of chapter summary). The following textbook **excerpt** (selected passage) comes from the chapter, "Families," which appears in *Sociology: A Brief Introduction* by Alex Thio.

Terms and definitions:

Par. 1 *diligently:* applying effort consistently

Par. 2 *chivalrous:* courteous and gentlemanly

Par. 3 *spontaneity:* the quality of being ready at a moment's notice; *seclusive:* isolated

Par. 4 *courting:* dating that leads to marriage; *"playing the field":* casually dating a number of people

Par. 5 *nuclear family:* a family consisting of a father, a mother, and their children

Par. 6 *irrationally:* illogically; *intrinsic:* essential, inner; *extrinsic:* outer; *pragmatic:* practical; *overt:* open and observable

Par. 7 *fervent:* passionately sincere

Preparing for Marriage
by Alex Thio

In the *introduction,* the writer of the textbook section introduces the main ideas of the section.

The first *subsection* (which focuses on one of the main ideas) is identified by boldface. Clearly, the writer will focus on dating practices. This subsection is part of the body of the textbook selection.

1   Most people do not consciously prepare themselves for marriage or diligently seek a person to marry. Instead, they engage in activities that gradually build up a momentum that launches them into marriage. They date, they fall in love, and in each of these steps they usually follow patterns set by society.

2   **The Dating Ritual**   Developed largely after World War I came to an end in 1918, the U.S. custom of dating has spread to many industrial countries. It has also changed in the United States in the last two decades. Before the 1970s, dating was more formal. Males had to ask for a date at least several days in advance. It was usually the male who decided where to go, paid for the date, opened doors, and was supposed to be chivalrous. The couple often went to an event, such as a movie, dance, concert, or ball game.

3   Today, dating has become more casual. In fact, the word "date" now sounds a bit old-fashioned to many young people. Usually you do not have to call somebody and ask for a date. "Getting together" or "hanging

around" is more likely. Spontaneity is the name of the game. A young man may meet a young woman at a snack bar and strike up a brief conversation with her. If he bumps into her a day or two later, he may ask if she wants to go along to the beach, to the library, or to have a hamburger. Males and females are also more likely today than in the past to hang around—get involved in a group activity—rather than pair off for some seclusive intimacy. Neither has the responsibility to ask the other out, which spares them much of the anxiety of formal dating. Getting together has also become less dominated by males. Females are more likely than before to ask a male out, to suggest activities, pay the expenses, or initiate sexual intimacies. Premarital sex has also increased, but it tends to reflect true feelings and desires rather than the need for the male to prove himself or for the female to show gratitude (Strong and DeVault, 1992).

The names and years appearing in parentheses (Strong and DeVault, 1992) are references to research used by Thio in the textbook.

4   The functions of dating, however, have remained pretty constant. It is still a form of entertainment. More important, dating provides opportunities for learning to get along with members of the opposite sex—to develop companionship, friendship, and intimacy. Finally, it offers opportunities for courting, for falling in love with one's future spouse. "Playing the field" does not lead to a higher probability of marital success, though. Those who have married their first and only sweetheart are just as likely to have an enduring and satisfying marriage as those who have married only after dating many people (Whyte, 1992).

Note the word "finally." This signals the writer's final point and concluding remark about dating.

5   **Romantic Love**   Asked why they want to get married, Americans usually say, "Because I am in love." In U.S. society, love between husband and wife is the foundation of the nuclear family. In fact, young people are most reluctant to marry someone if they do not love the person even though the person has all the right qualities they desire. . . .

The second subsection (which focuses on a main idea from the introduction) is identified by boldface as well. This subsection is a part of the body of the textbook selection.

6   But does romantic love really cause people to choose their mates irrationally? Many studies have suggested that the irrationality of love has been greatly exaggerated. An analysis of these studies has led William Kephart and Davor Jedlicka (1988) to reach this conclusion: "Movies and television to the contrary, U.S. youth do not habitually fall in love with unworthy or undesirable characters. In fact, [they] normally make rather sound choices." In one study, when people in love were asked, "Does your head rule your heart, or does your heart rule your head?" 60 percent answered, "The head rules." Apparently, romantic love is not the same as infatuation, which involves physical attraction to a person and a tendency to idealize that person. Romantic love is less emotionalized, but it is expected to provide intrinsic satisfactions, such as happiness, closeness, personal growth, and sexual satisfaction. These differ from the extrinsic rewards offered by a pragmatic loveless marriage—rewards such as good earnings, a nice house, well-prepared meals, and overt respect.

Notes

The writer wraps up
this subsection with a
concluding remark.

7   In the United States over the last 30 years, the belief in romantic love as the basis for marriage has grown more fervent than before. In several studies in the 1960s, 1970s, and 1980s, college men and women were asked, "If a person had all the other qualities you desired, would you marry this person if you were not in love with him/her?" [In the 1980s], as opposed to earlier decades, a greater proportion of young people [said] no (Simpson, Campbell, and Berscheid, 1986).

A CLOSER LOOK AT THE PARTS

Like the essay, the textbook chapter contains the basic elements of academic writing—introduction, body, and conclusion. However, there is a difference between the essay "Women Play the Roles Men Want to See" and the textbook selection "Preparing for Marriage." Textbook chapters often contain section headings and subheadings in bold to keep information clearly organized. It's easy to see how such headings work.

Under the general heading of "Preparing for Marriage," the author gives a quick overview of the section. The two subsections, "The Dating Ritual" and "Romantic Love," which offer different aspects of the main topic, are presented in an organized manner—one topic at a time. Textbook headings and subheadings show the general topic of the section, give easy references to specific information, and help readers anticipate what sections will be about.

Activity

Examining Headings and Subheadings

1. The heading of this textbook section is "Preparing for Marriage." Highlight the two subheadings. Notice that the two subheadings (or subsections) are introduced in the opening paragraph of the section. Explain how the writer sets up the two subsections in the introduction.

2. Examine a chapter of another textbook. (Look at a history, psychology, sociology, or other textbook that presents large sections of information.) Read the chapter, then write down the chapter's headings and subheadings. Explain how the writer has organized the information under headings and subheadings.

The Introduction and Thesis

Textbook sections and chapters—like the essay—contain an introduction that lets the reader know what information will be covered. In fact, it's important for the textbook writer to state the **thesis** or main idea of each chapter clearly so that students can follow the chapter discussion easily.

Activity

Identifying the Thesis

After rereading the introduction, in your own words, write down the thesis of "Preparing for Marriage." What does the introduction tell you the excerpt will be about?

The Body Paragraphs

The body paragraphs of a textbook chapter often begin with topic sentences like those in the essay. They are followed by support in the form of examples, details, quotations, and other evidence.

Activity

Identifying Topic Sentences

Review the body paragraphs in "Preparing for Marriage" and then complete the tasks below.

1. Highlight the topic sentence(s) in each body paragraph. (Keep in mind that sometimes it takes more than one sentence to introduce the paragraph topic.) Then, in your own words, write down what each paragraph is about.

2. Also in your notebook, make a "specific support" list. Go back through the selection and write down examples, details, quotations, and other forms of support. Which of the paragraphs contains the most support? Share your findings with a classmate.

The Conclusion

Most textbook chapters end with a summary. You may have noticed, for example, that Chapter 1 of *Connections* ends with a summary of

Notes   the entire chapter. However, within each section or subsection of a chapter, you should be able to identify a concluding remark or two that draws that section or subsection to a close.

Activities

Examining the Conclusion

Review the concluding remarks in each subsection of "Preparing for Marriage." Does Thio repeat all of the main points of the body paragraphs from "The Dating Ritual"? What does Thio want you to learn about dating? Does Thio repeat the main points of "Romantic Love"? What does he want you to learn about romantic love?

Comparing the Structures of Academic Writing

1. Compare the structures of Thio's "Preparing for Marriage" and Bandur's "Women Play the Roles Men Want to See." How are their shapes similar? How are they different?

2. Compare the structure of "Preparing for Marriage" to the structure of a chapter or section in another college textbook. How are their shapes similar? How are they different? Does the section you've chosen contain headings and subheadings similar to those in "Preparing for Marriage"?

THE WRITER'S PURPOSE AND AUDIENCE

Although the essay "Women Play the Roles Men Want to See" was written to convince women to resist fulfilling stereotypes, the textbook selection "Preparing for Marriage" was written to inform. If you look back through the selection, you will see that Thio has compiled source information (studies and research) and has presented concepts differently than Bandur. As you respond to the questions that follow, consider why Thio's writing would serve a different audience and purpose than Bandur's might.

Questions for Critical Thought

"Preparing for Marriage"

1. According to Thio, do most people consciously prepare for marriage? What leads people to eventually marry?

2. How has dating in the United States changed in the last thirty years? What was it like before the 1970s? In what ways is it different today? What hasn't changed about dating? What's dating really for?

3. According to Thio, what is "the foundation of the nuclear family"?

4. What part, if any, does romantic love play in American marriages, according to Thio's findings?

5. What is Thio's purpose in writing "Preparing for Marriage"? Who would be his audience? Explain how Thio's purpose and audience differ from Bandur's.

Journal Assignment

Making the Writing-Reading-Critical Thinking Connection

Compare dating, romantic love, and marriage in the past and present. Is dating today the same as it was in your parents' or grandparents' youth? Did romantic love play a part in their choices of mates? Do you consider romantic love to be important to your own relationships? In your notebook, write about what you believe to be the ideal approach to love and/or marriage based on what you've read and experienced.

UNDERSTANDING THE STRUCTURE OF JOURNALISTIC WRITING

Besides academic writing, there are other forms of professional writing, such as journalism (news writing and reporting), that you probably encounter on a daily basis. If you read the newspaper or a weekly or monthly magazine, then you've already come across many different types of writing. In this section, you will examine a type of newspaper article called the feature story.

EXAMINING A FEATURE STORY

A feature story is a newspaper article that presents and discusses a timely issue. It does not follow the same format as the essay or textbook chapter. News writers know that they must "hook" their readers with an interesting opening statement. Once they snag their audience, they must provide manageable "bites" of information because busy readers are probably reading their papers over morning coffee. In fact, that's one of the reasons the paragraphs are short, sometimes only a sentence or two in length.

Notes   Another reason for the short paragraphs has to do with the way a newspaper is laid out into columns (several long, vertical rows of writing on a news page). Newspaper columns are long and thin, so paragraphs must be kept short. Otherwise, a paragraph might go on for an entire column, which could result in readers losing their place in the reading. Finally, journalistic style doesn't call for the same level of explanation and development that academic style requires, so shorter paragraphs are acceptable.

The feature story "He Turns Boys into Men" appears below. In it, writer Jeffrey Marx focuses on former NFL star Joe Ehrmann's work with inner-city youth and a program Ehrmann started called Building Men for Others.

Terms and definitions:

Par. 1 *taut:* tense

Par. 2 *hobbled:* broken down physically

Par. 23 *empathy:* identifying with and/or understanding another person's circumstances or feelings

Par. 33 *obituary:* a notice placed in the newspaper to announce the death of an individual; it usually contains a biographical summary and funeral arrangements

He Turns Boys into Men*
by Jeffrey Marx

Jeffrey Marx is a Pulitzer Prize winner and author of the book *Season of Life.*

1   Young faces usually filled with warmth and wonder are now taut with anticipation and purpose. Eyes are lasers. Hearts are pounding. This is nothing unusual for the final minutes before a high school football game. But a coach and his players are about to share an exchange that is downright foreign to the tough-guy culture of football.

2   The coach, Joe Ehrmann, is a former NFL star, now 55 and hobbled, with white hair and gold-rimmed glasses. Still, he is a mountain of a man. Standing before the Greyhounds of Gilman School in Baltimore, Ehrmann does not need a whistle.

3   "What is our job as coaches?" Ehrmann asks.

4   "To love us!" the Gilman boys yell back in unison.

5   "What is *your* job?" Ehrmann shouts back.

6   "To love each other!" the boys respond.

7   The words are spoken with the commitment of an oath, the enthusiasm of a pep rally.

8   This is football?

9   It is with Ehrmann. It is when the whole purpose of being here is to totally redefine what it means to be a man.

10   This is lofty work for a volunteer coach on a high school football field. It is work that makes Ehrmann the most important coach in America.

11   In his eighth season at Gilman, Ehrmann's résumé is anything but ordinary for a defensive coordinator. After 13 years in professional football, most of them as a defensive lineman for the Baltimore Colts, he retired in 1985 and began tackling much more significant challenges. As an inner-city minister and founder of a community center known as The Door, Ehrmann worked the hard streets of East Baltimore. He also co-founded a Ronald McDonald House for sick children and launched a racial-reconciliation project called Mission Baltimore. Now he's a pastor at the 4000-member Grace Fellowship Church and president of a national organization that supports abused children.

12   "He's a lot of things to a lot of people," says Maryland Gov. Robert I. Ehrlich Jr. "He's really an opinion leader. And what I love about Joe—it's not just the messages. It's the messenger. He's a very unique man. Gentle. Principled. Committed. And effective."

13   Aside from the X's and O's of football, everything Ehrmann teaches at Gilman stems from his belief that our society does a horrible job of teaching boys how to be men and that virtually every problem we face can somehow be traced back to this failure. That is why he developed a program called Building Men for Others, which has become the signature philosophy of Gilman football.

14   The first step is to tear down what Ehrmann says are the standard criteria—athletic ability, sexual conquest and economic success—that are constantly held up in our culture as measurements of manhood.

15   "Those are the three lies that make up what I call 'false masculinity,'" Ehrmann says. "The problem is that it sets men up for tremendous failures in our lives. Because it gives us this concept that what we need to do as men is compare what we have and compete with others for what they have."

16   "As a young boy, I'm going to compare my athletic ability to yours and compete for whatever attention that brings. When I'm older, I'm going to compare my girlfriend to yours and compete for whatever status I can acquire by being with the prettiest or the coolest or the best

girl I can get. Ultimately, as adults, we compare bank accounts and job titles, houses and cars, and we compete for the amount of security and power that those represent."

17 "We compare, we compete. That's all we ever do. It leaves most men feeling isolated and alone. And it destroys any concept of community."

18 Ehrmann offers a simple but powerful solution. His own definition of what it means to be a man—he calls it "strategic masculinity"—is based on only two things: relationships and having a cause beyond yourself.

19 "Masculinity, first and foremost, ought to be defined in terms of relationships," Ehrmann says. "It ought to be taught in terms of the capacity to *love* and *be loved*. It comes down to this: What kind of father are you? What kind of coach or teammate are you? What kind of son are you? What kind of friend are you? Success comes in terms of relationships."

20 "And then all of us ought to have some kind of cause, some kind of purpose in our lives that's bigger than our own individual hopes, dreams, wants and desires. At the end of our life, we ought to be able to look back over it from our deathbed and know that somehow the world is a better place because we lived, we loved, we were other-centered, other-focused."

21 How is all of this taught within the context of football?

22 From the first day of practice through the last day of the season, Ehrmann and his best friend, Head Coach Biff Poggi, bombard their players with stories and lessons about being a man built for others.

23 They stress that Gilman football is all about living in a community. It is about fostering relationships. It is about learning the importance of serving others. While coaches elsewhere scream endlessly about being *tough*, Ehrmann and Poggi teach concepts such as empathy, inclusion and integrity. They emphasize Ehrmann's code of conduct for manhood: accepting responsibility, leading courageously, enacting justice on behalf of others.

24 "I was blown away at first," says Sean Price, who joined the varsity as a freshman and is now a junior. "All the stuff about love and relationships—I didn't really understand why it was part of football. After a while, though, getting to know some of the older guys on the team, it was the first time I've ever been around friends who really cared about me."

25 Four hours before each game, the Gilman players file into a meeting room for bagels, orange juice and Building Men 101. Ehrmann and Poggi tell their players they expect greatness out of them. But the only way they will measure greatness is by the impact the boys make on other people's lives.

26 Ultimately, the boys are told, they will make the greatest impact on the world—will bring the most love and grace and healing to people—by

constantly basing their actions and thoughts on one simple question: What can I do for *you*?

27   That explains the rule that no Gilman football player should ever let another student—football player or not—sit by himself in the school lunchroom. "How do you think that boy feels if he's eating all alone?" Ehrmann asks his players. "Go get him and bring him over to your table."

28   There are other rules that many coaches would consider ludicrous. No boy is cut from the Gilman team based on athletic ability. Every senior plays—and not only in lopsided games. Coaches must always teach by building up instead of tearing down. As Ehrmann puts it in a staff notebook: "Let us be mindful never to shame a boy but to correct him in an uplifting and loving way."

29   Whenever Ehrmann speaks publicly about Building Men for Others— usually at a coaching clinic, a men's workshop or a forum for parents— someone inevitably asks about winning and losing: "All this touchy-feely stuff sounds great, but kids still want to win, right?"

30   "Well, we've had pretty good success," Ehrmann says. "But winning is only a byproduct of everything else we do—and it's certainly not the way we evaluate ourselves."

31   Unless pressed for specifics, Ehrmann does not even mention that Gilman finished three of the last six seasons undefeated and No. 1 in Baltimore. In 2002, the Greyhounds ranked No. 1 in Maryland and climbed to No. 14 in the national rankings.

32   Much more important to Ehrmann is the way that his team ends each season when nobody else is watching. Before the last game, each senior stands before his teammates and coaches to read an essay titled "How I Want to Be Remembered When I Die."

33   Here is something linebacker David Caperna—reading from his own "obituary"—said last year: "David was a man who fought for justice and accepted the consequences of his actions. He was not a man who would allow poverty, abuse, racism or any sort of oppression to take place in his presence. David carried with him the knowledge and pride of being a man built for others."

34   The most important coach in America sat back and smiled. Win or lose on the field of play, Joe Ehrmann had already scored the kind of victory that would last a lifetime.

A CLOSER LOOK AT THE PARTS

Although it doesn't have the same structure as the essay or textbook chapter, the newspaper article does contain some similar components: an introduction, body, and conclusion.

Activity

Labeling the Parts

Go back through "He Turns Boys into Men," and in the "Notes" column label the introduction, body, and conclusion. (Remember, an introduction may be longer than one paragraph.)

Get Involved!

Bring in a front-page newspaper article that you believe has a strong lead. Be prepared to share your article and describe to classmates what the writer has done to draw you into the article.

The Introduction Is Called the Lead

Whereas the essay contains a more formal introduction, a newspaper article begins with what is called the lead. The lead, the opening statement of an article, is often an intriguing or dynamic sentence or two designed to interest the reader. At other times, it is a statement of fact or explains the main point of the article. Without a clever or engaging lead, journalists (news writers) risk losing their audience. In "He Turns Boys into Men," Marx presents a captivating lead.

Activities

Examining the Lead

Review the first paragraph of "He Turns Boys into Men." What does Marx do to draw the reader into the article? Did his opening paragraph make you want to read more? Why, or why not?

Identifying the Thesis

Now that you've examined the lead, reread the first ten paragraphs of the article. With a partner, discuss what you believe the article is about. Look for and then highlight the sentence or sentences (in paragraphs 1–10) that describe what the article is about.

The Body Paragraphs Are Shorter

The body paragraphs of a newspaper article are shorter than those appearing in an essay. You may have noticed, in fact, that some paragraphs are only one sentence long. As in the essay, each new paragraph identifies a shift in an idea or thought. But newspaper articles contain paragraph breaks for other reasons as well. Journalists break for new paragraphs or keep paragraphs short in a newspaper article for a number of reasons:

1. to signal a shift in an idea or thought (just like in the essay);

2. to set off a quotation or a set of facts;

3. to identify shifts in dialogue (when one person stops talking and another begins talking);

4. to emphasize a certain idea or make a dramatic or significant point;

5. to keep the paragraph from going on too long (since newspaper articles are arranged in slim columns, paragraphs must be kept short); or

6. to offer the busy reader manageable bites of information.

Activities

Examining Paragraph Breaks

With a classmate, move through the article "He Turns Boys into Men" and write reason 1, 2, 3, 4, 5, or 6 (from the list above) next to each new paragraph to identify the probable reason for the paragraph shift.

Examining Paragraph Support

In the "Notes" column, make a list of the types of support that appear in the body of the article. This could include examples, quotations, statistics, personal testimony, or other forms of evidence.

The Conclusion

In the conclusion of a newspaper article, the writer tries to bring his ideas full circle. Most often, the feature story ends with a final thought or quotation rather than a summary of the main points.

Activities

Examining the Conclusion

Review the final few paragraphs of the article, especially paragraphs 31–34. Explain how Marx concludes his feature story. What final thought would you say Marx wants to leave with his reader? Explain.

Notes

THE WRITER'S PURPOSE AND AUDIENCE

The journalist has the same goal as any other writer—to convey a particular message to his reader. In "He Turns Boys into Men," Marx presents a new way to think about masculinity. By introducing the reader to Joe Ehrmann and his approach to coaching football, Marx offers the reader the opportunity to reconsider how we prepare boys to become men in our society. Consider Marx's perspective and approach as you answer the questions that follow.

Questions for Critical Thought

"He Turns Boys into Men"

1. According to Marx, what is Joe Ehrmann's reason for coaching football at Gilman School in Baltimore?

2. In what ways is football different at Gilman than at most other schools?

3. Ehrmann talks about the difference between "false masculinity" and "strategic masculinity." How does Ehrmann define each of these terms?

4. Ehrmann says, "Our society does a horrible job of teaching boys how to be men." Do you agree or disagree with his statement? Explain.

5. He also claims "that virtually every problem we face" is a result of society's failure to teach boys how to be men. Do you agree or disagree? Explain.

6. What are the two things that Ehrmann says it takes to be a man? What is modern society's concept of what it means to be a man, according to Ehrmann?

7. Describe Ehrmann's course, Building Men 101. What are some of the lessons taught in the class? Do such lessons seem appropriate for a football squad? Why, or why not?

8. Ehrmann didn't bring up Gilman's record of wins and losses. Why not? Do you think he's right to keep the focus off the team's wins and losses? Explain.

9. In what ways has Ehrmann's approach affected the boys he coaches? What evidence does Marx include to show how the boys have changed under Ehrmann's leadership?

> ### *Journal Assignment*
>
> ### *Making the Writing-Reading-Critical Thinking Connection*
>
> Write a response to those who ask Ehrmann this question (see paragraph 29): "All this touchy-feely stuff sounds great, but kids still want to win, right?"
>
> Think about how Ehrmann answers this question. Think about your own reaction to Ehrmann's approach. What would you say to those who ask this question?

BUILDING SUMMARY SKILLS

Now that you've learned how academic and journalistic writing work, you're ready to learn how to summarize these forms of writing. As you learn to summarize, you'll develop the ability to produce condensed versions of documents for study purposes, class assignments, and workplace reports.

What Is a Summary?

A **summary** is basically a *concise retelling of the main points of a longer piece of writing.* Your job in writing a summary is to relay the author's most important points without including your own opinion on the subject. (Although your opinion isn't included when you are writing a summary, your opinion is a welcome and important part of reading questions, journal responses, essays, and other written assignments.)

Points to Remember About Summaries

- Summaries should be much shorter than what you are summarizing.
- Summaries should include all main points and important supporting details—not just what you liked best. Nonessential details and examples should be left out.

Notes

Plagiarism is the act of using someone else's words as your own without giving proper credit to the author. If you use a word-for-word phrase or sentence from the original, you must place it in quotation marks and credit the author.

- Summaries should include, when possible, the author's name and the title of what you're summarizing (and the date and place of publication, if available).
- Summaries should be written in your own words (paraphrased), not copied—to avoid *plagiarizing* the author's work. (You may include an occasional quotation for impact.)
- Summaries should not include your reactions to the text.

A Sample Summary

Before writing the summary, you'll examine what a summary looks like and how it works. First, you'll read a brief essay from the textbook *Essentials of Sociology: A Down-to-Earth Approach*, Seventh Edition. Then you'll examine a list of main ideas and important supporting ideas drawn from the reading. Finally, you'll read a summary that incorporates these ideas in order to relay the author's most important points.

Terms and definitions:

Par. 1 *ingenious:* clever and original; *homely:* unattractive

Par. 4 *permeate:* to spread throughout or fill; *bestows:* presents

Beauty May Be Only Skin Deep, But Its Effects Go On Forever: Stereotypes in Everyday Life*
by James M. Henslin

The date appearing in parentheses (1993) refers to the year in which Snyder conducted his study.

1   Mark Snyder, a psychologist, wondered whether **stereotypes**—our assumptions of what people are like—might be self-fulfilling. He came up with an ingenious way to test this idea. He (1993) gave college men a Polaroid snapshot of a woman (supposedly taken just moments before) and told them that he would introduce them to her after they talked with her on the telephone. Actually, the photographs—showing either a pretty or a homely woman—had been prepared before the experiment began. The photo was not of the woman the men would talk to.

2   Stereotypes came into play immediately. As Snyder gave each man the photograph, he asked him what he thought the woman would be like. The men who saw the photograph of the attractive woman said that they expected to meet a poised, humorous, outgoing woman.

---

*From James M. Henslin, *Essentials of Sociology: A Down-to-Earth Approach*, 7th edition. Published by Allyn and Bacon, Boston, MA. Copyright © 2007 by Pearson Education. Reprinted by permission of the publisher.

The men who had been given a photo of the unattractive woman described her as awkward, serious, and unsociable.

3   The men's stereotypes influenced the way they spoke on the telephone to the women, who did not know about the photographs. The men who had seen the photograph of a pretty woman were warm, friendly, and humorous. This, in turn, affected the women they spoke to, for they responded in a warm, friendly, outgoing manner. And the men who had seen the photograph of a homely woman? On the phone, they were cold, reserved, and humorless, and the women they spoke to became cool, reserved, and humorless. Keep in mind that the women did not know that their looks had been evaluated—and that the photographs were not even of them. In short, stereotypes tend to produce behaviors that match the stereotype. . . .

4   Although beauty might be only skin deep, its consequences permeate our lives (Katz 2005). Beauty bestows an advantage in everyday interaction, but it also has other effects. For one, if you are physically attractive, you are likely to make more money. Researchers in both Holland and the United States found that advertising firms with better-looking executives have higher revenues (Bosman et al. 1997; Pfann et al. 2000). The reason? The researchers suggest that people are more willing to associate with individuals whom they perceive as good-looking.

The names and dates appearing in parentheses are references to particular research studies.

List of main ideas and important supporting ideas:

- James M. Henslin wrote "Beauty May Be Only Skin Deep, But Its Effects Go On Forever," which focuses on the long-term effects of stereotyping.
- He examines a study by Mark Snyder on stereotyping.
- Snyder wanted to see if stereotypes might be "self-fulfilling."
- Snyder developed a unique way to test his idea by using college-age men to evaluate snapshots of pretty and homely women to see if the photos would influence their interaction with the women.
- Then Snyder had the men talk to the women on the phone.
- The men thought they were talking to the women in the photos, but they weren't.
- The women didn't know the men had been shown fake photos of them, nor did they know that the men had judged them based on these photos.
- Snyder found out that the men's attitudes affected their telephone conversations with the women.

- The men were warm toward the women they thought were pretty and cool toward the women they thought were homely.
- The women responded to the men's warmth or coolness in the conversation, proving that the conversation was influenced by what the men thought the women looked like.
- Henslin refers to one study which suggests that, "although beauty may be only skin deep, its consequences permeate our lives."
- He cites other researchers who have discovered that people's careers and salaries are influenced by how they look.
- Henslin says this is because people like being around good-looking people.
- Henslin believes that stereotypes have long-term effects on people's lives.

Summary   In the essay "Beauty May Be Only Skin Deep, But Its Effects Go On Forever," sociologist James M. Henslin reports on the long-term effects of stereotyping. In order to make this point, Henslin shares some surprising results of a study conducted by psychologist Mark Snyder. Snyder had been interested in finding out whether people buy into stereotyping, so he developed a method for testing this idea using a group of college-age men and a set of photographs. Snyder showed each man a photograph of either an attractive or unattractive woman and told him that he would be meeting the woman in the photo after a brief telephone conversation with her. Before each man spoke to the woman on the telephone, Snyder asked the man what he thought she would be like. The men who saw the photo of a pretty woman thought she would be smart and funny. But those who saw the photo of a homely woman thought she would be dull and boring. Following this, Snyder told each man he would be speaking to the woman in the photograph—even though that was not true. The women had no idea that these photos had been shared or their personalities had been discussed. As the men spoke to the women, Snyder discovered that those who thought they were talking to a pretty woman were funny and engaging while those who believed they were talking to a homely woman were serious and cold. Henslin says that Snyder's results reinforce other studies that suggest more attractive people tend to get better jobs and make higher earnings. Citing another study, Henslin says, "although beauty may be only skin deep, its consequences permeate our lives."

WRITING THE ACADEMIC SUMMARY

Notes

As you examined how the typical essay or textbook chapter is constructed, you discovered that general information appeared in certain places and specific information in others. You learned, for instance, that in most cases the introduction offers an overview of the essay or chapter, so it contains mainly general information.

Note: Summaries may be more than one paragraph long depending on the length of the original document. However, the summary assignments in this chapter call for a single paragraph.

You've learned, too, that each body paragraph usually (though not always) begins with a topic sentence, a general statement that tells what the paragraph will be about. This topic sentence is followed by details and examples, specific information that helps prove the main point of the paragraph. And you've examined the process one writer went through to identify main ideas and summarize Henslin's "Beauty May Be Only Skin Deep, But Its Effects Go On Forever."

Now you're ready to develop your summary writing skills. While similar to the writing process you practiced in Chapter 1, the summary writing process contains a couple of unique steps. The five steps of the process are described here:

Step 1:   Distinguishing between general and specific information

Step 2:   Identifying the main points

Step 3:   Drafting the summary

Step 4:   Revising the summary

Step 5:   Editing the summary

You'll read about and practice each of these steps in the activities and summary assignments that follow.

Distinguishing Between General and Specific Information

Learning to tell the difference between general and specific statements is the first step in learning to summarize academic writing. Most of the academic writing you'll encounter contains both general and specific information. General statements usually give the reader an overview of the essay or a particular paragraph. Specific statements offer examples, statistics, quotations, or other forms of evidence to support the more general statements. Why is it important for you to be able to distinguish between general and specific information? As you develop this skill, you'll begin to see how main ideas appear in various forms of writing. This will help you understand your readings, prepare for exams, and summarize.

Notes

Read this paragraph from the essay titled, "The Modern Family." (*Note:* General information has been identified by a "G" in the "Notes" column, and specific information has been identified by an "S.")

G   During the 1950s, the Cleavers on the television show *Leave It to Beaver* epitomized the American family. In 1960, over 70 percent of all American households were like the Cleavers: made up of a breadwinner father, a home-

S   maker mother, and their kids. Today, "traditional" families with a working husband, [a homemaker], and one or more children make up less than 15 percent of the nation's households. And as America's families have changed, the image

G   of the family portrayed on television has changed accordingly. . . .

—*James Kirby Martin et al., from* America and Its People

The topic sentence of this paragraph offers a general statement about what the authors believe a typical American family used to be like. This statement is followed by specific information in the form of statistics—"In 1960, over 70 percent of all American households were like the Cleavers"—and a description of the roles played by members of the traditional American family: "a breadwinner father, a home-maker mother, and their kids." The statistical information and description are followed by a final general statement suggesting that images on television reflect changes in the American family.

Activity

Distinguishing Between General and Specific Information in "The Modern Family"

1. Read the paragraph below. (This is another paragraph from the essay, "The Modern Family.")

Profound changes have reshaped American family life in recent years. In a decade, divorce rates doubled. The number of divorces today is twice as high as in 1966 and three times higher than in 1950. The rapid upsurge in the divorce rates contributed to a dramatic increase in the number of single-parent households. . . . The number of households consisting of a single woman and her children has tripled since 1960. A sharp increase in female-headed homes has been accompanied by a startling increase in the number of couples cohabitating outside of marriage. The number of unmarried couples living together has quadrupled since 1970.

2. Write "G" beside general statements and "S" beside specific statements.

3. Write down any words or phrases (such as "for example") that indicate that specific support will follow.

SUMMARIZING AN ESSAY

You've learned that distinguishing between general and specific information is the first step of an effective summary writing process. Now that you've practiced this step on the paragraph, you're ready to practice it on an essay. Once you've completed this step, you'll move on to Steps 2 through 5 as you write your first summary.

Summary Assignment #1

Write a one-paragraph summary of Maggie Bandur's "Women Play the Roles Men Want to See" (pages 41–42).

Step 1

Distinguishing Between General and Specific Information in "Women Play the Roles Men Want to See"

1. Return to the essay "Women Play the Roles Men Want to See." As you review the essay, mark general statements with "G" and specific statements with "S."

2. Underline or highlight words and phrases (such as "for instance") that indicate that specific support follows.

Identifying the Main Points

Now that you've marked the general and specific pieces of information in "Women Play the Roles Men Want to See," you're prepared to identify the main ideas Bandur presents in her essay. Remember, main ideas most often appear in general statements. So you'll want to pay close attention to the sentences you marked "G" in Step 1.

Step 2

Identifying Main Points in "Women Play the Roles Men Want to See"

1. Look back at how you've marked the general and specific statements in "Women Play the Roles Men Want to See." Which statements appear to be the most important, or main, ideas? Highlight only these statements and review them carefully. Leave out details.

2. Now set the essay aside and from memory make a list of these main ideas. (You don't need to quote them exactly. In fact, you should put these main points in your own words.)

3. Go back to the essay and double-check to see that you've included all of the main points. Add necessary information to your list.

Drafting the Summary

Once you have made a list of the main points, you are ready for Step 3, writing your summary. Remember that your summary should

- open with a sentence (or two) that introduces the essay and explains, in general, what it's about;

- provide an overview of the piece;

- include all of the main points (even those you may not agree with) and the most important supporting points; and

- end with the author's conclusions on the subject.

Step 3

Drafting a Summary of "Women Play the Roles Men Want to See"

Drawing from your list of main ideas, draft your summary of "Women Play the Roles Men Want to See." Be sure to include a topic sentence that contains the title and author of the essay and explains in general what the essay is about. Follow the topic sentence with Bandur's main ideas and most important supporting points. Add a final sentence that provides the author's conclusions on the subject.

Revising the Summary

After completing a draft of your summary, it's time to move to Step 4 of the process. To do this, you must look back at the document you're summarizing to make sure you have accurately explained the main ideas as the author intended. If you discover that you have not explained an idea correctly, then you need to revise (rewrite) parts of your summary to more accurately reflect the main ideas presented in the original piece.

Step 4

Revising Your Summary of "Women Play the Roles Men Want to See"

Return to "Women Play the Roles Men Want to See." Compare the main ideas that you highlighted to those you have relayed in your summary. Have you explained the most important points accurately? If not, revise your summary to better reflect the main ideas in the original.

Editing the Summary

By now, your summary paragraph should have a strong topic sentence and contain the main ideas and most important supporting points of the essay you're summarizing. When you've reached this point, you're ready to correct sentence and spelling errors.

Step 5

Editing Your Summary of "Women Play the Roles Men Want to See"

Ask a friend or classmate to read your summary paragraph to you. If your reader struggles with a word or sentence, then you need to look carefully to determine if there's a sentence or spelling error. Correct the errors you can. If there are errors you aren't sure how to fix, ask your instructor or a tutor to explain how you can fix them.

SUMMARIZING A TEXTBOOK CHAPTER

Earlier in this chapter, you studied the structure of a textbook chapter. You learned that, like the essay, it contains an introduction, supporting body paragraphs, and a conclusion (or chapter summary). As in the

Notes

essay, general statements in a textbook chapter tend to appear in the introduction, in the topic sentences of the body paragraphs, and in the conclusion. These general statements offer the reader an overview of the chapter, a subsection of the chapter, or individual paragraphs. Specific statements contain examples, statistics, details, and other forms of evidence that support the general statements.

Unlike the essay, the textbook chapter (because of its length) is often divided into smaller subsections in order to keep information neatly organized and make it easier to follow. Still, chapter subsections adhere to the same academic writing structure as the essay. You'll find that you can distinguish between general and specific ideas, identify main points, and summarize subsections of a chapter just as you would an essay.

Summary Assignment #2

> *Write a one-paragraph summary of Alex Thio's "Preparing for Marriage" (pages 46–48).*

Step 1

Distinguishing Between General and Specific Information in "Preparing for Marriage"

1. Return to the essay "Preparing for Marriage." As you review the textbook passage, mark general statements with "G" and specific statements with "S."

2. Underline or highlight any words or phrases (such as "for example") that indicate that specific support follows.

Step 2

Identifying Main Points in "Preparing for Marriage"

1. Review the general and specific statements you identified in Step 1. Highlight only those statements that appear to be the main ideas.

2. Now set the textbook passage aside and from memory make a list of these main ideas.

3. Return to the textbook passage and double-check to make sure that you've included all of the main points. If you've missed important information, add it to your list.

Step 3

Drafting a Summary of "Preparing for Marriage"

Drawing from your list of main ideas, draft your summary of "Preparing for Marriage." Be sure to include a topic sentence that contains the title and author of the textbook passage and explains in general what the passage is about. Follow the topic sentence with Thio's main ideas and most important supporting points. Add a final sentence that provides the author's conclusions on the subject.

Step 4

Revising Your Summary of "Preparing for Marriage"

Return to "Preparing for Marriage" and compare the main ideas you highlighted in the textbook passage to those you've included in your summary. Have you included all of the main ideas? And have you explained them as the author presented them? If not, revise your summary so that it contains all the main ideas as the author presented them.

Step 5

Editing Your Summary of "Preparing for Marriage"

Ask a friend or classmate to read your summary paragraph to you. If your reader struggles with a word or sentence, then you need to look carefully to determine if there's a sentence or spelling error. Correct the errors you can. If there are errors you aren't sure how to fix, ask your instructor or a tutor to explain how you can fix them.

WRITING THE JOURNALISTIC SUMMARY

Earlier in this chapter, you discovered the ways in which journalistic writing differs from academic writing. You learned, for example, that most newspaper or magazine articles begin with a lead that is followed by short body paragraphs, which may or may not have topic sentences.

Such articles often conclude with a final remark or a quotation that reinforces the lead.

You may be surprised to find out that you will use the same five steps that you followed for summarizing academic writing when you summarize journalistic writing. The steps appear here for review:

Step 1:   Distinguishing between general and specific information

Step 2:   Identifying main points

Step 3:   Drafting the summary

Step 4:   Revising the summary

Step 5:   Editing the summary

SUMMARIZING AN ARTICLE

The following summary assignment will give you the opportunity to apply what you've learned about journalistic writing and practice the summary writing process.

Summary Assignment #3

Write a one-paragraph summary of Jeffrey Marx's "He Turns Boys into Men" (pages 52–55).

Distinguishing Between General and Specific Information

When you studied the feature story, you learned that the body paragraphs of newspaper and magazine articles are usually short, and paragraph shifts can occur for a variety of reasons. These are important points to remember when summarizing journalistic writing. Unlike the body paragraph of an essay or textbook chapter, the body paragraph of an article may or may not contain a topic sentence or main idea. Keep this difference in mind as you distinguish between general and specific ideas in "He Turns Boys into Men."

Step 1

Distinguishing Between General and Specific Statements in "He Turns Boys into Men"

Return to the article "He Turns Boys into Men." As you read, mark general statements with "G" and specific statements with "S."

Identifying the Main Points

In distinguishing between general and specific information, you are preparing to write your summary. Remember, the main ideas in a magazine or newspaper article usually appear in general statements just as they do in academic writing. Identifying these main ideas is the second step of the summary process.

Step 2

Identifying Main Points in "He Turns Boys into Men"

1. Look back at how you've marked general and specific statements in "He Turns Boys into Men." Which statements appear to be the most important, or main, ideas? Highlight only these statements and review them carefully. Leave out details for now.

2. Set the article aside, and from memory write a list of the main points. (Don't worry about getting them down word for word. These should be in your own words.)

3. Return to the article and check to see if you've included all of the main points on your list. Add any you left out.

Drafting the Summary

Putting the main points into paragraph form is Step 3. Keep in mind that a summary should begin with a statement that gives an overview of the article and includes the article's author and title. In order for a summary to be effective, it must include all of the main points and end with the author's conclusions.

Step 3

Drafting a Summary of "He Turns Boys into Men"

Draft a summary using the list of main ideas you wrote down in Step 2. In a topic sentence, introduce the author, title, and overall main idea of the article. Follow with the most important points. End your summary with the author's conclusions on the subject.

Revising the Summary

After writing a draft of your summary, it's important to return to the article and check to make sure that you have explained the author's main ideas accurately. This is Step 4 of the process.

Step 4

> **Revising Your Summary of "He Turns Boys into Men"**
>
> Review the article "He Turns Boys into Men." Compare the main ideas you highlighted earlier to those that appear in your summary now. Have you included the most important points? Have you relayed them as the author did? If not, revise your summary to agree with the original.

Editing the Summary

By now, your summary paragraph should have a strong topic sentence and contain the main ideas and most important supporting points of the article you're summarizing. When you've reached this point, you're ready to correct sentence and spelling errors.

Step 5

> **Editing Your Summary of "He Turns Boys into Men"**
>
> Ask a friend or classmate to read your summary paragraph to you. If your reader struggles with a word or sentence, then you need to look carefully to determine if there's a sentence or spelling error. Correct the errors you can. If there are errors you aren't sure how to fix, ask your instructor or a tutor to explain how you can fix them.

PRACTICING SUMMARY SKILLS

Knowing how to summarize will help you at work, at home, and in your classes. On the job, you may be asked to summarize documents and reports. At home, you might have to summarize the problems you have had with a product in a letter to the Better Business Bureau. In your classes, you will probably be asked to write summaries of textbook chapters or essays, which will help you strengthen study skills and prepare for tests.

Activity

Put Your New Summary Skills to Work

1. Choose a section from one of your textbooks from another class, and then write a paragraph summary. Be prepared to show your instructor the actual section in your textbook as well as how you marked general and specific information and identified main ideas. (This is a good way to get a jump on your reading for other classes.)

2. Choose a magazine or newspaper article, and then write a paragraph summary. In addition to your summary, be prepared to show your instructor the actual article and how you marked general and specific information and identified main ideas.

TIME TO REFLECT

Journal Assignment

Your Progress as a Writer, Reader, and Critical Thinker

Spend a few minutes *reviewing* sections of the chapter that you found interesting or helpful. Look back at any notes you took, comments in the "Notes" column, journals, activities, and readings. *Think* about your summary skills and how they are improving already. *Write* down those things you've learned from this chapter that you hadn't known before. In what ways will you *apply* this new knowledge?

SUMMARY OF CHAPTER 2

In Chapter 2, as you considered the themes of gender roles, stereotypes, and relationships you also

- examined the structure of academic and journalistic writing,
- practiced the five steps to writing an effective summary, and
- practiced summarizing academic and journalistic texts.

Notes

VERB TENSE

Thus far in your sentence work, you've practiced identifying verbs, and you've considered the differences between action, linking, and helping verbs. In this section, you'll learn about a unique characteristic verbs possess that makes identifying them easier.

Verbs Tell Time

Verbs possess a unique characteristic: They tell time. **Verb tense** tells when the action (or linking) takes place. The simple verb tenses are the past, present, and future tenses. You should know, too, that verbs are the only words that change form when the tense changes.

Here are some examples of how verbs change when the tense changes.

Today I <u>walk</u>.   Today I <u>sing</u>.

Yesterday I <u>walked</u>.   Yesterday I <u>sang</u>.

Tomorrow I <u>will walk</u>.   Tomorrow I <u>will sing</u>.

Practice #1   Grandmother, the Feminist

Read this paragraph, and then answer the questions that follow.

My grandmother was a feminist of her own design. She kept the living room clean, organized, and beautifully decorated. The appearance of the living room was important to her because she often served afternoon tea to local politicians. The rest of the house, however, was never clean. She baked wonderful cookies and pies to serve to guests. On the other hand, she never cooked dinner for her family. Many years ago, she said to me that she was interested in local and foreign politics. She said, "I had to be a good hostess in order to be involved in interesting political discussions. But I was never a good housekeeper. Your grandfather understood me. He didn't like coming home to no dinner. However, our marriage survived because he let me be me."

1. When did most of the action in this paragraph take place? (Today? In the past? In the future?)

2. How do you know? Write down specific words from the paragraph that help you understand when the story occurs.

3. Did you find all of the words that help you understand when the story occurs? Check with a classmate.

4. Are the verbs in the present tense, past tense, or future tense? Underline verbs twice.

Verb Tense

Practice #2   Manipulating Verb Tense

1. Rewrite the paragraph in Practice #1 as though the events are happening right now. Remove words as necessary.
2. Underline the verbs twice.
3. What tense are the verbs in now?

Practice #3   The Woman of My Dreams

- Read the following paragraph.
- Rewrite it in the future tense. To make verbs tell *future* time, add *will* before the **base form** of the verb. The base form of a verb is the verb with no special endings like *-ed* or *-ly*. At the beginning of the paragraph, change *today* to *tomorrow*.
- Underline your future tense verbs twice. Be sure to underline the entire verb (*will* + _____).

Example: She <u>understands</u> physics. (present tense)
            She <u>*will*</u> <u>understand</u> physics. (future tense)

Today I met the woman of my dreams. She wants to split all the responsibilities right down the middle. She pays for half of everything. She asks me out sometimes. On other occasions, I plan the dates. She spends time alone with her friends. She encourages me to go out with my friends. She is a confident, secure woman. I appreciate those qualities.

Remember, verbs tell time:

- All verbs can change tense.
- Only verbs can change tense.

To figure out if a word is a verb, use the **test of time.** This means that you place the word *today, yesterday,* or *tomorrow* at the beginning of a sentence and see which word (or words) change. Any word that changes is a verb. (Don't be fooled by words that *look* like verbs. Use the test of time.)

    Here is an example of how you could use the test of time to figure out the verb of this sentence:

Notes

Many couples attend the marriage workshop.

- *Yesterday,* many couples attended the marriage workshop.
- *Today,* many couples attend the marriage workshop.
- *Tomorrow,* many couples will attend the marriage workshop.

The only word that changes in these sentences is *attend,* so *attend* must be the verb.

VERB IMPOSTERS AND PREPOSITIONAL PHRASES

Imposter #1: Present Participles (-ing *Words*)
Imposter #2: Infinitives (To + *Verb Combinations)*
Prepositional Phrases

Using the test of time can really help when searching for the verb, and knowing which words are verbs can help you avoid a variety of sentence errors. Besides using the test of time to identify verbs, you should also be aware of two kinds of **imposters**—words that look like verbs but really aren't. When searching for the verb in a sentence, you can make your task easier by eliminating the imposters.

Imposter #1: Present Participles (-ing *Words)*

A word ending in *-ing* like *snowing* or *talking* is called a **present participle.** Present participles cannot change tenses, so they cannot be verbs all by themselves. However, present participles can work as verbs *if* they get some help. In the following sentences, you'll find a present participle that is not a verb and then one that is a verb.

a. <u>Communicating</u> is important to a healthy marriage.

b. Marge and Kevin <u>are communicating</u> better.

In sentence *a, communicating* cannot change tense and still make sense in the sentence. Therefore, it isn't a verb. It does not make sense to say, "[Yesterday] communicated is important to a healthy marriage."

In sentence *b, are communicating* can change tense to *were communicating* or *will communicate* when we use the test of time. The following sentences do make sense.

Marge and Kevin were communicating better.

Marge and Kevin will communicate better.

Thus, *are communicating* acts as a verb in sentence *b*. *Note:* When you have a helping verb and another word, only the helping verb will change *tense* although the other word may change *form*. (For example, compare *were communicating* to *will communicate*.)

Practice #4   **The House Husband**

Put brackets around the present participle imposters in the paragraph below. Then underline the verbs twice.

Many men are choosing the role of "house husband" today. Dusting, vacuuming, and cooking are just some of the daily chores the house husband is responsible for. On weekdays, he rises at 6:00 A.M. to cook breakfast and drive the children to school. Then he spends his afternoons running errands and driving the children to after-school activities. He devotes his evenings to helping the children with their homework and then to tucking them into bed. Around midnight, after stapling all the PTA newsletters, he finds himself ready to fall into bed. Although he considers it exhausting, he finds his chosen profession rewarding at the same time.

Imposter #2: Infinitives (To + Verb Combinations)

An **infinitive** is a phrase that consists of *to* + a verb. Infinitives cannot change tenses, so they cannot be verbs. In these examples, complete verbs are underlined twice and the infinitives are in brackets.

Some women <u>choose</u> [to enter] traditional career fields.

Others <u>break</u> gender barriers [to become] firefighters or police officers.

I <u>want</u> [to study] psychology.

Jason <u>has offered</u> [to share] his lecture notes.

Notes

Practice #5   A Business Leader Speaks

- Read the following paragraph.
- Put brackets around the infinitives and present participle imposters.
- Rewrite each sentence and change the tense to future tense. Begin the paragraph with *tomorrow*.
- Notice that the infinitives and present participle imposters don't change. They cannot change tense. Therefore, they cannot be verbs.
- Underline the verbs twice.

   A group of business leaders spoke at a special lunch for business majors attending the University of California, Berkeley. I was one of those people giving a speech. I didn't focus my speech on which business classes to take. And I didn't focus on which magazines or newspapers to read. Instead, I emphasized the importance of learning to write well. My intention was to get business majors to realize the importance of good communication and thinking skills.

Prepositional Phrases

You now know that you must ignore imposters when looking for verbs. A **prepositional phrase,** which is a group of words consisting of a preposition and its object, is another group of words that you can eliminate when searching for verbs.

How can you spot prepositional phrases? Although there are many prepositions, you can learn to recognize them. They usually suggest location, time, or belonging. In the following examples, the preposition is in italics and the object follows.

Location	Time	Belonging
in the dark woods	*at* four o'clock	*by* William Shakespeare
at the old farm	*before* noon	*of* my family
on the table	*after* dark	

The *object* of the preposition follows the preposition and may consist of one or more words.

Sometimes words in a prepositional phrase may look like verbs. However, words in a prepositional phrase cannot be the verb(s) for the sentence.

Consider this sentence:

For many, beauty rates above brains as the most important personal asset.

Finding the verb in this sentence can be a little tricky. But if you place brackets around any prepositional phrases, you'll find the verb is easier to identify. You can put brackets around *For many, above brains,* and *as the most important personal asset.* Only *beauty* and *rates* remain. The only word here that will change tense when you use the test of time is *rates.* So *rates* must be the verb.

[For many], beauty <u>rates</u> [above brains] [as the most important personal asset.]

Here's a reference list of common prepositions in alphabetical order:

about	*but*	*outside*
above	*by*	*over*
across	*concerning*	*past*
after	*down*	*plus*
against	*during*	*regarding*
along	*except*	*since*
amid	*following*	*than*
among	*for*	*through*
around	*from*	*to*
as	*in*	*toward*
at	*inside*	*under*
before	*into*	*underneath*
behind	*like*	*until*
below	*near*	*up*
beneath	*of*	*upon*
beside	*off*	*with*
between	*on*	*within*
beyond	*onto*	*without*

Practice #6   Identifying Verbs and Nonverbs

In the paragraph that follows, put brackets around present participle imposters, infinitive imposters, and prepositional phrases. Underline the verbs twice. Use the *test of time* to test verbs when necessary. The first sentence is done for you.

Verb Imposters and Prepositional Phrases

Notes

It <u>is</u> time [for us] [to change]. For too long, society has judged people by the way they look. People living by this standard ask too much of themselves and others. They think being beautiful is the primary goal of life. Because of this, they spend countless hours and lots of money on the physical and not enough time on the intellectual or spiritual. Many young women take the idea of beauty too far. For example, some begin to starve themselves in order to look like supermodels. Others are convinced that breast implants or a nose job will make them more acceptable by society's standards. Looking good is not a bad goal. But it should not be the only goal. And it should not be the standard by which we measure a person's worth.

Practice #7   Verbs and Nonverbs in Bandur's Paragraph
In the paragraph from Bandur's column that follows, put brackets around present participle imposters, infinitive imposters, and prepositional phrases. Underline the verbs twice. Be careful to include helping verbs and exclude imposters. (Use the test of time to identify verbs when you are in doubt.)

A favorite assignment of media courses is to have students analyze advertisements. Without fail, some boy will bring in a picture from the Victoria's Secret catalog as an example of the objectification of women. Does it objectify women? Considering how many sex-starved, male dorm residents steal the mailroom's copies to check out the scantily clad women wearing submissive, come-hither looks, I would have to say "yes." The male-dominated society's lack of respect for women is alive and well!

Notes

Your Own Writing: Verb Imposters and Prepositional Phrases

- Copy two paragraphs from your own writing (a journal or summary).
- Underline the verbs twice.
- Put brackets around present participle imposters. (Remember, if the present participle has a helping verb, it is working as a verb.)
- Put brackets around infinitives.
- Put brackets around prepositional phrases.

Using **Connections** *Online with* **mywritinglab**

For more practice identifying verb imposters and prepositional phrases, log onto www.mywritinglab.com to access the online resources for *Connections*, Third Edition.

Verb Imposters and Prepositional Phrases

CHAPTER 3

Examining the Reading Process

Main Topics

- Examining the PARTS of the reading process

- Practicing the reading process

- Responding to texts

- Using the dictionary and building your vocabulary

- Reading about people's roles in society

- Identifying subjects in your sentences

Calvin and Hobbes   by Bill Watterson

I LOVE MY SCHOOL BOOKS. JUST THINK! PRETTY SOON WE'LL HAVE READ **ALL** OF THIS!

I LIKE TO READ AHEAD AND SEE WHAT WE'RE GOING TO LEARN NEXT. IT'S SO EXCITING TO KNOW STUFF.

HAVING A BOOK IS LIKE HAVING A GOOD FRIEND WITH YOU.

IF YOU FLIP THE PAGES OF **MY** BOOK, AN ANIMATED T. REX DRIVES THE BATMOBILE AND EXPLODES!

SOMETIMES I THINK BOOKS ARE THE ONLY FRIENDS WORTH HAVING.

Notes

Reading is the process of gathering meaning from letters, words, and sentences. In this chapter, you'll learn strategies that will help you better understand and remember what you read. In addition, as you read and absorb information about style, vocabulary, and writing technique, you'll begin to apply what you've learned to your own writing. Quite simply, the more you practice your reading skills, the better your reading and writing will become.

THE PARTS OF AN EFFECTIVE READING PROCESS

Experienced readers aren't necessarily speed readers. In fact, they take their time when reading and often reread to reach understanding. They use what's known as the **reading process,** a series of steps that helps them comprehend (understand) and retain (remember) what they have read. This process may be divided into five basic **PARTS,** or stages. As you begin to practice using the PARTS of the reading process, you will become a more confident reader.

Preview

Experienced readers **preview** their reading by looking at author, title, length, and topic sentences. They also review any subheadings, charts, pictures, or diagrams that accompany the reading. This previewing helps prepare them for the information to come.

Anticipate

During the preview stage, experienced readers **anticipate** (guess) what the reading will be about. Then as they read through the first time, they think about what will logically come next. Readers who have these expectations when they read stay interested and focused.

Read and Reread

During their first read, successful readers move through the text quickly. They jot down questions and note words they don't recognize, although they won't answer these questions or look up definitions yet. Then they reread slowly, answer their own questions, and look up the meanings of any words they don't know or haven't figured out. At this stage, readers also take the time to highlight important points and make written comments in the margins of the reading or on note paper.

As you read through this text, be sure to use the "Notes" column to record your questions, any new terms, and comments.

Think Critically

Experienced readers also think critically about their reading. They discuss important points or answer critical thinking questions as they begin to "make sense" of the reading. These activities help readers understand the author's message and purpose, remember important ideas, and examine writing techniques that they can use in their own writing.

Summarize

Finally, experienced readers take the time to **summarize** (restate in their own words) so that they can easily review the main points of their reading.

This process may seem like hard work if you've never done it before. However, as you become a more experienced reader, you'll begin to use the PARTS of the reading process without even thinking about them.

Get Involved!

Interview a reading instructor on your college campus (or review your notes or textbook if you are currently in a reading class). Create a list of five important tips for effective reading to share with your classmates.

> ### *Journal Assignment*
>
> #### *Responding to Calvin and Susie*
>
> Review Bill Watterson's *Calvin and Hobbes* comic strip on page 82. Which of the two characters, Calvin or Susie, appears to be the more experienced reader? How does each character feel about books? Are both views valid? What have you learned about reading and about readers from this strip?

ENGAGING IN THE READING PROCESS

To help you see how the reading process works, you'll look at one reader's preview, anticipation, and first reading of "The Struggle to Be an All-American Girl," written by Elizabeth Wong. After reviewing the first two parts of the reading process, you'll read the article yourself. Then you'll complete the stages of the reading process by rereading, thinking critically about, and summarizing the writer's main points.

One Reader's Preview and Anticipation

[*The reader's thoughts are italicized and in brackets.*] The reader's written responses appear in plain text.

Preview   [*This column appeared in the newspaper, so I expect short paragraphs and few topic sentences. I'll look quickly at the title, the author, and the first two paragraphs to get an idea of what the column is about.*] The title suggests that the writer is struggling because she wants to be an "all-American girl." As I look over the column, I can see that the writer's mom made both of her children attend Chinese school. Also, the writer's first name is Elizabeth, but her last name is Wong. So her parents may be from China, but she was probably born in America. Maybe that's why she's struggling.

Anticipate   Overall, Wong seems to be frustrated. It looks like she doesn't want to learn Chinese. I'm guessing that she didn't want to be connected to her heritage.

[*As I read, I'll underline words that I plan to look up. I'll also place questions in the "Notes" column that I plan to answer when I read through the second time.*]

One Reader's First Read

Following the preview and anticipation stages of the process, the reader reads through the column quickly, jotting questions in the margin and highlighting or underlining unknown words.

Activity

The First Read

Read "The Struggle to Be an All-American Girl." As you read, look at one reader's questions in the "Notes" column and notice which vocabulary words the reader has underlined.

The Struggle to Be an All-American Girl
by Elizabeth Wong

This column appeared in the *Los Angeles Times* in 1980.

1   It's still there, the Chinese school on Yale Street where my brother and I used to go. Despite the new coat of paint and the high wire fence, the school I knew 10 years ago remains remarkably, <u>stoically</u> the same.

Notes

I'm wondering why Wong's mother insisted they learn Chinese against their will.

2   Every day at 5 P.M., instead of playing with our fourth- and fifth-grade friends or sneaking out to the empty lot to hunt ghosts and animal bones, my brother and I had to go to Chinese school. No amount of kicking, screaming, or pleading could <u>dissuade</u> my mother, who was solidly determined to have us learn the language of our heritage.

3   Forcibly, she walked us the seven long, hilly blocks from our home to school, depositing our defiant tearful faces before the stern principal. My only memory of him is that he swayed on his heels like a palm tree, and he always clasped his impatient twitching hands behind his back. I recognized him as a repressed maniacal child killer, and knew that if we ever saw his hands we'd be in big trouble.

4   We all sat in little chairs in an empty auditorium. The room smelled like Chinese medicine, and imported faraway mustiness. Like ancient mothballs or dirty closets. I hated that smell. I favored crisp new scents. Like the soft French perfume that my American teacher wore in public school.

5   Although the emphasis at the school was mainly language—speaking, reading, writing—the lessons always began with an exercise in politeness. With the entrance of the teacher, the best student would tap a bell and everyone would get up, <u>kowtow</u>, and chant, "sing san ho," the phonetic for "How are you, teacher?"

6   Being ten years old, I had better things to learn than <u>ideographs</u> copied painstakingly in lines that ran right to left from the top of a *moc but,* a real ink pen that had to be held in an awkward way if blotches were to be avoided. After all, I could do the multiplication tables, name the satellites of Mars, and write reports on *Little Women* and *Black Beauty.* Nancy Drew, my favorite book heroine, never spoke Chinese.

7   The language was a source of embarrassment. More times than not, I had tried to <u>disassociate</u> myself from the nagging loud voice that followed me wherever I wandered in the nearby American supermarket outside Chinatown. The voice belonged to my grandmother, a fragile woman in her seventies who could outshout the best of the street vendors. Her humor was <u>raunchy</u>, her Chinese rhythmless, patternless. It was quick, it was loud, it was unbeautiful. It was not like the quiet, lilting romance of French or the gentle refinement of the American South. Chinese sounded <u>pedestrian</u>. Public.

Why does Wong think Chinese is pedestrian? What does she mean by pedestrian?

8   In Chinatown, the comings and goings of hundreds of Chinese on their daily tasks sounded <u>chaotic</u> and <u>frenzied</u>. I did not want to be thought of as mad, as talking gibberish. When I spoke English, people nodded at me, smiled sweetly, said encouraging words. Even the people in my culture would cluck and say that I'd do well in life. "My, doesn't

she move her lips fast," they would say, meaning that I'd be able to keep up with the world outside Chinatown.

9   My brother was even more <u>fanatical</u> than I about speaking English. He was especially hard on my mother, criticizing her, often cruelly, for her pidgin speech—smatterings of Chinese scattered like chop suey in her conversation. "It's not 'What it is,' Mom," he'd say in exasperation. "It's 'What is it, what is it, what is it!'" Sometimes Mom might leave out an occasional "the" or "a," or perhaps a verb of being. He would stop her in mid-sentence: "Say it again, Mom. Say it right." When he tripped over his own tongue, he'd blame it on her: "See, Mom, it's all your fault. You set a bad example."

Why was Wong's brother so bothered by his mother's mistakes in English?

10   After two years of writing with a *moc but* and reciting words with multiples of meanings, I finally was granted a cultural divorce. I was permitted to stop Chinese school.

11   I thought of myself as <u>multicultural</u>. I preferred tacos to egg rolls; I enjoyed Cinco de Mayo more than Chinese New Year.

Why was she allowed to stop going to Chinese school? Why is she sad at the end? Didn't she get what she wanted?

12   At last, I was one of you; I wasn't one of them.

13   Sadly, I still am.

REREAD, THINK CRITICALLY, AND SUMMARIZE

Reread   Following a quick first read, the reader reads the column a second time, slowing down to consider the writer's meaning more closely. Then the reader looks up meanings of unfamiliar terms and answers her own questions from the first reading.

Activity

Reread

Reread Wong's essay, looking up the meanings of any words you don't know or can't figure out. Write definitions in your notebook, in the "Notes" column, or on notecards. Also, write responses to the first reader's questions in the "Notes" column.

Think Critically   As you read through the article a second time, you should have begun to carefully consider the writer's message and purpose. This stage of the process also involves answering critical thinking questions and/or discussing important points with classmates after you have completed your second read.

Notes

Questions for Critical Thought

"The Struggle to Be an All-American Girl"

1. Why would Wong's mother have wanted her children to attend Chinese school?

2. Why might Wong have rebelled against going to Chinese school? In your opinion, should she have been forced to attend? Why, or why not?

3. What are some of the reasons Wong seemed to be embarrassed by her grandmother's Chinese? Are these the same reasons Wong's brother became upset when their mother made mistakes in English?

4. The title of the article suggests that Wong was "struggling to be an all-American girl." What does she mean by this? Did she reach her goal? What evidence does she offer as proof?

5. What does Wong mean in paragraph 10 when she says, "I finally was granted a cultural divorce"? Does the word *divorce* accurately describe what happened?

6. Why does Wong use the word *sadly* in paragraph 13? In your opinion, does she have reason to be sad?

7. Because Wong's article appeared in a newspaper, we can assume that it was directed at a general audience. In your opinion, what message does she wish to share with her audience?

Summarize   Finally, it's a good idea to summarize what you've read. As you discovered in Chapter 2, summarizing not only helps you remember what you've read, but it also can be a resource for your own writing.

Activity

Summarize

Summarize Wong's article. Remember that when you are summarizing a newspaper article, you need to look for main ideas rather than topic sentences. Write a list of these main ideas. Then write a brief summary of the article. Be sure to include author, title, and place of publication.

RESPONDING TO READING

A **response** is a thoughtful reaction to what you've read. In a response, the writer refers back to the article, essay, or textbook chapter, and then comments on the most important or most intriguing ideas. It differs from the more organized summary, which requires the writer to include only the author's main points. Also, a response differs from the essays you'll be writing. In an essay, the writer states a thesis in the introduction and then supports that thesis in the paragraphs that follow. In a response, the writer has the freedom to move from one idea to another and back again, perhaps to explore several aspects of an issue or just to think on paper. You've been writing responses as you've worked your way through the first two chapters of this text. When you're asked to write your opinion in the form of reading questions, journals, or other assignments, you're writing a response.

Journal Assignment

Respond to "The Struggle to Be an All-American Girl"

Write a 10- to 15-minute response to Wong's article. You might write about the importance of your own cultural heritage, an experience of your own that is similar to or different from Wong's, or another issue connected to the article.

BUILDING YOUR VOCABULARY

One of the most important benefits of reading is improving your vocabulary. Your vocabulary will naturally grow as you look up new terms and figure out words as you read. But if you haven't had much practice using the dictionary, looking up words can be pretty frustrating, especially when there are several possible definitions listed for a single word. Also, new words are easy to forget if you don't have a plan for reviewing them. In the following discussion, you'll learn some techniques for developing your vocabulary.

Using the Dictionary to Find Word Meanings

If you were unsure of what *pedestrian* means in paragraph 7 of Wong's article, then you probably looked it up in your dictionary.

> The voice belonged to my grandmother, a fragile woman in her seventies who could outshout the best of the street vendors. Her humor was raunchy, her

Chinese rhythmless, patternless. It was quick, it was loud, it was unbeautiful. It was not like the quiet, lilting romance of French or the gentle refinement of the American South. Chinese sounded *pedestrian*. Public.

This entry is from *The American Heritage® Dictionary:*[*]

pe·des·tri·an (pə-dĕs′trē-ən) *n.* A person traveling on foot; a walker. *adj.* **1.** Of, relating to, or made for pedestrians: *a pedestrian bridge.* **2.** Going or performed on foot: *a pedestrian journey.* **3.** Undistinguished; ordinary: *pedestrian prose.* [From Latin pedester, pedestr-, *going on foot,* from pedes, *a pedestrian,* from pēs, ped-, *foot;* see ped- in Indo-European roots.]

When you look at a dictionary entry, you can't just pick any part of the entry and apply that information to the word and sentence you are interested in. *Pedestrian,* for example, can be a noun (person, place, or thing) or an adjective (a word used to describe a noun). The *n* (meaning noun) and *adj* (meaning adjective) in the entry tell us that. In order to choose the correct meaning, you have to figure out how the word you want to define is being used. In the quotation, *pedestrian* is being used as an adjective because it describes the noun *Chinese.*

Once you know how the word is being used, then you can look at the possible definitions. Three are listed following *adj.* Numbers 1 and 2 relate to someone walking, but you can see that the sentence doesn't refer to walking. However, number 3 offers a different meaning: "Undistinguished; ordinary." These two words help describe how her grandmother's Chinese sounded to Wong. It sounded ordinary and unimportant. Remember, when looking up a word like *pedestrian,* you should think about how it works in the sentence.

You should also consider the words and sentences surrounding *pedestrian.* For example, look at the word *public,* which follows *pedestrian* in paragraph 7. When something is *public,* it's exposed to all. It's not special. Wong's use of *public* following *pedestrian* emphasizes the idea that her grandmother's Chinese sounded ordinary and unimportant to Wong. Then consider how Wong describes other languages and dialects in the same paragraph: "the quiet, lilting romance of French" and "the gentle refinement of the American South." Words such as *refinement* and *romance* contrast with *pedestrian* and *public,* revealing that Wong thought other languages were beautiful in comparison to her grandmother's. By considering the surrounding words and sentences, you're better able to understand what *pedestrian* means and how Wong felt.

---

[*]Copyright © 2006 by Houghton Mifflin Company. Reproduced by permission from *The American Heritage Dictionary of the English Language,* Fourth Edition.

Activity

Finding Meanings in the Dictionary

The paragraph that follows is from a personal essay, "Navigating My Eerie Landscape Alone," in which writer Jim Bobryk talks about living with blindness. (You'll read the entire essay later in this chapter.) Practice your dictionary skills by finding definitions for the words in italics.

> I was driving home for lunch on what seemed to be an increasingly foggy day, although the perky radio deejay said it was clear and sunny. After I finished my lunch, I realized that I couldn't see across the room to my front door. I had battled *glaucoma* for 20 years. Suddenly, without warning, my eyes had *hemorrhaged*.

Write down the definitions for these terms. Explain how knowing these terms helps you better understand what happened to Jim Bobryk.

Finding Definitions in the Writing

Often, unfamiliar words in a reading are immediately followed by their definitions. This is particularly true in a textbook when the writer must introduce several new concepts within a single chapter. Note how the definition follows the term *feminism* in this example:

> The struggle for women's rights has been a long and hard-fought battle in the United States. The first major wave of **feminism,** *an ideology aimed at eliminating patriarchy in support of equality between the sexes,* was linked to the pre–Civil War abolitionist movement.
>
> —*William E. Thompson and Joseph V. Hickey, from*
> *"Feminism: The Struggle for Gender Equality"*

Recognizing Context Clues

In addition to using your dictionary or finding definitions in the text, you should try to figure out the meaning of an unfamiliar word by looking at the **context,** the writing in which the word appears. This means that you think about the entire sentence in which the unfamiliar word appears, and you consider the sentences before and after it. Nearby words and other sentences often give you clues about what the unknown word means.

For example, the word *patriarchal* in the following textbook excerpt on the Puritans might be unfamiliar to you. Consider what this word means by looking at the sentence that precedes it.

Families cared for the destitute and elderly; they took in orphans; and they housed servants and apprentices—all under one roof and subject to the authority of the father.

The Puritans carried *patriarchal* values across the Atlantic and planted them in America. . . .

—*James Kirby Martin et al., from "Seventeenth-Century Roles for Puritan Men, Women, and Children"*

In this case, the last phrase of the first paragraph, "all under one roof and *subject to the authority of the father,*" sets up the idea of *patriarchal* values. Now that you see this connection, it is clear that the term *patriarchal* connects to the idea that males were in charge of the Puritan family.

Reexamine the paragraph example from the previous section, "Finding Definitions in the Writing" (reprinted again below). Note that though the word *feminism* has been defined in the example, there are at least two other words, *ideology* and *patriarchy,* that you may find unfamiliar.

The struggle for women's rights has been a long and hard-fought battle in the United States. The first major wave of **feminism,** *an ideology aimed at eliminating patriarchy in support of equality between the sexes,* was linked to the pre–Civil War abolitionist movement.

However, you may have recognized that the word *patriarchy* is a form of the word *patriarchal,* which you've already discovered has something to do with males being in charge. So now you can see that feminism means "eliminating male superiority" (patriarchy) in favor of supporting "equality between the sexes." When figuring out words in context, then, you should look for variations of words you already know. In this case, the only other term you would need to look up would be *ideology.* But before you do, ask yourself what other words might be forms of this term.

Activity

Finding Meaning in Context

Read the paragraph that follows. Look at the context of the word *matrilineal.* What discussion follows the introduction of this term? Based on the sentences surrounding it, what do you think it means?

Meghalaya, a district tucked away in the remote northeastern corner of India, is home to the Khasi, one of the largest surviving matrilineal societies in the world. In this hill tribe of nearly 650,000, descent is traced through the mother's line and women have an honored place in the society. Here, baby girls are quite welcome, and, some argue, even more highly prized than boys. Since the woman's family holds the cards when arranging a marriage, the question of dowry—paying a man's family for accepting the "burden" of a wife—would never even arise. No social stigma is attached to women, whether they choose to divorce, remarry, or stay single.

—Kavita Menon, from "In India,
Men Challenge a Matrilineal Society"

Notes

Figuring out a word in context will save you time and energy while developing your critical thinking skills. However, the most important reason to develop this skill is so that you'll gain a better understanding of the meaning of the word and how it works in a particular sentence, paragraph, or essay.

Keeping a Vocabulary Notebook

Assign a section of your notebook to vocabulary. Writing down new words, definitions, and other related information will help you build your vocabulary. But writing down such information is not enough. To help you make these terms a part of your life, you need to review your vocabulary section regularly. You must also practice using these new words in your own writing.

Use the vocabulary section of your notebook to write down and define unfamiliar words you come across in all of your classes—not just your English class. Your list should contain

- the sentence that the word appeared in,
- the meaning in context (if possible),
- how the word works in the sentence, and
- the dictionary definition.

Here is an example of how to list a word.

dissuade

"No amount of kicking, screaming, or pleading could <u>dissuade</u> my mother, who was solidly determined to have us learn the language of our heritage."

I know that "persuade" means to convince someone to do something. "Dissuade" must mean to make someone not do something.

The new term

The sentence in which the term appeared

Definition based on context

Type of word	Verb
Pronunciation	Pronunciation: (dĭs•wād')
Definition	Definition: To deter from course or action.
Other forms	Other forms of the word: dissuader (noun)
Word meaning in context—in your own words	Paraphrased: Nothing Wong did could keep her mother from insisting that Wong and her brother learn Chinese.

Notes

Activity

Vocabulary Notebook

Return to Elizabeth Wong's article, "The Struggle to Be an All-American Girl." Write any words that were new to you in the vocabulary section of your notebook. Be sure to include the definition as well as other related information. In addition, log any other new terms from this section, "Building Your Vocabulary." Consider logging the following terms: *pedestrian, glaucoma, hemorrhaged, patriarchal* or *patriarchy,* and *matrilineal.*

Remember, writing this information will help you learn new words and review and study them. Also, you must *practice using your new words* if they are to become a part of your expanding vocabulary. Try using these new words as you answer questions or respond in journal assignments. In the chapters to come, plan to include them in your essays.

PRACTICING THE READING PROCESS

So far in this chapter, you've studied the PARTS of the reading process and explored some strategies for using the dictionary and building your vocabulary. You're ready now to begin practicing what you've learned. In the reading assignments that follow, you'll encounter some of the writing structures you explored in Chapter 2. In addition, you'll have the opportunity to practice and develop your reading-writing-critical thinking connection as you explore people's roles in society.

READING THE PERSONAL NARRATIVE

In "The Struggle to Be an All-American Girl" earlier in the chapter, you encountered a type of writing called the personal narrative. In a **personal narrative,** an individual recounts an event or series of events from his or her own life, usually to make a point or to help the reader better understand an issue. In Wong's case, she retold her story about wanting to be "an all-American girl" so that she could tell what she had learned from her experience—that it's important to remember your own cultural heritage. In the essay that follows, writer Jim Bobryk shares his personal experience.

Reading Assignment: *"Navigating My Eerie Landscape Alone"*

Preview This is a personal narrative that appeared in a popular magazine. You can assume that it will follow journalistic format, with shorter paragraphs and few topic sentences. Review the title, the quotation underneath the title, and the first two paragraphs.

Anticipate What do you think this personal narrative will be about? Use the "Notes" column to record your answer.

Read Now read the entire article quickly and continue to anticipate as you read. Highlight unfamiliar terms and jot down any questions in the margins. (Remember, because you're reading quickly, it's all right not to understand everything the first time through.)

Navigating My Eerie Landscape Alone*
by Jim Bobryk

This *Newsweek* article, by writer and executive Jim Bobryk, appeared on March 18, 1999.

"Unless I ask for help, strangers are so afraid of doing the wrong thing that they do nothing at all."

1   Now, as I stroll down the street, my right forefinger extends five feet in front of me, feeling the ground where my feet will walk.

2   Before, my right hand would have been on a steering wheel as I went down the street. I drove to work, found shortcuts in strange cities, picked up my two daughters after school. Those were the days when I

---

*Jim Bobryk, "Navigating My Eerie Landscape Alone." From *Newsweek*, March 18, 1999. © 1999 Newsweek, Inc. All rights reserved. Used by permission and protected by the Copyright Laws of the United States. The printing, copying, redistribution, or retransmission of the Material without express written permission is prohibited.

Notes

ran my finger down a phone-book page and never dialed Information. When I read novels and couldn't sleep until I had finished the last page. Those were the nights when I could point out a shooting star before it finished scraping across the dark sky. And when I could go to the movies and it didn't matter if it was a foreign film or not.

3   But all this changed about seven years ago. I was driving home for lunch on what seemed to be an increasingly foggy day, although the perky radio deejay said it was clear and sunny. After I finished my lunch, I realized that I couldn't see across the room to my front door. I had battled glaucoma for 20 years. Suddenly, without warning, my eyes had hemorrhaged.

4   I will never regain any of my lost sight. I see things through a porthole covered in wax paper. I now have no vision in my left eye and only slight vision in my right. A minefield of blind spots make people and cars suddenly appear and vanish. I have no depth perception. Objects are not closer and farther; they're larger and smaller. Steps, curbs and floors all flow on the same flat plane. My world has shapes but no features. Friends are mannequins in the fog until I recognize their voices. Printed words look like ants writhing on the pages. Doorways are unlit mine shafts. This is not a place for the fainthearted.

5   My cane is my navigator in this eerie landscape. It is a hollow fiberglass stick with white reflector paint and a broad red band at the tip. It folds up tightly into four 15-inch sections, which can then be slipped into a black holster that attaches to my belt with Velcro.

6   Adults—unless they're preoccupied or in a hurry—will step aside without comment when they see me coming. Small children will either be scooped up apologetically or steered away by their parents. Only teenagers sometimes try to play chicken, threatening to collide with me and then veering out of the way at the last moment.

7   While I'm wielding my stick, strangers are often afraid to communicate with me. I don't take this personally—anymore. Certainly they can't be afraid that I'll lash at them with my rod. (Take *that,* you hapless sighted person! Whack!) No, they're probably more afraid *for* me. Don't startle the sword swallower. Don't tickle the baton twirler.

8   The trick for the sighted person is to balance courtesy with concern. Should he go out of his way or should he get out of the way? Will his friendliness be misconstrued by the disabled as pity? Will an offer of help sound patronizing? These anxieties are exaggerated by not knowing the etiquette in dealing with the disabled. A sighted person will do nothing rather than take the risk of offending the blind. Still, I refuse to take a dim view of all this.

9   When I peer over my cane and ask for help, no one ever cowers in fear. In fact, I think people are waiting for me to give them the green light to help. It makes us feel good to help.

10   When I ask for a small favor, I often get more assistance than I ever expect. Clerks will find my required forms and fill them out for me. A group of people will parade me across a dangerous intersection. A sales-clerk will read the price tag for me and then hunt for the item on sale. I'm no Don Juan, but strange (and possibly exotic) women will take my hand and walk me through dark rooms, mysterious train stations and foreign airports. Cabbies wait and make sure I make it safely into lobbies.

11   It's not like it's inconvenient for friends to help me get around. Hey, have disabled parking placard—will travel. Christmas shopping? Take me to the mall and I'll get us front-row parking. Late for the game? *No problema.* We'll be parking by the stadium entrance. And if some incon-siderate interloper does park in the blue zone without a permit, he'll ei-ther be running after a fleeing tow truck or paying a big fine.

12   Worried about those age lines showing? Not with me looking. Put down that industrial-strength Oil of Olay. To me, your skin looks as clean and smooth as it was back in the days when you thought suntanning was a good idea.

13   So you see, I'm a good guy to know. I just carry a cane, that's all.

14   None of this is to make light of going blind. Being blind is dark and depressing. When you see me walking with my cane you may think I'm lost as I ricochet down the street. But you'll find more things in life if you don't travel in a straight line.

Notes

Reread   Once you've completed a first reading, read Bobryk's narra-tive a second time. Slow down to answer your own questions and look up the meanings of any words you don't know or can't figure out. Add these to the vocabulary section of your notebook.

Here is a list of words to get you started. Be sure to include any other unfamiliar terms and definitions. (You may skip any of the terms that you're familiar with already.)

Par. 3: glaucoma; hemorrhaged

Par. 4: porthole; minefield; mannequins

Par. 5: eerie

Par. 7: wielding

Par. 8: misconstrued; etiquette

Par. 11: interloper

Par. 14: ricochet

Think Critically, Summarize, and Respond   The questions and activi-ties that follow will help you develop your reading skills as you com-plete the reading process.

Notes

Questions for Critical Thought

"Navigating My Eerie Landscape Alone"

1. What caused Jim Bobryk to lose his sight?

2. Bobryk explains that his cane is now his "navigator." What does he mean by this?

3. In what ways has Bobryk's life changed as a result of his losing his eyesight?

4. Bobryk explains that "strangers are often afraid to communicate" with him, but when he asks for assistance, he finds that people are more than willing to help. How does he account for these different forms of treatment?

5. Identify two places in the article where Bobryk uses humor to make his point. Why would a writer use humor to make a serious point?

6. Bobryk states, "I'm a good guy to know. I just carry a cane, that's all." What does he want his audience to understand from this statement?

7. Bobryk's article appeared in *Newsweek* magazine. Who would most likely be included in his audience? What overall point or message do you believe Bobryk conveys in this article?

Activity

Summarize "Navigating My Eerie Landscape Alone"

After making a list of the main points and most important supporting points, write a summary of Bobryk's article. Be sure to include author, title of article, and where it was published. Also include a general statement telling what the article is about, followed by its main points. When you've finished a draft of your summary, return to the article to check for accuracy and revise as necessary.

Get Involved!

Rent and watch the film *At First Sight* (1999) starring Val Kilmer and Mira Sorvino and directed by Henry Winkler. In the film, a blind man has an operation that gives him sight. Prepare to discuss in your next class how the main character's life changes as a result of the operation. Also be ready to discuss how this character's experience compares to the real-life experience of Jim Bobryk.

Journal Assignment

Respond to "Navigating My Eerie Landscape Alone"

Take ten to fifteen minutes to respond to Bobryk's article. You might comment on Bobryk's use of humor in the piece. (Look back at paragraphs 7, 9, 10, and 11.) You could write about a similar experience of your own or of someone you know. You might also write about what you have learned from Bobryk's article.

READING A POEM

While the first two writers in this chapter, Wong and Bobryk, both chose the personal narrative to explore their roles in society, the next writer chose poetry. Sometimes students feel intimidated by poetry. They may think it will be too difficult to understand. However, we have all been exposed to and enjoyed a variety of poetic forms from our infancy. From childhood rhymes and lullabies to the poetic speeches of Martin Luther King, Jr. and our favorite song lyrics, poetry is all around us. Chapter 8 will give you an opportunity to carefully analyze poetry and music and write an essay explaining your interpretation of a poem or song. In this chapter, your goal will be to apply the reading process to a poem and, perhaps, write a paragraph in response.

Here are a few unique characteristics about poetry and some reading strategies. When you read poems, expect ambiguity (uncertainty). This means that there will be more than one way to interpret most poems. The meaning may not be crystal clear, so your class discussions should be very interesting. Visually, poems will look different from essays and articles. The writer might not use any capital letters or any punctuation. The writer will probably not use complete sentences. Poems can be very long—hundreds of pages—or very short. They may or may not rhyme. You will want to keep an open mind—just as you do when you hear your favorite artist perform a new song—and read the poem more than once. As with the following poem, poets often use few words, but they choose their words very carefully in order to create specific images and messages. You'll want to read carefully, thinking about the writer's word choices.

Reading Assignment: *"Refugee Ship"*

Preview   Read the title and the first two **stanzas**.

Anticipate   What do you think this poem will be about? What kind of mood or message do you think it has? Use the "Notes" column to record your thoughts.

Read   Quickly read the poem one time, marking unknown terms and jotting down any questions you have.

Stanzas are the paragraphs in poems.

Notes

Refugee Ship

Lorna Dee Cervantes (b. 1954)

Cervantes is a poet, editor, and teacher of Native American and Mexican ancestry.

Cornstarch is a powder that cooks use to thicken soups, sauces, and puddings. When cornstarch is added to water, the water becomes thicker, slippery, and cloudy.

The Spanish words *mi abuelita's* mean "my grandmother's."

A refugee ship is a boat carrying people who are fleeing to another country for safety.

1   like wet cornstarch
I slide past *mi abuelita's* eyes
bible placed by her side
she removes her glasses
the pudding thickens

2   mama raised me with no language
I am orphan to my Spanish name
the words are foreign, stumbling on my tongue
I stare at my reflection in the mirror
brown skin, black hair

3   I feel I am a captive
aboard the refugee ship
a ship that will never dock
a ship that will never dock

Reread   Reread more slowly and use the "Notes" column to record images and meanings that come to mind. Answer any questions you have and look up the meanings of any words you don't know or can't figure out. Add these to the vocabulary section of your notebook. Finally, read the poem aloud and record any further ideas in the "Notes" column.

Think Critically, Summarize, and Respond   The questions, activity, and journal assignment that follow will help you continue to explore and think critically about the meaning in Cervantes' poem.

Questions for Critical Thought

"Refugee Ship"

1. What is your general reaction to this poem? How does it make you feel? What words create this feeling?

2. "Cornstarch" might connect to more than one image here. Explain how it connects to the speaker. With your classmates, explore how "cornstarch" and "pudding" might connect to the grandmother. Why does "the pudding thicken" when she removes her glasses?

3. What other important word or words show up in stanza 1 to tell us something about the grandmother? Describe your image of the grandmother in this poem.

4. What do you think Cervantes means when she says, "I am orphan to my Spanish name / the words are foreign, stumbling on my tongue"?

5. What do you think the speaker is saying in the last stanza?

Notes

The slash (/) in "name / the words" tells us where one line of the poem ends and another line begins.

Activity

Summarize "Refugee Ship"

In two or three sentences, tell someone who has never read "Refugee Ship" what the title is, who the author is, and what this poem is basically about.

Journal Assignment

Respond to "Refugee Ship"

Take ten to fifteen minutes to respond to Cervantes' poem. You might discuss how you feel about poetry in general and whether or not you enjoyed Cervantes' poem specifically. Do any of the lines, images, or messages in this poem connect to your life? Explain. Or you might write a message back to the speaker in this poem. What would you say to this person?

READING A TEXTBOOK CHAPTER

In Chapter 2 you studied the structure of textbook chapters. You know that this type of writing follows basic essay format and contains an introduction and clear thesis that lead the reader through the chapter. A textbook chapter's body paragraphs usually consist of topic sentences followed by supporting details and explanations. Most end with at least a concluding remark. This section includes an excerpt (portion) of a chapter from a history textbook that explores people's roles in our society.

Reading Assignment: *"Seventeenth-Century Roles for Puritan Men, Women, and Children"*

Preview   This segment comes from a history textbook, so you know that it will follow the expected format of a clear introduction, body paragraphs, and concluding remarks. Review the title, author, and introductory information. Then read the opening paragraphs as well as the topic sentences throughout the piece.

Get Involved!

Before reading this textbook excerpt, go to the library or the Internet and gather information about the Puritans. Share the information with your classmates.

Anticipate   After reviewing the introduction and topic sentences, what do you believe this textbook selection will be about? Use the "Notes" column to record your answer.

Read   Quickly read through the excerpt. Anticipate what information will appear next as you read. Be sure to highlight unfamiliar terms and write any questions you may have in the margins.

Seventeenth-Century Roles for Puritan Men, Women, and Children
by James Kirby Martin et al.

This selection appeared in the history textbook, *America and Its People.*

1   The early Puritans looked at their mission as a family undertaking, and they referred to families as "little commonwealths." Not only were families to "be fruitful and multiply," but they also served as agencies of education and religious instruction as well as centers of vocational training and social welfare. Families cared for the destitute and elderly; they took in orphans; and they housed servants and apprentices—all under one roof and subject to the authority of the father.

2   The Puritans carried *patriarchal* values across the Atlantic and planted them in America. New England law, reflecting its English base, subscribed to the doctrine of *coverture,* or subordinating the legal identity of women in their husbands, who were the undisputed heads of households. Unless there were prenuptial agreements, all property brought by women to marriages belonged to their mates. Husbands, who by custom and law directed their families in prayer and scripture reading, were responsible for assuring decency and good order in family life. They also represented their families in all community political, economic, and religious activities.

3   Wives also had major family responsibilities. "For though the husband be the head of the wife," the Reverend Samuel Willard explained, "yet she is the head of the family." It was the particular calling of mothers to nurture their children in godly living, as well as to perform many other tasks—tending gardens, brewing beer, raising chickens, cooking, spinning, and sewing—when not helping in the planting and harvesting of crops.

4   Most Puritan marriages functioned in at least outward harmony. If serious problems arose, local churches and courts intervened to end the turmoil. Puritan law, again reflecting English precedent, made divorce quite difficult. The process required the petitioning of assemblies for bills of separation, and the only legal grounds were bigamy, desertion, and

adultery. A handful of women, most likely battered or abandoned wives, effected their own divorces by setting up separate residences. On occasion the courts brought unruly husbands under control, for example, a Maine husband who brutally clubbed his wife for refusing to feed the family pig. There were instances when wives defied patriarchalism, including one case involving a Massachusetts woman who faced community censure for beating her husband and even "egging her children to help her, bidding them knock him in the head."

5   Family friction arose from other sources as well, some of which stemmed from the absolute control that fathers exercised over property and inheritances. If sons wanted to marry and establish separate households, they had to conform to the will of their fathers, who controlled the land. Family patriarchs normally delayed the passing of property until sons had reached their mid-twenties and selected mates acceptable to parents. Delayed inheritances help to explain why so many New Englanders did not marry until several years after puberty. Since parents also bestowed dowries on daughters as their contributions to new family units, romantic love had less to do with mate selection than parental desires to unite particular family names and estates.

6   Puritans expected brides and grooms to learn to love one another as they went about their duty of conceiving and raising the next generation of children. In most cases spouses did develop lasting affection for one another, as captured by the gifted Puritan poetess Anne Bradstreet in 1666 when she wrote to her "dear and loving Husband":

> If ever two were one, then surely we.
> If ever man were lov'd by wife, then thee;
> If ever wife was happy in a man,
> Compare with me the women if you can.

7   Young adults who openly defied patriarchal authority were rare. Those who did could expect to hear what one angry Bay Colony father told his unwanted son-in-law: "As you married her without my consent, you shall keep her without my help." Also unusual were instances of illegitimate children, despite the lengthy gap between puberty and marriage. As measured by illegitimate births, premarital sex could not have been that common in early New England, not a surprising finding among people living in closely controlled communities and seeking to honor the Almighty by reforming human society.

Reread Complete a second, slower reading of the textbook excerpt. Respond to questions you wrote in the margins during your

Notes

first reading. Look up terms and record their definitions in your notebook.

Consider adding the following terms to your vocabulary list. Remember to try to figure out the word in its context. Then use the dictionary to verify its meaning.

Par. 1: "little commonwealths" (look up the term "commonwealth"); apprentices

Par. 2: patriarchal; coverture; prenuptial agreement

Par. 5: dowries

Think Critically, Summarize, and Respond You will continue the reading process in the following activities as you think critically, summarize, and respond to what you've read.

Questions for Critical Thought

"Seventeenth-Century Roles . . ."

1. The reader is told that Puritan society was a patriarchal society. Explain how this society operated.

2. Look up the word *commonwealth*. Write out the meaning. Explain what you believe the authors mean when they say Puritan families operated as "little commonwealths."

3. What does the command "be fruitful and multiply" mean? Where might this command have come from? Why did the Puritans believe and obey it?

4. According to the selection, what were the husband's responsibilities or duties in the early Puritan household? What were the wife's?

5. Look back at the term *coverture* and its definition in paragraph 2. How were Puritan women affected by the doctrine of coverture?

6. Describe what early Puritan marriages were like. Did they seem to work? What happened if trouble developed in a Puritan marriage?

7. Did romantic love play a large part in the selection of a mate in those days? Why, or why not?

8. What might have happened to a son or daughter who rebelled against his or her father's wishes in marriage?

9. Was premarital sex a common occurrence in early Puritan New England? Why, or why not?

10. In what ways has the American family changed since early Puritan times?

11. Who would be the audience for this piece? What is the authors' purpose in presenting this reading to this particular audience?

Activity

Summarize "Seventeenth-Century Roles . . ."

Write a summary of this excerpt. Because it follows essay form, you can check for a thesis in the introduction and main ideas in the topic sentences. Begin by listing the most important points. Open your summary with the excerpt's overall main idea. Follow with the most important points. Look back at the excerpt to make sure you've included all of the main ideas. Don't forget to identify the author, title, and textbook.

Journal Assignment

Respond to "Seventeenth-Century Roles . . ."

Spend ten to fifteen minutes responding to this excerpt. Consider the positive and negative aspects of love and marriage in the past and present. Think about how modern views compare to Puritan views. You might write about what you believe to be the ideal approach to love and/or marriage. You might write about a time when love and marriage worked best, or respond to something else in the text that interests you.

Paragraph Assignment: Societal Roles and Expectations

All of the readings in this chapter discuss people's roles in society and their identities. Wong's personal narrative explores what it is like for a girl of Chinese heritage to grow up in American society. In his personal narrative, Bobryk explains how his role and identity changed when he became blind. The speaker in Cervantes' poem is also caught between two worlds. The last reading, a textbook excerpt, explains how gender determined people's roles in early American Puritan society.

Write a paragraph in which you respond to one of these prompts:
• In what ways are Wong's feelings similar to the speaker's in Cervantes' poem?

- How are the endings in Wong's essay and Cervantes' poem different?
- How does Bobryk's attitude differ from that of the speaker's in Cervantes' poem?
- Drawing on the textbook chapter "Seventeenth-Century Roles" and your own experiences, give two examples of how women's roles have changed since Puritan times.

Predrafting

If you feel strongly about one of the prompts in the writing assignment or if your instructor has asked all students to focus on one particular prompt, write freely in response to it. If you are unsure about which prompt you want to write about, write freely about all four. Share your freewriting with classmates and share ideas. You may also want to discuss these questions with classmates:

- Which topic are you most interested in?
- What do you need to tell your audience so that readers will understand your topic?
- What will your main idea be?
- What evidence or information can you use from the readings to support your main idea? (You can quote a sentence or line from the readings.)

Drafting

Create a topic sentence that tells your reader what you will be discussing in your paragraph. As you create your first draft, think about what your audience needs to know. Supply the basic facts (title, author, genre) before getting into specific information. You will be making statements—expressing your opinions and interpretations—and then you will need to back up those statements with specific facts and details from the readings and, perhaps, your own experiences.

Revising

Remember, in the revising stage, you think about adding, deleting, and moving information. Don't worry about editing and polishing yet.

Consider these questions as you revise:

- Does your paragraph begin with a strong topic sentence? A strong topic sentence can be seen as the "perfect umbrella" for your ideas. It should be broad enough to cover everything you have to say, but not so broad that it's hard to hold up.
- Do you offer specific support from the readings so that your reader will understand and believe you?

Editing

Once you feel confident about the content of your paragraph, you can begin to polish. Read your paragraph aloud and listen for sentences that don't sound right. Check your spelling—when in doubt, look up the word in the dictionary!

Also, consider these questions:

- Are you using strong action verbs whenever possible?
- Do you have strong, clear subjects?
- Have you avoided "there" sentences whenever possible?
- Are your subjects and verbs next to one another?
- Have you avoided using the passive voice whenever possible?
- Are there any new vocabulary words that you can use in your paragraph?

TIME TO REFLECT

Journal Assignment

Your Progress as a Writer, Reader, and Critical Thinker

Think about the chapter and the skills you have developed, then respond in your journal by discussing

- new reading skills you have begun to develop,
- how using the reading process will help you become a better reader and writer,
- the kinds of writing activities you found most helpful, and
- new reading and writing goals.

SUMMARY OF CHAPTER 3

In Chapter 3, you have examined the strategies used by effective readers and the PARTS of an effective reading process:

Preview

Anticipate

Read and reread

Think critically

Summarize

You have also

- contemplated and responded to a variety of challenging readings about people's roles in society,

- learned to use your dictionary and search for context clues to discover meanings of unknown words and phrases,

- learned the importance of retaining new words to build your vocabulary, and

- started logging definitions in a section of your notebook for easy review.

As you continue to practice the stages of the reading process and become a more experienced reader, you'll not only see your reading skills improve, but your writing and critical thinking skills as well.

INTRODUCTION TO SUBJECTS

Identifying Subjects
Subjects Are Nouns or Pronouns
-ing Words Can Be Subjects
Subjects and Prepositional Phrases
Multiple Subjects

Now that you have learned the importance of verbs and how to identify them in your sentences, it's time to turn to the next major ingredient of a sentence: the *subject*. The subject of a sentence is the person or thing the sentence is about. The subject performs the action expressed by the verb, or it is linked to other information by the verb. In these examples, the verbs are underlined twice and the subjects are underlined once:

I <u>wrote</u> an essay.

My <u>classmates</u> <u>gave</u> me suggestions.

At the end of class, the <u>instructor</u> <u>collected</u> our drafts.

Identifying Subjects

To identify the subject of a sentence, ask, "Who?" or "What?" about each verb. In the following example, the verb is underlined twice.

I <u>like</u> funny books.

Question: Who *likes?*

Answer: *I*

The answer to your question is the subject of that sentence.

I <u>like</u> funny books.

One verb can have more than one subject, and one subject can have more than one verb.

Elizabeth Wong and Amy Tan <u>write</u> about Chinese culture.

Question: Who *writes?*

Answer: *Elizabeth Wong and Amy Tan*

<u>Elizabeth Wong</u> and <u>Amy Tan</u> <u>write</u> about Chinese culture.

The essay <u>entertains</u> and <u>informs</u> readers.

Question: What *entertains and informs?*

Answer: *essay*

The <u>essay</u> <u>entertains</u> and <u>informs</u> readers.

Notes

Sometimes it is easier to find the subject if you ask "Who?" or "What?" after the entire *predicate*. The predicate of a sentence is the verb and all the words attached to the verb.

To help me study vocabulary, I <u>created some vocabulary flashcards</u>.

Question: Who *created some vocabulary flashcards?*

Answer: *I*

To help me study vocabulary, <u>I</u> <u>created some vocabulary flashcards</u>.

Practice #1   Jim Bobryk's Essay

- In the following sentences, identify the verbs and underline them twice.
- Remember not to let "imposters" fool you. Infinitives like *to win* won't be verbs. Present participles (words ending in *-ing*) can be verbs only if they have helping verbs with them. Be sure to underline the whole verb.
- Then, ask the "Who?" or "What?" question, identify the subjects, and underline them once.

Example: Jim Bobryk lost his sight.

Jim Bobryk <u>lost</u> his sight.

Question: Who <u>*lost his sight?*</u>

Answer: *Jim Bobryk*

- <u>Jim Bobryk</u> <u>lost</u> his sight.

1. I added the word *glaucoma* to my vocabulary list.
2. Unfortunately, sighted people are sometimes afraid to help blind people.
3. Bobryk's essay reminded me to look beyond a person's disability.
4. People don't want to be reduced to just one characteristic.
5. For instance, I don't want to be labeled by just my skin color.
6. I am many things: a man, a father, a sports enthusiast, a restaurant manager, and an Italian American.
7. No one wants to be discriminated against.

8. The *Newsweek* article educated people about the feelings of at least one disabled person.

9. I would like to learn to use humor in my writing.

10. An entertaining essay will keep a reader's interest.

11. Bobryk's description of losing his sight was vivid and frightening.

Subjects Are Nouns or Pronouns

The subject in a sentence is either a noun or a pronoun. As you may know, a **noun** names a person, place, thing, or idea: tree, book, happiness, Mom, Fred, fighting. A **pronoun** is a word that can take the place of a noun: it, he, she, me, I, you, we, us, they. (See pages 219–227 for more on pronouns.) In the following sentences, the nouns and pronouns are highlighted. If they are used as subjects, they are also underlined once. Verbs are underlined twice.

I reread the article.

Jessie found the main points after reading it again.

The instructor reminded us to edit carefully.

Practice #2   The Study Group
In the following sentences

• find the verbs and underline them twice,
• highlight all nouns and pronouns, and
• ask the "Who?" or "What?" question and underline the subjects once.

1. The instructor assigned four readings on water pollution.
2. Four students decided to form a study group.
3. The students followed the reading process.
4. First, they previewed and anticipated.
5. Then, they read the articles quickly, marking unknown words.
6. Next, they reread the articles, looking up definitions and making notes in the margins.
7. Finally, the students met to discuss the readings.
8. Frank summarized each reading.

Notes

9. He did a good job of finding most of the main points.
10. The other students took notes and added some missing points.
11. Susan asked a few questions about one of the readings.
12. She had found some of the technical vocabulary to be confusing.
13. Stuart had created some practice questions for them to work on.
14. On the day of the exam, they felt well prepared.

-ing *Words Can Be Subjects*

You have learned that *-ing* words cannot be verbs unless they have helping verbs. So what are *-ing* words when they don't have helping verbs? Well, they can act as nouns and in some of those cases they can be subjects. Another name for an *-ing* word that is working as a noun is **gerund**.

In the following sentences, the *-ing* word (gerund) is working as an *-ing* noun but not as a subject. The nouns (gerunds) are highlighted. The subjects are underlined once, and the verbs are underlined twice.

I enjoy skiing.

Lisa and Sam love driving to the coast.

The doctor suggested counting sheep.

In the following sentences, the *-ing* words (gerunds) are nouns, and they are working as subjects. The subjects are underlined once, and the verbs are underlined twice.

Writing this paper was a challenge.

Editing takes patience.

Drinking too much coffee is not good for me.

Practice #3   Writing

1. Highlight all of the nouns in sentences *a–d*.

   a. The class discusses the topic.
   b. The student writes in his journal.
   c. The instructor assigns a reading.
   d. The student reads the essay and answers the discussion questions.

2. Some of the nouns you highlighted in sentences *a–d* are also the subjects of those sentences. Underline the verbs in those sentences

Introduction to Subjects

twice, and then ask your "Who?" or "What?" questions to find the subjects. Underline the subjects once.

3. Underline the verbs in the following sentences twice, and then ask your "Who?" or "What?" questions to find the subjects. Underline the subjects once. You may want to discuss these sentences with your classmates.

   a. Writing takes a lot of time.
   b. Expressing your thoughts is not always easy.
   c. However, communicating with the written word gives you power.
   d. Reading is another key to power.

4. Look at one of your readings from this class or from another class and find two more sentences that have *-ing* words as the subjects. Write these sentences down. Underline the verb twice and the subject once.

Subjects and Prepositional Phrases

Remember, a prepositional phrase consists of a preposition, its object, and any words in between. In these examples, the preposition is underlined and the object is highlighted.

    <u>in</u> the brick building
    <u>on</u> the neighbor's roof
    <u>by</u> the author
    <u>for</u> one week

When you are looking for the subject of a sentence, you will want to ignore the prepositional phrases because your subject cannot be in a prepositional phrase. In the following sentences, the subjects are underlined once. The verbs are underlined twice, and the prepositional phrases are in brackets.

    <u>Grading standards</u> [at their school] <u>are</u> tough.
    <u>Computers</u> [in the classroom] <u>are</u> an asset [to writing students].
    A <u>tutor</u> [from one of the learning centers] <u>helps</u> dedicated students.
    [In his article], <u>Francis</u> <u>explained</u> the significance [of the statistics].

Introduction to Subjects

Notes

Practice #4   Puritans and Kids
In the following sentences

- underline the verb twice,
- put brackets around the prepositional phrases,
- ask your "Who?" or "What?" question, and
- when you find the subject, underline it once.

   The first sentence is done for you.

[In "Seventeenth-Century Roles for Puritan Men, Women, and Children,"] the <u>authors</u> <u>describe</u> Puritan family life. Perhaps we could learn something from the Puritans. Men shouldn't have such absolute power in a family. In marriages, men and women should make decisions together. Kids should be involved in some of the discussions. However, as a society, we should teach kids to respect the experience of their elders. Young people can learn from the successes, problems, and failures of their parents. The trick is to listen. In the reading, the authors explained the Puritan method of parental control: delaying inheritance. That method wouldn't work today. However, parents should think about making things too easy for kids. Young adults should earn trust and independence.

Multiple Subjects

Writing sentences with more than one subject can help you say things more clearly and make your writing more interesting. For example, if you wanted to tell readers that three famous people have affected your life in a similar way, you could write three separate sentences:

   Helen Keller inspired me because she had a disability but still achieved so much. Franklin Delano Roosevelt inspired me because he had a disability but still achieved so much. Steven Hawking inspired me because he had a disability but still achieved so much.

Of course, you wouldn't want to be so repetitive in your writing. A better choice would be to create a sentence with multiple subjects.

> Helen Keller, Franklin Delano Roosevelt, and Steven Hawking inspired me because they had disabilities but still achieved so much.

Notice that the plural pronoun *they* had to be substituted for the singular pronouns, and *disability* had to become *disabilities*.

Punctuation Rule #1

Put commas between items in a series.

- Helen Keller, Franklin Delano Roosevelt, and Steven Hawking inspired me because they had disabilities but still achieved so much.

Here is another example:

- I bought eggs, milk and cheese at the store.
  (A comma before the *and* is optional with a list.)

Practice #5   Dating, Marriage, and Sex Education

For each set of sentences, write a new sentence that has multiple subjects. Remember to apply Punctuation Rule #1.

Example: Dating practices have been the focus in our health class for the last few weeks. Marriage has been the focus in our health class for the last few weeks. Sex education has been the focus in our health class for the last few weeks.

- Dating practices, marriage, and sex education have been the focus in our health class for the last few weeks.

Note: Verbs may change form when you create sentences with multiple subjects. For example, a verb like *has* would change to *have*.

1. In the 1600s, Puritan ministers spoke out against premarital sex. In the 1600s, the government spoke out against premarital sex. In the 1600s, parents spoke out against premarital sex.

2. Today, television influences our views on relationships. Today, music influences our views on relationships. Today, movies influence our views on relationships.

3. Education is an important part of preventing teen pregnancy. Open communication between parents and children is an important part of preventing teen pregnancy.

Notes

4. My grandparents' experience with dating was different than mine. My parents' experience with dating was different than mine.

5. After attending the training seminar, the principal had a better plan for dealing with sex education. After attending the training seminar, the school nurse had a better plan for dealing with sex education. After attending the training seminar, the teachers had a better plan for dealing with sex education.

THE HARD-TO-FIND SUBJECT

Implied Subjects
Subjects in Questions
Subjects in **There** *Sentences*

In the last section, you learned that subjects are nouns or pronouns. Sometimes an *-ing* word can function as a noun and subject. You also learned that a sentence can have more than one subject but that no subject will be in a prepositional phrase.

This section will help you find subjects that may seem hidden in a sentence (or that may seem to not exist at all).

Implied Subjects

Look at the following sentences. The verbs are underlined twice.

Study these statistics. Prepare a report for the committee. Be prepared to explain the pay discrepancy. Review your ideas with the personnel director. Present your ideas at the next meeting.

In the paragraph above, who is supposed to do all the work? The sentences in the paragraph are called *command sentences*. **Command sentences** give someone work to do. They give directions. Command sentences do not have stated subjects: they have **implied subjects.** The implied subject is "you."

[You] study these statistics. [You] prepare a report for the committee. [You] be prepared to explain the pay discrepancy. [You] review your ideas with the personnel director. [You] present your ideas at the next meeting.

The Hard-to-Find Subject

Practice #6   Equal Pay

In the following sentences, underline the verbs twice. Underline the subjects once. If the subject is implied, write *you* at the beginning of the sentence and underline the *you*.

Example: Review the punctuation rules before editing.

- [*You*] Review the punctuation rules before editing.

1. You should write a research paper on gender equality in the workplace.
2. Go to the Department of Labor's Web site.
3. You will find useful statistics.
4. Talk to our business professor.
5. She will give you some good articles to read.
6. Consider interviewing some men and women in your dad's corporation.
7. Check the college library for useful books.
8. Ask the librarian for assistance.
9. Remember to use the writing process.
10. Keep a good record of your sources.

Subjects in Questions

You've seen that finding a subject in a command sentence can be a little tricky. Finding the subject in a question can be tricky too. Just remember that often the subject and verb won't be in their usual positions. For example, look at these questions. The verbs are underlined twice and the subjects are underlined once.

Did you read Jackson's essay?

Do you agree with him?

Which experts believe in bilingual education?

What happens to the verb in the first two questions? (Answer this question in the margin and share your response with your classmates.) To make finding the subject and verb easier, sometimes you can change a question into a statement. (Notice that the question word *which* is dropped in the third example.)

Notes

You <u>did read</u> Jackson's essay.

You <u>do agree</u> with him.

<u>Experts</u> <u>believe</u> in bilingual education.

Practice #7   Questions About Workplace Equality

In the following questions, underline the verbs twice and the subjects once. Change the questions into statements if you have any difficulty identifying the verb and subject. (Also, remember that you can use the test of time to find verbs, and you can use the "Who?" or "What?" question to find subjects.)

1. Why are male teachers paid more than female teachers in our district?
2. Where can I find a copy of the federal Equal Pay Act?
3. Why are men more willing to do the more dangerous jobs?
4. Why do social workers make less than probation officers?
5. Is a woman with kids less likely to devote herself to the job than a man with kids?
6. Did you read the statistics about women earning more college degrees than men?
7. How can we encourage more men to go to college?
8. Do we need a campaign to urge women to enter higher-paying fields?
9. Would you be good at negotiating higher pay for yourself?
10. Should we take action on this issue?

Subjects in There *Sentences*

You may be used to sentences that start with the subject and have a verb shortly after the subject. A sentence that starts with *there* is a little different. In the following sentences, the subjects are underlined once and the verbs are underlined twice.

There <u>are</u> many <u>ways</u> to write a paragraph.

There <u>are</u>, however, a few key <u>steps</u>.

There <u>is</u> the planning <u>stage</u>.

As you may have noticed, *there* is never the subject. To help you find the subject in a sentence that begins with *there*, you may want to bracket *there,* infinitives, and prepositional phrases. (To review infinitives and prepositional phrases, see pages 76–81.)

[There] <u>is</u> the crucial <u>step</u> [of rewriting], too.

[There] <u>are</u> <u>tutors</u>, <u>instructors</u>, and <u>books</u> [to help] you.

Practice #8   Paragraphs and Reading

In the following sentences, underline the verbs twice and underline the subjects once. Bracket *there* and any infinitives and prepositional phrases you find.

1. There are three parts to a paragraph.
2. There are the topic sentence, body, and wrap up.
3. There is a process for writing a paragraph.
4. There is also a process for reading.
5. There are the previewing and anticipating steps.
6. There is the reading and rereading step.
7. There is the think critically step.
8. There is the summarize step.

STYLE TIPS

From this point forward in *Connections,* you'll find Style Tips at the end of the chapters. You've begun to learn the basic grammar terms: nouns, pronouns, subjects, verbs, predicates, and prepositional phrases. With these terms in your vocabulary, you can have meaningful discussions with your tutor or instructor about your sentences and learn to avoid fragments, run-ons, and other grammatical errors.

However, just because a sentence is grammatically correct doesn't mean that it has good style or that it is clear. While writing style is, to a degree, a matter of personal preference, most writers agree on the basics: Writing should be clear, informative, and varied.

Here is an overview of our style advice:

• Readers respond well to directness. This means that the writer should choose strong verbs and clear subjects, and the writer should place the subjects and verbs next to one another in the usual order (subject then verb).

Notes

Style Tips

Style Tips

Notes

- Readers like writing that isn't cluttered with unnecessary words.

- Readers like a mix of long and short sentences. They want the writer to vary how sentences begin. They want the writer to occasionally interrupt a sentence or embed a thought—smoothly. They want some of the sentences in a piece of writing to include details and descriptions.

- Readers want help moving from one point to another.

These are the style points you will learn throughout this book. Of course, style is something you pay attention to during the editing step of your writing process. Don't worry about style while you are exploring, drafting, and revising.

Style Tip #1
Use strong subjects and verbs whenever possible and place them carefully in your sentences.

This means you should

- choose action verbs whenever possible,

- choose subjects that can perform the action, or can at least name a specific entity, and

- place the subject and verb directly next to one another and in the usual order: subject then verb. (Of course, in questions, the order will be reversed.)

In Chapter 1 you got a taste of editing for style when you focused on using action verbs on pages 34–35. Now let's take that kind of editing a step further. In the exercise called "Paragraphs and Reading" on page 119, the sentences don't follow Style Tip #1. They are grammatically correct, but they do not have good style. None of the sentences have action verbs, and the verbs come before the subjects in all of the sentences. In most cases, *there* sentences are not stylistically strong.

Practice #9
Revise the sentences below. (The first three are borrowed from Practice #8.) Revise them so that they don't start with *there*. You will probably want to create new subjects and new verbs in each sentence. Aim to stick close to the original meaning, but feel free to liven up the sentences. The first five come with helpful hints.

Example: There are many ways to write a paragraph.

- I <u>know</u> many ways to write a paragraph.
  or
- <u>Writers</u> <u>can approach</u> a paragraph assignment many different ways.

1. There are three parts to a paragraph. (*Hint:* Make *paragraph* the subject. *Paragraph* can be a strong, clear subject. Then use the action verb *has*.)

2. There is a process for writing a paragraph. (*Hint:* Add a whole new word to the sentence. Use *I* as a strong subject. Use *have learned* or *have been practicing* as the action verb.)

3. There is also a process for reading. (*Hint:* Try using *I* again as a subject and see what action verb makes sense to you.)

4. There was a very intelligent man talking about heritage and our roles in society. (*Hint:* Reduce the number of words in this sentence; find the word that should be the action verb and make it the verb of the sentence; find the noun that should be the "actor" or the "subject." You can change the ending on a word if you want to.)

5. There is a lot of information in this report. (*Hint:* Try using the action verb *contains*. Ask yourself "What contains a lot of information?" and make your answer the subject.)

6. There are two people who could tell me more about my heritage.

7. There is a dusty diary in my grandmother's attic.

8. There were lessons in traditional Indian dances at our community center.

9. There were some interesting images in that poem.

10. There was a question that I had about interpreting the poem.

As you learned earlier, the verb and subject will never be in a prepositional phrase. In fact, to have the clearest style, you'll want to keep an eye out for those prepositional phrases and stop them from separating your subject and verb. Sometimes you can't avoid it, and the prepositional phrase will get between your subject and verb, but usually you can find another arrangement.

Three of the sample sentences from page 113 would have better style if we just moved the prepositional phrases. The verbs are underlined twice and the subjects once. The prepositional phrases are bracketed.

Notes

Grading standards [at their school] are tough.

This sentence would have better style if the subject and verb weren't separated by the prepositional phrase.

[At their school], grading standards are tough.

Or

Grading standards are tough [at their school].

In both of the style revisions, we moved the prepositional phrase. In one version, we moved it to the front of the sentence. In the other version, we moved it to the end of the sentence.

The next sample sentence from page 113 has the same problem. A prepositional phrase is separating the subject and verb.

Computers [in the classroom] are an asset [to writing students].

This sentence would be better if we got rid of the first prepositional phrase completely. We can take a piece of the prepositional phrase and place it in front of the subject.

Classroom computers are an asset [to writing students].

Keep in mind that prepositional phrases are not bad. Often, writers need them in order to fully explain ideas. Our advice is to look at where you place the useful prepositional phrases and to get rid of the ones that aren't useful.

Style Tip #2
Don't use more words than needed.

This tip isn't telling you to leave out details and descriptions. Those are necessary in well-developed writing. This tip is telling you to watch out for words that don't actually add any meaningful information to your sentences. At the editing step, you should eliminate those unnecessary words.

The next sentence would be better off with no prepositional phrase. The phrase adds unnecessary words to the sentence. You can take a piece of one prepositional phrase and place it in front of the subject.

A tutor [from one of the learning centers] helps dedicated students.

This sentence would be clearer if written this way.

A learning center tutor helps dedicated students.

Practice #10

The sentences in this exercise are grammatically correct but have poor style. Follow the style suggestions presented so far to write sentences that have better clarity and style.

1. The <u>roles</u> of women <u>were</u> very limited in the seventeenth century. (Problem: The subject and verb are separated by a prepositional phrase. Get rid of the phrase by changing *The roles of women* to *Women's roles.*)

2. <u>Household chores</u> in the days of the Puritans <u>were</u> much more difficult than chores today. (Problem: The subject and verb are separated by two prepositional phrases. Move the phrases to the beginning of the sentence.)

3. Even the <u>steps</u> for washing clothes <u>were</u> more difficult. (Problem: The subject and verb are separated by a prepositional phrase. Make *washing clothes* the subject and change the verb from *were* to *was*. This means you'll be eliminating the current subject *the steps* and the preposition *for.*)

4. The <u>members</u> of the Puritan society <u>had</u> to obey the laws of the courts and the church. (Problems: The subject and verb are separated by a prepositional phrase; there are unnecessary words in this sentence; the verb could be stronger. The writer doesn't need to say *the members of the Puritan society.* Replace all of those words with *Puritans.* Also, the writer might want to change *had to obey* to *obeyed.* This changes the meaning slightly, but give it a try anyway. Your new sentence will be shorter, clearer, and more direct.)

5. The <u>people</u> of these early colonies <u>supported</u> many English traditions. (Problem: The subject and verb are separated by a prepositional phrase. Replace *the people of these early colonies* with a simpler, more direct subject: *Early colonists.*)

Practice #11

Improve the style in the following sentences by making sure that a prepositional phrase *does not* come between the subject and verb.

Notes

Consider these options:

- move the prepositional phrase to another part of the sentence,
- take a piece of the prepositional phrase and place it in front of the subject, or
- eliminate the prepositional phrase completely.

Any change is acceptable if your sentence still communicates basically the same idea and has better style. You'll want to discuss your improved sentences with classmates. You and your classmates will come up with a variety of solutions.

1. The price of the airline tickets was expensive.
2. My relatives from Germany shared many wonderful stories with us. (*Hint:* You might want to change *Germany* to *German.*)
3. The habits of my relatives were a little different than ours.
4. The presents from my cousins were made by hand.
5. My practice of showering before and after work seemed excessive to my aunt and uncle.
6. The dialect in my grandmother's village is hard for me to understand.
7. The main topic of conversation during the first two hours was the hot weather here.
8. The request from my cousin was for me to come visit soon.
9. One of my goals in the future is to travel.
10. The traditions of my family are important to me.

Action verbs add life and interest to your sentences. However, they can also be used a little differently and lose their energy. Compare the sentences below.

I <u>wrote</u> the letter to my aunt.

The sentence above has a strong action verb and a clear subject that can perform the action. Now consider a slightly different sentence.

The <u>letter</u> to my aunt <u>was written</u> by me.

This second sentence is written in the **passive voice.** *Passive voice* means that the person or thing that should be the subject is hidden somewhere in the sentence and is receiving the action instead of performing it.

Passive voice doesn't break any grammar rules, and sometimes you need to use it. However, most of the time you should avoid passive voice because it causes you to break at least two style rules. In passive voice

- you don't have a subject that can perform the action, and

- you usually have more words than you need.

The next sentence is written in the passive voice. (In all of the following examples, the verbs are underlined twice, the subjects are underlined once, and the prepositional phrases are bracketed.)

The book was loaned [to me] [by my grandfather].
The verb in this sentence is *was loaned*. The subject is *book*. However, the *book* can't *loan* anything. The sentence should be revised so that *grandfather* becomes the subject.

My grandfather loaned the book [to me]. (Notice that the verb changed slightly from *was loaned* to *loaned* and there are fewer words overall in this more stylish sentence. Passive voice requires more words—words that aren't really helpful.)

The house was owned [by my great uncle].
The verb is *was owned*. The subject is *house*. However, the *house* can't own anything. The sentence should be revised so that *my great uncle* becomes the subject.

My great uncle owned the house.

Their conversation was interpreted [by my bilingual cousin].
The verb is *was interpreted*. The subject is *their conversation*. However, *the conversation* can't actually *interpret* anything. The sentence should be revised so *my bilingual cousin* becomes the subject.

My bilingual cousin interpreted their conversation.

Practice #12
In the following sentences, underline the verbs twice and the subjects once, and put brackets around the prepositional phrases. All of the sentences are written in passive voice, so your second step is to rewrite the sentences so that they are no longer passive. (In each sentence, you will find a word in one of the prepositional phrases that could be moved to become a strong, clear subject.)

1. A complicated idea was explored by that poem.
2. An interesting image of old age was created by that poet.

Notes

3. "The Long Way Around" was performed by The Dixie Chicks.

4. The message in "The Long Way Around" can be connected by me to the themes in this chapter.

5. A rap song was brought into class by one of my classmates.

6. An interesting interpretation of the rap song was given by my classmate.

7. The drawing about gender and racial roles was created by my roommate.

8. A small sketch of Rosie the Riveter was added by me to the bottom of his drawing.

9. Some very helpful comments on my paragraph were offered to me by my great tutor.

10. The quality of my paragraph was improved by the writing process.

Your Own Writing: Using Strong Subjects and Verbs

Pick a sentence from a journal, summary, or paragraph that doesn't yet have good style. Write the sentence down and then use Style Tips #1 and #2 to make it stronger and clearer.

Using Connections *Online with* mywritinglab

For more practice with subjects, log onto www.mywritinglab.com to access the online resources for *Connections,* Third Edition.

Examining the Essay Writing Process

Main Topics

- Examining the essay writing process

- Communicating your ideas about advertisements and evil characters

- Identifying phrases and clauses in your sentences

- Achieving sentence variety with phrases and clauses

RUBES by Leigh Rubin

With his deadline fast approaching, Harvey resorts to the unconventional.

By permission of Leigh Rubin and Creators Syndicate, Inc.

In the past, people often assumed that good writing was a matter of genetics—either you were born a Hemingway, or you weren't. Fortunately, good writing is not a result of special writing genes, nor is it a matter of knowing "the tricks." Good writing is largely the result of taking the right steps, of using an effective writing process.

You can think of this process as being similar to what you might do if you were preparing a presentation at work. The presentation doesn't simply appear. You must research your topic, gather information and props, plan the sequence of information, and perhaps write out a script.

Similarly, each writer must (and can) develop an effective writing process in order to produce effective essays. You've practiced some of this process already as you've written paragraphs in Chapters 1–3. Now it's time to examine the writing process in greater detail as you prepare to write your first essays of the term.

THE STAGES OF AN EFFECTIVE WRITING PROCESS

The writing process can be broken into stages that you'll begin using in this chapter.

Discuss and Engage

You'll talk about the general topic and begin to get involved in it.

Read, Discuss, Think Critically

You'll read, discuss the readings, and think critically about the readings and how they relate to the writing assignment.

Explore the Writing Assignment

You'll carefully review the actual writing assignment and explore what kind of information should go into your essay. You may also take the time at this stage to outline and plan your essay.

Draft

You'll write a complete essay. The essay will probably be rough, so you'll have to work on the draft and improve it.

Revise

You'll change and improve the draft. You might add information, delete information, and move ideas around.

Edit

You'll work on sentence structure, usage, punctuation, and spelling. This is the "polishing" stage.

Points to Remember About the Writing Process

- The writing process stages will not always happen in this exact order. They may overlap, and some stages may need to be repeated.

- Approaching an essay assignment as a series of steps will actually make your task easier. You will be able to take your essay assignment one step at a time.

- All writers have some kind of writing process. Some processes are more effective than others and make writing easier, so it's important to refine your process until it works well for you.

Journal Assignment

Your Writing Process, Past and Future

The comic strip *Rubes* on page 127 addresses the frustration writers sometimes feel as deadlines approach. In his desperation, Harvey is ready to try anything to get the ideas out of his head and onto the page.

In your notebook, respond to the scene. Have you ever felt like Harvey? If so, share some of the strategies you used to break through writer's block. If not, what advice would you share with someone who's struggling with writer's block?

Also in your notebook, describe the writing process you have used until now. Consider some of the following questions:

- What do you do before you begin to write?
- Do you talk to anyone about your assignment?
- Do you handwrite your ideas on a notepad first?
- Do you compose on a word processor or computer?
- Do you usually write more than one draft?
- Are there certain steps that you must improve or add to your process? Explain.

Developing an Effective Writing Process

Analyzing your past writing process and thinking about how to improve your writing process are important activities. Of course, the next step is to begin *practicing* an effective writing process.

Notes

In this chapter, you will be offered three writing assignments. These assignments will help you begin to sharpen and refine your reading, writing, and critical thinking processes as you analyze some challenging subjects: advertising and the human character.

Writing Assignment #1: *Analyzing Advertisements*

In this assignment, you'll sharpen your critical thinking skills as you analyze a selection of advertisements. This analysis will require you to study the details of the ads so that you can draw conclusions about the ads and the motives of the advertisers.

Here, in brief, is the writing assignment that you are preparing for:

Write an essay in which you analyze one advertisement by discussing the strategies the advertiser is using to make the product "appeal" to buyers. Comment on how successful you think the advertisement is.

Keep this assignment in mind as you dig deeper into the issue of advertisements and prepare to write.

Save all the writing you do in preparation for your writing assignments. This writing will become your **process package,** a collection of work—including class notes, all brainstorming, an outline, a rough draft, and more. This process package will represent the writing process that takes you from initial ideas to a finished essay.

Discuss and Engage

Research shows that this is one of the stages of the writing process that some writers skip. These writers jump into writing their papers before they discuss and think about the topic even though they would never consider making an important decision such as purchasing a new car without discussing their options with experts, friends, or family members. They would take the time to discuss the various makes and models (Ford Explorer versus Jeep Grand Cherokee), extras (CD player, air conditioning, passenger air bags), and price before purchasing their vehicles. Otherwise, they might end up dissatisfied or even with a "lemon."

Discussion, planning, and critical thinking are also important when writers are given essay topics. Writers who discuss their topics with classmates, their instructor, a tutor, friends, or family members before writing are more satisfied with their papers than those who do not. In addition, these writers save time in the long run because they have taken time at the beginning to get to know the topic before they start to write.

Non Sequitur

Notes

NON SEQUITUR © 1997 Wiley Miller. Dist. by
UNIVERSAL PRESS SYNDICATE. Reprinted with
permission. All rights reserved.

Activities

Discuss Advertisements

Discuss with your class advertisements that you remember and why you remember them.

- In what ways did the advertisements appeal to you?

- Do you remember some advertisements because they didn't appeal to you?

- Do you sometimes buy products because of the advertisements you've seen?

- Are advertisers always straightforward and honest in the way that they advertise?

Review the *Non Sequitur* cartoon above.

- What product are the characters looking to sell?

- What tricks will they use?

Get Involved!

With a classmate, visit AdAge.com's Web site, www.adage.com/ century/ad_icons, to view "The Top 10 Advertising Icons of the Century." Take notes on the top ten icons and bring your notes to class for discussion.

Notes

- Why is this funny?
- Why does the second man say, "We?"

> ### *Journal Assignment*
> #### *Review Discussion*
> Think about your class discussion and write down your thoughts about advertisements. This is an opportunity to express your thoughts privately and freely. (Refer back to your journal when you're ready to begin drafting your essay.)

Read, Discuss, Think Critically

In this stage, you gather information by reading material related to the topic. Inexperienced writers often worry that they do not have anything to say about an assigned topic. These writers need to realize (through discussions and journal writing) that they already know *something* about an assignment although they probably need more information on the subject (often gained through reading).

Returning to our analogy of buying a car, it would be wise to "read up" on the car you intend to buy before following through with the purchase. You may want to know, for example, what *Consumer Reports* or *Car and Driver* has to say about the car's performance, value, or gas mileage. Once you become knowledgeable on the subject, you will be better prepared to make a purchase. In the same way, the more you know about your writing topic, the better prepared you are to write about it.

Reading Assignment: *The Advertisements*

(The questions and suggestions that follow will help you continue to use some of the PARTS of the reading process.)

Preview   Quickly review the following advertisements and think about the kinds of readers the advertisers are trying to attract.

Anticipate   Next to each advertisement, write down a guess about what kind of magazine the advertisement might show up in. Can you name a specific magazine for each advertisement?

Read and Reread   Carefully study the details of the advertisements. Notice that four of the ads are modern and would be found in a variety of popular magazines. The other two, however, are vintage ads, which means they're older ads that represent products of another era. As you read each ad, pay attention to the words, for they were carefully chosen by the advertisers. Also, note the objects and the people (their clothes, postures, facial expressions). Mark interesting parts or words in the advertisements and make notes about both the advertisements and who you think the intended audience might be. Do you want to change any of your earlier guesses about where each advertisement came from?

Notes

Activity

Discuss Selected Advertisements

In groups, discuss what you see in each advertisement. What sorts of words are used? What is (or is not) in the picture? If there are people, what do they look like? What sorts of expressions and clothes do they wear? How are the advertisers manipulating you? What kind of audience will respond best to the advertisement and want to buy the product? (Think about gender, age, ethnicity, economic status, and so on.) Are the advertisers relying on stereotypes?

Now consider the differences between the modern and vintage ads. What similarities do they share? How are they different?

Examine just the vintage ads. Can you think of a modern example of either ad? If so, how does the modern version of the ad differ from the vintage version? (Be sure to take notes during your class discussion.)

Get Involved!

Find an advertisement that would be interesting to analyze and bring it to class for discussion.

Journal Assignment

Review Discussion

Think about your group discussion and review your notes and the advertisements. Now write down your thoughts. (Answer as many of the previous questions as you can, and add any other thoughts.) Exchange this journal with one or more classmates. When you read someone else's, simply say, "Thank you," when you return the journal to the author. Don't criticize or discuss.

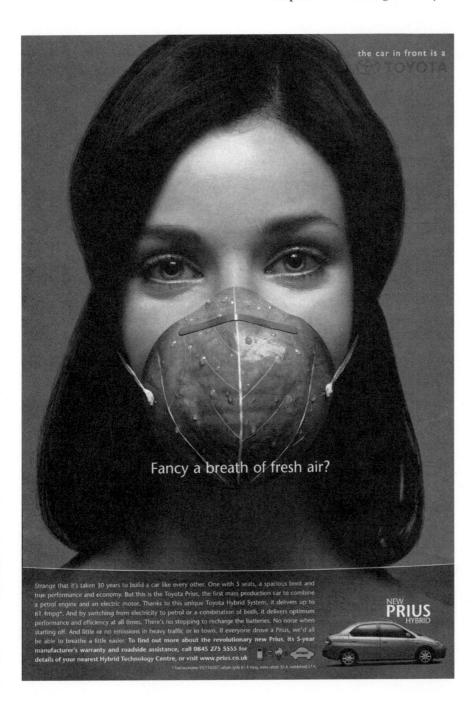

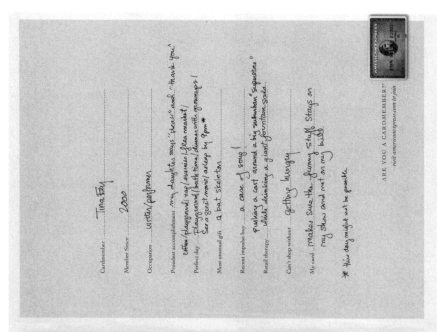

i ran along side until i felt he didn't need me. then...i let go. immediately, i wanted to grab hold again but he was gone. two wheeling for the first time ever. and as we celebrated over lunch, him munching on Chicken McNuggets® made with white meat, fresh Apple Dippers and a low-fat milk jug* and me enjoying the Southwest Salad with warm cilantro-lime glazed chicken, i thought about driver's licenses and girlfriends and college and enjoyed the moment even more.

Beauty and Health cry out "Save your teeth!"
DOUBLE MINT GUM enjoyed daily helps you to do this by
increasing the flow of life-blood to the roots and gums.

Notes

Explore the Writing Assignment

At this stage, you and your classmates will carefully study the writing assignment. (No one wants to finish an assignment only to find out that he or she wrote "off topic.") It is at this point that you and your classmates can discuss how you might respond to the essay topic. What is the assignment asking? What kind of main point do you want to focus on? How will you prove your main point? Are you unclear about any facts? Talk with other people to help you think through the topic and help you make good choices as you begin writing.

Activities

Review the Writing Assignment

Here, again, is your writing assignment. Review it carefully before continuing. Underline the important terms in the assignment.

> *Write an essay in which you analyze one advertisement by discussing the strategies the advertiser is using to make the product "appeal" to buyers. Comment on how successful you think the advertisement is.*

Get Involved!

With a classmate, go to the following Web site to examine a series of Virginia Slims cigarette commercials from 1969: www.archive.org/details/tobacco_leo 23e00. Make a list of the strategies used in the commercials to make cigarette smoking appealing to women. Be ready to discuss these strategies in class.

Choose an Advertisement

Choose an advertisement you would like to write about. (*Note:* It is acceptable to change your mind later about which advertisement to write about, but you will save yourself some time if you first carefully consider your choices.) Choose an advertisement that you find interesting and that has a number of features you want to think about and study.

Explore the Advertising Assignment

Explore the topic. Review and discuss the assignment with your classmates and consider these critical thinking questions:

1. What advertisement do you want to focus on? Why?

2. What sort of information needs to be in your essay? What doesn't?

3. What will you say? In what order will you state your points?

4. What kinds of details and explanations will you give?

Analyze an Advertisement

On a separate sheet of paper, make a chart similar to the one that follows. To further analyze your advertisement, list strategies (such as wording, color, or placement of objects) and answer the questions provided.

Advertiser's strategies	How does the strategy work?	How effective is it?
1.		
2.		
3.		
4.		

Brainstorm   When you have read and thought about the topic, made notes, and discussed your ideas with classmates, you may want to let your thoughts flow freely on paper. This is called **freewriting,** which is one type of **brainstorming.** Looking back periodically at the advertisement and the assignment, let yourself write freely with no interruptions or worries about corrections. This can help you discover what points most interest you about a certain topic. The key is to let yourself write freely for as long as you can, even repeating ideas, because the ideas you repeat may be the ideas that most intrigue you. These are the ideas that might become the focus of your essay.

Activity

Brainstorming

Focusing on the current writing assignment and the advertisements you have been studying, write freely for as long as you can. Let your mind wander, but periodically look back at the assignment to remind yourself of what you will be writing an essay about. If you run out of ideas, look back at your class notes and reread what you've already written. Remember, it's okay to repeat yourself when you're freewriting.

Create Your Thesis Statement   The thesis is the sentence at the end of your introduction that expresses the main idea of your essay. In this

Notes

sentence, you tell your reader precisely what you're planning to explain or prove in your essay and why it's important. Keep in mind that the thesis sentence should directly respond to the **essay assignment** (also known as the **essay prompt**). It may take a few attempts before you're able to create a sentence that clearly states your essay plan. In fact, as you develop your essay, you may need to return to your thesis to further refine it during the drafting or revising stages of the process. Writing a good thesis statement requires using your critical thinking skills as you decide what you'll focus on and what you'll explain or prove.

Activity

Creating a Thesis

Sometimes it's helpful to change the essay assignment, or prompt, into a question, if it isn't already a question. For example, your current essay topic is

> *Write an essay in which you analyze one advertisement by discussing the strategies the advertiser is using to make the product "appeal" to buyers. Comment on how successful you think the advertisement is.*

If you turned this into a question, it might read like this:

> *What strategies is the advertiser using [in the ad you've chosen] to make the product appeal to buyers, and how successful is the advertisement?*

Your answer to this question could become your thesis statement.

Now, focusing on the advertisement you have chosen, write down some possible answers to this question. Share your responses with classmates or a tutor. Work on polishing the sentence so that it clearly communicates your main idea. Remember that it's okay to come back later and improve your thesis statement.

Outline Another helpful tool for writers is the **outline.** An outline can be a formal and thorough list of all the major and supporting points in an essay, or it can be a quick list of just the major points to be covered. The benefit in creating an outline is to make a plan for yourself so that you stay focused on your main idea and on ideas that directly support it. When creating an outline, think about what your major points will be and what order these points should be in. You'll need to use your critical thinking skills as you choose what to include and what to leave out of your essay.

Some writers spend a lot of time perfecting their outlines—listing major points, supporting points, and details. These writers revise and perfect their outlines until the entire essay is just about written. Other writers start with a rough, quick outline—listing the thesis and topic sentences—and then begin drafting the essay, looking at the outline just to see if they are staying on track. These writers may drift away from their outlines and decide that drifting away is okay because the outlines weren't quite right for what they have decided to say. Some of these writers take the time to revise their outlines as a way of checking their drafts for good organization, focus, and development.

The goal with an outline is to make a plan first before diving into an essay. If you think about your thesis and what your major supporting points should be, you are more likely to stay on track and not get lost in many other related topics. Also, you can use an outline as a tool for sharing your ideas. That is, before writing an entire draft, you can test out your ideas by simply showing your outline to a reader and getting feedback.

Activity

Outline

Write down your thesis statement at the top of a page. Then make a list of supporting ideas. Again, you'll have to experiment and use your critical thinking skills as you decide what your major points should be. If you want to, add some notes under each major supporting point to remind yourself of the details you will use from the advertisement.

Share this outline with a classmate or tutor to see if you are responding clearly and directly to the writing assignment.

Draft

When you have discussed a topic, read about it, discussed related readings, thought critically about the topic and readings, and written an outline, it's time to begin drafting your essay.

Write a draft that you'll want to share with your classmates, a tutor, or your instructor. It should be complete—with an introduction, body, and conclusion. This complete draft will naturally be imperfect.

Notes

You'll have opportunities later in your writing process to rearrange ideas, add ideas, or even take out some ideas if they don't fit. Keep your audience in mind as you write your draft, and repeat any earlier steps of your writing process as necessary. (For example, if you feel that midway through your essay you have run out of things to say, go back and look at the advertisement again, review your class notes, or talk to a classmate or tutor.)

Consider completing your draft on a computer so that you don't have to retype the entire essay after each improvement.

Activity

Draft Your Advertisement Essay

Draft your essay about the advertisement you selected. (Be sure to use the notes, chart, and outline you've made so far.) Remember that you're writing an essay to a reader who has never seen your advertisement before, so in your introduction summarize what you see in your advertisement and what you believe the advertiser is trying to accomplish. In the body of your essay, support what you have said in your introduction by exposing the strategies the advertiser uses. Be specific. In your conclusion, comment on the effectiveness of the advertisement.

Activity

Study a Student Sample

The following is a student essay on one of the popular "Got Milk?" ads. Read the introductory paragraph closely. Underline the sentence that appears to be the thesis. (Remember, the thesis tells the reader what the writer plans to explain or prove in the essay and why.) Then consider what you think is good about this student's introduction. Answer the questions that follow.

Got Milk?

1 The advertisement I chose to analyze is advertising the dairy product milk. It appeared in *Rolling Stone* magazine. The person who is promoting the product is the late-night talk show host Conan O'Brien. Conan is sitting at a desk in a classroom wearing blue jeans that are cuffed way up, high tops, and a striped T-shirt. He looks like he is portraying a little kid. He has a little kid innocent look on his face, and he is also wearing a milk mustache that

goes along with the caption that reads under the picture, "Where's your mustache?" Next to the picture of Conan is a little paragraph that states why Conan likes to drink milk and how drinking milk can benefit a person. To convince people to buy milk in this advertisement, the advertiser successfully uses tricks such as colors, words, an eye-catching setting, and a celebrity.

2 The first trick the advertiser uses to get people to buy milk is a celebrity to promote the product. For anyone who watches late-night television, Conan O'Brien should look familiar. People who like him will read the advertisement, and maybe they will think that if Conan O'Brien drinks milk, they should too. If the advertiser had used an ordinary person in the advertisement, I don't think as many people would look at it because it would not catch their eye.

3 The advertiser uses words in this advertisement to draw people in. People see the short paragraph next to the familiar face of Conan O'Brien, and they want to read it. A person might figure that since it is a comedian advertising the product, whatever is written next to the picture will be funny. That is certainly true in this case. Most people would probably read the advertisement knowing they're in for a good laugh.

4 Another trick that the advertiser uses to convince people to buy milk in the advertisement is the use of colors. The advertisement contains an array of different colors. The shirt that Conan is wearing stands out because it is brighter than the colors in the background. The milk carton that is sitting on the desk really stands out because it is brighter than the colors in the background and is the only item in the picture that contains the color red. The advertiser wants the milk carton to stand out because that is exactly what is being advertised. The white milk mustache that Conan is wearing in the advertisement also stands out. This is the first thing a person would probably notice when looking at the ad.

5 The last trick the advertiser uses in the ad to get people to notice the product is the eye-catching setting. For anyone who went to grammar school, the setting should look very familiar. There is the huge blackboard, desks, and little chairs, all typical items a person would see in a classroom. The setting would catch the eye of a person because there is a grown man, Conan, dressed up like a little kid,

sitting on a very small chair at a desk in a classroom. It looks funny and would not be something a person sees everyday in life. 6 Overall, I would say that the advertiser is very successful in convincing people to buy milk in this ad. The ad is very humorous along with informational. It's straight to the point, and I think the celebrity they chose to advertise their product was a good one.

—*Jennifer Arch, student writer*

There are many ways to introduce an essay, and Jennifer found a way that worked well for her. Respond to the following questions in your notebook and be prepared to discuss your responses with classmates.

1. What do you particularly like about this introduction? What good decisions did Jennifer make?

2. An introduction to an essay should tell you *what* the topic of the essay is and *why* the reader should read the essay. (What will the reader learn from reading the essay?) Can you find the *what* and *why* in this introduction? Underline the parts that you find, and then discuss them with your class.

3. An introduction usually has a thesis (a sentence that states the main idea). Do you see Jennifer's thesis? Where? Underline her thesis.

4. Now look at each of her body paragraphs. Explain how each of the body paragraphs (2–5) supports Jennifer's thesis.

Revise

Revising means *reseeing* what you have written and then *rewriting* it to make it better. It involves using your critical thinking skills to make choices and rearrange parts of your essay to help "make sense" of the topic. As you revise, you may need to add more information to help the reader see your point. Or you may need to delete information that does not fit. The revising stage overlaps with the previous stage because each time you revise (or rewrite), you'll end up with a new draft.

Take a moment now to look back at Jennifer's essay about the "Got Milk?" advertisement. Think about suggestions you might make to help Jennifer improve her essay. For example, you could suggest that Jennifer reorganize her body paragraphs to reflect the order of the strategies presented in her thesis statement. As Jennifer revised, she would think about her thesis statement and make sure her body paragraphs followed that order.

Points to Remember About Revision

- All writers need to revise. Revision is a normal and healthy part of the writing process.
- Effective revising requires the writer to think about audience and to use his or her critical thinking skills to decide what necessary changes need to be made.
- All writers need feedback on their work. Even professional writers have editors and friends comment on their work before publishing it. Be sure to share your writing with classmates and other readers.
- Effective writers take pride in their work, making it their own. This means that although they consider others' advice, they do not let others take over their work.

Activity

Share Your Writing

Find a classmate to work with. Read each other's essays and discuss the following questions in relation to each essay:

- Does your introduction tell *what* your essay is about and *why* your reader should read it?

- Have you given your reader enough details? Will he or she be able to "see" the advertisement in his or her mind?

- Have you told your reader what strategies the advertiser is using?

- Do you support your statements about the strategies with proof from the advertisements, such as words or images?

- Have you clearly expressed how successful you feel the advertiser was in making the product appealing?

- Make a list of things you want to change in your essay. Start with the most important.

Begin revising your essay. Focus on one problem area at a time. Write more than one new draft. (Each time you revise, your essay will probably get better.)

Edit

When you have revised your paper to the point that you feel confident about its organization and development of ideas, then it's time to begin editing your essay. This is the stage where writers work on spelling, punctuation, and grammar to make sure their sentences are grammatically correct.

Activity

Edit Your Advertising Essay

When you feel your essay says everything you want it to (or when your deadline is nearing), then begin "polishing" it. (*Note:* Many writers feel that they could go on improving an essay forever—that's normal.) It's a good idea to have your instructor or tutor show you one area you need to work on (for example, making sure you've used complete sentences throughout). Also remember to check your spelling.

Writing Assignment #2: *Creating an Advertisement*

In this assignment, you'll create your own advertisement and analyze it. You'll exercise your critical thinking skills and practice your reading and writing processes as you consider your audience and your goals as an advertiser.

Here, in brief, is the writing assignment that you are preparing for:

Create an advertisement to promote a product of your choice. Then, write an essay in which you analyze your own advertisement.

Keep this assignment in mind as you dig deeper into the issue and prepare to write.

Discuss and Engage

Activity

Discuss Creating an Advertisement

Discuss with your classmates products you might want to sell and the types of people who would be interested in buying these products. (Think about selling your favorite cereal, perfume, shampoo, or car, for example.) Be specific. Also, discuss ways to get the attention of different groups of people.

Journal Assignment

Products, Buyers, and Hooks

Think about products, buyers, and *hooks* (ways to grab consumers' attention). Write down some possible products you'd like to advertise. Describe the people you would be trying to attract with each product and how you might do that. Think about the people, props, colors, and words you might use. Write about more than one advertisement you could create. (This journal is for your eyes only.)

Read, Discuss, Think Critically

Remember that at this stage of your writing process you should gather more information and consider other people's thoughts on your subject.

Reading Assignment: *"When Advertising Offends: Another Look at Aunt Jemima"*

(The questions and suggestions that follow will help you continue to use some of the PARTS of the reading process.)

Preview   Before you read, note when and where this essay was published. Read the title and introduction. Read and highlight the topic sentences.

Anticipate   What do you anticipate this essay will be about? Use the "Notes" column to record your thoughts.

Read and Reread   Read the essay quickly and mark unfamiliar words. Then reread the essay more slowly, interacting with the text by making comments in the "Notes" column and highlighting important points. Define unknown words.

When Advertising Offends: Another Look at Aunt Jemima
Based on Westerman (1989) and Simpson (1992)
by John J. Macionis

This essay comes from a college sociology textbook, *Sociology*.

1   Commercial advertisers want to sell products. However, some old ad campaigns are becoming counterproductive because they offend their audience by portraying categories of people in inaccurate and unfair ways.

Notes

2   A century ago, the vast majority of consumers in the United States were white people, and many were uneasy with growing racial and cultural diversity. Businesses commonly exploited this discomfort, depicting various categories of people in ways that were clearly condescending. In 1889, for example, a pancake mix first appeared featuring a servant mammy named "Aunt Jemima." Although somewhat modernized, this logo is widely used in the mass media, and the product continues to hold a commanding share of its market. Likewise, the hot cereal "Cream of Wheat" is still symbolized by the African-American chef Rastus, and "Uncle Ben" is familiar to millions of households as a brand name for rice. But to many people, use of such caricatures—which, after all, originally depicted the black slaves or servants of white people—is racially insensitive at best.

3   Changes in advertising have occurred in recent decades in all the mass media. The stereotypical Frito Bandito, long familiar to older television viewers, was abandoned in 1971 by Frito-Lay (a company, ironically, whose first product was a corn chip invented by a Latino living in San Antonio). The characterization of Latinos as bandits or outlaws, embodied in the bumbling cartoon figure of Frito Bandito, discredited an entire segment of the population. A host of other such images have also disappeared as businesses in the United States confront a new reality: the growing voice and financial power of minorities, who represent a market worth one-half trillion dollars a year. Taken together, Americans of African, Latino, and Asian descent represent 20 percent of the population and may constitute a national majority by the end of the next century. And, just as important, the share of the minority population that is affluent is steadily increasing.

4   Businesses are responding to the growing financial power of minorities. In the last ten years businesses have doubled their spending on advertising aimed at African Americans to about $1 billion annually. The results of this policy shift have been encouraging for the businesses involved—far higher sales—and pleasing to people who have historically found little to like in commercial advertising.

Questions for Critical Thought

"When Advertising Offends . . ."

1. Find the thesis statement in this essay and underline it. What is the main point of this essay? Write it down in your own words.

2. What stereotypes are discussed in this essay?

3. It could be argued that advertisers must rely on stereotypes to some degree. Usually these stereotypes are harmless, although obviously some stereotypes can be hurtful. Respond to this idea of "harmless" versus "hurtful" stereotypes.

4. When you write your advertisement, will you be relying on any stereotypes? Is this okay? Explain.

5. One of the stylistic strengths of this essay is the use of **transitions**, words that add **coherence** to the essay. *(In a coherent essay, all the ideas fit together and support the thesis.)* In paragraphs 1 and 2, you can find the following words that help the different ideas flow and fit together: *however, for example, although, likewise,* and *but.* Explain how the author used each transition to show how all the ideas fit together. (For example, how does *however* in the first paragraph help us move from the first sentence to the second? What does *however* tell us?) Discuss each of the five transitions mentioned above.

Journal Assignment

Ideas About Writing an Ad

Write down your thoughts about creating an advertisement.

1. What is the hardest part about creating a good advertisement? What is the easiest part?

2. What products are you considering advertising, and how is the audience different for each one?

3. If the audience is large, how might you create your ad for an audience of a specific magazine?

4. What will attract each different audience?

Exchange journals with a classmate, and when you've finished reading, say, "Thank you."

Explore the Writing Assignment

Here is a more detailed description of your writing assignment.

Create an advertisement to promote a product of your choice, and write an essay in which you analyze your advertisement. You may sketch the ad yourself or put together pictures from other advertisements. Be sure to make it clear in your sketch (or collage) what colors you would use, what the people would look like (expressions, clothes, posture, gender, ethnicity, age), and what props you would use. And, of course, write some interesting text to sell your product. Then, in your essay, describe the ad you have created, and explain what audience you are trying to attract and how you are trying to attract it. What strategies are you using?

Activity

Explore the Assignment

Discuss the following questions with your classmates:

1. What product will you sell?

2. What audience will you try to attract?

3. What strategies will you use?

Create Your Advertisement

Be thoughtful and creative as you design your advertisement. After you have created your advertisement, show it to friends and classmates and ask them what strategies they see you using. Are these effective strategies? Are your friends and classmates right? Do you need to change your advertisement at all?

Brainstorm   With your advertisement completed, it's time to begin the second part of your assignment. Focus now on the part that says, "Analyze your own advertisement." You may want to think of the prompt as a series of questions:

• How would you analyze your advertisement?

• What strategies are you using, and are they effective?

• Who is your audience?

Write freely and answer these questions, but don't feel limited to them. Remember that when you are brainstorming, you want to let your thoughts wander a bit.

Create Your Thesis   Use your brainstorming notes, readings, journal entries, and class notes to experiment with thesis statements. You want to find a sentence that clearly explains what your essay will focus on and what you'll be explaining or proving in your essay.

Outline   When you've created a thesis statement you're satisfied with, begin listing ideas that will support your thesis statement. Decide what your main supporting points should be and create topic sentences that express these points. Consider the best way to organize your topic sentences. Can you use any transitions to help with coherence (*however, for example, likewise*)?

Draft

As you begin to draft your essay, refer to your outline, but feel free to vary from it if you need to. In the introduction, describe your advertisement, giving enough detail so that your audience will "see" your ad. Also, explain who your intended audience is and what you hope to accomplish with this advertisement. (Remember to give your reader a sense of what is coming and why your essay is worth reading.) In the body of your essay, support your introduction by explaining the strategies you have used in the ad. In your conclusion, explain what you hope the reader has learned from your essay.

Revise

Enter this stage with an open mind. Assume that you will find some weaknesses in your draft *and* that you will find ways to improve and strengthen your essay.

Activity

Share Your Writing

Work with a classmate and discuss the following questions as they relate to your essays:

- Do you have a thesis? Does your introduction tell *what* your essay is about and *why* your reader should read it?

- Have you given your reader enough detail? Will he or she be able to "see" the advertisement in his or her mind?

- Have you told your reader what strategies you are using? Have you explained why you are using these particular strategies? Who is your audience?

- Have you used any transitions to help your ideas flow (*however, for example, likewise*)?

Notes

> Make a list of things you want to improve in your essay. Start with the most important.

Edit

Now begin "polishing" your essay. Carefully check for typing errors, spelling errors, and any other errors you tend to make. Also, review your essay for sentence variety. You may also want to consider these questions after completing the sentence work at the end of this chapter (pages 163–182).

- Have you used coordinators, transitions, and subordinators to add variety and to clarify relationships between ideas in your essay?
- Can you add useful information to your essay by including prepositional or participial phrases in some of your sentences?

Writing Assignment #3: "The Most Evil Character"

> In this assignment, you'll examine the decisions people make and the values reflected by those decisions. You'll exercise your critical thinking skills and practice your reading and writing processes as you analyze the story that follows.
>
> Here, in brief, is the writing assignment that you are preparing for:
>
> *Write an essay in which you analyze the story "The Most Evil Character" and determine who is the most evil of all the characters.*
>
> Keep this assignment in mind as you dig deeper into the topic and prepare to write.

Discuss and Engage

Activity

Making Decisions

> Discuss with your classmates some decisions you've had to make recently. What decisions were easy? What decisions were hard? Did any of these choices reflect your values? What do you value in people? What are important characteristics that you think people should have?

> ### *Journal Assignment*
>
> #### *Review Class Discussion*
>
> Write down your answers to these questions: What do you value in peo-ple? What are important characteristics that you think people should have? You may also want to write down what your classmates said and what you thought about their comments. (This journal is for your eyes only. Refer back to this journal when you are getting ready to write your essay.)

Read, Discuss, Think Critically

Reading Assignment: *"The Most Evil Character"*

Preview Note that this selection is not an essay. It is a fictional story used by teachers and students as a way to discuss people's values and decision-making skills. (The style of the writing here is, of course, different from that of academic essays.) Read the title and the first few sentences.

Anticipate What do you anticipate this story will be about? Use the "Notes" column to record your thoughts.

Read and Reread Read the story quickly and mark unfamiliar words. Then reread the story more slowly, interacting with the text by making comments in the "Notes" column and highlighting im-portant points. Define unknown words.

The Most Evil Character
(author unknown)

1   Jack is in his third year of college and doing passing but below-average work. His mother has been insisting that he plan to enroll in law school and become an attorney, like his father. Angry at him for not receiving better grades, she has told him that under no circumstances will he get the car or the trip that he has been promised unless his average goes up one full grade. Although Jack has done slightly better work this term, he has been having trouble with his psychology course, especially with the term paper. Twice he has asked for a conference (not during office hours, the time of which conflicts with another class he cannot miss) with his teacher, but Professor Brown has told him that he is not being paid to run a private tutoring service. So Jack postpones writing the pa-per and finally puts it together hastily the night before it is due. Then

Professor Brown calls him in and tells him that the paper is disgraceful and that he has no chance of getting a passing grade or even an incomplete unless he submits a more acceptable essay by 9 A.M. the next day. Jack tries to explain his situation and his mother's demands, and he asks for some more time to revise the paper, but his teacher is inflexible and says, "You probably don't belong in college anyway." Since there is no way that Jack is going to be able to produce the revised essay on time, he decides to salvage the car and the trip by getting somebody to write it for him. He has heard about Victor, a recent graduate who always needs money. Victor agrees and, after some haggling about the fee, he writes an acceptable paper overnight. A few days after Professor Brown has accepted the paper and given Jack his grade, Jack gets a call from Victor, who says that, unless he gets double the original fee, he will reveal the entire transaction to Professor Brown and the dean. Jack does not have the money and cannot tell his parents.

Activities

Summarize the Story

Write a summary of "The Most Evil Character." What are the main points, the facts, and the names that you need to remember?

Who Is the Worst? The Best? Why?

Discuss the reading with your classmates. First, review the facts about what happened. (Refer to your summary.) Then begin discussing how the characters in the story rank. Who is the worst character, and why? Who is the best/most innocent character, and why? What does all of this suggest about your values?

Journal Assignment

Review Class Discussion

Immediately after your class discussion, write down your thoughts.

1. How do you feel about the characters in the story? Why?

2. How do your classmates feel? Why?

3. Did any of your classmates change your opinions? Did any of your classmates disagree with you?

4. How did your values influence your rating of the characters?

   Exchange journals with a classmate, and when you've finished reading, say, "Thank you."

Explore the Writing Assignment

Here is a more detailed description of your writing assignment.

> *Write an essay for a reader who has never read "The Most Evil Character."*
> *Briefly summarize for the reader what happens in the story. Then tell the*
> *reader what your judgment of the characters is. Who do you think is the most*
> *evil character, and who is the least evil? Where do the other characters rank?*
> *Also, explain why you have made these judgments.*

Activities

Explore the Assignment

Discuss with your classmates what kind of information you think you need
to put in your essay. Perhaps you want to make a list. What will your judgments be? How will you explain your judgments? What will come first in
your essay? Second?

Charting Your Thoughts

As a way of organizing your thoughts, make a chart similar to the one that
follows, and use it to gather information. Compare your chart with your
classmates'. (Keep in mind that it's not necessary for your charts to agree.)

Character	Deed	Judgment (Why?)
1.		
2.		
3.		
4.		

Notes

Character	Deed	Judgment (Why?)
5.		
6.		

Create Your Thesis   When you begin to work on your thesis for this assignment, review the writing assignment carefully and then ask yourself these questions: What do I want my audience to know after they have read my essay? What main point should stick in the reader's mind? You may want to summarize the assignment (in writing or out loud to a tutor) and explain what it is asking for. Summarizing and explaining will help you clarify what you must focus on with your thesis (and in your essay). Then experiment with sentences until you find one that would function well as a thesis statement.

Outline   Write your thesis statement at the top of a blank page and review, again, your writing assignment, journal entries, notes, and chart. What major points should you cover in your essay to support your thesis? Under your thesis statement, make a list of possible points to cover. Use your critical thinking skills to decide which of these points should be made into topic sentences. Take your time in creating thoughtful topic sentences. Create an outline by writing these topic sentences beneath your thesis statement on the first page.

Draft

Refer to your outline as you begin drafting. In your introduction, you'll need to summarize the story for the reader and establish your position on who is the most evil character. In the body of your paper, you'll want to explain and prove why that person is the most evil. You'll also want to show how the other characters rank, and why. In your conclusion, discuss the values that you are supporting. Your goal is to complete an essay with an introduction, body paragraphs, and conclusion.

Activity

Study a Student Sample

The following is an introductory paragraph from a student's essay. Read it carefully and underline what you think works well. Then answer the questions that follow.

> "The Most Evil Character" is a story about a college student named Jack with mediocre grades who tries to live up to both his mother's and Professor Brown's expectations. With the help of Victor, "a recent graduate who always needs money," Jack achieves his goal by less than honest means. We will now examine the characters from the most to the least evil.
>
> —*Miguel Viera, student writer*

1. What do you think Miguel did particularly well?

2. If a reader had never read "The Most Evil Character," would this introduction be clear? Why, or why not?

3. Does this writer have a clear thesis? If so, where?

Activity

Study a Student Sample

In the next student sample, you'll read the first body paragraph from another student's essay. (This student's thesis was "I intend to prove that Victor is 'The Most Evil Character' in this story." This thesis was the last sentence in the introduction.) Then answer the questions that follow.

First body paragraph:

> Jack's mom wanted him to become a lawyer, like his father. *Setting Limits,* by Robert J. MacKenzie, Ed.D., says that "the exploration is the most important part. . . . Teens need to try out new roles, new values and beliefs, new relationships and commitments." She did not give him that chance. Instead, she promised him a car and a trip to pursue the career of her choice. Because his grades were not commendable, she warned him that if he did not bring his average up one grade he would not receive the offering, and this became his first ultimatum.
>
> —*Keisha Harris, student writer*

Notes

1. This paragraph has a number of strengths. What do you think Keisha did well?

2. Study Keisha's paragraph. What is Keisha proving in this paragraph? Write your own topic sentence for this paragraph. (Remember, your topic sentence should show how this first body paragraph connects to the idea expressed in the thesis.)

Activity

Study a Student Sample

In the next student sample, you'll read a concluding paragraph from yet another student's essay. As you read it, think about what a conclusion should do and mark the parts of the conclusion that you like best. Then answer the questions that follow.

> To wrap it all up, Jack by far is the most evil person, in my opinion. He has created his own mess. He needs to stop and take a long look at his life, also his situation and fix it no matter what the outcome may be. Mom and Victor need to get real lives and stop the blackmail games. Professor Brown maybe could be a bit less open in his own personal opinion of his student's life outside of his classroom. As for dad and the dean they are just names thrown into a situation that they were not directly a part of.
>
> —*Ruth Hathaway, student writer*

1. From reading this concluding paragraph, can you tell what Ruth's thesis probably was? If yes, write a thesis for her essay.

2. From this concluding paragraph, can you tell what Ruth's main supporting points might have been? Write topic sentences (in your own words) for body paragraphs that might work in her essay.

3. Will the conclusion in your essay be anything like Ruth's? Explain.

Revise

Use your critical thinking skills and find strengths and weaknesses in your own writing *before* you hear what others think. This will help you become an independent writer.

Then, when you do have a classmate or a tutor read your essay, listen carefully. But *you* make the decisions about what to change and what not to change. You are in control of your own writing.

Activity

Share Your Writing

Find a classmate to work with. Read each other's essays and discuss the following questions as they relate to your essays:

- What concerns do you have about your essay?

- Have you summarized the events of the story?

- Have you ranked the characters in order to show who is the *most* evil?

- Is it clear who the *least* evil character is?

- Do you support and explain your ideas?

- Do your ideas flow from one sentence to the next and from one paragraph to the next? Does each point clearly connect to the thesis?

- Does the essay contain an introduction, body paragraphs, and a conclusion?

Make a list of things you want to change in your essay. Start with the most important. Are there certain things that your instructor wants you to focus on when you revise?

Begin revising your essay. Focus on one problem area at a time. Write more than one new draft.

Edit

Now begin "polishing" your essay. Carefully check for typing errors, spelling errors, and any other errors you tend to make. Also, review your essay for sentence variety. You may also want to consider these questions after completing the sentence work at the end of this chapter (pages 163–182):

- Have you used coordinators, transitions, and subordinators to add variety and to clarify relationships between ideas in your essay?

- Can you add useful information to your essay by including prepositional or participial phrases in some of your sentences?

TIME TO REFLECT

> ### *Journal Assignment*
>
> ### *Your Progress as a Writer, Reader, and Critical Thinker*
>
> Reflect on the skills you have strengthened in this chapter. Write a journal entry in which you discuss
>
> - what you have learned in this chapter,
> - the skills you are improving,
> - the skills you feel need more work,
> - changes in your reading process, and
> - changes in your writing process.
>
> Also respond to this question: How have the essay writing assignments in this chapter sharpened your critical thinking skills?

SUMMARY OF CHAPTER 4

This chapter has focused on understanding and effectively using the stages of the essay writing process.

Discuss and engage

Read, discuss, and think critically

Explore the writing assignment

Draft

Revise

Edit

As you have studied advertisements, advertising strategies, and evil characters, you have162

- used your reading, writing, and critical thinking skills; and
- seen the advantages of using an effective essay writing process.

Your tasks as a writer are easier when you approach writing as a process. In addition, your writing will be clearer, better organized, and more developed. Using the writing process effectively is key to writing well.

CLAUSES AND PHRASES

The Independent Clause
Using Coordinating Conjunctions
Punctuating Correctly with Coordinating Conjunctions
Using Semicolons and Transitions
The Dependent (or Subordinated) Clause
Punctuating Correctly with Dependent Clauses
Understanding Phrases
Prepositional Phrases
Participial Phrases
Punctuating Correctly with Participial Phrases

Thus far in *Connections*, you have focused primarily on verbs and subjects—two key ingredients in sentences. Now, you'll turn your attention to two larger sentence units: the clause and the phrase.

Understanding clauses and phrases will help you avoid errors like run-on sentences. In addition, learning to use clauses and phrases effectively will help you add variety to your sentence structure. Good writing will have short sentences and long sentences. Short sentences can help you make powerful, direct statements, but too many short sentences will bore your reader and make your writing seem too simple. Longer sentences allow you to explain the complexity of an issue. They help you to show the relationships between ideas. Of course, too many long sentences might tire your reader and make your writing seem unbalanced. This chapter will help you create the right balance of short and long sentences in your essays.

The Independent Clause

A **clause** is a group of words with a subject and a verb. There are two kinds of clauses—independent and dependent. The **independent clause** can stand on its own and is the same thing as a complete sentence. (Remember, a *complete sentence* is a group of words with a subject and verb that expresses a complete idea.) Here are independent clauses with the subjects underlined once and verbs underlined twice.

Today, we focused on the writing process.

My tutor helps me with each step in the writing process.

I like to discuss my writing ideas with my spouse.

A simple independent clause can be very useful. If you have provided enough information and support, a simple sentence like "Jack is the most evil character" can make your point clearly and dramatically.

Using Coordinating Conjunctions

To add variety to your writing and to help show the relationships between your ideas, you can join two independent clauses and make one longer sentence. A **coordinating conjunction** is a word that can join independent clauses. (These words are also called *coordinators*.)

There are seven coordinating conjunctions, which you will study here briefly. You will get more practice with these in Chapter 8. You can remember them by remembering the acronym FANBOYS.

An *acronym* is a word that is created by using the first letters of other words. For example, you may have heard people say "ASAP" when they mean "as soon as possible." FANBOYS is an acronym also.

For   And   Nor   But   Or   Yet   So

When you want to join two independent clauses with one of the FANBOYS, you need to choose one that accurately expresses the relationship between the ideas you are joining.

For: expresses a relationship of *effect-cause*. The idea in the first sentence is the effect. The idea in the second sentence is the cause.
Joseph hurried to the store, <u>for</u> he desperately wanted the new home theater system.

And: expresses a relationship of *addition*. The idea in the first sentence is added to the idea in the second sentence.
The advertisement called the new CD/DVD home theater system the key to throwing a great party, <u>and</u> Joseph loved parties.

Nor: expresses a relationship of *negative addition*. The idea in the first sentence is negative, and another negative idea is added in the second sentence. (Notice that the subject and verb in the second independent clause are not in their usual order.)
Unfortunately, Joseph didn't actually have enough cash for the purchase, <u>nor</u> did he have any room left on his credit card.

But: expresses a relationship of *opposition*. The idea in the first sentence is in opposition to the idea in the second sentence.
He asked his roommate to loan him the money, <u>but</u> his roommate wouldn't do it.

Or: expresses a relationship of *alternatives*. The idea in the first sentence is one option. The idea in the second sentence is another option.
He could save up his money for the next few months, <u>or</u> he could call his parents for a loan.

Yet: expresses a relationship of *opposition*. The idea in the first sentence is in opposition to the idea in the second sentence.

The advertisement made the sound system seem so necessary, <u>yet</u> Joseph didn't want to go further into debt.

So: expresses a relationship of *cause-effect*. The idea in the first sentence causes the idea in the second sentence.

Joseph decided to save up for the home theater system, <u>so</u> he went to the bank and opened a savings account.

Punctuating Correctly with Coordinating Conjunctions

When you are using coordinating conjunctions to join independent sentences, remember the following rule.

Punctuation Rule #2

When you join independent clauses with a coordinating conjunction, you need to put a comma after the first independent clause.

- She spent a lot of time thinking about shopping, for she was a slave to advertising.
- My kids don't watch much television, yet they still seem to know about all the newest toys and sugared cereals.

Sometimes writers choose to begin sentences with coordinators. This adds a slight emphasis to the sentence that begins with the coordinator:

Cassidy doesn't go shopping much. And she particularly dislikes people who constantly talk about shopping.

Practice #1   Creating an Advertisement

On a separate piece of paper, join the independent clauses below using carefully chosen coordinators (FANBOYS). Remember to put a comma after the first independent clause. (Don't use the same coordinator twice.)

Example: I have never analyzed an advertisement before.
　　　　 I do not know much about creating an advertisement.

- I have never analyzed an advertisement, nor do I know much about creating an advertisement.

1. My mom loaned me a bunch of magazines. I want to study how advertisers manipulate their audiences.

Remember that when you use *nor* to join independent clauses, the subject and verb will not be in their usual positions. Also, the negative word in the second sentence must be dropped. In the example, *not* has been dropped.

Clauses and Phrases

Clauses and Phrases

Notes

2. In class, we made a great list of products to advertise. I can only choose one.

3. Advertising baby strollers could be interesting. I may choose to advertise briefcases for women.

4. For a stroller advertisement, pastel colors would be best. I would emphasize safety and beauty with my words.

5. Most briefcases are okay for either gender. I think I could create an advertisement that women would be especially drawn to.

6. The briefcase advertisement shouldn't be too feminine. It should not be sexy.

7. The stroller advertisement might be more fun. I think I will choose that one.

Practice #2   Miracle Product

On a separate piece of paper, join the independent clauses below using carefully chosen coordinators (FANBOYS). Remember to put a comma after the first independent clause. (Don't use the same coordinator twice.)

1. You should try this new product. It will make you feel like a new person.

2. Your skin will glow. Your hair will be shiny.

3. At first, you might think it is too expensive. You won't think so after you see what this product can do for you.

4. You won't find this product in your local stores. You can't order it online.

5. Call this phone number now. You can get a month's supply before we run out.

6. You can give us your credit card number. You can send a check in the mail.

7. When you get your jar of Magic Mud, you may think this is just ordinary wet dirt. We promise that it is a unique mixture of minerals, vitamins, rare plant oils, water, and garden soil.

Using Semicolons and Transitions

Another way to join independent clauses is to use a semicolon. A semicolon is as strong as a period. Use a semicolon when the ideas in each independent clause are closely related.

I studied the advertisement carefully; I was preparing to analyze it.

Sheila is an artist; she loved creating her advertisement.

You can also use a transition with a semicolon. A transition is a word or phrase that helps show the relationship between two ideas. It acts like a bridge between independent sentences. Transitions like *however, therefore,* and *then* cannot join independent clauses with a comma like coordinators do, but you can use them with semicolons. Note that the semicolon separates the sentences and a comma follows the transition. You are actually combining two punctuation rules when you use transitions in this manner.

The advertisement was directed at women; *however,* I think men will pay attention too.

He clearly stated his goal for the advertising campaign; *therefore,* the staff knew exactly how to proceed.

Punctuation Rule #3

You may use a semicolon to separate two complete sentences.

- Three people at the advertising agency worked on the ad; they liked bouncing ideas off of one another.

Punctuation Rule #4

Follow an introductory word or phrase with a comma.

- <u>Then,</u> they got together to exchange their ideas.

Note: Punctuation Rules #3 and #4 are both applied when you join two complete sentences with a semicolon and transition.

- The three people on the project drafted their own ads; <u>then,</u> they got together to exchange their ideas.

Here is a list of common transitions:

also, furthermore, next, similarly, in addition, likewise: express addition of similar ideas

consequently, therefore, thus, as a result: express cause-effect

Notes

however, otherwise, in contrast: express opposition

then, next, finally, now, first, second, third: express time

for example, such as, for instance: indicate an example is coming

---

Practice #3   Advertising (and Transitions)

On a separate piece of paper, create the sentences described below.

Example: Join these sentences with a semicolon.

The advertisement used bold colors and the words "dynamic" and "successful." It would appeal to people seeking power and prestige.

- The advertisement used bold colors and the words "dynamic" and "successful"; it would appeal to people seeking power and prestige.

1. Join these sentences with a semicolon.

   The advertising staff discovered that the target audience watched a lot of prime-time television. They decided to use television stars to promote the product.

2. Join these sentences with a semicolon.

   Baby food manufacturers like to advertise in women's magazines. Mothers buy more baby food than other people do.

3. Join these sentences with a semicolon and one of these transitions: *therefore, however,* or *then.*

   The perfume manufacturer wanted women to believe that the new fragrance would make them sexier. The advertisement showed a beautiful half-naked woman in bed.

4. Join these sentences with a semicolon and one of these transitions: *therefore, however,* or *then.*

   The advertising firm did a phone survey. The staff had a better idea about who is interested in the product.

5. Join these sentences with a semicolon and one of these transitions: *however, similarly,* or *consequently.*

   Harrison loved creating advertisements. Samantha felt there was something dishonest about the whole business.

6. Join these sentences with a semicolon and one of these transitions: *similarly, in contrast,* or *consequently.*

Clauses and Phrases

> I wanted to encourage people to spend more money on diamond engagement rings. My advertisement suggests that spending more money means your love is deeper.
>
> 7. Join these two sentences with a semicolon and one of these transitions: *therefore, similarly,* or *then.*
>
> I really enjoyed searching for just the right words for my advertisement. My classmate, Tim, loved experimenting with color and props.

The Dependent (or Subordinated) Clause

The **dependent** or **subordinated clause** is a group of words that contains a subject and verb but cannot stand on its own. It is *not* a complete sentence.

When <u>Cecilia</u> <u>looked</u> at the advertisement.

Even though <u>I</u> <u>read</u> magazines frequently.

Because <u>Neil</u> <u>believed</u> every advertisement.

The words *when, even though,* and *because* change the independent clauses into dependent clauses. If you read the dependent clauses carefully aloud, you will hear how they sound "unfinished."

Subordinators are words that can attach to independent clauses and make them dependent (or subordinated). Here is a list of subordinators:

although

because

even though

if

since

though

when

while

You cannot use a dependent clause by itself. A dependent clause standing alone is called a **fragment,** or an incomplete sentence. However, joined to independent clauses, dependent clauses can be very useful because they allow you to express complex ideas and the relationships between those ideas.

Notes

When will allow you to tell your reader that two ideas are connected by time.

> <u>When I studied the words more closely</u>, I could see how the advertiser was trying to manipulate me.

Since allows you to express a cause-and-effect relationship or a time relationship.

> <u>Since I had so many ideas for this essay</u>, I had to spend a lot of time planning and organizing my thoughts. (cause and effect)

> I haven't written an essay <u>since I was a senior in high school</u>. (time)

While allows you to express a relationship of opposition or of time.

> <u>While I have never relied on outlines</u>, I actually found one helpful with this assignment. (opposition)

> <u>While listening to the class discussion</u>, I got some good ideas for my own essay. (time)

Even though, *though*, and *although* allow you to tell your reader that one idea is the opposite of another.

> <u>Even though my target audience is male sports fans</u>, I believe that women will like my ad also.

Because allows you to tell your reader that the ideas have a cause-and-effect relationship.

> <u>Because my tutor said I was trying to cover too much in my second paragraph</u>, I decided to break that paragraph into two.

If allows you to tell your reader that the ideas have a conditional relationship.

> You might discover more ideas to write about <u>if you start by discussing your assignment with your tutor</u>.

Punctuating Correctly with Dependent Clauses

There are two punctuation rules to remember with dependent clauses.

> ### Punctuation Rule #5
>
> *When you begin a sentence with a subordinated or dependent clause, you must put a comma after the subordinated (or dependent) clause.*
>
> • <u>Because I didn't have enough to say about the bicycle ad</u>, I decided to write about the jewelry ad.

Punctuation Rule #6

If the subordinated clause comes after the independent clause, you do not need a comma.

- I decided to write about the jewelry ad <u>because I didn't have enough to say about the bicycle ad</u>.

Practice #4 Advertising (and Dependent Clauses)

On a separate piece of paper, join the sentences with an appropriate subordinator from the following list:

although

because

even though

if

since

though

when

while

- In some sentences, put the dependent clause first. In other sentences, put the dependent clause second.
- Underline the dependent clause.
- Do not use a subordinator more than once.
- Don't forget to use commas when necessary.

Example: You don't start your essay soon. You won't finish in time!

- <u>If you don't start your essay soon</u>, you won't finish in time!

1. My classmates gave me some good suggestions. I asked for their advice on my essay.
2. I thought the advertisement was very effective. It skillfully played on my emotions.
3. I decided to take some art classes. My new goal was to go into advertising.
4. I took notes. I watched the advertisements on television.
5. Martha was afraid of public speaking. She did a really good job presenting her advertisement to the class.

Notes

6. You don't draw well. You can create a collage by cutting items out of magazines.

7. Music would make my advertisement so much better. We're supposed to focus on print ads, not on television or radio ads.

Practice #5   An Evil Character

On a separate piece of paper, join the sentences with an appropriate subordinator from the following list:

although

because

even though

if

since

though

when

while

- In some sentences, put the dependent clause first. In other sentences, put the dependent clause second.
- Underline the dependent clause.
- Do not use a subordinator more than once.
- Don't forget to use commas when necessary.

1. My roommate made excuses for not having enough money to pay her share of the rent. She really made me mad.

2. She didn't have the money. She went shopping and bought shoes for $200.

3. I think people should admit their mistakes. They make bad decisions.

4. The mistake might cause a problem for me. I can easily forgive someone who apologizes sincerely.

5. I am human too and will make my own mistakes. I know it is important to forgive people.

6. I really wanted to yell at her. I held my tongue and promised myself that I'd get a new roommate at the end of the semester.

7. She really put me in a bad spot. I wouldn't call her evil.

Clauses and Phrases

Practice #6   Creating Sentences with Clauses

On a separate piece of paper, create original sentences that fit the descriptions below. Your sentences must be on the same topic as your current reading or writing assignment.

1. Create one sentence for each coordinating conjunction. (You'll be creating seven different sentences.)
2. Create one sentence using a semicolon.
3. Create one sentence using a semicolon and a transition word or phrase.
4. Create a sentence that has an independent clause and a subordinated clause that begins with *if*. Put the subordinated clause first and underline it. (Remember to use a comma.)
5. Create a sentence that has an independent clause and a subordinated clause that begins with *because*. Put the subordinated clause second and underline it. (Remember, do not use a comma when the subordinated clause comes second.)

Understanding Phrases

A **phrase** is a group of words that is missing a subject, a verb, or both. Phrases are very useful to writers because they allow writers to insert critical pieces of information into sentences. Phrases are one key to writing longer, more sophisticated, more expressive sentences. Understanding phrases is also important in avoiding sentence fragments.

Here are some examples of phrases—groups of words missing one or more sentence ingredients:

worrying about his grade

on his chemistry test

for her parents' approval

embarrassed by the scandal

at the prestigious college

from the cameras

If a writer were to use one of these phrases by itself, the writer would be creating a fragment. However, these phrases can be inserted into independent clauses, creating nicely shaped, sophisticated sentences that will add variety and interest to an essay:

Notes

Worrying about his grade, Kyle decides to cheat on his chemistry test.
Susan was desperate for her parents' approval.
Embarrassed by the scandal, the students at the prestigious college hid their faces from the cameras.

Prepositional Phrases

In Chapter 2 you learned that a *prepositional phrase* is a group of words made up of a preposition and its object. A *preposition* is a word that suggests position, location, direction, condition, or time. An *object* is the noun that follows the preposition. Sometimes a prepositional phrase will include descriptive information too (between the preposition and the object). In these examples, the preposition is underlined once and the object is underlined twice.

at the college

in the overcrowded, noisy classroom (note that *overcrowded* and *noisy* describe the object)

after much thought (*much* describes the object)

There is neither a subject nor a verb in a prepositional phrase. Prepositional phrases, however, are very useful because they add information to sentences and often help the writer avoid unnecessary repetition. These sentences, for example, suffer from unnecessary repetition.

The movie addressed the issue. The movie was on HBO. The issue of cheating was the topic. The cheating was on college campuses.

This is a better sentence that uses prepositional phrases. (Prepositional phrases are bracketed.)

The movie [on HBO] addressed the issue [of cheating] [on college campuses].

Practice #7   **Cheaters**

Add the prepositional phrases to each sentence to make longer, more complex sentences. Bracket the prepositional phrases in your new sentences.

Example:

Many students accept cheating.

as a normal part

of college

- Many students accept cheating [as a normal part] [of college].

1. Some are worried.
   of my friends
   about getting
   into the best graduate schools

2. To keep up, they think that they must cheat too.
   with their dishonest classmates

3. A news commentator said our public officials are partly to blame because they often cheat.
   on television

4. Lately, many CEOs have been found guilty.
   of major companies
   of cheating

5. However, I keep hearing the old saying, "Two wrongs don't make a right."
   from my childhood

6. I'm afraid.
   of the long-term effects
   of such widespread cheating

7. What can we look forward to if many make it?
   of our future doctors, lawyers, military officers, and professors
   through school
   by cheating

Participial Phrases

A **participial phrase** consists of a present or past participle and the words attached to that participle. (Participial phrases can include prepositional phrases.)

Present participles end in -*ing*:

talking

focusing

questioning

hoping

Clauses and Phrases

Notes

Here are those same present participles in participial phrases:

> talking to my classmates
>
> focusing intently
>
> questioning their ideas
>
> hoping for a better future

Past participles usually end in *-ed,* but sometimes they have an irregular form:

> concerned
>
> written (irregular)
>
> questioned
>
> chosen (irregular)

Here are those same past participles in participial phrases:

> concerned by the new study
>
> written clearly
>
> questioned by my peers
>
> chosen by the voters

Participial phrases can add interesting information to sentences and often help the writer express ideas with fewer sentences. In this section, you'll focus on participial phrases that describe nouns. Consider the following sentences:

> I was talking to my classmates. I learned that they don't approve of cheating.
>
> Callie was focusing intently on her exam. She didn't notice her classmate looking at her answers.
>
> The dean is concerned about cheating. The dean buys a new antiplagiarism software program.
>
> I was questioned by my peers. I felt ashamed of my actions.

The following revised sentences are more interesting and would add nice sentence structure variety to an essay:

> <u>Talking to my classmates,</u> I learned that they don't approve of cheating.
>
> <u>Focusing intently on her exam,</u> Callie didn't notice her classmate looking at her answers.
>
> <u>Concerned about cheating,</u> the dean buys a new antiplagiarism software program.
>
> <u>Questioned by my peers,</u> I felt ashamed of my actions.

Although participial phrases can be used in a number of positions in sentences, in this chapter, you'll focus on participial phrases that begin sentences. Note that in the following examples the participial phrases describe a noun that immediately follows. The participial phrase has a single underline. The noun has a double underline. (*Hint:* This is the sentence pattern to follow: Participial phrase, noun + verb + completing information.)

<u>Working all night,</u> <u>Frieda</u> finished her essay.

<u>Taking his time with the revision,</u> <u>Tom</u> created a persuasive analysis.

<u>Irritated by the noise,</u> the <u>student</u> moved to a different part of the library.

Punctuating Correctly with Participial Phrases

A participial phrase that comes at the beginning of a sentence is also called an introductory phrase. When you begin a sentence with such a phrase, remember the following rule.

Punctuation Rule #4 (Review)
Follow an introductory word or phrase with a comma.

- <u>Working all night,</u> Frieda finished her essay.

Practice #8 "The Most Evil Character"

- Underline the participial phrases that are describing nouns.
- Use a double underline to mark the nouns each phrase describes.

(You may find infinitives and prepositional phrases within the participial phrases.)

Example: Determined to do well on the assignment, Jess sought the help of a tutor.

- <u>Determined to do well on the assignment,</u> <u>Jess</u> sought the help of a tutor.

1. Hoping for the car and the trip, Jack paid someone else to write his essay.

Notes

2. Wanting more money, Victor blackmailed Jack.

3. Angered by Jack's lack of effort, the professor had little sympathy for Jack.

4. Asked to analyze each character, the student made a chart describing their actions and motives.

5. Looking for more information, the student listened carefully to the class discussion.

Practice #9   Using Participial Phrases

On a separate piece of paper, write new sentences that include the participial phrases given. (*Hint:* Place the participial phrases at the beginning of the new sentences.)

Example: Oscar knew he had to pay closer attention to creating a clear thesis and useful topic sentences.
Reflecting on the instructor's comments on the previous essay

• Reflecting on the instructor's comments on the previous essay, Oscar knew he had to pay closer attention to creating a clear thesis and useful topic sentences.

1. James decided who the most evil character is.
   Considering his own morals and values carefully

2. Sam asked some classmates to get together for a study session.
   Finding it difficult to get started on the essay

3. Veronica spent double her usual amount of time editing her essay.
   Wanting to show some significant improvement

4. Francesca changed her major to philosophy.
   Realizing her love for philosophical discussions

5. Lyle decided to go play a game of hoops.
   Tired of thinking and writing

6. Charise did some independent research.
   Determined to liven up her paper

7. The professor spoke up against the antiplagiarism software.
   Worried that the school would be sending a message of no trust

8. Elise found some areas in her essay that needed to be more fully developed.
   Reading her essay aloud

Clauses and Phrases

Practice #10   Creating Sentences with Phrases
Part One: Create five original sentences that have prepositional phrases in them.

- The sentences must connect to the topics of your current reading and writing assignments.
- Bracket the prepositional phrases.

Part Two: Create five original sentences that begin with participial phrases.

- The sentences must connect to the topics of your current reading and writing assignments.
- Underline the participial phrases.

(*Hint:* This is the sentence pattern to follow: participial phrase, noun + verb + completing information.)

STYLE TIPS

In this chapter, you have learned to use coordinators, transitions, sub-ordinators, participial phrases, and prepositional phrases to add more variety and meaning to your sentences. As stated earlier, readers don't want all short or all long sentences. They want variety, and they want help seeing how ideas connect to one another. So, when you are editing your writing, step back, look carefully at your sentences, and remember Style Tips #3 and #4.

Style Tip # 3
Add variety to your sentence structure.

Style Tip # 4
Provide the necessary connections between ideas and show how ideas relate to one another.

Practice #11   Vintage Ads
The following paragraph sounds a bit choppy, and the relationships between the ideas aren't always clear. Read the paragraph and look for places where you might apply Style Tips #3 and #4 by joining

Notes

sentences with coordinators (FANBOYS), subordinators, and transitions. Write out your improved paragraph.

> Modern and vintage ads are quite different from each other. The modern ads have few words. The vintage ads often have 100 to 200 words of text. A vintage ad for gum explained how fresh the gum tastes and how important it is to have fresh breath when you are looking for that someone special. The modern ad for Wrigley's Double Mint gum just showed pretty twin women and said "Double the fun." I like the vintage ads more. The message is more innocent. The drawings are more artistic.

Practice #12   Seeking Beauty

The following paragraph sounds a bit choppy and the relationships between the ideas aren't always clear. Read the paragraph and look for places where you might apply Style Tips #3 and #4 by using coordinators, subordinators, and transitions. Write out your improved paragraph.

> We've been studying advertisements and the messages they send. I have begun to look at ads differently. I read beauty magazines. I see a lot of advertisements for cosmetics and accessories. I used to look at the ads and just yearn for the products advertised. I think to myself, Do I really need that item to be happy or attractive? I realize I have been manipulated over the years into spending more money than I should have. I think I've spent too much time worrying about my outward appearance. I should start reading *Newsweek* and skipping over the ads.

Practice #13   Humor Sells

The following paragraph sounds a bit choppy and the relationships between the ideas aren't always clear. Read the paragraph and look for places where you might apply Style Tips #3 and #4 by using participial phrases and prepositional phrases. You'll be deleting some words as you take the participial phrases and prepositional phrases out of some sentences and work them into the other sentences. Write out your new, improved paragraph.

Example: Create a single, more interesting sentence out of these two.

- I was listening to the radio. I heard five minutes of ads and only two minutes of music.
- Listening to the radio, I heard five minutes of ads and only two minutes of music.

Example: Create one more interesting sentence out of these two.

• I found an excellent ad. The ad was in *Time* magazine.

• In *Time* magazine, I found an excellent ad.
or

• I found an excellent ad in *Time* magazine.

I was skimming the pages of my favorite newspaper. I saw a funny ad. A copier appeared to be running down the street. The copier was in the center of the page. The copier had a woman's purse sitting on top. I could see a woman who looked as if she'd been knocked down. The woman was in the background. The advertisers were selling the idea that a bad copy machine is stealing your money. It requires repairs too often. I love humorous ads.

Your Own Writing: Clauses and Phrases

Review one of the journals, summaries, or essays you have written and look at the sentence structure.

• How many of your sentences are short? How many are long? Highlight the short sentences.

• Have you expressed complex ideas by joining independent clauses with commas and coordinators, semicolons, or semicolons followed by transition words? Circle coordinators, semicolons, and transition words.

• Have you used any subordinators? Circle subordinators.

• Have you used any prepositional phrases? Bracket the prepositional phrases.

• Do any of your sentences begin with participial phrases? Underline any participial phrases that start sentences.

Rewrite a few sentences from the journal, summary, or essay that you have selected, improving the variety in your sentence structure. Use coordinators, subordinators, transition words, semicolons, prepositional phrases, and participial phrases. You may even decide to add new information. Here are some of the coordinators, subordinators, and transitions you can choose from:

Coordinators: for, and, nor, but, or, yet, so

Subordinators: if, since, while, though, although, even though, because, when

Notes

Transitions: therefore, however, then, similarly, in contrast, consequently

Highlight the improved sentences in the revised version of your journal, summary, or essay (or paragraph from an essay).

Using Connections *Online with* mywritinglab

For more practice with clauses and phrases, log onto www.mywritinglab .com to access the online resources for *Connections,* Third Edition.

Employing the Connections

This section contains five chapters. Each devoted to a different contemporary theme, Chapters 5–8 ask you to connect the reading, writing, and critical thinking processes as you write essays. Then, Chapter 9 challenges you to apply your skills to a variety of in-class essay topics.

Writing About Heroes

Main Topics

- Focusing your writing

- Communicating your ideas about heroes

- Using pronouns effectively

- Understanding parallel structure

CALVIN AND HOBBES © 1988 Watterson. Dist. by UNIVERSAL PRESS SYNDICATE.

One of the first things readers expect from academic paragraphs and essays is for the writing to be focused. When we speak, we often wander from one topic to another. That's acceptable in speech. (Consider the stand-up comedian who can begin talking about his mother-in-law and end up talking about car repair.) However, in academic writing, your audience expects you to choose a subject and stay focused on it. This requires you to think critically about your topic and your own writing. Every writer must make choices about what to say and how to say it so that the audience doesn't get distracted from the main message. In this chapter, you'll explore the topic of heroes and then write a focused definition and essay about a hero.

FOCUSING YOUR WRITING

Imagine that your photography instructor asks you to photograph one person in a crowd of people. He wants you to study a crowd and choose one face that interests you. You go downtown during the week-day lunch hour and watch people as they go to lunch, do their shopping, and so on. Then, after you make your choice, you take a close-up photograph, making sure that this person's face is in perfect focus. Everyone around this person is blurry.

Courtesy of Milenko Vlaisavljevic.

Notes   Writing an essay is similar to this type of photography. You are given a topic (a crowd), you explore your options (the many faces), and then, using your critical thinking skills, you choose one manageable, interesting point to make (the best face). Finally, you write your essay about that point only, leaving out all distracting information. (One person is in focus, and all the rest are blurry.) This kind of focus helps your reader stay interested and understand what you want to explain or prove.

Focusing the Paragraph

A **focused paragraph** will have a clear, informative topic sentence that tells the reader what the main idea of the paragraph is. This sentence should not be too broad or too narrow. That is, it must be broad enough to express an idea worth developing in a paragraph, but it shouldn't be so broad that the reader has a hard time telling where your writing is going next.

The sentences that follow the topic sentence are called the body of the paragraph, and these sentences will clearly support the topic sentence. This support can be in the form of examples, statistics, details, explanations, comparisons, or other forms of evidence. In addition, a paragraph may have a wrap-up sentence that closes the paragraph by summarizing points made or restating the main idea.

All of the sentences in the well-focused paragraph must stick to and support the main idea in the topic sentence. To achieve this clear focus, good writers use the writing process: they brainstorm, draft, and revise. Throughout the process, they make choices. For example, if a student who has been reading about and discussing heroes in class wants to write a paragraph on why a particular athlete is a hero, he may need to write down a list of ideas and many trial topic sentences before finding a main idea he is comfortable with. After he has a topic sentence (a main idea), he drafts the paragraph and makes choices about which ideas support his topic sentence the best. When he adds information that strengthens the paragraph and takes out information that doesn't, he is revising effectively and improving the focus of the paragraph.

Activity

Miguel's Focused Paragraph

Read the following paragraph.

(This is the third paragraph in an essay about Roberto Clemente. The second paragraph focused on how well Clemente played baseball and on his dedication to the sport.)

In the same manner that Roberto played baseball with all his heart and soul, he also gave to all those who were less fortunate than him. In Puerto Rico he had a baseball clinic where he donated all of the equipment and spent much of his off-time teaching children the fundamentals of baseball. Roberto also donated large amounts of money to children's charity. He understood how much he meant to children and people in general, took his role as a leader of youth very seriously, and always held himself to a higher standard.

—*Miguel Viera, student writer*

1. Write *T.S.* next to the topic sentence. Highlight the part of the sentence that announces what this paragraph will focus on.

2. Write *S* next to specific pieces of support in the body of the paragraph that stay focused on the topic sentence. Note how the topic sentence and specific pieces of support work together to create a focused paragraph.

3. Why would the following topic sentence be *less* effective for Miguel's paragraph?

Roberto Clemente had other good qualities.

Focusing the Essay

A **focused essay** relies on a thoughtful thesis statement (the sentence at the end of the introduction that announces the main idea of the essay). A writer must read, discuss, think, brainstorm, draft, and revise to find the thesis statement that expresses a focused idea worth developing. Sometimes a writer must return to earlier steps in the writing process to find a good, focused thesis. For example, a writer might be in the middle of writing an essay when she realizes that part of her essay doesn't seem to support her thesis. If this happens, the writer must use her critical thinking skills and make some choices. Should the thesis be changed? Should certain ideas she has written down be left out of the essay? Perhaps she needs to go back and take another look at her brainstorm and outline. The writer must stay sensitive to the reader's need for focus.

Of course, the thesis isn't the only part of the essay that is important to focus. The topic sentence of each body paragraph and each

Notes   piece of support should clearly relate to the thesis. Good topic sentences in a focused essay often repeat key terms from the thesis and always announce a major point that directly supports the thesis.

Activities

A Focused Outline: Malcolm X

Consider this outline for a well-focused essay on a hero.

Thesis: Malcolm X is a hero to me because of the strength he showed in his fight to improve his life and the lives of others.

Topic sentence for body paragraph #1: First of all, he had the strength to turn away from the life of street crime he knew so well and become a respectable citizen.

Supporting information—explain:
He had been involved in crime for a long time.
His friends were all criminals.
He had to turn his back on everything he knew well.
He reached out to family and religion.

Topic sentence for body paragraph #2: Malcolm X also drew on great inner strength when he taught himself to read and write in prison.

Supporting information—explain:
He read and copied the entire dictionary.
He read many, many books.
He studied late at night (broke curfew).

Topic sentence for body paragraph #3: After deepening his understanding of his Muslim religion, Malcolm X showed great strength as he moved away from separatist beliefs and fought to create a peaceful, multiracial community.

Supporting information—explain:
He traveled to Mecca.
He learned the truth about his religion.
He courageously changed his views about separating blacks and whites.

Topic sentence for body paragraph #4: Finally, I admire Malcolm X's strength and determination to help the black race.

Supporting information—explain:

His life revolved around politics.
He didn't work to get rich.
He spoke honestly.

Topic sentence for conclusion: Overall, I see Malcolm X as a hero because he showed such strength as he evolved from a poor, uneducated criminal to a leader of people.

1. Highlight the key words in the thesis statement that tell the reader what the essay will be about.

2. Highlight the words in each topic sentence that show that the topic sentence connects directly to the thesis.

Checking the Focus: "My Dad"

Study the thesis and notes that follow.

Thesis: My father is a hero in our neighborhood.

The thief who stole my friend's car was caught by an alert neighbor.
My uncle, who lives down the street, had his house broken into three times before the neighborhood watch program began. Since we started the program, he hasn't had a single problem.
My father became an important man in our neighborhood when he organized a neighborhood watch program and helped reduce crime in the neighborhood.
He helped clean up all the broken glass, old newspapers, and tires that littered the neighborhood.
He took charge because my brother got hurt playing in the empty lot next door.
We walked door-to-door, talked to people about the way our neighborhood looks, and organized a clean-up day.
Also, my father made our neighborhood a more attractive place to live.
My dad is an outstanding golfer, and he plays basketball too.

1. Which of the sentences here might make good topic sentences for an essay that focuses on the thesis statement the student wrote?

2. Which sentences might act as support to which topic sentences?

3. Which of the ideas don't connect clearly to the thesis?

Notes

> 4. Rewrite the sentences showing how you might group them to create an outline for an essay.

Points to Remember About Focus

As you work through this chapter and think about focusing your writing, remember these points:

- When you first start the writing process, let your mind wander and explore many different ideas.
- Spend plenty of time brainstorming, reviewing readings, and talking to classmates before you choose a focus for your essay.
- Allow yourself to change the focus of your essay if your thesis isn't working for you.
- When you revise, think critically about what you've written. Do your words communicate a focused idea to the reader?

INVESTIGATING HEROES

This section of the chapter is the beginning of your writing process. You'll discuss heroes. Then you'll read about heroes and discuss the readings. Toward the middle of the chapter, you'll find two writing assignments and support and advice as you complete the writing process.

Discuss and Engage

We've all heard about superheroes—Batman, Superman, Wonder Woman, Spiderman, the Power Rangers, even Underdog. These characters have certain human qualities that we admire and think of as heroic. However, they also have superhuman abilities, such as X-ray vision, which help them perform heroic feats. Film heroes also have extraordinary qualities—sometimes to the point of being superhuman. Think about, for example, a film hero's ability to fight off five attackers, dodge hundreds of bullets, and jump out a window just before a bomb explodes (and look good while doing it). Although you'll be writing about real-life heroes in this chapter,

let's consider for a moment what we love about superheroes and
film heroes.

Journal Assignment

Calvin and Hobbes

In the *Calvin and Hobbes* comic strip on page 184, Calvin pretends to be
a superhero named Spiff. Study the comic strip and think about the qualities Spiff seems to have. What heroic qualities has Calvin's imagination
created?

Activities

Superheroes

Discuss with your classmates what you admire about various superheroes.
Create a chart similar to the one below to record your class discussion
notes. Then answer the class discussion questions.

Get Involved!

Bring a superhero
comic book to class and
explain what heroic
qualities the characters
have.

Superhero	Heroic or Admirable Qualities	Superhuman Abilities
Superman		

1. What heroic or admirable qualities do these heroes share?

2. How do their superhuman abilities differ from their heroic qualities?

3. In your opinion, why do we enjoy our superheroes?

   (*Note:* Remember to take notes during class discussion.)

Film Heroes

Before we move on to "real-life" heroes, think about film heroes. Most people love to watch men and women in films who act, look, and live like heroes. Take a few minutes to consider this kind of hero.

Notes

> Discuss with your classmates some of your favorite film heroes. Who are they? In what films do they perform? What makes them heroes? Do film heroes look and act a certain way? How are film heroes different from real-life heroes? Explain. (Be sure to take notes.)

Real-Life Heroes   Studying superheroes and film characters helps us begin thinking about what makes a hero, but what about "real-life" heroes? These include the famous (public) heroes as well as the private (personal) heroes. Do they share certain qualities? What do public and private heroes have in common?

As you begin to define heroes, consider what these students had to say about them.

A hero is a person who has shared or done some good deeds in a country or in the world. Heroes may risk their lives and some even die for their own fellow men. They're often written about and remembered through history.

—*Diony Fernandez, student writer*

A hero can be any person on this planet, who, without ever thinking about it, goes to the rescue of his fellow man. I'd like to think that each of us has been a hero at one time or another in our lives, and didn't even realize it. A hero is a person who is sensitive to the feelings of others, and receives the pleasurable satisfaction of being able to help as their reward. A hero is that one person who wasn't noticed, recognized, or sometimes even thanked. The real hero receives his or her rewards within because they don't want to be known as a hero.

—*Maria Gonzales, student writer*

A hero is a person who goes above and beyond what any normal person can do. It's a person who works for what he or she believes in and helps others to be better people in society.

—*Doris Maysonet, student writer*

Activities

Identifying the Characteristics of Public Heroes

If you ask a group of people to list their favorite heroes, certain names keep showing up. Consider these names:

Maya Angelou	John F. Kennedy
Bono	Martin Luther King, Jr.
César Chávez	Rosa Parks
Marie Curie	Jackie Robinson
Albert Einstein	Eleanor Roosevelt
Mahatma Gandhi	Mother Teresa
Bill Gates	Harriet Tubman
Angelina Jolie	George Washington

Now, discuss with your classmates what you admire about some of these public heroes. Create a chart similar to the one that follows and list some names and admirable qualities. Then respond in your notebook to the questions after the chart.

Public Heroes	Heroic or Admirable Qualities

1. What heroic qualities do these famous people share?

2. What kinds of heroic acts have these famous people performed?

3. What are the differences between a hero and a "normal" person?

4. Are there less obvious heroes among us in society, people who don't perform dramatic acts of bravery but who could still be considered heroes? Explain.

5. How would you define the term *hero?*

Identifying the Characteristics of Private or Personal Heroes

Think about people who aren't famous but who are considered heroes. The New York City firefighters are a good example. They risked (and many lost) their lives helping innocent victims escape the World Trade Center disaster of September 11, 2001. They've become famous following the disaster, but before September 11, they were performing heroic deeds without much notoriety. There are many other people who could be called heroes for their acts of strength and courage. Perhaps you know of a private citizen who has acted heroically.

Discuss with your classmates what you admire about private citizens who exhibit heroic qualities. Create a chart similar to the one below and list some names and heroic or admirable qualities these people possess. Then respond in your notebook to the questions after the chart.

Personal Heroes	Heroic or Admirable Qualities

1. What heroic qualities do the private citizens on your list share?

2. What kinds of heroic acts have these people performed?

3. What are the differences between a private citizen we might call a hero and a "normal" person?

4. Add to your definition of the term *hero* to account for the private citizen you might consider a personal hero.

Journal Assignment

Reviewing Your Hero Discussions

Write about your class discussions. Were there any important heroes left out of your discussions? Write about the heroes and heroic qualities that interest you most. Also, write about any heroes in your own life or in your community.

Activity

Definition Paragraph

Write a focused paragraph in which you define a hero. Your topic sentence should announce the focus of your paragraph, and all of your body sentences should support this topic sentence. Remember to use the writing process (brainstorm, make choices, plan, draft, revise, edit). Keep this paragraph. You might want to include all or part of it in your essay.

Writing Assignment #1: Paying Tribute to a Personal Hero

Notes

Here, in brief, is the writing assignment that you are preparing for.

Write an essay in which you define what a hero is and then prove that an individual person you know is a hero. Focus on only one person, and focus on only those qualities that make him or her a hero. Consider including information you find through talking to family members or friends who know or have known the individual.

Keep this assignment in mind as you proceed to dig deeper into the issue of heroes and prepare to write.

Get Involved!

Rent and watch the film *Schindler's List* (1993) starring Liam Neeson, Ben Kingsley, and Ralph Fiennes and directed by Steven Spielberg. In your next class meeting, share your reactions to the film and discuss what it has to say about heroes as well as the Holocaust.

Read, Discuss, Think Critically

This section of the chapter offers a personal essay written about a family friend. The student author of the essay describes this man and the qualities and actions that made him a hero.

Reading Assignment: "A Chinese Hero"

Preview   Read the title and the information directly beneath the title. Then read the introductory paragraph and each of the topic sentences.

Anticipate   What guesses can you make about the style, structure, and quality of this essay? What do you think this essay will be about?

Read and Reread   Read the essay once quickly, marking unknown terms. Then reread the essay, responding to Liu-Fong's ideas in the "Notes" column and highlighting important points. Define unknown terms.

A Chinese Hero
by Yvonne Liu-Fong

College student Yvonne Liu-Fong wrote this essay for her English class at Cosumnes River College in Sacramento, California.

1   Heroes come in different forms. Superman, the Power Rangers, and He-Man were all fearless, courageous, and persevering. They are children's heroes. Mother Teresa, Princess Diana, and Dr. Martin Luther King Jr. were all unselfish, generous, and kind. They each were almost as perfect as God

in the eyes of the world. The soldiers currently in Iraq are sacrificing their precious lives serving for the United States of America. They are all brave heroes. My hero, Kim Toy, is 88 years old and retired. I know about him through my parents. My parents were editors and publishers of an overseas Chinese monthly magazine. They acted as liaisons for Kim Toy, who donated many funds to Chinese organizations. Stories of Mr. Toy's generosity were often written about in my parents' magazine. He has done charitable work throughout his life. In being so charitable, he sacrifices a comfortable life to help and educate other Chinese people.

2   Even today, Kim Toy continues to do more charitable work daily. He was a U.S. soldier serving in the southern Pacific Ocean during World War II. After World War II, he worked as a merchant marine and traveled the world. He retired at age 65 and made his permanent home in San Francisco, California. After settling in a small apartment, charitable work became Mr. Toy's full-time job. Every morning, he volunteered to clean the streets of Chinatown in San Francisco. While cleaning, he reminded others to properly dispose of garbage into nearby public trash containers. When Mr. Toy reached his mid-80s, he had to give up the "cleaning" job because his hands could not handle heavy work. Therefore, he now voluntarily sells Chinese newspapers from a bookstore on Jackson Street. He encourages everyone in Chinatown to spend two quarters on newspapers to find out what is going on in the world. Kim Toy is the type of individual who cannot sit still at home. As long as he can move, he wants to do something to benefit people.

3   Kim Toy is especially passionate about educating Chinese people. He sacrificed his comfortable life to support educational organizations. Mr. Toy's income comes from his pension. His lifestyle is frugal. He usually shops for food in the late afternoon when the markets reduce prices. He might buy a bundle of bananas for a dollar. He hardly ever shops for clothes for himself. He doesn't have any luxury furniture in his small studio apartment. However, he saves every penny so that he can use it in the places of real need for others. In 1992, Mr. Toy returned to his hometown in Taishan, China, for the first time since leaving his homeland. When he learned that Taishan City had just built its first television broadcasting station, he donated $10,000 to the TV station without hesitation. He believes Chinese people should continually educate themselves in order to make a better life. This local TV station had just been only one of a new technology used for education media. In 1995, he saved up another $30,000 and donated it to the Taishan City School District to be used for scholarship funding for students. Even in his own retirement years, he often journeyed to San Francisco State University and visited foreign students from China. He listened to their problems and tried to help them out. He always encouraged students to go back

to China after graduation from the United States. "China needs new knowledge to become stronger," Kim Toy would always advise.

4   Kim Toy not only donates money to education, but also helps other less fortunate people with their daily necessities as well. Many newcomers from China choose to stay in San Francisco when they first arrive in the United States because the language barriers prevent them from finding jobs. When Mr. Toy knows someone new has arrived, he always sends a bag of rice and some food to that newcomer's family. He feels happy as long as he is able to help people. Last year, when my parents told him Taishan City was planning to build its first senior citizen home, Mr. Toy donated $2,000. He told my parents: "Wait until the end of 2004; I will save up another $10,000. I will donate this to the senior citizen home." On his meager income, he is willing to commit himself to save up the large amount of money and give it away to others. In my world, I hear people say "Wait until after income tax; I will have money to buy a new car." On the other hand, I see people spend $10,000 for a vacation or a party, but people wouldn't spend it to help others.

5   Although Kim Toy has never done anything as dramatic or heroic as saving someone's life, he is a bona fide hero. He cares for Chinese people with his heart and soul. He is my idea of a Chinese hero.

Questions for Critical Thought

"A Chinese Hero"

1. Explain how Liu-Fong began her essay. How did she pull her readers in and get her audience focused on her topic?

2. Underline Liu-Fong's thesis and her topic sentences. Note how the topic sentences connect to and support the thesis. In your own words, what will she focus on in each paragraph?

3. One of the strengths of Liu-Fong's essay is the amount of specific, detailed support. List three or four examples of specific support from her body paragraphs.

4. Liu-Fong thought carefully about what order to put her body paragraphs in. What do you think her reasoning was behind the organization?

5. Liu-Fong does a nice job connecting her conclusion to her introduction. Explain how she does this.

6. Liu-Fong does a nice job of balancing pronouns and proper nouns. For example, she doesn't use "Mr. Toy" too much. Nor does she

let us forget who "he" is in this essay. Liu-Fong creates a nice balance by going back and forth between "Mr. Toy" and "he." Pick one of her body paragraphs and underline each "Mr. Toy" you find and circle each "he" you find.

7. Reflecting on the strengths of Liu-Fong's essay, name one or two things you want to keep in mind as you write your essay.

Journal Assignment

Personal Heroes

Write down your thoughts about heroes in general. Then write about one or two more personal heroes in a bit more detail. Why do they interest you? What impresses you about them? Exchange your journal with classmates, and when you are done reading your classmates' work, simply say, "Thank you" when returning their journals.

Explore the Writing Assignment

Here, again, is the writing assignment that you are preparing for.

> *Write an essay in which you define what a hero is and then prove that an individual person you know is a hero. Focus on only one person, and focus on only those qualities that make him or her a hero. Consider including information you find through talking to family members or friends who know or have known the individual.*

It's important to explore your options before planning or drafting. The first topic you think of for an essay may not be the best. If you take the time to explore your options, you may find a topic that is even more interesting or worthwhile than the first one that popped into your head. You'll be putting considerable time into writing this essay, so give yourself the chance to find a personal hero to write about who truly interests you. (Be sure to choose a personal hero—not a public hero. The second writing assignment in this chapter addresses public heroes.)

Brainstorm   Spend ten to twenty minutes and write freely about individuals you know personally or have heard about who have performed heroic deeds. Write as much as you can about each hero. If there is a person you are interested in but don't know much about, write down questions you have about that person. Also write down where you can go to find some answers. (Consider interviewing other family members or friends who may have known the person.) When you have finished brainstorming, write down the name of the person you think you will write about and explain why you have chosen to focus on this person.

Gather Information About Heroes   Find some information on the person you have chosen. You may already have information (from personal experience or from listening to family stories over the years). If you don't have enough information, go to those who knew this person and ask for the basic facts (date of birth, place of birth, education, accomplishments, and date of death—if applicable). Then identify the admirable qualities and actions that make you consider this person a hero. Take notes as you speak to family and friends. If you quote a sentence or two from someone you interviewed, practice your quoting skills. (See pages 492–493 for information on using quotations in your essay.)

Think Critically About Your Choice of a Hero   Do you still want to write your essay about the person you chose? Why, or why not? Why is the person you've chosen considered a hero? If you have decided *not* to write about the person, you should go back and look at your brainstorming. Then talk to your instructor or a tutor. Think about why your first choice turned out to be unsatisfactory. Then make a new choice and find information on this new person.

Narrow Your Brainstorming   Once you have chosen your personal hero and gathered some basic information, you should write freely for approximately thirty minutes about anything connected to this person. Let your mind wander and don't worry about what you write. A good brainstorming session is long and full of many different ideas. Some of the ideas will prove useful and others will not, but now is not the time to make those choices.

When you have finished your brainstorming, use your critical thinking skills and highlight the ideas that seem most likely to prove that the person you've chosen to write about is a hero.

Consider Your Audience   Before you actually begin thinking about your thesis or outline, you should consider who is in your audience and what they want to know. Thinking about your audience will help you begin to focus your thoughts and determine what must be included in your essay.

Notes

Activities

Audience—Group Work

Write one to three sentences in which you state the name of your hero, how you know this person (or know about this person), and why this person is a hero. Read this information to your group. Then, ask each other the following questions:

1. What do you know about my hero?

2. What would you like to know about my hero?

3. Do you think the person I have chosen is a hero?

When you have answers to these questions, write down your own description of a larger audience. Who is in your audience? What do they know and not know about the hero you have chosen? Will you have to persuade your readers that your hero is, indeed, a hero? Assume that your audience extends beyond your classroom. What kinds of information about heroes in general do you want to share with this larger audience? What specific information about your hero seems important?

Speak Your Mind

Share your responses to the following prompts with a classmate. (Be sure to make notes so that you can use this information when you outline and draft your essay.)

1. My definition of a hero is . . .

2. The person I have chosen as a hero has the following characteristics (he or she doesn't have to have all the characteristics in the hero definition) . . .

3. The main points I should cover in my essay are . . .

4. I probably don't need to mention the following information in my essay:

Create Your Thesis Remember that a thesis statement is the sentence that expresses the main idea of your essay. It usually comes at the end of your introduction, and everything else in the essay should connect to and support this thesis. Obviously, it is an important element in your essay. You'll want to experiment with different ways of expressing your main idea. While you are experimenting with the thesis statement, you'll find that you are thinking critically about exactly what you want to prove in your essay.

Review the writing assignment, your brainstorming, activities, and class notes and write a thesis statement for your essay. You may need to write a few thesis statements before you create one that expresses your ideas well. Share your thesis statement with your classmates, tutor, and instructor. Ask them what they expect your essay to be about. Think critically about what they say and about your own reaction to your thesis statement. Is it too broad? Too narrow? Your thesis should give your reader a clear sense of where your essay is going and why.

Outline After revising and polishing your thesis statement, copy it down on a clean piece of paper and experiment with possible topic sentences for your essay. (*Note:* For a well-focused essay, your topic sentences must clearly support your thesis.) Be careful of topic sentences that give facts rather than state the main idea of a paragraph. For example, a topic sentence that says, "He was born in 1852," does not give the reader a good sense of what that paragraph will be about. Such a sentence also does not show how the paragraph will support the idea that "he" is a hero. Your topic sentences will probably each focus on a different heroic quality you see in your hero.

Revise your topic sentences until they seem clear and effective. List them beneath your thesis statement. You may also want to list a few pieces of support under each topic sentence to remind yourself of the type of information that will go into the body of each paragraph. Share this outline with classmates, a tutor, or your instructor. Can your reader(s) tell what your essay will be about? Does everything connect to your thesis?

Feel free to change and revise your outline at any time during your writing process. The outline should be a guide, not something that forces you to state something you are no longer satisfied with.

Draft

At this stage of the writing process, you want to create a complete essay (introduction, body, and conclusion). However, remember that this is a work in progress, and you should not try to make the draft perfect. Striving for perfection at this stage will probably just make you worry about every word you put on paper. You will have the chance to revise later. In fact, you, like many writers, may write many drafts—each one better than the previous one.

When you are ready to draft your essay, remember that you should assume that your reading audience doesn't know very much, if anything, about the hero you are focusing on, so it's your job to provide important information about this person and why he or she is a hero. Your introduction should define heroes and generally explain why the person you selected is considered a hero. In your body paragraphs, describe in more detail the different heroic qualities your personal hero possesses. In your conclusion, tell your reader what you've learned from writing this essay and what you want the reader to learn from it.

Revise

This is the stage in the writing process in which you change and improve your draft. As you complete this stage, you may find that you actually produce a number of drafts. It is important to have someone review your work and respond to your ideas. Don't worry about sentence corrections yet. Put your energy into improving the *focus, development,* and *organization* of your essay.

Activity

Share Your Writing

Find a classmate to work with. Discuss the following questions as they relate to your essay.

- Do you have a clear definition of what a hero is?

- Do you focus on just one person in your essay?

- Do you focus on only those qualities that make your person a hero? (For example, you might remember your mother making great lemon meringue pies when you were a kid, but you wouldn't mention that in your essay because it doesn't explain why she is a hero.)

- Is there enough specific evidence that this person is a hero? Do you have enough facts? Do you need to find out more about this person?

- Check the coherence of your essay. Will your reader see how each piece of information connects to your point that this person is a hero?

Edit

Now is the time to work on polishing your sentences. The goal is to make your ideas clear and to project a professional image so that your reader will respect your work.

Read your essay aloud and look (and listen) for awkward spots and typographical errors.

Review your essay again, slowly, sentence by sentence, and consider the following:

- Are there any errors that you tend to repeat? Focus on them one at a time.
- Is there a certain area your instructor wants you to focus on?
- Are there any misspelled words? Use spell check on your computer, or get out your dictionary and look up any words you are uncertain about. Do this early enough so that if you need it, you can get help from a tutor or instructor.

Specific words to be aware of in this assignment include the following:

- hero/heroes (notice that the singular form doesn't have an *e* on the end),
- the name of your hero, and
- the names of places and events (like your hero's birthplace, and so on).

You may also want to consider these questions after completing the sentence work at the end of the chapter:

- Are you using pronouns to improve the flow and coherence of your essay without overusing them?
- Do your pronouns agree in number with their antecedents?
- If any of your sentences contain lists, are you using parallel structure?
- Have you quoted any sources (relatives or friends you interviewed)? If so, be sure to identify the source and place direct quotations in quotation marks. (See "Using Outside Sources" on pages 489–494 for review.)

Writing Assignment #2: Honoring Our Public Heroes

Here, in brief, is the writing assignment that you are preparing for.

Write an essay about a heroic public figure. Focus on only one person, and focus on only those qualities that make him or her a hero. Prove to your audience why and how that person fits the definition of "hero." Be sure to include information you find through research.

Keep this assignment in mind as you proceed to dig deeper into the issue of heroes and prepare to write.

Read, Discuss, Think Critically

Two additional readings about heroes follow. The first discusses a well-known hero from the civil rights movement and heroes in general. The second describes a modern-day hero in Burma.

Reading Assignment: *"Civil Rights Movement Was the Sum of Many People"*

Preview   Read the first three paragraphs.

Anticipate   What do you think this article will be about? Write your response in the "Notes" column.

Read and Reread   Read the entire article, marking unknown terms. Then reread more slowly and use the "Notes" column to record your responses to the essay. Mark important and interesting points and define unknown terms.

Civil Rights Movement Was the Sum of Many People
by Paul Rogat Loeb

This article by Paul Rogat Loeb, who authored *Soul of a Citizen: Living with Conviction in a Cynical Time*, appeared in the *Sacramento Bee* on January 16, 2000.

1   Seattle—We learn much from how we present our heroes. A few years ago, on Martin Luther King Jr. Day, I was interviewed on CNN. So was Rosa Parks, by phone from Los Angeles.

2   "We're very honored to have her," said the host. "Rosa Parks was the woman who wouldn't go to the back of the bus. She wouldn't get up and give her seat in the white section to a white person. That set in motion the yearlong boycott of city buses in Montgomery. It earned Rosa Parks the title of 'mother of the civil rights movement.'"

3   I was excited to hear Parks' voice and to be part of the same show, but it occurred to me that the host's description—the story's familiar rendition—stripped the Montgomery boycott of its most important context.

4   Before the fateful December day in 1955 when Parks refused to obey a law designating segregated seating on buses, she had spent 12 years helping lead the local NAACP chapter, along with union activist E.D. Nixon, from the Brotherhood of Sleeping Car Porters; teachers from the local Negro college; and a variety of members of Montgomery's African American community. Parks allowed her arrest to be used to spark a boycott, which was led by King. That 382-day boycott ended on Dec.

20, 1956, when the U.S. Supreme Court declared segregated seating on city buses unconstitutional.

5   The summer of 1954, Parks had attended a 10-day training session at Tennessee's labor and civil rights organizing school, the Highlander Center, where she'd met an older generation of civil rights activists and discussed the Supreme Court's *Brown* decision banning "separate but equal" schools.

6   Parks didn't make a spur-of-the-moment decision that gave birth to the civil rights movement. She was part of an existing force for change when success was far from certain. Her tremendously consequential act might never have occurred without all the humble and frustrating work she and all the others had been doing. Her initial step of involvement 12 years before was just as courageous and critical as the moment she refused to move further back in the bus.

7   People such as Parks shape our models of social commitment. Yet the conventional retelling of her story creates a standard so impossible to meet, it may actually make it harder for us to get involved.

8   This portrayal suggests that social activists come out of nowhere to make sudden, dramatic stands. It implies that we make the greatest impact when we act alone, or at least alone initially; that anyone who takes a committed public stand, or at least an effective one, has to be a larger-than-life figure—someone with more time, energy, courage, vision or knowledge than any normal person could ever possess. The beliefs pervade our society, in part because the media rarely represent historical change as the work of ordinary human beings.

9   Parks' real story conveys a far more empowering moral. In the 1940's, she goes to a meeting and then another. Hesitant at first, she gains confidence as she speaks out. She keeps on despite a profoundly uncertain context as she and others act as best they can to challenge deeply entrenched injustices with little certainty of results. Had she and others given up after her 10th or 11th year of commitment, we might never have heard of Montgomery.

10   Once we enshrine our heroes on pedestals, it's difficult for mere mortals to measure up. When individuals speak out, we're tempted to dismiss their motives, knowledge and tactics as insufficiently grand. We fault them for not being in command of every fact and figure. We fault ourselves as well for not knowing every detail, or for harboring uncertainties and doubts. We find it hard to imagine that flawed human beings might make a critical difference in worthy social causes.

11   Our culture's misreading of Parks' story hints at a collective amnesia in which we forget the examples that might most inspire our courage and conscience. Most of us know next to nothing of the old grass-roots movements in which ordinary men and women fought to preserve freedom,

expand the sphere of democracy and create a more just society: the abolitionists, the populists, the women's suffrage campaigns, the union movements that ended 80-hour work weeks at near starvation wages. These movements could teach us how their participants successfully shifted public sentiment, challenged entrenched institutional power and found the strength to persevere. But their stories are buried.

12   In the prevailing myth, Parks decides to act on a whim, in isolation. She's a political innocent. The lesson seems to be that if any of us suddenly got the urge to do something equally heroic, that would be great. Of course most of us don't, so we wait our entire lives to find the ideal moment.

13   Parks' journey suggests that change is the product of deliberate, incremental action, whereby we join together to try to shape a better world. Sometimes our struggles will fail, as did many earlier efforts of Parks, her peers and her predecessors. Other times they may bear modest fruits. And at times they will trigger a miraculous outpouring of courage and heart—as happened with her arrest and everything that followed. Only when we act despite all our uncertainties and doubts do we have the chance to shape history.

Questions for Critical Thought

"Civil Rights Movement Was the Sum of Many People"

1. Following a journalism model, some of Loeb's paragraphs are short. He often uses more than one paragraph to make a single point. He uses paragraphs 1, 2, and 3 as the introduction. Reread those first three paragraphs and highlight (or copy down) paragraph 3. This is his thesis.

2. What is his main point in paragraphs 4, 5, and 6?

3. What is his main point in paragraphs 7 and 8?

4. Loeb begins paragraph 9 with this sentence: "Parks' real story conveys a far more empowering moral." Reread the entire paragraph and then explain what *moral* he is referring to in that first sentence of paragraph 9.

Moral can mean "message," "lesson," or "rule."

5. What is his main point in paragraph 10?

6. Now look back at the thesis you marked in paragraph 3. Put Loeb's thesis into your own words.

7. What is Loeb's purpose in writing this essay? Who is his audience? What do you think Loeb wants to accomplish with this essay?

8. Reread paragraph 11. Is there a modern issue that you care about, one that you would give your time and energy to? Explain.

Notes

Reading Assignment: *"Aung San Suu Kyi"*

Preview   Read the title and the topic sentence in each paragraph.

Anticipate   What do you anticipate this reading will be about? What will the author say about Aung San Suu Kyi? Use the "Notes" column to record your thoughts.

Read and Reread   Read the entire essay and highlight unknown terms and interesting points. Then reread more slowly and write your responses in the "Notes" column. Mark important points and define unknown terms.

Aung San Suu Kyi
by Carol Einstein

Aung San Suu Kyi is pronounced Ong San Sue Chee

1   For over fifteen years, Aung San Suu Kyi has fought to bring democracy to Burma (also known as Myanmar), her native country. Although the party she helped establish, the National League for Democracy, won a landslide victory in the 1990 national elections, the military government refused to hand over power and continues to control the country. Suu Kyi has spent years under house arrest for her pro-democracy work. Her family is not allowed to visit or have any contact with her. She can leave the country whenever she wishes, but once she goes she will not be allowed back. Knowing this, Suu Kyi refuses to leave. Yet she is not bitter, writing, "We must all understand that there is great merit in sacrificing for others and that by so doing we live the full life. . . . To live the full life one must have the courage to bear the responsibility."

2   The youngest of three children, Aung San Suu Kyi was born in Rangoon, (also known as Yangon), the capital of Burma. Her father, Aung San, is revered throughout Burma as the father of the nation. During the 1940s, he led the struggle for independence from British colonial rule and from the Japanese who occupied Burma during World War II. When the war ended in 1945, Aung San negotiated with the British government for Burma's independence. Tragically, he and almost his whole cabinet were gunned down in 1947, just before Burma gained independence on January 4, 1948. A jealous political rival had planned the assassination.

Get Involved!

Go to *Time.com* to read about "The People Who Share Our World," located at www.time.com/time/specials/2007/time100. Be ready to discuss some of the people mentioned when you return to class.

3   After her husband's death, Daw Khin Kyi, Suu Kyi's mother, was appointed director of social welfare in Burma's new independent government.

Notes

In 1961, Daw Khin Kyi became Burma's ambassador to India, and Suu Kyi went with the family to Delhi, the Indian capital. She was raised as a Buddhist and, with her mother's encouragement, often assisted the Buddhist monks in their ceremonies. She had riding and piano lessons, but her favorite activity was reading. After finishing high school, Suu Kyi studied political science at Delhi University. She became an admirer of Mahatma Gandhi and a firm believer in the principles of nonviolence, which Gandhi had lived by.

4   In 1964, Suu Kyi entered Oxford University, in England, where she decided to study politics, philosophy, and economics. Later, she told a reporter that she would have preferred to study English, Japanese, or forestry, but she thought a knowledge of economics and politics would be more helpful, if she ever returned to work in her own country. Friends remember her as being interested in different cultures and devoted to Buddhism and to her country's cultural traditions.

5   Even though Suu Kyi was only two years old when her father died, she never forgot him. While she was at Oxford, she gathered a large collection of books and papers in Burmese and English about her father. Later she wrote, "It was only when I grew older and started collecting material on his life that I began to learn how much he achieved in his thirty-two years. I developed an admiration for him as a patriot and statesman. Because of this strong bond I feel a deep responsibility for the welfare of my country."

6   Suu Kyi graduated from Oxford in 1967 and moved to New York City, where she worked for the United Nations. During her time at Oxford, she had become friends with Michael Aris, another student. After his graduation, Aris moved to the Himalayan kingdom of Bhutan to become the private tutor of the children of the royal family. Aris and Suu Kyi dated by mail. Suu Kyi sent 187 letters to Bhutan from New York in the eight months before they married. In many of the letters, she reminded him that one day she would have to go back to Burma. She wrote, "I only ask one thing, that should my people need me, you would help me to do my duty by them."

7   After their marriage in 1972, the couple returned to England, where their two sons, Alexander and Kim, were born. While her husband taught at Oxford University, she raised the boys, and in her free time, read about her father's life. In 1984, she wrote a biography of him, and in 1985, she traveled to the University of Kyoto in Japan to continue research on his life. Later her husband wrote, "Some would say she became obsessed with the image of the father she never knew." Suu Kyi says that she developed a strong identification with him because they shared many views.

8   Even though Burma was no longer her home, she often traveled there to visit her mother. Suu Kyi saw with her own eyes the country's poor economy, the hardships of the people, and the crooked dictatorship of the military government, which had seized power in 1962 and continued to rule the country. Then, in March 1988, she received a phone call that changed her life. She learned that her mother had had a severe stroke. Two days later Suu Kyi was at her mother's bedside in Rangoon. When she arrived, the capital was very tense. Independently, groups of students were demonstrating against the government, and the police were shooting at them. By June 1988, several hundred people had died.

9   In July, Ne Win, the country's absolute leader, resigned and chose the most reactionary of his friends, General Sein Lwin, to lead the Burma Socialist Program Party. When the party refused to allow a vote on Burma's future, Suu Kyi's house became a center of political planning. Suu Kyi later said, "As my father's daughter, I felt I had a duty to get involved." Tens of thousands of people filled streets in the capital and in towns throughout the country to protest. Many carried posters with a photograph of Aung San Suu Kyi. Often, the army fired into the unarmed crowds. Between August 8 and August 13, about three thousand people were killed.

10   On August 26, 1988, Suu Kyi made her first public appearance. About five hundred thousand people came to Shwedagon Pagoda, Burma's most sacred shrine, to hear her. Although she had spent most of her life outside of Burma, she spoke perfect Burmese and dressed in traditional Burmese clothing. The crowd saw a resemblance to her father: she looked like him, spoke like him, and had his air of powerful authority. Suu Kyi quickly set herself apart from other possible leaders by offering a vision for the country's future. Up to that point a broad movement of people had been united only by widespread hatred for the military government. She told her audience that all people had basic human rights and that one of the most important of these was the right to choose one's government. Suu Kyi asked the military leaders to take their proper role as protectors of the people.

11   The military government, of course, knew she was a threat to its power. On September 18, the leaders of the armed forces established a council as the top political authority. It forbade political demonstrations and gatherings of more than four persons and announced that citizens could be arrested and sentenced without a trial. On the other hand, it promised to hold free elections and said that people could form political parties. The next morning, just as they had done during the past weeks, the demonstrators took to the streets, clearly disobeying the new laws. In a three-day period about one thousand people were killed.

12   Throughout all the turmoil, Suu Kyi nursed her mother until Daw Khin Kyi died in December 1988. For the funeral, which thousands of people attended, Suu Kyi's husband and sons were granted permission to enter Burma. For a short time, the family was reunited.

13   Suu Kyi helped found the National League for Democracy and became its secretary-general. Traveling around the country, she encouraged people in their fight for freedom, human rights, and democracy. At first, the government did not stop her when tens of thousands of people came to hear her. Within a few months, though, the army began arresting her supporters. On April 5, 1989, she was nearly killed by six soldiers who had been ordered to shoot her. Staying calm, she asked her supporters to step aside and then walked straight toward the soldiers. At the last moment, a high-ranking officer canceled the order to shoot. Later, when asked about the incident, Suu Kyi said, "It seemed so much simpler to provide them with a single target than to bring everyone else in."

14   As the months passed, Suu Kyi's activities became too much for the dictatorship. On July 20, 1989, eleven truckloads of armed troops blocked her from leaving her house. Her telephone lines were cut, and she was placed under house arrest. Her sons were already visiting her and her husband arrived shortly after her detention. But when they left for England in September, the military rulers denied them permission to re-enter the country and cut off any contact by mail.

15   In May 1990, the parliamentary elections took place. The National League for Democracy, Suu Kyi's party, won over eighty percent of the vote, but the military rulers refused to honor the results. The following year, Suu Kyi received the Nobel Peace Prize. In announcing the award, the Norwegian Nobel Committee said, "Suu Kyi's struggle is one of the most extraordinary examples of civil courage in Asia in recent decades."

16   Suu Kyi has been in detention in one form or another for the past fifteen years. Her contact with the outside world is cut off. In a rare interview in 1994, Suu Kyi said that isolation is not difficult. She realizes that other people have suffered more and have died in the struggle for freedom. In 1995, when she was temporarily freed from house arrest, she worked quickly to revive the democracy movement that had basically died out during her long detention. Whenever she tried to travel outside Rangoon to meet with party members, the military stopped her car. To protest, Suu Kyi would remain in her car for days until she was finally forced to return to her home. Once, after Suu Kyi had spent thirteen days in her car, one of her party officials described this confrontation as a "war of endurance." The government has tried to break her determination in other ways, too. In 1999, when her husband discovered that he was dying of cancer, he repeatedly asked the Burmese government

for permission to enter the country to visit his wife one last time, but the authorities turned down every request. He died in England in 1999 without their meeting again.

17   Over the years, Suu Kyi has used different means to keep her movement alive, but she has had fewer ways to do it. Her party members have been forced to stop their activities or have been jailed or killed. She has never given up her nonviolent "battle of wills" with the military, hoping to draw the attention and support of foreign governments to her struggle. At the beginning of her quest for democracy in her country, Suu Kyi said, "We should do what we believe is right, even if we are afraid." Today, Suu Kyi continues her courageous struggle against tyranny.

Questions for Critical Thought

"Aung San Suu Kyi"

1. In paragraph 2, what does *revered* mean?

2. Who is Mahatma Gandhi and what did he do (see paragraph 3)?

3. In paragraph 5, what does *statesman* mean? And what does it mean to care about the "welfare of my country"?

4. In paragraph 8, find and copy down the sentence that shows parallel structure (see pages 227–234 for information on parallelism).

5. How did Einstein organize her ideas in this biographical essay?

6. What is Einstein's purpose in writing this essay?

7. In what ways could Aung San Su Kyi be considered a hero?

8. What adjectives would you use to describe Suu Kyi?

9. If you were to write a hero essay on Suu Kyi, which facts would you focus on when proving she is a hero?

10. What might be good topic sentences for the body paragraphs of an essay that proves Suu Kyi is a hero?

11. What would your thesis be?

Journal Assignment

Studying Our Public Heroes

What are some of the similarities and differences between Rosa Parks and Aung San Suu Kyi? When you've finished writing, exchange your journal with classmates, and when you are done reading your classmates' work, simply say, "Thank you" when returning their journals.

Explore the Writing Assignment

Here, again, is the writing assignment that you are preparing for.

> *Write an essay about a heroic public figure. Focus on only one person, and focus on only those qualities that make him or her a hero. Prove to your audience why and how that person fits the definition of "hero." Be sure to include information you find through research.*

Now it's time to explore your options even further. As you've probably discovered, the first topic you think of for an essay may not be the best. When you take the time to explore your options, you often find a topic that is even better than the first. Because you'll be putting considerable time into writing this essay, be sure to select a public hero you really want to know more about. (Be sure to keep source notes throughout the writing process so that you'll be able to cite your sources easily when you write your essay.)

Brainstorm   Spend ten to twenty minutes writing freely about as many public heroes as you can think of. Refer to the list on pages 192–193 to help you get started. Also, refer to your class notes and the readings in this chapter. What do you know about each hero? If there is a person you are interested in but don't know much about, write down questions you have about that person. When you have finished brainstorming, evaluate the names that have come up. Narrow the list to the person you most admire. Write down why you admire this person.

Gather Information About Heroes   Locate information on the person you have chosen. You may already have information (from essays in this book, materials at home, or readings from your instructor). However, if you don't have enough information, go to the library (or the Internet) and research this person. Find out the basic facts (date of birth, place of birth, education, accomplishments, and date of death— if applicable). Then identify the qualities and actions that make this person a hero. Take notes and record your source information (author, title, and source). Use your own words. Do not copy your research sources. If you find a sentence or two in a source that is worth quoting, practice your quotation skills. (See pages 489–494 for help in using outside sources.)

Think Critically About Your Choice of a Hero   Evaluate why the person you researched is considered a hero. If you have decided *not* to write about the person you researched, you should return to your brainstorming, select another candidate from your list, and then research that person. You may want to talk to your instructor or a tutor. Think about why your first choice turned out to be unsatisfactory. Then make a new choice and find information on this new person.

Narrow Your Brainstorming   Once you have chosen a hero and gathered some basic information, freewrite for thirty minutes on your hero. Let your mind wander and don't worry about what you write. Some of the ideas will prove useful, and others will not, but now is not the time to make those choices.

When you have finished your brainstorming, go back, use your critical thinking skills, and highlight the ideas that seem most promising to you.

Consider Your Audience   Before drafting your thesis or outline, you should consider who your audience is and what they want to know. Thinking about your audience will help you begin to focus your thoughts and determine what must be included in your essay.

Notes

Activities

Audience

In small groups, share the name of your hero; then, ask each other the following questions:

1. What do you know about my hero?

2. What would you like to know about my hero?

3. Do you think the person I have chosen is a hero?

When you have answers to these questions, write down your own description of a larger audience. Who is in your audience? What do they know and not know about the hero you have chosen? Will you have to persuade your readers that your public hero is, indeed, a hero? Assume that your audience extends beyond your classroom. What kinds of information about heroes in general do you want to share with this larger audience? What specific information about your hero seems important? What distinguishes your hero from other public figures?

Notes

> ## Speak Your Mind
>
> Share your responses to the following prompts with a classmate. (Be sure to make notes so that you can use them when you outline and draft your essay.)
>
> 1. My definition of a hero is . . .
>
> 2. The person I have chosen as a public hero has the following characteristics (he or she doesn't have to have all the characteristics in the hero definition) . . .
>
> 3. The main points I should cover in my essay are . . .
>
> 4. I probably don't need to mention the following information in my essay:

Create Your Thesis   Your thesis statement is the sentence that expresses the main idea of your essay. As you've learned, it usually comes at the end of your introduction. The body paragraphs of the essay should connect to and support this thesis. To create a successful thesis, you'll want to experiment with different ways of stating your main idea. While you are experimenting with the thesis statement, you'll find that you are thinking critically about exactly what you want to prove in your essay.

Review the writing assignment, your brainstorming, activities, and class notes and write a thesis statement for your essay. You may need to write a few thesis statements before you develop the one that best expresses who your hero is and why. Share your thesis statement with your classmates, tutor, and instructor. Ask them what they expect your essay to be about. Think critically about what they say and about your own reaction to your thesis statement. Is it too broad? Too narrow? Your thesis should give your reader a clear sense of where your essay is going and why.

Outline   After revising and polishing your thesis statement, copy it down on a clean piece of paper and experiment with possible topic sentences for your essay. (*Note:* For a well-focused essay, your topic sentences must clearly support your thesis.) Be careful of topic sentences that give facts rather than state the main idea of a paragraph. For example, a topic sentence that says, "He was born in 1852," does not give the reader a good sense of what that paragraph will be about. Such a sentence also does not show how the paragraph will support the idea that "he" is a hero. Your topic sentences will probably each focus on a different heroic quality you see in your hero.

Notes

Revise your topic sentences until they seem clear and effective. List them beneath your thesis statement. Also list a few pieces of support under each topic sentence to remind yourself of the type of information that will go into the body of each paragraph. Outside information would fit well in the body of your essay. (To avoid plagiarism, be sure to use quotation marks around words taken directly from sources and always include in your essay where you found the information.)

Share this outline with classmates, a tutor, or your instructor. Can your reader(s) tell what your essay will be about? Does everything connect to your thesis?

Feel free to change and revise your outline at any time during your writing process. The outline should be a guide, not something that forces you to state something you are no longer satisfied with.

Draft

Now it's time to write a complete draft of your essay (introduction, body, and conclusion). Since this is a work in progress, you don't have to make the draft perfect. Remember that you will have the chance to revise later. In fact, you, like most writers, will write many drafts, each showing improvement over the previous one.

As you write, you should assume that your readers have probably heard of the public hero you've chosen, though they may not know many details about the hero's deeds. So it's your job to provide important information about this person and why he or she is a hero. Your introduction should define public heroes and generally explain why the person you selected is considered a hero. In your body paragraphs, describe in more detail the different qualities the hero you've chosen possesses. You may want to turn to "Using Outside Sources" on pages 489–494 for some pointers on using quotations. That section also reminds you that most quotations need to be followed by an explanation so that your reader understands the quotation and its relationship to your main point. In your conclusion, tell your reader what you've learned from writing this essay and what you want the reader to learn from it.

Revise

This is the stage in the writing process in which you change and improve your draft. As you complete this stage, you may find that you actually produce a number of drafts. It is important to have someone review your work and respond to your ideas. Don't worry about sentence corrections yet.

Activity

Share Your Writing

Find a classmate to work with. Discuss the following questions as they relate to your essay:

- Do you have a clear definition of what a public hero is?

- Do you focus on just one person in your essay?

- Do you focus on only those qualities that make your person a hero? (For example, George Washington may have been an excellent card player, but you wouldn't mention that in the essay because it doesn't explain why he is a hero.)

- Is there enough specific evidence that this person is a hero? Do you have enough facts? Do you need to do more research?

- Check the coherence of your essay. Will your reader see how each piece of information connects to your point that this person is a hero?

Edit

Now that you've revised your essay and have cited sources correctly, it's time to work on polishing your sentences. The goal is to make your ideas clear and to project a professional image so that your reader will respect your work.

Read your essay aloud and look (and listen) for awkward spots and typographical errors.

Review your essay again, slowly, sentence by sentence, and consider the following:

- Are there any errors that you tend to repeat? Focus on them one at a time.

- Is there a certain area your instructor wants you to focus on?

- Are there any misspelled words? Use spell check on your computer, or get out your dictionary and look up any words you are uncertain about. Do this early enough so that if you need it, you can get help from a tutor or instructor.

  Specific words to be aware of in this assignment include the following:

- hero/heroes (notice that the singular form doesn't have an *e* on the end),

- the name of your hero, and

- the names of places and events (like your hero's birthplace, and so on).

  You may also want to consider these questions after completing the sentence work at the end of the chapter:

- Are you using pronouns to improve the flow and coherence of your essay without overusing them?

- Do your pronouns agree in number with their antecedents?

- If any of your sentences contain lists, are you using parallel structure?

- Are you using outside sources correctly? (See "Using Outside Sources" on pages 489–494 for examples.)

Notes

TIME TO REFLECT

> ### *Journal Assignment*
> ### *Your Progress as a Writer, Reader, and Critical Thinker*
> Write in your journal your reflection on any or all of the following:
>
> - Have your reading and writing processes continued to change and improve? Explain.
> - What reading and writing skills do you feel really good about?
> - What skills are you most concerned about?
> - Are you using any of the tutoring resources on campus?

SUMMARY OF CHAPTER 5

In this chapter, you have studied the role of *focus* in effective writing. You have

- considered how topic sentences and thesis statements help writers focus their writing,

- seen how important critical thinking is in creating a focused piece of writing, and
- practiced your ability to focus your thoughts on paper while you communicated your own ideas about what makes a hero and who is a hero.

PRONOUNS

Identifying Pronouns
Identifying Antecedents
Avoiding Unclear Pronoun References
Avoiding Pronoun Disagreement and Sexist Language

A pronoun is a word that can be used instead of a noun in a sentence. (Remember, a noun is a person, place, thing, or idea: *Jim, store, chair, happiness.*) Knowing about pronouns gives you more options when you write because you won't have to use the same nouns over and over. You'll be able to use pronouns in their place. This section will help you identify and then use pronouns correctly (avoiding errors such as pronoun disagreement and sexist language). In addition, you'll study **synonyms** (words that have similar meanings), which can also help you add variety to your writing.

Identifying Pronouns

Pronouns come in five different forms: subject, object, possessive, relative/interrogative, and indefinite.

Subject form	I, he, she, it, they, we, you
Object form	me, him, her, it, them, us, you
Possessive form	my/mine, his, her/hers, its, their/theirs, our/ours, your/yours
Relative/Interrogative form	who, that, which
Indefinite form	somebody/someone, everybody/everyone, each, neither, either, anybody/anyone

In the following sentences, pronouns are underlined.

I (subject form) asked him (object form) if I (subject form) could borrow his (possessive form) copy of Malcolm X's autobiography.

After reading her (possessive form) suggestions on my (possessive form) draft, I (subject form) realized that Samantha was a pretty good critic.

Notes

Jackie was a nurse <u>who</u> (relative form) gave <u>her</u> (possessive form) heart to <u>her</u> (possessive form) patients.

<u>Everybody</u> (indefinite form) can learn from <u>her</u> (possessive form) dedication.

Practice #1   Rosa Parks

Read the following passage aloud. Then, reread the passage and put boxes around the pronouns you find. (The paragraph comes from "Civil Rights Movement Was the Sum of Many People.")

> Parks didn't make a spur-of-the-moment decision that gave birth to the civil rights movement. She was part of an existing force for change when success was far from certain. Her tremendously consequential act might never have occurred without all the humble and frustrating work she and all the others had been doing. Her initial step of involvement 12 years before was just as courageous and critical as the moment she refused to move further back in the bus.

1. Cross out every *she* in the passage that refers to Parks and write in *Parks*. Also cross out every *her* and write in *Parks'*.
2. Read the paragraph aloud the way you have rewritten it. How does the paragraph sound without using *she* or *her*?

As you can see (and hear), pronouns are important so that writing doesn't become repetitive.

Identifying Antecedents

An **antecedent** is the noun a pronoun refers to. It is important for pronouns to have clear antecedents so that the reader knows to whom you are referring. Think of an *antecedent* as an "ancestor" (someone who came before you). Pronouns must have *antecedents* just as people must have *ancestors*. In the following sentences, the pronouns are boxed and the arrows point to the antecedents.

My father first showed an interest in caring for animals when he was only 5 years old.

The children all cheered when they saw Mickey Mouse.

In the paragraph that follows, the pronouns are boxed and there are arrows going from the pronouns to the underlined antecedents. (The paragraph comes from "Aung San Suu Kyi.")

On August 26, 1988, Suu Kyi made her first public appearance. About five hundred thousand people came to Shwedagon Pagoda, Burma's most sacred shrine, to hear her. Although she had spent most of her life outside of Burma, she spoke perfect Burmese and dressed in traditional Burmese clothing.

Practice #2   **Heroes**

In the sentences below, put boxes around the pronouns and draw arrows to the antecedents. Notice how the pronoun/antecedent relationship helps us see the connections between different sentences. This improves the flow and coherence of the writing. (The sentences come from "Civil Rights Movement Was the Sum of Many People" and "Aung San Suu Kyi.")

Remember, a *coherent* piece of writing has ideas and sentences that fit together smoothly and logically.

1. Parks' real story conveys a far more empowering moral. In the 1940's, she goes to a meeting and then another. Hesitant at first, she gains confidence as she speaks out. She keeps on despite a profoundly uncertain context as she and others act as best they can to challenge deeply entrenched injustices with little certainty of results. Had she and others given up after her 10th or 11th year of commitment, we might never have heard of Montgomery. (Par. 9, "Civil Rights Movement Was the Sum of Many People")

2. Suu Kyi helped found the National League for Democracy and became its secretary-general. Traveling around the country, she encouraged people in their fight for freedom, human rights, and democracy. At first, the government did not stop her when tens of thousands of people came to hear her. (Par. 13, "Aung San Suu Kyi")

3. As the months passed, Suu Kyi's activities became too much for the dictatorship. On July 20, 1989, eleven truckloads of armed troops blocked her from leaving her house. Her telephone lines were cut, and she was placed under house arrest. (Par. 14, "Aung San Suu Kyi")

Avoiding Unclear Pronoun References

If a pronoun does not have a clear antecedent, an instructor may use the phrase "unclear pronoun reference." There are a few exceptions. For example, when you use pronouns like "I," "everyone," and "anyone," an antecedent is not necessary because your reader will not be confused by these pronouns. This sentence, however, suffers from an unclear pronoun reference:

> My father and my classmate both liked my hero essay. However, he said I should remove a few details that seemed more distracting than helpful.

Who suggested the change? The father or the classmate? In this situation, the writer needs to make the antecedent clear. The writer might do this without repeating words. For example, if it is the father that made the suggestion, the writer can use a synonym like "dad" instead. A word is a *synonym* of another if it means basically the same thing. Here is the revision:

> My father and my classmate both liked my hero essay. However, Dad said I should remove a few details that seemed more distracting than helpful.

Here's another example of an unclear pronoun reference:

> After my brother finished boot camp, my dad visited him at the base. He was so happy about this.

Who does *he* refer to? The brother or the father? And what does *this* refer to? Finishing boot camp or visiting? Here is one way of revising the sentence:

> After my brother finished boot camp, my dad visited him at the base. Dad was so proud of my brother and so pleased to see him.

Or

> After my brother finished boot camp, my dad visited him at the base. My brother was thrilled to see my dad.

Obviously, these two ways of revising result in sentences that express very different ideas. It is up to the writer to provide clear antecedents (clear pronoun references) so that the reader will understand the writer's point. So, keep in mind that you must be careful that pronouns refer directly to clear antecedents. In addition, don't use *this* to refer to complex ideas or events.

Practice #3   Oprah, A Modern Hero

The following paragraph has some unclear pronoun references and some unnecessary repetition.

- Read the paragraph aloud and listen for unclear pronoun references and repetition.
- Read the additional directions that follow the paragraph.
- On a separate piece of paper, rewrite the paragraph using pronouns and synonyms to make this paragraph clearer and less repetitive.
- Read the paragraph aloud again and notice the improvement in flow when the pronoun references are clear and there is less repetition.

> One of the most obvious signs that Oprah is a modern hero is her charitable acts. Oprah frequently gives guests on Oprah's show great gifts like pajamas, books, cameras, and even trips to Disneyland. More importantly, Oprah started the Angel Network to which people donated their spare change. With a viewing audience as large as Oprah's, Oprah collected millions of dollars and used the money for scholarships for underprivileged kids. On Oprah's own, Oprah has given hundreds of thousands of dollars to colleges and students. In a country where celebrities make so much money and yet we still have people living in poverty, I admire Oprah for this.

- Replace repetitive nouns with appropriate pronouns.
- Use "the Queen of Daytime" as a synonym for Oprah once.
- Be sure to replace "this" in the last sentence with a word or phrase that makes the meaning of the paragraph clear. Remember, writers shouldn't use *this* to refer to complex ideas or events. (You and your classmates will probably come up with different solutions and slightly different ideas of how the paragraph should end. That's okay. Discuss your ideas.)

Avoiding Pronoun Disagreement and Sexist Language

Pronouns must have clear antecedents, and the pronouns must agree in number with those antecedents. If the antecedent is singular, the pronoun

Notes

must be singular. If the antecedent is plural, the pronoun must be plural. Note that "indefinite" pronouns are always singular.

Singular Pronouns	Plural Pronouns
He, she, it	We, they
My, mine, his, hers	Their, theirs
Somebody, someone, everybody, everyone, each, neither, either, anybody, anyone	

The antecedents and pronouns are marked in the following sentences.

I consider <u>Harriet Tubman</u> a hero. She took great risks to help other people.

The underground railroad Tubman created was not really underground; it was really just a series of complex routes and "safe houses" that brought the slaves to freedom.

All of the slaves who took the underground railroad were successful. They made it to the North, and from there they could go to Canada.

An easy error to make is using *they* when the antecedent is *singular*:

A *person* doesn't have to be perfect to be a hero. *They* are human.

The antecedent to *they* in the example is *person. Person* is singular; *they* doesn't work because *they* is plural. Instead, the writer should use *he, she,* or *he or she.* Traditionally, writers have used *he* or *him* when the gender of the person is unknown. However, this can seem sexist:

An effective social worker needs to enjoy his vacation time to avoid getting burned out.

It isn't accurate to suggest that all social workers are men. To make your antecedents and pronouns agree in number *and* avoid sexist language, consider these solutions.

- Change the antecedent to plural and then use the plural pronouns *they* or *their.*

    Effective social workers need to enjoy their vacation time to avoid getting burned out.

Pronouns

- Keep the singular antecedent and use *he or she* or *his or her*.   N o t e s

An effective social worker needs to enjoy his or her vacation time to avoid getting burned out.

Occasionally, you may find that you want a singular antecedent and pronoun to make your idea clear and persuasive. In the following paragraph, using *he or she* would make the paragraph awkward and wordy because *he or she* would have to be stated so many times. Changing the antecedents and pronouns to the plural would be okay, but using a singular pronoun might make the paragraph seem less vague and more interesting. In such a case, the writer would choose either the female pronoun or the male pronoun and then stick with it.

> A teacher who wants to make a difference in students' lives must continue to learn, change, and grow. The teacher needs to take classes and attend seminars to learn new approaches to learning because researchers are always gathering new information. Updating <u>her</u> knowledge is, of course, only the first step for the dedicated teacher. <u>She</u> will have to use this knowledge by changing <u>her</u> approaches and updating <u>her</u> teaching materials. Such a teacher will have greater empathy for <u>her</u> students as they struggle to learn, for <u>she</u> will be struggling and growing right along with them.

Practice #4   Heroes and Pronouns

The following sentences have pronoun agreement problems. On a separate piece of paper, rewrite these sentences and make the changes described.

Example: A <u>person</u> who wants to be a firefighter needs to consider how <u>they</u> deal with high-pressure situations. (Revise the sentence so that both the antecedent and pronoun are plural.)

- People who want to be firefighters need to consider how they deal with high-pressure situations. (Notice that more than just the antecedent had to be changed in this sentence. *Wants* changed to *want*, *firefighter* changed to *firefighters*, and *needs* changed to *need*. Make all necessary changes in the exercises that follow.)

  1. A <u>hero</u> may go unnoticed. <u>They</u> might do wonderful things that don't make headlines. (Revise the sentences so that both the antecedent and the pronoun are plural.)

2. You may know a <u>person</u> who has helped change your neighborhood. <u>They</u> may have started a neighborhood watch program, or perhaps <u>they</u> look out for the kids in the neighborhood who have parents who work all day. (Revise the sentences so that both the antecedent and the pronouns are singular. Use *he or she* as your pronouns.)

3. This type of <u>person</u> may sacrifice many hours of <u>their</u> own time in order to keep your neighborhood happy and safe. (Revise the sentences so that both the antecedent and the pronoun are singular. Use *her* as your pronoun.)

4. <u>Someone</u> found my wallet. <u>They</u> dropped it off at my house with a note that said, "Have a nice day." (Revise the sentences so that both the antecedent and the pronoun are singular. Use *he or she* as pronouns.)

5. A <u>volunteer</u> at the animal shelter will need to be tender and strong. <u>They</u> need to care about animals but also be prepared for the sad truth that some of the animals will not survive. (Revise the sentences so that both the antecedent and the pronoun are plural.)

You and your classmates will come up with different solutions to 6–10. You may want to discuss your choices.

6. A person who volunteers their time to help clean up oil spills or other environmental hazards is a hero in my book. (Find the antecedent and pronoun that don't agree in number. Decide if they should both be plural or singular and then make the corrections.)

7. Anybody who understands this computer accounting system would be an asset to our volunteer organization. They could really help us clean up this bookkeeping mess. (Find the antecedent and pronoun that don't agree in number. Decide if they should both be plural or singular and then make the corrections.)

8. A doctor who flies to foreign countries to donate their time and help suffering people should be recognized as a hero. (Find the antecedent and pronoun that don't agree in number. Decide if they should both be plural or singular and then make the corrections.)

9. I would like to meet a politician who focuses on what their constituents want instead of what the special interest groups want. (Find the antecedent and pronoun that don't agree in number. Decide if they should both be plural or singular and then make the corrections.)

10. I don't think a person is a hero if they do a good deed only to be noticed and praised. (Find the antecedent and pronoun that don't agree in number. Decide if they should both be plural or singular and then make the corrections.)

Practice #5   Creating Sentences with Pronouns

Create the sentences described below.

1. Write two sentences, one that has an antecedent and one that uses *he* to refer to that antecedent. (Draw an arrow from *he* to the antecedent.)

2. Write two sentences, one that has an antecedent and one that uses *she* to refer to that antecedent. (Draw an arrow from *she* to the antecedent.)

3. Write two sentences, one that uses *a person* as the antecedent and one that has a pronoun that refers to *a person*. (Draw an arrow from the pronoun to the antecedent.)

4. Write two sentences, one that has an antecedent and one that uses *they* to refer to that antecedent. (Draw an arrow from *they* to the antecedent.)

PARALLELISM

Understanding and Identifying Parallel Structure
Creating Parallelism

Certain sentence structures are easier for readers to read, and these structures deliver your message more clearly. This section focuses on one such structure—*parallel structure*.

Understanding and Identifying Parallel Structure

Parallel structure is having two or more items in a sentence in similar grammatical form. For example, having a list of three *-ing* adjectives in your sentence demonstrates parallel structure. Having two infinitives in your sentence would also demonstrate parallel structure. The parallel items in the following sentence are all verb phrases.

Notes

The students were <u>discussing the general qualities of heroes</u>, <u>listing these qualities</u>, and <u>creating a definition of heroes</u>.

The parallel items in the following sentence are all *-ing* words working as subjects (gerunds).

<u>Protecting lives</u>, <u>serving others</u>, and <u>donating money</u> are all ways that a person might become a hero.

The parallel items in this sentence are all adjectives.

The film was <u>inspiring</u>, <u>frightening</u>, and <u>exciting</u>.

The parallel items in this sentence are all infinitives. The *to* is only stated once, but it works with all of the underlined words (*to help animals*, *to run in charity races*, *to donate money*).

Caroline loved <u>to help animals</u>, <u>run in charity races</u>, and <u>donate money</u>.

Practice #6   Beginning My Hero Essay

Underline the words or phrases that are parallel (similar in grammatical form). Use separate underlines for each item.

Example: The assignment requires that I define heroism, focus on one person, and prove that person is a hero.

- The assignment requires that I <u>define heroism</u>, <u>focus on one person</u>, and <u>prove that person is a hero</u>.

1. I discussed the assignment with my tutor, went to the library to do research, and started the draft.
2. My classmates said I need to make the introduction more interesting, supply more facts, and sharpen my topic sentences.
3. I had thought about writing about Jimmy Carter because he is still building houses for the poor and promoting the idea of peace.
4. I think I can find more information on the Internet, at the public library, and in my grandfather's collection of history books.
5. When I edit, I have to watch out for run-ons, comma splices, and fragments.

Creating Parallelism

When you are editing your writing, read your work aloud. Listen for awkward places and look for groups of words that you think should be parallel in form. Keep in mind that the parallel items must be similar in form but not necessarily in "size." That is, you might have three adjectives in a list; two might be single-word adjectives and one might be a multiword adjective phrase:

My father is <u>strong</u>, <u>adventurous</u>, and <u>committed to protecting the environment</u>.

The underlined items in this sentence are parallel even though one item is longer than the others.

The following examples show how to create parallel structures in the editing stage of the writing process. This first sentence does *not* have parallel structure. Look closely at the underlined parts.

Our group's mission is <u>to feed</u>, <u>house</u>, and <u>educating the homeless</u>.

The first two underlined items are infinitives:

Our group's mission is *to feed*.

Our group's mission is *to house*.

The last underlined item, *educating*, is a present participle. It ruins the parallel structure the writer started with. To make all items parallel, the writer could make the following revision:

Our group's mission is to <u>feed</u>, <u>house</u>, and <u>educate the homeless</u>.

As noted earlier, it is okay for the last underlined part to be longer than the first two. All three items are now infinitives: *to feed, to house, to educate.*

Now, consider this sentence that also does *not* have parallel structure.

She wrote an essay <u>defining heroism</u> and <u>to prove that Rosa Parks is a hero</u>.

The first part that is underlined is an adjective phrase. The second part is an infinitive phrase. To create parallelism, the writer could make both parts adjective phrases:

She wrote an essay <u>defining heroism</u> and <u>proving that Rosa Parks is a hero</u>.

You may have noticed that parallel items can share a lead-in word. For example, you don't have to repeat the *to* with infinitive phrases.

Jillian plans <u>to watch the film again</u>, <u>to take careful notes</u>, and <u>to discuss her ideas with her husband</u>.

You can write the *to* just once.

Jillian plans <u>to watch the film again</u>, <u>take careful notes</u>, and <u>discuss her ideas with her husband</u>.

Notes

Another point to keep in mind is that each item in a parallel list must fit smoothly with the words that come before the list. For example, the parallel items in the following list are all nouns (working as objects of the preposition *in*), but they *don't all fit* with the beginning of the sentence.

I found some great information in the school library, the public library, and the Internet.

You can say *in the school library* and *in the public library.* However, you can't say *in the Internet.* In this case, you would have to include the correct preposition before each noun.

I found some great information in the school library, in the public library, and on the Internet.

Practice #7 Creating Parallel Items in a List

Make the items in each group parallel in form. Discuss different solutions with classmates.

Example: drafting, revising, to edit

- drafting, revising, editing

1. on the Internet, in the encyclopedia, the new biography
2. discussing, explanation, analysis
3. escape, to succeed, hide
4. introducing, developing, conclusion
5. defining the word, to analyze his actions
6. fighting in wars, protecting U.S. citizens, to volunteer time
7. dynamic, going on adventures, brave
8. making choices, to be objective, to delete unnecessary information
9. in the newspaper, television, in the movie
10. frightening, forcefully, excite

Practice #8 Creating Parallelism in Sentences

On a separate piece of paper, rewrite the following sentences, correcting the parallelism error that is underlined.

Example: Before her famous arrest, Rosa Parks worked as a seamstress and serving as secretary for the NAACP.

Notes

- Before her famous arrest, Rosa Parks worked as a seamstress and served as secretary for the NAACP.

1. Aung San Suu Kyi is a caring mother, a skilled politician, and <u>supports only nonviolent action</u>.
2. Don Quixote is a fictional hero who fights windmills that he thinks are giants and <u>battling flocks of sheep that he thinks are armies</u>.
3. In my film class, we discussed how some heroes from films made in the 1950s were actually racist and <u>had sexist beliefs</u>.
4. In my hero essay, I need to define heroism, <u>applying this definition to one hero</u>, and stay focused on just the heroic qualities.
5. Carl has done a good job introducing his essay, stating a clear thesis, and <u>has stayed focused on his main points</u>.
6. Determined to choose an unusual hero, I searched the Internet, scoured the bookshelves at the college library, and <u>was asking my parents and grandparents for their suggestions</u>.
7. My goal with this essay is to improve my focus, devote more time to revising, and <u>editing carefully</u>.
8. <u>To participate in class discussions</u>, brainstorming, and planning have helped me come up with a good topic and stay focused on my topic.
9. To learn more about Gandhi, I watched a film, studied a few encyclopedia articles, and <u>was looking at Internet articles</u>.
10. My great grandfather helped feed, clothe, and <u>was hiding slaves</u>.

Practice #9 Adding a Parallel Item

On a separate piece of paper, rewrite the following sentences, inserting parallel items. (You will be inserting single words or phrases. Do not insert independent clauses.)

- Underline each parallel item in each sentence.
- Compare your answers with your classmates' answers. Discuss the differences.

Example: Not intending to eavesdrop, Clara listened to the single dad next door talking on the phone and _____ to someone that he didn't have any money for Christmas this year.

Parallelism

Notes

- Not intending to eavesdrop, Clara listened to the single dad next door <u>talking</u> on the phone and <u>explaining</u> to someone that he didn't have any money for Christmas this year. (The words *lamenting* or *complaining* would also have worked. In fact, there are a number of ways to complete this sentence.)

1. After hearing the conversation, Clara felt depressed and _____.

2. The young children deserved to _____ toys and enjoy the holiday season.

3. On a limited budget herself, Clara knew that she could only buy a few decorations and _____.

4. She decided to _____ a few neighbors, _____ some money, and surprise the little family.

5. Every neighbor she spoke with responded with joy and _____.

6. Making a detailed plan for decorating, the neighbors planned to buy Christmas lights, a tree, and _____.

7. Next they divided up the tasks of shopping for presents, _____ the house, and _____ the presents.

8. The family was thrilled when they returned home one day to find their house decorated with lights and their porch _____ with presents.

9. To top off the surprise, the neighbors came over with freshly baked _____ and homemade _____.

10. Later that evening the father said to Clara, "You are my hero for _____ of us and _____ so much time and energy to give my kids a Christmas they will never forget."

Practice #10   Sentence Combining and Parallelism

Parallel structures can help you avoid repetition. In the following exercises, cross out the words that don't need to be repeated and then create one sophisticated sentence using the joining word in parentheses. (Remember, Punctuation Rule #1 states that you must put commas between items in a series. See page 115 for a review of Punctuation Rule #1.)

Example:

A hero should be selfless.
A hero should be honest.
A hero should be courageous. (and)

• A hero should be selfless.
• ~~A hero should be~~ honest.
• ~~A hero should be~~ courageous. (and)
• A hero should be selfless, honest, and courageous.

1. Did you define heroism?
   Did you explain how your hero fits the definition?
   Did you provide details and examples? (and)

2. I discussed his childhood.
   I discussed his teen years.
   I discussed his adult years. (and)

3. Sheila found my introduction interesting.
   Sheila found my conclusion boring. (but)

4. The tutor asked me to clarify my definition of hero.
   The tutor asked me to add a few more examples.
   The tutor asked me to leave out the quote in paragraph four. (and)

5. I hate deleting ideas from my draft.
   I know that it is necessary. (but)

6. Parents should teach their kids the importance of volunteering.
   Parents should teach their kids the importance of speaking up for the underprivileged.
   Parents should teach their kids the importance of protecting the young. (and)

7. My children must call their grandparents once a week.
   My children must complete one community service project a year.
   My children must donate 10 percent of their weekly allowance to charity. (and)

8. Does a person become a hero on purpose?

Style Tips

Notes

> Does a person become a hero by chance?
>
> Does a person become a hero through fate? (or)
>
> 9. In the film *Hero*, Bernie LaPlante is funny.
>
> In the film *Hero*, Bernie LaPlante is not very likeable. (but)
>
> 10. Can a person be heroic once?
>
> Can a person be nonheroic the rest of the time? (but)

Practice #11   Create Original Parallelism

Create five sentences that demonstrate your knowledge of parallelism. (The sentences can be on different topics.) Underline each parallel item in each sentence.

STYLE TIPS

In this chapter, you have learned to use pronouns accurately and effectively. You have also practiced creating parallel structure in your sentences. Pronouns and parallelism will both help you follow Style Tips #2, #3, and #4.

Style Tip #2 (Review)
Don't use more words than needed.

Style Tip #3 (Review)
Add variety to your sentence structure.

Style Tip #4 (Review)
Provide the necessary connections between ideas and show how ideas relate to one another.

Practice #12   Editing, Pronouns, and Parallelism

Edit the following paragraph and apply Style Tips #2, #3, and #4 by using pronouns and parallelism effectively. You will find that the writer did not use enough pronouns, so the sentences sound a bit choppy and repetitive. You will also find sentences that are not grammatically correct because they have lists of items that are not parallel in structure yet. Finally, you'll find more words than you really need. By using a parallel structure, you can turn three sentences into one. (Rewrite your improved paragraph on another sheet of paper and compare your edited piece with a classmate's.)

> My girls, ages 2, 2, and 5, love Mulan, the lead character in Disney's film *Mulan*. A young Chinese girl, Mulan pretends to be a boy and, to the horror of Mulan's family, dresses as a soldier and running off to fight the Huns in Mulan's father's place. To bring honor to Mulan's family, Mulan is supposed to be a traditional Chinese young lady—feminine, quiet, beautiful, and shows skill in womanly tasks like serving tea and cooking. Mulan, however, is outspoken. Mulan is athletic. Mulan is headstrong. Mulan has Mulan's own ideas, and Mulan pursues them against many odds. Compared to some of the other "heroes" my girls have taken a liking to—Batgirl, Snow White, and Sleeping Beauty—I like Mulan quite a bit. I consider Mulan to be a positive role model.

Practice #13   Editing and Parallelism

In this paragraph, focus on the last three sentences, which contain too many words. Apply your knowledge of parallel structure and Style Tip #2 and turn those last three sentences into one clear, powerful sentence. (Rewrite your new, improved paragraph on another sheet of paper.)

> Yet, the girls know (especially my 5-year-old) that Mulan is "pretend," and as Dennis Denenberg, a professor of education at Millersville University of Pennsylvania points out, children need real heroes—people, not fictional characters. My girls should learn about other heroes, people who have lived. They should learn about people who have accomplished great deeds. They should learn about people who have made our world a better place.

Your Own Writing: Pronouns and Parallelism

Copy down a piece of your writing. (A journal entry is fine, but a paragraph from your hero essay would be even better.) Underline all the pronouns that you use. Check your use of pronouns. Correct any errors you find. (Keep an eye out for agreement errors and sexist language.) Should you replace any nouns with pronouns or synonyms to add clarity and variety and to improve coherence?

Style Tips

Notes

Also look for places where parallel structure could make your paragraph easier to read and less wordy. Pay close attention to any sentences that have two or more items in a series. Revise your paragraph.

Using **Connections** *Online with* **my**writing**lab**

For more practice with pronouns and parallelism, log onto www .mywritinglab.com to access the online resources for *Connections,* Third Edition.

CHAPTER 6

Writing About Television and the Media

Main Topics

- Developing your writing

- Evaluating the effects of television and the media

- Creating more expressive sentences with adjectives, adverbs, and prepositional phrases

JUMPSTART by Robb Armstrong

Copyright United Feature Syndicate Inc.

Notes

Essay assignments, like blueprints, are designed to guide students in developing their essays. An assignment outlines a basic plan for completing an essay, but it's up to the student to take that plan and build on it. In the same way that a building contractor transforms blueprints into a building, a writer focuses on the plan, organizes the development of the project, and then moves the project through different levels of development until it reaches completion.

Development is the process of moving from a basic idea to a fully expressive, well-supported main idea that communicates to a specific audience for a specific purpose. Although you have been practicing some forms of development through the lists, charts, journals, workshop questions, paragraphs, and essays you've written in earlier chapters, this chapter will teach you specific strategies for further developing your essay ideas as you write about the effects of television and the media on the family.

DEVELOPING YOUR WRITING

When writing a paper, it's possible to follow an assignment and give just enough information to prove the thesis. This kind of a paper usually leaves the reader wanting more. A developed essay, however, offers more than just the facts. It interests, persuades, enlightens, informs, or delights the reader because of the choices made by the writer, choices that enrich the writing and compel the reader to read. Such writing may contain a single, detailed, thoughtful example, or it might contain a layering of several examples, depending on the point the writer wants to make. The developed piece of writing also has a strong voice, one that says, "Listen to me. I have something important to say." In developing a piece of writing, the writer anticipates the reader's needs, supplies enough evidence to prove the main point, and expresses her opinion in a distinct voice.

As you have written your essays, you have been practicing several forms of essay development already. If you *analyzed* advertisements to explain how a particular ad worked, you practiced a form of development. Whenever you have *added examples* to support your paragraphs in your essays, you have practiced another form of development. As you began to *include your own opinion* and *explain your position* on an issue, you developed your essay. In *using and citing sources*, you practiced development. In fact, wherever you have added examples, made comparisons, offered research data, or shared personal experience that related directly to your thesis, you have developed your writing.

Examining Developed Paragraphs

In a developed paragraph, the writer includes evidence, analysis, and detail that support the topic sentence and enrich the paragraph discussion. Sometimes examples appear layered as the writer builds on the paragraph's main idea. This kind of paragraph communicates the main idea to the audience through precise examples, careful wording, and clear structure. In the examples that follow, you will see how experienced writers constructed well-developed paragraphs.

> Television is the most popular of the popular media. Indeed, if Nielsen research and other studies are correct, there are few things that Americans do more than they watch television. On average, each household has a TV on almost fifty hours a week. Forty percent of households eat dinner with the set on. Individually, Americans watch an average of thirty hours a week. We begin peering at TV through the bars of cribs and continue looking at it through the cataracts of old age.
>
> —*Joshua Meyrowitz, from "Television: The Shared Arena"*

You may have noticed that Joshua Meyrowitz's paragraph isn't long, yet it includes enough interesting information and focused support to prove his topic sentence—"Television is the most popular of the popular media." Though a well-developed piece of writing is usually longer than an undeveloped piece, the term *development* doesn't necessarily suggest length. It refers more to the choices made by the writer that enrich his writing and help prove the main idea.

One choice Meyrowitz made is to follow his topic sentence with statistics that will make the reader stop and think. It's shocking, for instance, to think that in the average household, the television is on almost 50 hours a week. That means that the television runs longer than most people's work week. Before the reader has a chance to react to this fact, Meyrowitz offers a second, even more sobering fact to reinforce the first. On the average, most individuals watch 30 hours of television per week. If statistics alone are not enough to convince you that television is the most popular form of media, the writer takes another approach, employing a creative example to make his point when he concludes that most people begin watching television as babies and continue watching into old age. If you take a moment to reflect on this

Notes

idea in terms of hours of viewing over a lifetime, then you would probably have to agree with Meyrowitz that television is more popular than any of the other popular media. Indeed, Meyrowitz makes a powerful statement about television by backing his topic sentence with statistics and a creative example.

Here is another well-developed paragraph.

Get Involved!

Read Christenson and Ivancin's full report on reality television at http://www.kff.org/entmedia/7567.cfm. Come to class prepared to discuss how the authors supported and developed their discussion of the effects of reality television on viewers.

All television conveys information, and reality TV is no exception. Moreover, a good deal of the information is potentially useful to the average viewer. For example, even though it unquestionably dwells primarily on the entertainment generated by its competitive elements, *The Biggest Loser* nonetheless conveys information about the role of diet and different types of exercise in weight loss. Even more information appears in the specialty cable shows *Honey We're Killing the Kids* and *Weighing In*. In *Honey*, a nutritionist convinces overweight, sedentary families to make lifestyle changes designed to make everybody (but especially the kids) healthier. In one episode, as the nutritionist helps the family clear the refrigerator of junk food, she finds a package of hot dogs and says: "Do you have any idea what's in these hot dogs? They're about 80% fat and loaded with salt!" She then talks about the connection of such foods to the father's Type II diabetes. (In contrast, the episodes of iTV's smoking-related *Cold Turkey* contained almost no information about the effects of tobacco use.)

—*Peter Christenson and Maria Ivancin, from*
The "Reality" of Health: Reality Television and the Public Health,
a discussion paper prepared for the Kaiser Family Foundation, 2006

Peter Christenson and Maria Ivancin rely on specific examples to make their point that reality television can, and sometimes does, offer helpful information to viewers. However, instead of layering statistics like Meyrowitz did in his paragraph, these authors layer examples in theirs. First, they introduce *The Biggest Loser* as a program that provides general information on diet, exercise, and weight loss. Second, they present a pair of "specialty" cable shows that contain more specific information about making significant lifestyle changes. They build on this example by offering a quotation that shows the type of help nutritionists share with families on these programs. Christenson and Ivancin end the paragraph with a contrasting example of a program that offers less health information to viewers.

Here is a third effectively developed paragraph.

Americans spend an enormous amount of time watching, listening to, or reading . . . various forms of media. The increases in media options in recent years has even led to an increase in "multitasking"—using more than one form of media at a time. Americans have about 7 hours of "leisure" time per day and about two-thirds of that time—more than 4 1/2 hours—is spent with mass media. Of this media time, about two-thirds—or about 3 hours—is spent watching television (PR Newservice Association, 2000). Over the course of a year, 3 hours a day adds up to 45 days of TV viewing! Imagine someone sitting in front of a television set 24 hours a day for a month and a half! Every year, that's how much TV the typical American watches. Of course, this accounts only for television viewing. If you add the time we spend listening to the radio, playing CDs, reading, surfing the Net, and using other media, it is easy to see that near-constant exposure to media is a fundamental part of contemporary life. Indeed, some argue that the media have become the dominant social institution in contemporary society, supplanting the older institutions such as the educational system and religion.

—David R. Croteau and William Hoynes, from
Media/Society: Industries, Images and Audiences, *2003*

In this paragraph from their book, which focuses on media and its effects on society, David Croteau and William Hoynes ask readers to think about how much time Americans spend with media and the potential effects of heavy media use. They present data on television viewing trends, helping the reader see the data from both a daily and yearly perspective. Then, building on their readers' growing awareness, the authors list the many other forms of media people may spend time with every day. Croteau and Hoynes have a reason for developing their paragraph. They're hoping to raise their readers' level of concern not only about media use, but also about how media may be replacing other social institutions.

Activity

Examining Developed Paragraphs

Think about the ways in which Meyrowitz, Christenson and Ivancin, and Croteau and Hoynes developed their paragraphs about television and media use.

1. Read each paragraph a second time.

2. In the "Notes" column, label the topic sentence(s) in each as well as the types of support (such as statistics, examples, and studies) used to prove each paragraph idea.

3. Write what you have learned about development from these paragraphs. Think about how the writers used precise examples, careful wording, and clear structure. At this point, how would you define *development?*

Using the Questions for Development

Writers interested in developing their paragraph (or essay) ideas fully often rely on a series of questions known as the **Questions for Development.** These common questions simply help remind writers to make sure they've answered all the reader's questions in their paragraphs (or essays). The questions are listed here for you to refer to as you write and revise.

WHO?	Who is involved?
	Who is affected?
	Who is interested?
	Who is my audience?
	Who believes this?
	Who said this?
WHAT?	What happened?
	What are the main issues?
	What else does my reader need to know?
	What can I explain further?
WHEN?	When did it happen?
	When is it a problem?
	When will it occur again?
	When will it be resolved?
WHERE?	Where did it occur?
	Where were the participants?
WHY?	Why is the issue important?
	Why did it happen this way?
	Why should you or I care?
	Why should my audience care?
HOW?	How did it happen?
	How does it work?
	How can the problem be resolved?

Asking these questions helps writers make sure they have fully explained, explored, and supported their paragraph ideas (or essay ideas). You may apply these Questions for Development at any stage of the writing process.

Activity

Your Favorite Television Series or Video Game

Using the Questions for Development, describe your favorite television pro-gram or video game in a paragraph (or two). Your goal is to develop your paragraph, making it so interesting that your reader will want to watch the program or play the game. If you write about a television series, be sure to tell when it's on, who's in it, what happens in a typical episode, where it's set (location), why you like it, how you first heard about it, and why you began to watch it. For a video game, include a description of the game and how to play it, how many players are involved, what kind of graphics are used, and what the object of the game is.

1. Rather than beginning your paragraph with the typical—"My favorite program or game is . . ."—spend a few minutes creating a topic sen-tence that will draw the reader's interest. Consider the following be-ginnings:

   - For those who love drama, [name of show] is worth watching.

   - Looking for action? Then you must play [name of game] . . .

   - Consistently funny, [name of show] . . .

2. As you support your topic sentence, you should try to anticipate your reader's questions and answer them fully.

3. Ask a classmate to read your paragraph(s) and identify any of the Questions for Development that haven't yet been answered.

4. Revise your paragraph, being sure to supply any missing information.

Examining a Developed Essay

Like the developed paragraph, the developed essay includes evidence, analysis, and details that help support the main idea and enrich the dis-cussion. The developed essay, however, is different from the developed paragraph because it addresses more than one significant point.

In developing the essay, the writer uses the same writing process practiced in the previous chapters. Naturally, the writer spends time brainstorming. Then, after discussion and research, she narrows the field of topics to a single topic of interest. From there, she creates a

Notes

thesis for her essay and then a list of ideas to support that thesis. She develops the most important ideas into body paragraphs when she drafts her essay.

After determining which ideas to develop into paragraphs, the writer considers which examples, studies, statistics, experiences, and other forms of evidence would best fit in these body paragraphs. As she drafts her essay, she strives to achieve a balance of evidence and discussion in each body paragraph. For example, if she includes a quotation by an expert, she follows that quotation with a sentence or two of explanation to help the reader understand the expert's opinion and to reinforce the particular paragraph idea. In doing so, she also reinforces the thesis of the essay. As she builds well-developed paragraphs that support the thesis, she achieves a well-developed essay containing a balance of evidence, carefully selected details, and discussion.

Activity

Study a Developed Essay

In the essay below, sociologist Ulla G. Foehr examines the factors that lead to an increase in media multitasking (using more than one form of media at the same time) among teens.

Predictors: Who Is Media Multitasking?
by Ulla G. Foehr

Foehr, a sociologist and media researcher, writes frequently about media and their effects on children. The following excerpt is from a multichapter research study written for The Henry J. Kaiser Family Foundation titled, *Media Multitasking among American Youth: Prevalence, Predictors, and Pairings.*

1   Before looking at how media affect teen behavior, it is critical to understand which teens multitask and with which media. Are all young people equally likely to media multitask, or do some have a higher propensity than others? This issue interests not only media scholars, but also media corporations and advertisers trying to capture the teen market.

2   . . . If all things are equal, adolescents who are exposed to more media are more likely to media multitask. This was an expected outcome [of the study]. As kids add more media activities to their limited free time, they must media multitask in order to accommodate them. In a

previous study (Roberts & Foehr, 2004), youths who were high users of print, computer or television spent more time with other media than youths who were moderate or low users of each of those media. In order for youths to spend such large amounts of time with media, some of that time must have been spent media multitasking. The authors hypothesized that those high media users were the ones most likely to multitask their media use.

3   Interestingly, computer placement near a television close enough to view TV from the computer is another strong predictor of media multitasking. . . . This predictor speaks to "opportunity" to multitask. Hence, simply the addition of a TV in the vicinity of the computer increases media multitasking.

4   Young people who like risk and adventure and are "sensation seekers" are more likely to media multitask. Sensation seekers are averse to boredom and generally seek adventure and exciting experiences. It follows, then, that sensation seekers are more likely to have multiple media "balls" in the air at any one time.

5   Young people who live in a highly television-oriented household are also more likely to media multitask. Households characterized as highly TV-oriented have no rules about TV, usually watch during meals and often leave the TV on regardless of whether anyone is watching. These circumstances naturally increase opportunity to media multitask.

6   Girls are more likely to media multitask than are boys. This may not come as a surprise given the general assumption that women are superior multitaskers (O'Connell, 2002; Shellenbarger, undated). Women have larger prefrontal cortexes (the part of the brain responsible for multitasking) and some suggest women's brain architecture makes them better multitaskers (Fisher, 1999). Evolutionary psychology makes the argument that women need to be better multitaskers; women's evolutionary role, caring for offspring, required that they juggle multiple activities, and those who were successful survived (Ellison, 2005). Girls today, perhaps genetically primed for it, multitask what is at the center of their environment: media. In fact, little research exists on multitasking proficiency; though research does confirm that women do multitask slightly more often (Schneider & Waite, 2005), there is very little research to support the idea that women are actually "better" multitaskers than men (Mahany, 2005). Nonetheless, the data analyzed for this report indicate that adolescent girls do spend more of their media time multitasking. This could have more to do with the media activities they choose (IM [instant messaging], email, websites and music) than with some inherent ability or drive to multitask.

Notes

Notes

7   Finally, not having a computer (compared to those who have a computer but cannot see a television) seems to be associated with less media multitasking, as would be expected given the role of the computer in providing opportunities to media multitask. . . .

8   Also noteworthy are the characteristics that did not influence media multitasking—the null findings. Race, age, income and education, often predictors of media use, were not significant predictors in this model. While race, age, income and education may predict media use, they do not appear to indicate the likelihood to media multitask. . . .

1. Reread the essay. Define any unknown terms. Now highlight the thesis sentence(s) in the opening paragraph. (At least a portion of the thesis here appears in question form.) In your notebook, write a sentence or two explaining what Foehr plans to prove in her essay.

2. Now move through paragraphs 2–8 and highlight topic sentences. In your notebook, explain what Foehr focuses on each paragraph. Then explain how each paragraph helps support the thesis.

3. In your notebook, list the kinds of support Foehr uses to develop each paragraph idea.

4. In which paragraph does Foehr offer the best balance of evidence and discussion? Explain how evidence and discussion develop that paragraph point.

5. Which paragraph contains the most effective detail? Explain how the detail helps develop that paragraph point.

6. Based on what you've learned in this segment of the chapter, how would you describe a well-developed essay?

DEVELOPING THE FOCUSED ESSAY

As you focus and develop your essays in this chapter, you will continue to engage in the same productive writing-reading-critical thinking process you have been practicing. Before you write, you'll read, discuss, think critically, brainstorm, research, and observe. You'll spend time gathering information, examining research, and analyzing studies. You'll think about personal experiences. In fact, having some of this material early in the process helps you consider your options and gives you a pool of information and research from which to draw support when developing your essay idea. Once you have determined your essay's focus, you'll begin the process of organizing and thinking critically about what information to include when developing your essay.

Points to Remember About Development

- Explore ideas and then narrow your focus before worrying about development. An idea is only worth developing if it is focused.
- Construct a thesis for your essay and decide what main points you'll need to address in body paragraphs in order to sufficiently support your thesis.
- Use examples, studies, statistics, experiences, and other forms of evidence to develop paragraphs and support the thesis of your essay.
- Include *only* the pieces of evidence that help you develop paragraph ideas and support the thesis of your essay.
- Create a balance between examples and discussion in your paragraphs.
- Include your own opinion and analysis of research, ideas, and issues.
- Include creative sentences and examples that help develop ideas.
- Use the Questions for Development to help you fully develop ideas.

INVESTIGATING THE EFFECTS OF TELEVISION

Most Americans living today grew up with a television in the home. In fact, ninety-nine out of one hundred American families own at least one television set, and many families own two or more. As a result of cable, some Americans have access to more than 250 stations on a daily basis. And in most households, the television is on for the better part of the day. Can so much exposure to television be good for us?

Discuss and Engage

Many experts are concerned over the possible negative effects of television on children and the family. Some believe that television has taken over families, stripping them of valuable time they once spent reading or interacting with each other. Others warn that children are being exposed to too much violence and sex via the screen. However,

Notes

other experts assert that television can have a positive impact if used as an educational tool or if monitored by responsible parents.

Journal Assignment

TV Violence

Return to the cartoon *JumpStart* on page 237. In writing, describe the cartoon for someone who hasn't seen it. Then explain the point cartoonist Robb Armstrong is making and your reaction to it. Consider these questions as you develop your response:

- Who is engaged in conversation in the comic strip? Where is the conversation taking place? What is the conversation about?
- What clues help the reader understand the cartoonist's message?
- Can you explain the cartoonist's humor? Why might the cartoon be considered funny?

Journal Assignment

TV Yesterday and Today

Thinking back to your childhood, you can probably remember watching a favorite program. Perhaps you grew up watching *The Fresh Prince of Bel-Air* or *The Wonder Years*. Or maybe as a young child you watched *Sesame Street* or *Mister Rogers' Neighborhood*.

1. Describe your early television viewing experiences. What programs did you watch as a child? Why? Describe your favorite program. Who starred in it? Where was it set? What happened during a typical episode?

2. Overall, do you believe you were influenced in a positive way by your early experiences watching television? Explain. Do you think your viewing experiences as a child had a negative effect? Explain. (If you didn't watch television as a youngster, explain what other activities took its place and their effects on you.)

3. Now describe your current television viewing experiences. What programs are you drawn to now? Why? Describe your favorite program.

4. In general, in what ways has television changed since your childhood? Are these changes positive or negative? Explain. (This journal is for your eyes only. Refer back to it when you begin to write your television essay.)

Writing Assignment #1: The Effects of Television

Here, in brief, is the writing assignment you are preparing for.

Write an essay in which you argue for or against Marie Winn's view of television and its effect on children and the family.

Read, Discuss, Think Critically

This section of the chapter offers you a single reading. It's a lengthy excerpt from a book, so plan your reading time well. The reading is organized with eight subheadings that have been numbered and appear in boldface print.

Reading Assignment: "The Trouble with Television"

Preview   Read the title, introductory material, and the eight subheadings in bold.

Anticipate   What do you anticipate this excerpt will be about? Use the "Notes" column to record your thoughts.

Read and Reread   Read the entire excerpt, being careful to highlight unknown terms and interesting points. Then reread more slowly and respond to the writing in the "Notes" column. Mark important points and define unknown terms.

The Trouble with Television
by Marie Winn

Marie Winn, mother of two and author of *Unplugging the Plug-In Drug* (1987), is known for her concern over television and its effect on the family. In this chapter from her book, she argues there are "eight significant ways" television affects children and families. She suggests that all families try a "No-TV Week" to break the TV habit.

Most Parents Worry About TV—But Not for the Right Reasons

My parents don't think I should watch as much TV as I do. They think a lot of the programs I watch are meaningless.

—*Fifth grader, P.S. 84, No-TV Week*

1   Of all the wonders of modern technology that have transformed family life during the last century, television stands alone as a universal source of parental anxiety. Few parents worry about how the electric light or the automobile or the telephone might alter their children's development. But most parents do worry about TV.

Notes

2   Parents worry most of all about the programs their children watch. If only these weren't so violent, so sexually explicit, so cynical, so *unsuitable,* if only they were more innocent, more educational, more *worthwhile.*

3   Imagine what would happen if suddenly, by some miracle, the only programs available on all channels at all hours of day and night were delightful, worthwhile shows that children love and parents wholeheartedly approve. Would this eliminate the nagging anxiety about television that troubles so many parents today?

4   For most families, the answer is no. After all, if programs were the only problem, there would be an obvious solution: turn the set off. The fact that parents leave the sets on even when they are distressed about programs reveals that television serves a number of purposes that have nothing to do with the programs on the screen.

5   Great numbers of parents today see television as a way to make child-rearing less burdensome. In the absence of Mother's Helper (a widely used nineteenth-century patent medicine that contained a hefty dose of the narcotic laudanum), there is nothing that keeps children out of trouble as reliably as "plugging them in."

6   Television serves families in other ways: as a time-filler ("You have nothing to do? Go watch TV"), a tranquilizer ("When the kids come home from school they're so keyed up that they need to watch for a while to simmer down"), a problem solver ("Kids, stop fighting. It's time for your program"), a procrastination device ("I'll just watch one more program before I do my homework"), a punishment ("If you don't stop teasing your little sister, no TV for a week"), and a reward ("If you get an A on your composition you can watch an extra hour of TV"). For parents and children alike it serves as an avoidance mechanism ("I can't discuss that now—I'm watching my program"), a substitute friend ("I need the TV on for company"), and an escape mechanism ("I'll turn on the TV and try to forget my worries").

7   Most families recognize the wonderful services that television has to offer. Few, however, are aware that there are eight significant ways television wields a negative influence on children and family life:

1. TV Keeps Families from Doing Other Things

The primary danger of the television screen lies not so much in the behavior it produces— although there is danger there—as in the behavior it prevents: the talks, the games, the family festivities and arguments through which much of the child's learning takes place and through which his character is formed. Turning on the television set can turn off the process that transforms children into people.[1]

---

[1]Urie Bronfenbrenner, "Who Cares for America's Children?" Address presented at the Conference of the National Association for the Education of Young Children, 1970.

8   Urie Bronfenbrenner's words to a conference of educators almost two decades ago focus on what sociologists call the "reduction effects" of television—its power to preempt and often eliminate a whole range of other activities and experiences. While it is easy to see that for a child who watches 32 hours of television each week, the reduction effects are significant—obviously that child would be spending 32 hours doing *something* else if there were no television available—Bronfenbrenner's view remains an uncommon and even an eccentric one.

9   Today the prevailing focus remains on improving programs rather than on reducing the amount of time children view. Perhaps parents have come to depend so deeply on television that they are afraid even to contemplate the idea that something might be wrong with their use of television, not merely with the programs on the air.

2. TV Is a Hidden Competitor for All Other Activities

Now that I couldn't watch TV I thought of other things to do. I read all the books that I had classified as "boring" and discovered how good they really were.
                                                                —*Sixth grader, Marshall, Missouri, Turn-Off*

10   Almost everybody knows that there are better, more fulfilling things for a family to do than watch television. And yet, if viewing statistics are to be believed, most families spend most of their family time together in front of the flickering screen.

11   Some social critics believe that television has come to dominate family life because today's parents are too selfish and narcissistic to put in the effort that reading aloud or playing games or even just talking to each other would require. But this harsh judgment doesn't take into consideration the extraordinary power of television. In reality, many parents crave a richer family life and are eager to work at achieving this goal. The trouble is that their children seem to reject all those fine family alternatives in favor of television.

12   To be sure, the fact that children are likely to choose watching television over having a story read aloud to them, or playing with the stamp collection, or going out for a walk in the park does not mean that watching television is actually more entertaining or gratifying than any of these activities. It does mean, however, that watching television is easier.

13   In most families, television is always there as an easy and safe competitor. When another activity is proposed, it had better be really special; otherwise it is in danger of being rejected. The parents who have unsuccessfully proposed a game or a story end up feeling rejected as well. They are unaware that television is still affecting their children's enjoyment of other activities, even when the set is off.

14   Reading aloud is a good example of how this competition factor works. Virtually every child expert hails reading aloud as a delightful family pastime. Educators encourage it as an important way for parents to help their children develop a love for reading and improve their reading skills. Too often, however, the fantasy of the happy family gathered around to listen to a story is replaced by a different reality: "Hey kids, I've got a great book to read aloud. How about it?" says the parent. "Not now, Dad, we want to watch 'The Cosby Show,'" say the kids.

15   It is for this reason that one of the most important *Don'ts* suggested by Jim Trelease in his valuable guide *The Read-Aloud Handbook* is the following:

> Don't try to compete with television. If you say, "Which do you want, a story or TV?" they will usually choose the latter. That is like saying to a 9-year-old, "Which do you want, vegetables or a donut?" Since *you* are the adult, *you* choose. "The television goes off at eight-thirty in this house. If you want a story before bed, that's fine. If not, that's fine too. But no television after eight-thirty." But don't let books appear to be responsible for depriving children of viewing time.[2]

3. TV Allows Kids to Grow Up Less Civilized

The Turn-Off showed us parents that we can say "no" without so many objections from the kids.

—*Mother, Buffalo, New York, Great TV Turn-Off*

16   It would be a mistake to assume that the basic childrearing philosophy of parents of the past was stricter than that of parents today. American parents, in fact, have always had a tendency to be more egalitarian in their family life than, say, European parents. For confirmation, one has only to read the accounts of eighteenth- or nineteenth-century European travelers who comment on the freedom and audacity of American children as compared to their European counterparts. Why then do parents today seem far less in control of their children than parents not only of the distant past but even of a mere generation ago? Television has surely played a part in the change.

17   Today's parents universally use television to keep their children occupied when they have work to do or when they need a break from child care. They can hardly imagine how parents survived before television. Yet parents did survive in the years before TV. Without television, they simply had to use different survival strategies to be able to cook dinner, talk on the telephone, clean house, or do whatever work needed to be done in peace.

---

[2]Jim Trelease, *The Read-Aloud Handbook* (Penguin, 1985).

18   Most of these strategies fell into the category social scientists refer to as "socialization"—the civilizing process that transforms small creatures intent upon the speedy gratification of their own instinctive needs and desires into successful members of a society in which those individual needs and desires must often be left ungratified, at least temporarily, for the good of the group.

19   What were these "socialization" strategies parents used to use? Generally, they went something like this: "Mommy's got to cook dinner now (make a phone call, talk to Mrs. Jones, etc.). Here are some blocks (some clay, a pair of blunt scissors and a magazine, etc.). Now you have to be a good girl and play by yourself for a while and not interrupt Mommy." Nothing very complicated.

20   But in order to succeed, a certain firmness was absolutely necessary, and parents knew it, even if asserting authority was not their preferred way of dealing with children. They knew they had to work steadily at "training" their child to behave in ways that allowed them to do those normal things that needed to be done. Actually, achieving this goal was not terribly difficult. It took a little effort to set up certain patterns— perhaps a few days or a week of patient but firm insistence that the child behave in certain ways at certain times. But parents of the past didn't agonize about whether this was going to be psychologically damaging. They simply had no choice. Certain things simply *had to be done,* and so parents stood their ground against children's natural struggle to gain attention and have their own way.

21   Obviously it is easier to get a break from child care by setting the child in front of the television set than to teach the child to play alone for certain periods of time. In the first case, the child is immediately amused (or hypnotized) by the program, and the parent has time to pursue other activities. Accustoming children to play alone, on the other hand, requires day-after-day perseverance, and neither parent nor child enjoys the process very much.

22   But there is an inevitable price to pay when a parent never has to be firm and authoritative, never has to use that "I mean business" tone of voice: socialization, that crucial process so necessary for the child's future as a successful member of a family, a school, a community, and a nation is accomplished less completely. A very different kind of relationship between parent and child is established, one in which the parent has little control over the child's behavior.

23   The consequences of a large-scale reduction in child socialization are not hard to see in contemporary society: an increased number of parents who feel helpless and out of control of their children's lives and behavior, who haven't established the parental authority that might

protect their children from involvement in such dangerous activities as drug experimentation, or from the physical and emotional consequences of precocious sexual relationships.

4. Television Takes the Place of Play

I always used to turn the TV on for my 2 1/2-year-old son Alexander in the morning. Then I noticed during No-TV week that he played in a different way all morning. He seemed less irritable—in a better mood—everything was entirely different. I realized it wasn't Alexander who wanted to watch TV—it was I who needed to turn it on for him.
—Parent, P.S. 84, New York City, No-TV Week

24   Once small children become able to concentrate on television and make some sense of it—usually around the end of their second year of life—it's not hard to understand why parents eagerly set their children before the flickering screen: taking care of toddlers is hard! The desperate and tired parent can't imagine *not* taking advantage of this marvelous new way to get a break. In consequence, before they are three years old, the opportunities of active play and exploration are hugely diminished for a great number of children—to be replaced by the hypnotic gratification of television viewing.

25   Yet many parents overlook an important fact: children who are suddenly able to sustain attention for more than a few minutes on the TV screen have clearly moved into a new stage of cognitive development—their ability to concentrate on TV is a sign of it. There are therefore many other new activities, far more developmentally valuable, that the child is now ready for. These are the simple forms of play that most small children enjoyed in the pre-television era: cutting and pasting, coloring and drawing, building with blocks, playing games of make-believe with toy soldiers or animals or dolls. But the parent who begins to fill in the child's time with television at this point is unlikely to discover these other potential capabilities.

26   It requires a bit of effort to establish new play routines—more effort, certainly, than plunking a child in front of a television screen, but not really a great deal. It requires a bit of patience to get the child accustomed to a new kind of play—play on his own—but again, not a very great deal. It also demands some firmness and perseverance. And a small amount of equipment (art materials, blocks, etc.), most of it cheap, if not free, and easily available.

27   But the benefits for both parent and child of *not* taking the easiest way out at this point by using television to ease the inevitable child-care burdens will vastly outweigh the temporary difficulties parents face in filling children's time with less passive activities. For the parent, the need for a bit more firmness leads to an easier, more controlled parent-child relationship.

For the child, those play routines established in early childhood will develop into lifelong interests and hobbies, while the skills acquired in the course of play lead to a sense of accomplishment that could never have been achieved if the child had spent those hours "watching" instead of "doing."

5. TV Makes Children Less Resourceful

Tuesday I got home from school and didn't get to watch any of those old reruns that I've seen a hundred times before. I did my homework right after school, then I practiced my clarinet and guitar.

—High school student, Richmond, Indiana, Turn-Off

28   Many parents who welcome the idea of turning off the TV and spending more time with the family are still worried that without TV they would constantly be on call as entertainers for their children. Though they *want* to play games and read aloud to their children, the idea of having to replace television minute-for-minute with worthwhile family activities is daunting. They remember thinking up all sorts of things to do when they were kids. But their own kids seem different, less resourceful, somehow. When there's nothing to do, these parents observe regretfully, their kids seem unable to come up with anything to do besides turning on the TV.

29   One father, for example, says, "When I was a kid, we were always thinking up things to do, projects and games. We certainly never whined to our parents, 'I have nothing to do!'" He compares this with his own children today: "They're simply lazy. If someone doesn't entertain them, they'll happily sit there watching TV all day."

30   There is one word for this father's disappointment: unfair. It is as if he were disappointed in them for not reading Greek though they have never studied the language. He deplores his children's lack of inventiveness, as if the ability to play were something innate that his children are missing. In fact, while the *tendency* to play is built into the human species, the actual *ability* to play—to imagine, to invent, to elaborate on reality in a playful way—and the ability to gain fulfillment from it, these are skills that have to be learned and developed.

31   Such disappointment, however, is not only unjust, it is also destructive. Sensing their parents' disappointment, children come to believe that they are, indeed, lacking something, and that this makes them less worthy of admiration and respect. Giving children the opportunity to develop new resources, to enlarge their horizons and discover the pleasures of doing things on their own is, on the other hand, a way to help children develop a confident feeling about themselves as capable and interesting people.

32   It is, of course, ironic that many parents avoid a TV Turn-Off out of fear that their children won't know what to do with themselves in the

absence of television. It is television watching itself that has allowed them to grow up without learning how to be resourceful and television watching that keeps them from developing those skills that would enable them to fill in their empty time enjoyably.

6. TV Has a Negative Effect on Children's Physical Fitness

Dear Diary:

Today instead of TV I did exercises. I kicked my legs 50 times and jumped up and down 50 times. Then I took a bath. Then I cut papers and drew. Then I did knitting five times. It did not turn out so good.

—Fifth grader, P.S. 84, No-TV Week

33   Not long ago a study that attracted wide notice in the popular press found a direct relationship between the incidence of obesity in children and time spent viewing television. For the 6–11 age group, "children who watched more television experienced a greater prevalence of obesity, or superobesity, than children watching less television. No significant differences existed between obese, superobese, and nonobese children with respect to the number of friends, their ability to get along with friends, or time spent with friends, alone, listening to the radio, reading, or in leisure time activities," wrote the researchers. As for teenagers, only ten percent of those teenagers who watched TV an hour or less a day were obese as compared to twenty percent of those who watched more than five hours daily. With most other variables eliminated, why should this be? The researchers provided a commonsense explanation: Dedicated TV watchers are fatter because they eat more and exercise less while glued to the tube.[3]

7. TV Has a Negative Effect on Children's School Achievement

One day my class was getting ready to have a science test. There was nothing to do during the Turn-Off Week so I studied instead. I got S–, a good grade. My parents were proud of me.

—Fourth grader, Marshall, Missouri, Turn-Off

34   It is difficult if not impossible to prove that excessive television viewing has a direct negative effect on young children's cognitive development, though by using cautionary phrases such as "TV will turn your brain to mush" parents often express an instinctive belief that this is true.

35   Nevertheless an impressive number of research studies demonstrate beyond any reasonable doubt that excessive television viewing has an

---

[3]W. H. Dietz and S. L. Gortmaker, "Do We Fatten Our Children at the Television Set? Obesity and Television Viewing in Children and Adolescents." *Pediatrics* 75 (1985: 807–12).

adverse effect on children's achievement in school. One study, for instance, shows that younger children who watch more TV have lower scores in reading and overall achievement tests than those who watch less TV.[4]

36   Another large-scale study, conducted when television was first introduced as a mass medium in Japan, found that as families acquired television sets children showed a decline in both reading skills and homework time.

37   But it does not require costly research projects to demonstrate that television viewing affects children's school work adversely. Interviews with teachers who have participated in TV Turn-Offs provide confirmation as well.

38   Almost without exception, these teachers testify that the quality of homework brought into class during the No-TV period was substantially better. As a fifth grade teacher noted: "There was a real difference in the homework I was getting during No-TV Week. Kids who usually do a good job on homework did a terrific job. Some kids who rarely hand in assignments on time now brought in surprisingly good and thorough work. When I brought this to the class's attention during discussion time they said, 'Well, there was nothing else to do!'"

8. Television Watching May Be a Serious Addiction

Every time I walked through the living room I longed to sit down, relax, and watch dumb reruns on TV. I think I was suffering from TV withdrawal symptoms. After a few days, though, I was used to doing other things with my time.

—Tenth grader, Marshall, Missouri, Turn-Off

39   A lot of people who have nothing but bad things to say about TV, calling it the "idiot box" and the "boob tube," nevertheless spend quite a lot of their free time watching television. People are often apologetic, even shamefaced about their television viewing, saying things like, "I only watch the news," or "I only turn the set on for company," or "I only watch when I'm too tired to do anything else" to explain the sizable number of hours they devote to TV.

40   In addition to anxiety about their own viewing patterns, many parents recognize that their children watch too much television and that it is having an adverse effect on their development and yet they don't take any effective action to change the situation.

41   Why is there so much confusion, ambivalence, and self-deception connected with television viewing? One explanation is that great numbers of

---

[4]S. G. Burton, J. M. Calonico, and D. R. McSeveney, "Effects of Preschool Television Watching on First-Grade Children." *Journal of Communication* 29, no. 3 (1979: 164–70).

Notes

television viewers are to some degree addicted to the *experience* of watching television. The confusion and ambivalence they reveal about television may then be recognized as typical reactions of an addict unwilling to face an addiction or unable to get rid of it.

42   Most people find it hard to consider television viewing a serious addiction. Addictions to tobacco or alcohol, after all, are known to cause life-threatening diseases—lung cancer or cirrhosis of the liver. Drug addiction leads to dangerous behavioral aberrations—violence and crime. Meanwhile, the worst physiological consequences of television addiction seem to be a possible decline in overall physical fitness, and an increased incidence of obesity.

43   It is in its psychosocial consequences, especially its effects on relationships and family life, that television watching may be as damaging as chemical addiction. We all know the terrible toll alcoholism or drug addiction takes on the families of addicts. Is it possible that television watching has a similarly destructive potential for family life?

44   Most of us are at least dimly aware of the addictive power of television through our own experiences with the medium: our compulsive involvement with the tube too often keeps us from talking to each other, from doing things together, from working and learning and getting involved in community affairs. The hours we spend viewing prove to be curiously unfulfilling. We end up feeling depressed, though the program we've been watching was a comedy. And we cannot seem to turn the set off, or even not turn it on in the first place. Doesn't this sound like an addiction?

Questions for Critical Thought

"The Trouble with Television"

1. What main points does Winn make to support her view that television has a negative effect on the family?

2. Winn has developed each of her points over several paragraphs (except for point 6, which she developed in a single paragraph). Which of her points appears best developed? Why? List the evidence, examples, and details she used to support this point. What other forms of support could she have used to make her point even better?

3. Which of Winn's points appears less developed or weaker than the others? What kinds of evidence might help to prove these points?

4. Which of her points do you agree with most? Explain why. What evidence does she use to help prove this point? Are there other forms of support that she could have used to strengthen her argument?

5. Which of her points do you disagree with most? Explain why. What evidence does she use to help prove this point? How might you *rebut* (argue against) the point?

6. Examine Winn's use of outside sources in paragraphs 8 and 15. How did she integrate her sources in each case?

7. Identify Winn's audience. To whom is she speaking in the piece? What is her purpose for writing?

8. How does your own view of television compare to Winn's?

Notes

Get Involved!
Watch a child's TV program. Make notes. What channel did the program appear on? What is the title of the program? What do you think the intended age group is? What positive and negative qualities did you see in the program? Report back to your class.

> *Journal Assignment*
>
> **Considering Winn's View**
>
> Think about the concerns Winn has raised regarding television and its effect on children and families. Think about your own television viewing habits as well as the habits of those in your family. Write a response in the form of a letter to Winn telling her, overall, what you think of her ideas and suggestions. Exchange your journal with a classmate or two. After reading someone else's journal, just say, "Thank You," when you return it.

Explore the Writing Assignment

Here, again, is the writing assignment you are preparing for.

> *Write an essay in which you argue for or against Marie Winn's view of television and its effect on children and the family.*

Activities

Summary and Response

One method of exploring is to look more closely at each of Winn's arguments. In the activity that follows, you'll use your summary and response skills as you address Winn's arguments one at a time. Complete this activity on a separate sheet.

Summary of Introduction

1. **TV Keeps Families from Doing Other Things**
   (List main points.)

Do you agree or disagree that TV keeps families from doing other things? How? Why? Use examples from your own experience to develop your response.

2. TV Is a Hidden Competitor for All Other Activities
   (List main points.)

Do you agree or disagree that TV is a hidden competitor? If so, in what ways does it compete? Whom or what does TV compete with?

3. TV Allows Kids to Grow Up Less Civilized
   (List main points.)

Do you agree or disagree that kids who watch TV grow up less civilized? Offer specific examples to support your response.

4. Television Takes the Place of Play
   (List main points.)

Do you agree or disagree that TV takes the place of play? What kinds of activities does TV interfere with? Discuss specific observations you've made.

5. TV Makes Children Less Resourceful
   (List main points.)

Do you agree or disagree that children lose their resourcefulness because of TV? What evidence do you have to support your point?

6. TV Has a Negative Effect on Children's Physical Fitness
   (List main points.)

Do you agree or disagree that TV takes the place of physical activity and causes children's fitness to suffer? Offer specific examples to prove your point.

7. TV Has a Negative Effect on Children's School Achievement
   (List main points.)

Do you agree or disagree that children's achievement falls short because of television? If so, in what areas? How? Why? What evidence does Winn use to support this point?

8. Television Watching May Be a Serious Addiction
   (List main points.)

What does it mean to be addicted to something? Do you agree or disagree that people may become addicted to TV?

Discuss your views with classmates.

Observing Children's Viewing Habits

To further explore the topic, conduct an observation and record data on the viewing habits of children and families you know.

Over a period of three to five days, observe a child's television habits. Apply your Questions for Development. Who is the child? What are the child's viewing habits? When does the child watch television most? Least? Where does the child sit while viewing? Does the child appear to enjoy TV? How does the child behave while viewing? Why does the child view TV? Do any of Winn's concerns appear to hold true?

Interviewing Families

To gather additional information on families' viewing habits, conduct interviews with parents.

Using the Questions for Development, compose a set of interview questions that addresses Winn's concerns. Interview three to five parents from different families. Note where similarities and differences occur in their viewing habits.

Sample Questions:

- When do you watch television most? Least?

- How many hours do you (and your family) watch television daily/weekly?

- Do you monitor your children's viewing habits? When? Why? How? Which programs, if any, are off-limits?

- What do you see as the positive aspects of television?

- What are the negative aspects of television?

Be careful to keep your source information (who says what) in case you want to cite any of the adults as sources in your essay.

Brainstorm   Write freely about Marie Winn's concerns and other possible effects of television on children and the family. Don't worry about deciding which side of the issue you are on right now. Although Winn asserts there are "eight significant ways" that television affects the family, you should not argue for or against all eight points. Instead, write on two or three of the issues that interest you most. It might help to review your summary/response sheets to see which of the arguments you found most important. Also review your journal entries and your activities.

When you have finished writing, review your brainstorming and decide which side you want to take on the issue(s). Highlight the parts of your brainstorming you think might be useful when writing your essay.

Consider Your Audience   Imagine your audience as a group of concerned parents. It might help to visualize the PTA at a local elementary school. Which of Winn's concerns about television, children, and the family would you discuss with them? What might be some of their concerns? How would you address the concerns of those who disagree with your view? Direct your argument toward those who might be swayed by your discussion. Make a list of things to keep in mind when writing for your audience.

Create Your Thesis   Your thesis should reflect that you have narrowed the scope of your essay to focus on two or three of Winn's arguments. Also note that you are being asked to argue *for or against* Winn's position. Your position should be clearly stated in your thesis. Experiment with thesis statements until you find one that expresses your position and what you intend to focus on in your essay.

Outline   With your thesis in mind, list the two or three points that you intend to argue in your essay. Under each point, note the kind of support you will use to develop your idea. You should also consider what your opponent (the person on the other side) might say about each point and how you would respond. Now you're ready to draft a rough outline that shows how you will organize all of this information.

Here are some ways for you to consider organizing your arguments:

- Offer least important ideas first and most important ideas last.
- Present least interesting ideas first and most interesting ideas last.
- Alternate your views and your opponent's views.
- Present all of your opponent's views (divided into different paragraphs), then all of your views (divided into different paragraphs).

Draft

Using your summary/response sheets, your notes, the reading, your journal entries, your brainstorming notes, and your outline as guides, begin drafting your essay. In your introduction, you should introduce the two or three most important issues raised by Winn and tell whether you agree or disagree with them. In your body paragraphs, address these points one at a time, explaining and supporting your position with examples, personal experience, research, and discussion. Also, be sure to address your opponent's concerns. In your conclusion, remind your reader where you stand in regard to Winn's opinions.

Revise

Activity

Share Your Writing

As you work with a classmate, consider the following:

- Have you established your position in the introduction? Remember that your task is to show that you either agree or disagree with Winn.

- Can your reader see your organizational pattern? Have you addressed the arguments one at a time? Is it clear which paragraphs contain pro or con arguments?

Here is an example of a topic sentence for a **pro argument** (an argument in favor of):

> In her article, Winn argues that television keeps families from doing things together, and I agree.
>
> —*Allison Baxter, student writer*

Here is an example of topic sentences for a **con argument** (an argument against):

> Marie Winn said that television could become an addiction, which could be compared to a drug addiction. I strongly disagree.
>
> —*Lynita Harris, student writer*

- Have you developed/supported your ideas fully? Use any of the Questions for Development that help.

    WHO?   Who is involved?
           Who is affected?
           Who is interested?
           Who is my audience?
           Who believes this?
           Who said this?

WHAT?   What happened?
         What are the main issues?
         What else does my reader need to know?
         What can I explain further?
WHEN?   When did it happen?
         When is it a problem?
         When will it occur again?
         When will it be resolved?
WHERE?   Where did it occur?
         Where were the participants?
WHY?   Why is the issue important?
         Why did it happen this way?
         Why should you or I care?
         Why should my audience care?
HOW?   How did it happen?
         How does it work?
         How can the problem be resolved?

• Have you included examples or personal experience to support your ideas?

Review the following paragraph to see how one student effectively used personal experience to develop a body paragraph idea.

In her article Winn argues that television keeps families from doing things together, and I agree. Just recently, I realized that the big square box has kept me from doing things with my own children. For example, on our way home from school, my oldest son would ask me to play Monopoly with him after dinner, and of course I would agree to play. Some time after dinner, he would come to me with the board, and remind me that I had said I would play the game with him, but most of the time I would say, "Not right now. My show is on," and I would ask if we could play a little later. When he returned again with the game, I would say, "It's too late to play tonight. We will play tomorrow evening, I promise." This was very painful for my son, and I did have every intention of playing with him. I just got too involved in that mindless box.

—*Allison Baxter, student writer*

You may also want to consider these questions after completing the sentence work at the end of the chapter (pages 294–310):

- Have you used concessions—*though, although,* or *even though*—when you need to make one argument appear more important or stronger than another?

Example of a concession:

> Although I agree with most of Winn's article, I don't agree that TV has a negative effect on a child's academic achievement.
>
> —*Parris Ray, student writer*

- Have you used transitions to move the reader smoothly from one idea to the next and to provide **cohesion** (unity) throughout your essay?

In addition, address the following questions about using sources in your essay:

- Have you integrated and identified your own research findings in your essay?

- Have you included publication information for sources? Have you cited sources correctly? (See "Using Outside Sources," pages 489–494.)

Note: If you have any concerns about your essay at this stage of the writing process, be sure to talk them over with your instructor or a tutor.

Activity

Study a Student Sample

Read the student essay below and prepare to discuss it with your classmates.

The Strength of Television

According to the article, "Attention Span—How TV Produces Overstimulated, Underactive Kids" in the *Sacramento Bee*, "The average U.S. household has 2.24 television sets, and the television is on an average of 6 hours, 47 minutes daily in those homes." That's a lot of TV. But do parents really know the negative influence that it has on children and family life? Marie Winn, the author of *Unplugging the Plug-In Drug* and a mother of two, has argued in her book that there are "eight significant ways" television affects children and families. I agree with Winn's views on television and its effect on children and parents. In the following paragraphs I will discuss three of the more interesting points out of the eight that Winn talks about in her book.

First, I believe that TV has a negative effect on children's school achievement. I agree with Winn when she said, "It is difficult if not impossible to prove that excessive television viewing has a direct negative effect on young children's cognitive development." She is saying that there is no exact reason why television has a direct negative effect on the minds of young children, but there have been recent studies that help support her point. For example, in Japan, a large-scale study has found that as families acquired television sets, children showed a decline in both reading skills and time spent on homework. Low reading skills may be the result of watching TV rather than reading or writing. Also, less time spent on homework may result in the lack of understanding of future assignments; therefore, a child may receive low test and quiz grades. In my opinion when a child is at school, that means there is no television. No television means that more time would be spent doing their homework. If they are at home, that means there is television. Where television is present, there is a chance of it being turned on and viewed while in the process of doing homework or studying.

Next, I firmly agree with Winn when she argues that television has a negative effect on children's physical fitness. Researchers in a recent study found that "[d]edicated TV watchers are fatter because they eat more and exercise less while glued to the tube." In a class lecture, my instructor Ms. Johnson quoted this statistic, "More than 60 percent of TV ads are for sugared cereal, candy, fatty foods, and toys." These kinds of products grab the attention of young children; the mixture of unhealthy foods and television may be a harmful combination. Most of the time when a child is watching television they are plopped right in front of the TV on the floor or the couch. In this situation, no physical activity is occurring. There may be a good chance that the child is eating a snack or drinking while watching television. I doubt that the child is eating a healthy snack or drink. I believe this is where the parents need to step in. The parents can feed their children healthy snacks like fruits or vegetables while the kids watch TV. Also, the parents can set up times when a child needs to exercise before or after watching television.

Finally, I strongly agree that television can be very addictive if children are exposed at a young age. An addiction is a compulsive need for and use of a habit-forming substance (i.e., drugs, nicotine, alcohol, etc.). In this case, television is the "habit-forming substance." In point 8, Winn put it best when she said, "The great numbers of television viewers are to some degree addicted to the experience of watching television." I believe that the addiction to television may not be as harmful as drugs or alcohol, but it will affect you as you get older. I also believe that if kids are heavily exposed to television at a young age for prolonged amounts of time, then they too may become addicted. Then as they get older they won't know that they're addicted, and they will find it harder to go without television. In Chapter 6 of *Connections: Writing, Reading, and Critical Thinking* by Boeck and Rainey, the authors quote Joshua Meyrowitz, who says, "On average, each household has a TV on almost fifty hours a week. Forty percent of households eat dinner with the set on. Individually, Americans watch an average of thirty hours a week" (from "Television: The Shared Arena"). This means most children spend more time watching TV than they spend in school. Again, this is where I believe that the parents should take action. Besides worrying too much on the content of television, they should limit the amount of time a child watches TV. Limiting the amount of television being watched would lessen the chance of a possible uncontrollable addiction.

In conclusion, I find Winn's views to be strong and straightforward. The key to not letting the television take over the family is to establish clear communication between the children and parents. I feel that if a parent takes control of the situation (in this case, television), problems would be less likely to occur. Also, if parents regulate their children at a young age, then as the child gets older he or she may be less involved with the television.

—Paul Gregorio, student writer

Apply the same questions to Gregorio's essay that you applied to your own draft.

1. What is the writer's position? How many of Winn's points has the writer addressed?

2. What are the main points the writer makes in the essay? Is it clear which paragraphs contain pro or con arguments?

Notes

3. What kinds of support has the writer used to develop his main points? Are there any additional questions the writer might have addressed? (See page 242 for a list of the Questions for Development.)

4. Has the writer used a concession in his essay? Identify where a concession might be used effectively in this essay. (See pages 297–300 for information on concessions.)

5. Has the writer used transitions to move the reader smoothly from one idea to the next through the essay? Are there any places where a transition might provide more cohesion?

6. Has the writer included research in his essay? Has publication information been provided for sources? Have sources been cited correctly? Highlight an example.

7. If this writer were part of your workshop group, what praise would you offer his essay? Are there any revision suggestions you would like to make?

Edit

Now begin "polishing" your essay. Read your essay aloud and check for typing errors, spelling errors, and any other errors you tend to make. After completing the sentence work at the end of this chapter, consider these questions:

- Have you used subordinators, concessions, and transitions to create clear bridges between opposing ideas?
- Have you punctuated correctly when using subordinators, concessions, and transitions?

If you work with a tutor, ask the tutor to tell you how many (if any) and what types of errors you have made so that you can correct them.

Writing Assignment #2: Television: Good, Bad, or Tolerable?

Here, in brief, is the writing assignment you are preparing for.

Write an essay in which you discuss objectively the negative and positive effects of television. Come to a conclusion about what, if anything, should be done to minimize the negative effects of television and maximize the positive.

Read, Discuss, Think Critically

In this section, you'll consider two additional viewpoints on television. In "Guilt Free TV," writer Daniel McGinn presents some of the recent and more positive developments in children's programming. Then, in "Why We Tuned Out," Karen Springen explains why she and her husband have decided not to allow their children to watch television.

Reading Assignment: *"Guilt Free TV"*

Preview   This is a lengthy selection, so be sure to set aside plenty of time to complete a thorough reading process. Begin by reading the introduction and the topic sentences.

Anticipate   What do you think this article will be about? Write your response in the "Notes" column.

Read and Reread   Read the entire article, marking unknown terms. Then reread more slowly and use the "Notes" column to interact with the essay. Mark important and interesting points and define unknown terms.

Guilt Free TV*

In the beginning, there was Big Bird. Now, thanks to intense competition from Disney and Nick, there are more quality shows for preschoolers than ever.

by Daniel McGinn

This article appeared in the November 11, 2002, edition of *Newsweek*.

1   When Alicia Large was growing up, her parents rarely let her watch television. Even the Muppets were off-limits, she says, because her parents disliked the sexual tension between Kermit and Miss Piggy. Now 31 and raising her own sons—ages 2 and 3—Large views TV more benevolently. Her boys love *Dora the Explorer,* so when she takes them on errands, she draws a map—the bank, the grocery store—so they can track their progress as Dora does. Among Large's friends, kids' TV—what and how much are yours watching?—is a constant conversation. Yes, many parents still use TV as a babysitter. But increasingly, she says, parents are

Notes

Get Involved!
Go online to the
Children's Television
Workshop Web site
(www.ctw.org) to
examine the
supplemental activities
available to children
who watch *Sesame
Street.* What types of
activities appear on the
site? Which appear to
be more educational?
Which appear to be less
educational? Take notes
and be prepared to
discuss your findings in
class.

looking to TV to help them do a better job of raising kids. "Our generation is using it completely differently," she says.

2   Parents have felt conflicted about television since its earliest days.
Even Philo T. Farnsworth, TV's inventor, fretted over letting his son
watch cowboy shows, according to biographer Evan I. Schwartz. That
anxiety continues. In a survey released last week by Public Agenda,
22 percent of parents said they'd "seriously considered getting rid of
[their TV] altogether" because it airs too much sex and bad language.
But at the same time, for parents of the youngest viewers—ages 2 to
5—there are new reasons for optimism. Now that PBS, which invented
the good-for-kids genre, has new competition from Nickelodeon and
Disney, there are more quality choices for preschoolers than ever.

3   Inside those networks, a growing number of Ph.D.s are injecting
the latest in child-development theory into new programs. In Disney's
Stanley, meet a freckle-faced kid who's fascinated with animals; in one
episode, he and his pals explore the life and habitat of a platypus.
Nickelodeon now airs 4.5 hours of quality preschool shows daily (in addition to learning-free fare like *SpongeBob* for older kids). Shows like
Dora and *Blue's Clues* goad kids into interacting with the television set;
studies show this improves problem-solving skills. Even the grand-
daddy of this genre, *Sesame Street,* has undergone a makeover to better serve today's precocious viewers. The newcomers provide stiff
competition to Mister Rogers, whose show stopped production in
2000 (it still airs on PBS). But he welcomes his new TV neighbors. "I'm
just glad that more producers—and purveyors of television have signed
the pledge to protect childhood," says Fred Rogers, who now writes
parenting books.

4   That's the good news. The bad news is that working these shows
into kids' lives in a healthy way remains a challenge. Much of what kids
watch remains banal or harmful. Many kids watch too much. There are
also troubling socioeconomic factors at work. In lower-income homes,
for instance, kids watch more and are more likely to have TV in their
bedrooms, a practice pediatricians discourage. But even as some families choose to go TV-free, more parents are recognizing that television
can be beneficial. In the Public Agenda survey, 93 percent of parents
agree that "TV is fine for kids as long as he or she is watching the right
shows and watching in moderation."

5   When it comes to the right shows, *Sesame Street* remains the gold
standard. Last week, as the crew taped an episode for its 34th season,
the set looked comfortably familiar: while Telly and Baby Bear
worked on a skit near Hooper's Store, Snuffleupagus hung from the
rafters, sleeping under a sheet. The show's longevity is a testament to

the research-driven process founder Joan Ganz Cooney invented in the late 1960s. Then, as now, each season begins with Ph.D.s working alongside writers to set goals and review scripts. Any time there's a question—will kids understand Slimey the Worm's mission to the moon?—they head to day-care centers to test the material.

6   When *Sesame* began reinventing kids' TV in the early '70s, Daniel Anderson was a newly minted professor of psychology at the University of Massachusetts, Amherst. Like most child-development pros at that time, he assumed TV was bad for kids. Then one day Anderson taught his class that young children have very short attention spans. One student challenged him: "So why do kids sit still for an hour to watch 'Sesame Street'?" "I genuinely didn't know the answer," Anderson recalls. So he went to a lab and placed kids in front of TVs to find it.

7   What he found surprised him. Like most researchers, he assumed that fast-moving images and sounds mesmerized young viewers. But videotapes of kids' viewing showed that their attention wandered most during transitions between segments and when dialogue or plotlines became too complex. He hypothesized that even young children watch TV for the same reason adults do: to enjoy good stories. To test that theory, he sliced up *Sesame Street* skits so the plot no longer made sense. Even 2-year-olds quickly realized the story was amiss and stopped watching. Some knocked on the TV screen. Others called out: "Mommy, can you fix this?" Over years of research, Anderson reached a startling conclusion: "Television viewing is a much more intellectual activity for kids than anybody had previously supposed."

8   This research might have stayed hidden in psych journals if it hadn't been for the work of two equally powerful forces: the U.S. Congress and a purple dinosaur named Barney. In 1990 Congress passed the Children's Television Act, increasing demand for quality kids' shows. Then *Barney & Friends* was launched as a PBS series in 1992. Kids went wild, and merchandise flew off shelves. Until then, Nickelodeon and Disney had been content to leave preschool shows to the do-gooders at PBS. Now they saw gold. "The success of *Barney* just changed everybody's feeling—it became 'OK, we should be able to do that, too,'" says Marjorie Kalins, a former *Sesame* executive.

9   It was a profitable move. By 2001 Nick and Disney's TV businesses had generated a combined $1.68 billion in revenue, according to Paul Kagan Associates. Everyone admits that licensing money influences programming decisions. (Ironically, merchandisers at Nickelodeon lobbied against *Dora* because they believed that another show would generate more sales.) Ads and toys can detract from many parents' enthusiasm for the shows; no matter how much your kid may learn from *Sagwa* or

Rolie Polie Olie, the characters are hard to love when you can't get through Wal-Mart without a giant case of "I-WANT-itis."

10   Until there's a way to make shows free, that overcommercialization will continue. But for parents, there's some comfort from knowing that more TV producers are applying the latest research to make their shows better. This happened partly because researchers of Anderson's generation helped grow a new crop of Ph.D.s, who began graduating into jobs at *Sesame* and Nickelodeon. And like seeds from a dandelion blown at by a child, folks who'd trained at *Sesame* began taking root inside other networks. Anne Sweeney, who'd studied at Harvard with *Sesame* cofounder Gerald Lesser, interned with television activist Peggy Charren and spent 12 years at Nickelodeon, took over the Disney Channel in 1996. She hired a team (led by ex-Nick programmer Rich Ross) to design preschool shows. By 1999 Disney had a full block of little-kid programming it branded Playhouse Disney. Today it uses a 28-page "Whole Child Curriculum" detailing what shows should teach.

11   To see how research can drive these new-generation shows, come along, neighbor, as we visit a day-care center on Manhattan's Upper West Side. Dr. Christine Ricci sits in a child-size chair, holding a script and tapping a red pen against her lip. Ricci, who holds a psychology Ph.D. from UMass, is research director for *Dora the Explorer,* which airs on Nick Jr., Nickelodeon's preschool block. In each episode Dora, an animated Latina girl, goes on a journey with a monkey named Boots. Using a map to guide them (which helps kids' spatial skills), they visit three locations ("Waterfall, mountain, forest!" kids yell) and solve problems. As in *Blue's Clues,* Nick Jr.'s groundbreaking hit in which a dog named Blue and the host Joe help kids solve puzzles, *Dora* encourages kids to yell back at the screen (often in Spanish) or do physical movements (like rowing a boat).

12   Today Ricci shows 4-year-olds a crudely animated *Dora* episode slated for next season. As they watch, Ricci's team charts, moment by moment, whether the kids are paying attention and interacting with the screen. At first the kids sit transfixed, but during a pivotal scene (in which Swiper the fox, Dora's nemesis, throws a boot down a hole) their attention wanders. One child picks up a Magic Marker, and suddenly every child is seeking out toys. All the while the researchers scribble furiously. When the episode ends, an adult asks the children questions: "What color button on the fix-it machine matched the tire?" Their recall is astonishing. *Sesame Street* has done this kind of testing off and on since the '70s. Ricci's team, however, is relentless, testing and revising every *Dora* episode repeatedly.

13   The following afternoon, Ricci, *Dora* creator Chris Gifford and their team study a bar graph showing how kids interacted with the episode minute by minute. To boost the numbers, sometimes they suggest better animation. Sometimes they call for a better "money shot": a big close-up of Dora. Fixing one segment—"Only 15 out of 26 kids were still watching," Ricci informs them gravely—requires more drastic measures. Gifford stands up, motioning like a cheerleader, to suggest livelier movements to get kids moving along with Dora during a song. "So often when you work on a TV show for kids, you forget about your audience," Gifford says. "We've set up a system where we can't ignore them." Similar work goes on at *Blue's Clues.* Says Nick Jr. chief Brown Johnson: "It's science meets story."

14   For a parent, it's natural to get excited when kids shout back at the TV during *Dora* or dance to *The Wiggles,* a music-and-dance show that airs on Disney. That leads some parents to look at their TVs the way a previous generation looked to Dr. Spock. Colleen Breitbord of Framingham, Mass., sees these programs as so vital to the development of her children, 7 and 2, that she installed a TV in the kitchen so they can watch *Arthur* and *Clifford* while they eat. "They learn so much," Breitbord says. "I think children who don't have the opportunity to watch some of this excellent programming miss out." In Ansonia, Conn., Patti Sarandrea uses Playhouse Disney, Nick Jr. and PBS "to reinforce what I teach the kids: colors, shapes, counting." At 3 1/2, her daughter can count to 25. Thanks to *Dora,* her 18-month-old says "Hola."

15   As kids that young start tuning in, even *Sesame* is rethinking its approach. The show was originally designed for kids 3 to 5, but by the mid-1990s, many viewers were 2 or younger. The tykes seemed to tire of 60 minutes of fast-paced Muppet skits (the pacing was originally modeled after *Laugh-In* and TV commercials). So in 1999 *Sesame* introduced "Elmo's World," a 15-minute segment that ended every show. Even after that change, *Sesame* VP Lewis Bernstein noticed how today's little kids would sit still to watch 90-minute videotaped movies. So last February *Sesame* unveiled more longer segments. In "Journey to Ernie," Big Bird and Ernie play hide-and-seek against an animated background. Today ratings are up. The cast likes the new format, too. Before, stories were constantly cut short. "It was a little discombobulating," says Kevin Clash, the muscular, deep-voiced Muppet captain who brings Elmo to life. Now Elmo l-o-o-o-ves the longer stories.

16   So just how much good do these shows do? On a recent afternoon five undergrads sit around a table in the Yale University psychology department, playing a bizarre variation of bingo to try to find out. Together they watch three episodes of *Barney & Friends,* each filling in hash

marks on six sheets of paper. After each screening, they tally how many "teaching elements" they've counted. "I've got 9 vocabulary, 6 numbers . . . 11 sharing," says one student. Afterward Yale researcher Dorothy Singer will crunch the data and compare them with past seasons'. Her work has shown that the higher an episode's score, the more accurately children will be able to recount the plot and use the vocabulary words.

17   PBS does more of this postproduction "summative" research than other networks. Study after study shows *Sesame* viewers are better prepared for school. *Dragon Tales,* a *Sesame*-produced animated show, helps kids become more goal-oriented, and *Between the Lions,* a puppet show produced by Boston's WGBH, helps kids' reading. Nick research offers proof of the effectiveness of *Dora* and *Blue's Clues.* Disney doesn't do summative research; Disney execs say for now they'd rather devote resources to creating more shows for new viewers. Competitors suggest another reason: Disney's shows may not measure up. "It's scary to test," says *Sesame* research chief Rosemarie Truglio. "Maybe that's a piece of it—they're afraid."

18   Network-funded research won't change the minds of folks who say kids are better off with no television at all. That view gained strength in 1999, when the American Academy of Pediatrics began discouraging any television for kids under 2. But when you parse the pro- and anti-TV rhetoric, the two sides don't sound as far apart as you'd suspect. The pro-TV crowd, for instance, quickly concedes that violent TV is damaging to kids, and that too many kids watch too many lousy shows. The anti-TV crowd objects mostly to TV's widespread overuse. Like Häagen-Dazs, TV seems to defy attempts at moderation, they suggest, so it's safer to abstain entirely. They believe overviewing especially affects children because of what Marie Winn, author of *The Plug-In Drug,* calls the "displacement factor." That's when kids watch so much TV that they don't engage in enough brain-enhancing free play as toddlers or read enough during elementary school. Although pro-TV researchers say there are no data to support those fears, they agree it could be true. In fact, Anderson is currently conducting an experiment to measure whether having adult shows (like *Jeopardy!*) playing in the background interferes with children's play. Bad news, soap-opera fans: the early data suggest it might.

19   Even shows the academics applaud could be better. In his UMass office, Anderson pops in a videotape of *Dora.* It's one of the handful of shows that he advised during their conception. In this episode, Dora and Boots paddle a canoe down a river, around some rocks, toward a waterfall. Toward a waterfall? "If I'd read this script I'd have completely blocked this," he says, because it models unsafe behavior. Anderson has his arms

crossed, his eyebrows scrunched; occasionally he talks to the screen, like an NFL fan disputing a bad call. "Oh, God, another dangerous thing," he says as Dora and Boots canoe under downed tree limbs. He still likes *Dora,* but not this episode. "The education is a little thinner than I would wish, and it's a little dubious sending them on such a dumb journey." Then he watches *Bear* and *Blue's Clues,* still nitpicking but happier.

20   Even as the kids' TV environment improves, shortcomings remain. Only PBS airs educational shows for older elementary kids (examples: *Zoom* and *Cyberchase*). In focus groups, says Nickelodeon president Herb Scannell, older kids say they get enough learning in school; what commercial broadcaster is going to argue with the audience? Producers have other worries. Mitchell Kriegman, creator of *Bear in the Big Blue House,* says parents could grow too enamored of obviously educational, A-B-C/1-2-3–type shows. One of the most successful episodes of *Bear* involves potty training. "The [network's] reaction was 'Oh, my God, you can't say poop and pee on TV,'" Kriegman says. *Bear* did, and families loved it. Tighter curricula could dampen that creativity.

21   But those are worries for the future. For now, it's worth celebrating the improvements—however incremental—in shows for TV's youngest audience. Not everyone will want to raise a glass: like alcohol or guns, TV will be used sensibly in some homes and wreak havoc in others. Debating its net societal value will remain a never-ending pursuit. In the meantime parents live through these trade-offs daily. A recent issue of *Parenting* magazine offered the following question to help assess parenting skills: "I let my child watch TV only when . . . A) There's an educational show on public television, B) I have time to narrate the action for him . . . or C) I want to take a shower." The scoring code rates the answers: "A) Liar, B) Big fat liar, and C) You may not be perfect, but at least you're honest." As kids' TV raises the bar, parents who choose a different answer—D) All of the above—have a little less reason to feel guilty.

Questions for Critical Thought

"Guilt Free TV"

1. How has children's TV improved in recent years according to McGinn? Do you agree or disagree with his reasoning?

2. What are some of the negative effects mentioned in the article? Are there others not mentioned by McGinn? If so, explain.

3. What kinds of support does McGinn use to develop the idea that quality TV is being produced today?

4. What kinds of research is being done on children's TV? What do the sponsors of such research hope to find out? What are some of their goals in conducting research? Why might some avoid conducting research?

5. Besides the programming itself, what other problems might people have with children's TV? Why?

6. In paragraph 18, McGinn mentions Marie Winn's concern about TV's "displacement factor." Explain what this means and whether or not you agree this is a problem.

7. McGinn suggests that recent improvements in children's TV are "worth celebrating." Do you agree? Why, or why not?

Reading Assignment: "Why We Tuned Out"

Preview   Read the introduction and the topic sentences.

Anticipate   What do you think this article will be about? Write your response in the "Notes" column.

Read and Reread   Read the entire article, marking unknown terms. Then reread more slowly and use the "Notes" column to interact with the essay. Mark important and interesting points and define unknown terms.

Why We Tuned Out*

"When Jazzy was 1 year old, her babysitter asked if TV was OK. We thought about it, and we said, 'No.'"

by Karen Springen

This article appeared in the November 11, 2002, edition of *Newsweek*.

1   "What's your favorite TV show?" our girls' beloved ballet instructor asked each pint-size dancer in her class. Our oldest daughter, Jazzy, didn't know how to answer. She shrugged. Her moment of awkwardness results from a decision my husband, Mark, and I made five years

---

ago. We don't allow our kids to watch TV. Period. Not at home, not at friends' houses; and they don't watch videos or movies, either. We want our daughters, Jazzy, now nearly 6, and Gigi, 3, to be as active as possible, physically and mentally. So when a babysitter asked whether Jazzy, then 1 year old, could watch, we thought about it—and said no.

2   When we look at our inquisitive, energetic daughters, we have no regrets. And our reading of the research makes us feel even better. Nielsen Media Research reports that American children 2 through 11 watch three hours and 16 minutes of television every day. Kids who watch more than 10 hours of TV each week are more likely to be overweight, aggressive and slow to learn in school, according to the American Medical Association. For these reasons, the American Academy of Pediatrics recommends no TV for children younger than 2 and a maximum of two hours a day of "screen time" (TV, computers or videogames) for older kids. We are convinced that without TV, our daughters spend more time than other kids doing cartwheels, listening to stories and asking such interesting questions as "How old is God?" and "What makes my rubber ducks float?" They also aren't haunted by TV images of September 11—because they never saw them.

3   Going without TV in America has its difficult moments. When I called my sister, Lucy, to make arrangements for Thanksgiving, she warned that her husband was planning to spend the day watching football. We're going anyway. We'll just steer the girls toward the playroom. And some well-meaning friends tell us our girls may be missing out on good educational programming. Maybe. But that's not what most kids are watching. Nielsen Media Research reports that among children 2 through 11, the top-five TV shows in the new fall season were *The Wonderful World of Disney, Survivor: Thailand, Yu-Gi-Oh!, Pokemon* and *Jackie Chan Adventures.*

4   Will our happy, busy girls suffer because they're not participating in such a big part of the popular culture? Will they feel left out in school when they don't know who won on *Survivor?* "Kids are going to make fun of them," warns my mother-in-law. And a favorite child psychiatrist, Elizabeth Berger, author of *Raising Children with Character,* cautions that maintaining a puritanical approach may make our kids into social outcasts. "Part of preparing your children for life is preparing them to be one of the girls," she says. "It's awful to be different from the other kids in fourth grade."

5   Our relatives all watch TV. So did we. I was born in 1961, the year Newton Minow, then the chairman of the U.S. Federal Communications

Commission, called television a "vast wasteland." But I loved it. My sister, Katy, and I shared a first crush on the TV cartoon hero Speed Racer. Watching *Bewitched* and *The Brady Bunch* and, later, soap operas gave us an easy way to bond with our friends. Am I being selfish in not wanting the same for our children?

6   So far, our daughters don't seem to feel like misfits. We have no problem with the girls enjoying products based on TV characters. The girls wear Elmo pajamas and battle over who can sit on a big Clifford stuffed animal. From books, they also know about Big Bird, the Little Mermaid and Aladdin. And they haven't mentioned missing out on *Yu-Gi-Oh!* cartoon duels. Dr. Miriam Baron, who chairs the American Academy of Pediatrics committee on public education, says I'm helping our kids be creative, independent learners and calls our decision "awesome." And Mayo Clinic pediatrician Daniel Broughton, another group member, says that "there's no valid reason" the girls need to view television.

7   As the girls grow older, we can't completely shield them from TV anyway. We'll probably watch Olympic rhythmic gymnastics; the girls love it. And if Jazzy's favorite baseball team, the Cubs, ever make the World Series, we'll tune in. Last Monday Jazzy's music teacher showed *The Magic School Bus: Inside the Haunted House.* Though *Magic School Bus* is a well-regarded Scholastic product, I still cringed, wondering why the kids weren't learning about vibrations and sounds by singing and banging on drums. But I kept silent; I'd never require my kids to abstain in school. Like Jean Lotus, the Oak Park, Ill., mom who founded the anti-TV group the White Dot and who also reluctantly allows her kids to view TV in school, I'm wary of being seen "as the crusading weirdo." But some public ridicule will be worth it if I help get even a few people to think twice before automatically turning on the tube. Now it's time for me to curl up with the girls and a well-worn copy of *Curious George.*

Questions for Critical Thought

"Why We Tuned Out"

1. According to Springen, why did she and her husband ban TV in their home? What kinds of support does Springen use to develop the idea that she and her husband have made a positive decision for their family?

2. What kinds of activities do the Springens want their daughters to engage in?

3. In your opinion, how might the Springen's daughters benefit from their parents' decision? How might they suffer from their parents' decision? Explain.

4. Why might the Springens allow their daughters to enjoy the products based on TV characters but not allow them to view these characters on TV? Does this seem contradictory? Explain.

5. What advantages does Springen believe her children have that other children might not? Explain.

Journal Assignment

Considering McGinn's or Springen's View

Just as you wrote to Winn earlier in the chapter, take time now to write a letter to McGinn or Springen, letting him or her know whether you support and agree with his or her views or not. Consider your own viewing habits as well as what you've discovered about the viewing habits of others. Exchange your journal with a classmate, and when you've finished reading, say, "Thank you."

Explore the Writing Assignment

Here, again, is your writing assignment. Review it carefully before continuing. Underline the important terms in the assignment.

> *Write an essay in which you discuss objectively the negative and positive effects of television. Come to a conclusion about what, if anything, should be done to minimize the negative effects of television and maximize the positive.*

Activities

Charting the Negatives and Positives of Television

An effective way to generate, develop, and organize ideas is to complete charts on the negatives and positives of television. This will help you separate the arguments and reasons on both sides of the issue. Refer back to McGinn's and Springen's articles first, then to Winn's. On the first chart, list negative effects on the left, then support, proof, and examples on the right. On the second chart, list positive effects on the left, then support, proof, and examples on the right.

Negative Effects of TV	
Negative Effects Watching TV can lead to childhood obesity.	**Examples/Sources** "Kids who watch more than 10 hours of TV each week are more likely to be overweight . . . according to the American Medical Association." (from "Why We Tuned Out," Springen, par. 2)
Use additional pages as necessary.	
Positive Effects of TV	
Positive Effects Children learn from watching educational programs.	**Examples/Sources** Parents can select programs that reinforce what they are already teaching their kids like colors and shapes (from "Guilt Free TV," McGinn, par. 14)
Use additional pages as necessary.	

Look for Information at the Library and on the Internet

To further explore the topic, look for information on the effects of television.

1. Go to the library to find books and articles on the issue of television and its effect on children and the family. Here are some titles to get you started:

Gitlin, Todd. *Inside Primetime.*
Lemish, Dafna. *Children and Television: A Global Perspective.*
Minow, Newton N. *Making Television Safe for Kids.*
Signorielli, Nancy. *Sourcebook on Children and Television.*
Singer, Dorothy G., and Jerome L. Singer. *Handbook of Children and the Media.*
Winn, Marie. *The Plug-In Drug: Television, Computers, and Family Life.*
Winn, Marie. *Unplugging the Plug-In Drug.*

Notes

Note: You don't need to read the entire book to get information on the effects of television. Look in the table of contents at the beginning of the book for chapters that appear to be about the effects of television on children and the family. Also, refer to the index in the back of the text. Look up words such as *children, effects, family, education,* or *violence* to find specific sections that focus on these important issues. Apply the Questions for Development to what you read.

As you read sections from these books, be sure to take notes and write down source information—author, title, page numbers, and publication information. Then add new information to your positive and negative effects charts. (See pages 489–494 for more information on using outside sources.)

2. Spend some time on the Internet. Look for articles on "television and violence," "television and effects," or "television and children." (Ask a librarian for help if you have any trouble locating sources.) Apply the Questions for Development to what you read.

As you conduct your research, be sure to take notes and write down source information—author, title, Web address, and the date on which you retrieved the information. Add any new information to your positive and negative effects charts.

Brainstorm   Write freely about the positive and negative effects of television. Use this as an opportunity to look at both sides. Review McGinn's, Springen's, and Winn's pieces. Also, go back to your lists of the negative and positive effects of television and respond to the most important points on each list.

When you are done writing, review your brainstorming notes. Because you'll present a balanced paper showing both the positives and

Notes   negatives, focus on only two or three of the most important points for each side. Highlight these points for now.

Consider Your Audience   Imagine you are presenting an objective discussion to a group of concerned parents, teachers, and other members of the community. Whereas some would argue that television has a negative influence on children, others would point to the positive programming television has to offer. What difficulties might you face in fairly presenting both sides of the issue?

Create Your Thesis   Review the writing assignment. Note that the assignment asks that you present the negative and positive effects objectively. This means you should create a thesis that will allow you to present both sides of the issue. Your thesis should also show that you'll limit your discussion to the most important positive and negative effects.

Outline   Think about how you might organize the points you have highlighted in a way that will allow you to present both sides fairly. Draft an outline or make a list of the arguments you'll be presenting. Under each point, note the kind of support you'll use to develop your idea. Here are some options for organizing your essay effectively:

- Offer least important ideas first and most important ideas last.
- Present least interesting ideas first and most interesting ideas last.
- Alternate positive and negative effects.
- Present all positive effects (divided into different paragraphs), then all negative effects (divided into different paragraphs).

Draft

Using your positive effects and negative effects lists, reading notes, library or Internet sources, articles, journal entries, brainstorming notes, thesis statement, and outline, begin writing your essay. Your introduction should explain the basic conflicts between those who believe TV is a negative influence and those who believe the opposite. In your body paragraphs, present each side's concerns, but include only one main concern per paragraph. Be sure to develop each point with support in the form of evidence, details, examples, and discussion. In your conclusion, let your reader know what you believe should be done to minimize the negative and maximize the positive effects of television.

Revise

Activity

_____

Share Your Writing

As you work with a classmate, think about the following:

- Have you presented a fair discussion with both sides represented?

- Can your reader see your organizational pattern? Have you addressed the arguments one at a time? Is it clear which paragraphs show negative effects and which show positive ones?

- Have you developed your ideas fully? Apply any of the Questions for Development that help.

Note: Some questions have been altered so that they are specific to this assignment.

WHO?	Who is involved?
	Who is affected?
	Who is interested?
	Who is my audience?
	Who believes or says TV is a negative influence?
	Who believes or says TV is a positive influence?
WHAT?	What happened?
	What are the main arguments raised by McGinn?
	What are the main arguments raised by Springen?
	What else does my reader need to know?
	What can I explain further?
WHEN?	When is TV a problem?
	When is TV a benefit?
	When will the issues involving TV be resolved?
WHERE?	Where did the problem occur?
	Where were the participants?
WHY?	Why is the issue important?
	Why did it happen?
	Why should you or I care?
	Why should my audience care?
HOW?	How did it happen?
	How does it work?
	How can the problem be resolved?

You may also want to consider these questions after completing the sentence work at the end of the chapter (pages 294–310):

- Have you used transitions to move the reader smoothly from one idea to the next and to provide cohesion throughout your essay?

- Have you used concessions—*though, although, even though*—when you need to make one argument appear more important or stronger than another?

In addition, address the following questions about using sources in your essay:

- Have you brought in your own research findings?

- Have you included publication information for sources? Have you cited sources correctly? (See pages 489–494, "Using Outside Sources.")

Note: If you have any concerns about your essay at this stage of the writing process, be sure to talk them over with your instructor or a tutor.

Edit

Now begin "polishing" your essay. Read your essay aloud and check for typing errors, spelling errors, and any other errors you tend to make. After completing the sentence work at the end of this chapter, consider these questions:

- Have you used subordinators, concessions, and transitions to create clear bridges between opposing ideas?
- Have you punctuated correctly when using subordinators, concessions, and transitions?

If you work with a tutor, ask the tutor to tell you how many (if any) and what types of errors you have made so that you can correct them.

INVESTIGATING THE EFFECTS OF MEDIA MULTITASKING

In recent years, the concern over too much television has expanded to include the concern over too much "screen time" in general. Today, ninety-nine out of one hundred households have at least one television, and more than half of them also have home computers. On average, teens spend about $6\frac{1}{2}$ hours juggling media daily, according to a recent Kaiser Family Foundation study. A teen might surf the Internet or exchange e-mail while watching television. Or she might listen to her iPod while IMing (instant messaging) a friend. In addition, she may be attempting to complete her homework. No wonder parents, educators, and many health-care professionals are raising concerns over media multitasking (using more than one type of technology at the same time) and its potential effects on America's youth.

It's doubtful that today's teens would part with their computers, cell phones, or iPods willingly. Still, the issue of media multitasking and the potential for damage should not be ignored. In this assignment, you'll consider the possible effects of media multitasking on teens. You'll also explore what—if anything—might be done to prevent or lessen any negative effects.

Discuss and Engage

Parents, educators, and medical professionals argue that too much time spent with media may isolate teens, affect their ability to concentrate, or even disrupt their brain development. At the same time, these adults would admit that they envy the ease with which teens are able to engage and juggle several forms of media at a time.

Journal Assignment

Media Multitasking

Discuss these questions with classmates and take notes as you talk: What kinds of media do teenagers seem most interested in? What are some of the reasons teens use media? Why might they media multitask? What problems or advantages might media multitasking present for teens?

   Now write a journal entry in which you respond to the following questions: Have you ever used more than one form of media at a time? If so, what technologies were you using simultaneously and why? Describe any media multitasking problems you encountered and how you managed them.

Writing Assignment #3: The Effects of Media Multitasking on Our Youth

Here, in brief, is the writing assignment you are preparing for.

Write an essay in which you discuss objectively the effects of media multitasking (using more than one form of media at the same time) on young people. Come to a conclusion about what we should do to make the most of technology while protecting the future of our youth.

Read, Discuss, Think Critically

The *CBSNews.com* article that follows addresses the growing concern over media multitasking and its potential effects on teens. Follow the PARTS of the reading process as you study the article.

Reading Assignment: "This Is Your Brain Online"

Preview   Read the title and the first three paragraphs. Because this is a journalistic piece, the introduction and thesis are similar to what you would expect to see in a newspaper article.

Anticipate   What do you anticipate this article will be about? Use the "Notes" column to record your thoughts.

Read and Reread   Read the entire article. As you read, highlight unknown terms and interesting ideas so that you can return to them. Then reread more slowly. As you reread, define terms and comment on important ideas in the "Notes" column.

This Is Your Brain Online
by Amy Sara Clark

1   The high school sophomore who stays up all night adding to her blog. The 14-year-old who plays "Warcraft" for 12 hours at a stretch. The honors student who says she has no problem writing her English essay while IMing with her boyfriend and compiling iTunes play lists. Teens will swear up and down that the technology they won't turn off is harmless fun.

2   But what if they're wrong?

3   Only this much is certain: Teens are spending a lot of time hooked up—an average of $6^1/_2$ hours a day, according to a survey by the Kaiser Family Foundation. Parents, researchers, and educators are trying to figure out what all these hours plugged in are doing to their brains.

The Teen Brain As Construction Site

4   When considering whether damage is actually being done, the first thing to understand is that the teenage brain is an unfinished product, explains David Walsh, a psychologist and author of "Why Do They Act That Way? A Survival Guide to the Adolescent Brain for You and Your Teen." The brain continues to develop in spurts until we're about 25— something car insurance companies figured out a long time ago, and

which you may have noticed when your rates dropped after your 25th birthday.

5 "Experiences that have the greatest impact on the wiring of the brain are those that happen during the brain's growth spurts," he says. During those spurts, the nerve endings grow rapidly, a process called blossoming. During that time, the cells that fire strengthen networks. The ones that don't die back—it's called pruning.

6 Say a 2-year-old has chronic, untreated ear infections. Because his auditory functioning is being wired then, the child could end up with permanent hearing problems.

7 In the teenage years, says Walsh, one of the major circuits that's developing is the prefrontal cortex. "The circuits that are under construction during the teen years have to do with impulse control, management of aggression, emotional regulation, self regulation—a lot of 'executive functions' of the brain," he says. This might explain why your teen might suddenly storm out during breakfast or pick fights at school.

8 It's also the reason teenagers are famous for having to pull all-nighters, not thinking through the consequences of downloading porn onto mom's computer, or piercing their tongues. That's because the prefrontal cortex also handles planning, reasoning and social skills, says Jordan Grafman, who heads the cognitive neuroscience section at the National Institute of Neurological Disorders and Stroke. "It's what makes us human," he says—and because it's still developing, "it's very susceptible to trends and changes that happen during the adolescent years."

Doing Too Much?

9 Perhaps this sounds familiar: Your daughter says she's doing her homework, but you keep hearing her IM chime. She swears she "only spent five minutes" updating her blog. Those Mariah Carey songs she's downloading? That doesn't take any time at all.

10 Teens may think they're just taking little breaks, but David Meyer, a psychologist who directs the Brain, Cognition, and Action Laboratory at the University of Michigan, says they have no idea how much time they're really losing.

11 "I think there's a lot of mythology out there about how great multitasking is and that it's the sexy thing," Meyer says. He compares the image of the teen who can simultaneously IM with five friends while doing his homework with the Marlboro Man of the mid 20th century. "It's almost like smoking was in the '50s and '60s," he says, "It's a bunch of hype."

Notes

12   That's because multitaskers don't just lose the minutes they spend on sites such as Facebook; they also lose time getting reoriented with each interruption, says Meyer, whose lab has conducted experiments on multitasking for more than a decade. That means the homework itself can take between 25 and 400 percent longer depending on the complexity and similarity of the tasks.

13   Similarity? Yes. It turns out the worst kind of multitasking is between two related tasks, because they use the same parts of the brain. It's better, Meyer says, to switch from math to piano than, say, history to English.

14   That's why it's possible to fold laundry while listening to the stock report on the radio, he says. "They're relying on different kinds of information processing," he says, noting that the folding is a more automated task.

15   So how about talking on a cell phone and driving? While these may seem like different tasks, they both use the "talking" areas of the brain, Meyer says. Say you're driving in heavy traffic, he says. "You're reading signs and thinking what to do next. All this is talking to yourself."

16   Grafman, from the NIH [National Institutes of Health], says his problem with multitasking goes beyond concerns about safety or inefficiency.

17   "If you're constantly shifting around between tasks, then it's likely you can actually get pretty good at learning visual motor requirements for that shifting," he says. "But what does that cost you in terms of depth of knowledge?"

18   "These are frivolous, leisure time activities" he says, adding that he'd "love to compete against those kids for jobs or anything else [sic] they're not going to have the knowledge."

Questions for Critical Thought

"This Is Your Brain Online"

1. In the opening paragraph, Clark uses a series of three sentence fragments to draw us into the article. (Professional writers sometimes make a stylistic choice to use fragments.) Edit these three fragments—simply by removing one word in each sentence—to make them complete sentences. Which seems more effective to you—the fragments or the complete sentences?

2. Now examine the first three paragraphs (which act together as the introduction). What do you think Clark will focus on in the article?

3. Clark describes a variety of media activities that most teens would consider "harmless fun." What effects, if any, might these activities have on teens?

4. David Walsh, an expert cited in Clark's article, believes the teenager's brain is like "a construction site." Explain what he means by this. What evidence does Walsh use to support his point of view?

5. According to the article, what might happen if a young person's brain is stifled during a growth spurt?

6. What part of the brain is developing during the teen years and which mental functions relate to it?

7. Why might those who media multitask actually be losing time instead of gaining time, according to experts?

8. What kinds of evidence does Clark use to develop her essay? What additional evidence or information might she provide to develop her essay further?

Notes

Journal Assignment

Considering "This Is Your Brain Online"

Respond to Clark's article. Should parents and other concerned adults worry about the increase in media multitasking and its potential effects on our youth? What advice would you give to a parent who is worried?

Explore the Writing Assignment

Here, again, is the writing assignment you are preparing for:

> *Write an essay in which you discuss objectively the effects of media multitasking (using more than one form of media at the same time) on young people. Come to a conclusion about what we should do to make the most of technology while protecting the future of our youth.*

Activities

Charting the Effects of Media Multitasking

Referring back to "This Is Your Brain Online," make a list of some of the potential effects of media and media multitasking (both positive and negative) on teens. Next to each of the potential effects, list evidence you could use to show why it is a potential effect.

Notes

Looking for Information at the Library and on the Internet

1. Go to the library to find books and articles on the issue of media multitasking or the effects of media on young people. (Ask the librarian for help in conducting a search for books and articles if you're unsure of what to look for or where to look.)

   As you read the sources, be sure to take notes and write down source information—author, title, page numbers, and publication information. Add new information you find to your chart of potential effects. (See pages 489–494 for more information on citing sources.)

2. Spend some time on the Internet looking for articles on the subject. (If you need help with online research, return to the library and ask a librarian to help you conduct an online search.)

   As you find information, be sure to take notes and write down source information—author, title, Web address, and the date on which you retrieved the information. Add new information you find to your chart of potential effects.

Brainstorm   Write freely about the possible effects of media use and/or media multitasking on teens. Refer back to "This Is Your Brain Online" as needed. Also, return to your chart and any library information you found.

Consider Your Audience   Imagine your audience as a group of teens or adults who are concerned about the future of our youth. Chances are that most, if not all, use some forms of technology daily. Consider how best to approach them about the effects of media multitasking on our youth.

Create Your Thesis   Review the writing assignment. Note that you've been asked to discuss *objectively* the effects of media multitasking (using more than one form of media at the same time) on young people. Your thesis should reflect what you believe about the issue.

Outline   Think about how you might best organize your ideas. Draft an outline or make a list of the points you intend to make in your essay. Under each point, note the kind of support you'll use to develop your idea. Here are some options for organizing your essay:

- Offer least important ideas first and most important ideas last.
- Present least interesting ideas first and most interesting ideas last.

- Alternate positive and negative effects of media multitasking.
- Present all positive effects (divided into different paragraphs), then all negative effects (divided into different paragraphs).

Draft

Using your reading notes, chart of effects, brainstorming notes, journal entries, thesis statement, and outline, begin drafting your essay. Your introduction should explain the concern over the effects of media multitasking on our youth. Working from your outline of points, develop the body paragraphs of your essay. Be sure to include support in the form of evidence, details, examples, and discussion. In your conclusion, explain what you believe we should do to make the most of technology while protecting our youth.

Revise

Activity

Share Your Writing

As you read your classmate's essay, consider the following questions:

- Have you remained objective as you covered the most important effects of media multitasking?

- Can your reader see your organizational pattern? Have you limited each paragraph to one main idea? And have you fully developed each paragraph idea?

- Does your conclusion offer a clear recommendation about what can be done to reduce the negative effects of media multitasking?

Next, apply the Questions for Development to your essay to see where you might develop ideas even further (page 242).

You may also want to consider these questions after completing the sentence work at the end of the chapter (pages 294–310):

- Have you used transitions to move the reader smoothly from one idea to the next and to provide cohesion throughout your essay?

- Have you used concessions—*though, although, even though*—when you need to make one argument appear more important or stronger than another?

In addition, address the following questions about using sources in your essay:

- Have you brought in your own research?

- Have you included publication information for books and articles? Have you cited sources correctly? (See pages 489–494, "Using Outside Sources.")

Note: If you have any concerns about your essay at this stage of the writing process, be sure to talk them over with your instructor or a tutor.

Edit

Now begin "polishing" your essay. Read your essay aloud and check for typing errors, spelling errors, and any other errors you tend to make. After completing the sentence work at the end of this chapter, consider these questions:

- Have you used subordinators, concessions, and transitions to create clear bridges between opposing ideas?
- Have you punctuated correctly when using subordinators, concessions, and transitions?

If you work with a tutor, ask the tutor to tell you how many (if any) and what types of errors you have made so that you can correct them.

TIME TO REFLECT

Journal Assignment

Your Progress as a Writer, Reader, and Critical Thinker

Think about what you've learned about development in this chapter. Write a journal entry explaining what you've learned. You may want to think about these questions before you write.

- What should writers keep in mind when developing their paragraph or essay ideas?
- How do the Questions for Development help writers fully develop their ideas?
- What have you learned about developing an argument or discussion?

SUMMARY OF CHAPTER 6

In this chapter, you've strengthened your essay writing skills as you've practiced

- exploring ideas and then narrowing your focus to identify a thesis worth developing;
- selecting only the most significant main points to address in body paragraphs;
- relying on examples, studies, statistics, experiences, and other forms of evidence to develop paragraphs and support the thesis of your essay;
- including *only* the pieces of evidence that help you develop paragraph ideas and support the thesis of your essay;
- achieving a healthy balance between examples and discussion in your paragraphs;
- expressing your own opinion and analysis of research, ideas, and issues; and
- using the Questions for Development to help you fully develop ideas.

Notes

SUBORDINATORS, CONCESSIONS, AND TRANSITIONS

Reviewing Subordinators
Punctuating Correctly with Subordinators
Recognizing Emphasis
Making Concessions
Transitions
Punctuating Correctly with Transitions
Transitions That Interrupt Sentences
Punctuating Correctly with Interrupting Transitions

In this chapter, you're exploring the effects of media on children, teens, and the family. The first writing assignment asks you to argue. The second and third ask you to objectively discuss the negative and positive effects of television and the media. Thus, one of your challenges in this chapter is to discuss opposing ideas in a smooth, clear manner. You need to create bridges that explain the relationship between ideas.

There are many ways to create these bridges. This chapter will focus on two ways. The first method requires you to use a select group of subordinators that allow you to make concessions. The second method requires that you use transitions.

Reviewing Subordinators

See Chapter 4 for a complete review of subordinators.

In this section, you'll learn how to handle opposing ideas by using a group of subordinators that express opposition, and you'll learn how to place a subordinator in just the right place to make your position clearer and stronger.

Remember, the following subordinators express opposition:

although

even though

though

while

whereas

When you are discussing viewpoints that are different from one another—maybe even the opposite of one another—you can use these subordinators to build bridges between the ideas. The following sentences might be confusing with no bridge between them:

> Obesity is linked to television viewing. The cause-effect relationship between the two is not a strong one.

These sentences read more smoothly when a subordinator attaches to one of them, creating a dependent clause and warning the reader that the two ideas are in contrast to one another.

> <u>Although</u> obesity is linked to television viewing, the cause-effect relationship between the two is not a strong one.

The subordinator can also go between the two sentences.

> Obesity is linked to television viewing <u>although</u> the cause-effect relationship between the two is not a strong one.

Punctuating Correctly with Subordinators

In Chapter 4, you learned that there are two punctuation rules that apply to subordinated clauses. Remember that when a subordinator attaches to an independent clause (a sentence), the independent clause becomes dependent:

> I learned quite a bit from Winn's essay. (independent clause)
> <u>Although</u> I learned quite a bit from Winn's essay . . . (dependent clause)
> The point about resourcefulness was excellent. (independent clause)
> <u>Even though</u> the point about resourcefulness was excellent . . . (dependent clause)

To create a complete sentence, the dependent clause must attach to an independent clause:

> <u>Although</u> I learned quite a bit from Winn's essay, I disagreed with four important points.
> <u>Even though</u> the point about resourcefulness was excellent, I have serious objections to Winn's points about obesity and addiction.

How you punctuate a sentence with a dependent and independent clause depends on where the dependent clause is. Review these rules from Chapter 4:

Notes

> ## Punctuation Rule #5 (Review)
>
> *When you begin a sentence with a subordinated or dependent clause, you must put a comma after the subordinated (or dependent) clause.*
>
> - <u>Although</u> I learned quite a bit from Winn's essay, I disagreed with four important points.

> ## Punctuation Rule #6 (Review)
>
> *If the subordinated clause comes after the independent clause, you do not need a comma.*
>
> - I disagreed with four important points <u>although</u> I learned quite a bit from Winn's essay.

Recognizing Emphasis

So where should you place your subordinator? Does it matter which sentence it attaches to? Yes! It does matter. Where you place your subordinator is very important because one clause (and the idea in that clause) will get more emphasis than the other, so keep the following point in mind:

> When a sentence consists of a subordinated clause and an independent clause, the idea in the independent clause will come across with more emphasis. The subordinated clause is considered the weaker clause with the weaker idea.

Consider the following sentence (the independent clause is underlined):

> Although some kids might behave differently after watching violence on television, <u>most kids will not be affected</u>.

The writer is emphasizing that *most kids will not be affected*. In the next sentence, the writer is emphasizing possible dangers of violent television:

> Although most kids will not be affected, <u>some kids might behave differently after watching violence on television</u>.

Or

> <u>Some kids might behave differently after watching violence on television</u> although most kids will not be affected.

Practice #1   Emphasizing and Punctuating
In the following sentences,

- underline the independent clause—the independent clause expresses the idea that is being emphasized and
- check the punctuation, adding a comma when necessary.

Example: Although I try not to use the TV as a babysitter very often sometimes "plugging in" the kids is the only way for me to get a little peace.

- Although I try not to use the TV as a babysitter very often, <u>sometimes "plugging in" the kids is the only way for me to get a little peace.</u> (Notice the comma after the dependent clause.)

1. Even though I know I can't and shouldn't shelter my children from popular culture I limit their television viewing time in the hope that they won't emulate what they see on television.
2. Although my son prefers the violent cartoons he also enjoys educational shows like *The Magic School Bus.*
3. Television can teach kids basic school skills and even show them a variety of careers though television sometimes glamorizes criminal lifestyles.
4. I believe that the key to health and happiness is balance whereas my spouse tends to be more extreme.
5. I think the kids should be able to watch two hours of television a day while my spouse thinks that there should be no television until the weekend.

Making Concessions

Using subordinators to show emphasis is particularly helpful when you are writing an argumentative essay. These subordinators allow you to *make a concession* while still emphasizing your own point. **Making a concession** means that you acknowledge the other side's position. For example, assume that a writer is arguing in favor of turning the television off. In a desire to put forth a reasonable and educated tone, the writer wants to acknowledge that the opposition has some reasonable arguments. However, the writer wants to maintain an emphasis on his

Notes

own points. The subordinators *although, though, even though,* and *while* are particularly good for such a situation.

Examine the following sentences. The writer has placed the subordinator next to the ideas he wants to deemphasize. The independent clause is underlined.

Although I understand that kids might learn from educational television programs, <u>there are other, better ways to learn that don't carry the dangers of television viewing.</u>

Even though most kids probably recognize the "unreality" of television, <u>adults can't always tell how children are interpreting what they see and hear.</u>

Concessions are quite powerful when writing argumentative essays. The following exercises will give you some practice in manipulating subordinated clauses in order to show emphasis and make concessions.

Practice #2   Making Concessions

On a separate piece of paper, join the sentences below using the following subordinators: *although, even though, though,* and *while.* Use each subordinator at least once. Check your punctuation.

1. For the moment, assume that you support a No-TV Week. Placing your subordinators carefully, join the sentences and emphasize your position.

   a. One week of no television may not change everyone's perspective about television. It may wake up some kids and parents and result in some really wonderful changes for those families.

   b. My kids had a great time rediscovering old games and toys. The first few days without a television were pretty rough.

2. Now, assume that you do <u>not</u> support a No-TV Week. Placing your subordinator carefully, join the sentences so that you are expressing a concession, but still emphasizing your own position.

   a. I don't believe that it is necessary to turn off the television for a whole week. I do think we could cut back a bit.

   b. There are some kids who watch too much television. I think most kids at our school have too much homework and extracurricular activities to watch much television.

3. Assume that you want to argue that television has a negative effect on how kids perform at school. Placing your subordinator carefully, join the sentences so that you are expressing a concession, but still emphasizing your own position.

   a. Some kids respond well to educational television programs. I think even educational programs teach kids to be passive learners.

4. Assume that you want to express your support of educational television. Placing your subordinator carefully, join the sentences so that you are expressing a concession, but still emphasizing your own position.

   a. Some people will claim that television is not a good teacher. My child resisted learning her ABCs from me but loved the lessons on PBS.

5. Assume that you want to argue that television does not affect a child's resourcefulness. Placing your subordinator carefully, join the sentences so that you are expressing a concession, but still emphasizing your own position.

   a. My nephews have learned games and created their own craft projects after watching a preteen show on PBS. Winn says that television makes children less resourceful.

   b. A few may just stare at the screen and seem to get little benefit. The kids I observed had interesting things to talk about after watching their favorite shows.

Practice #3   Create Concessions

Choose from the following list of subordinators and create the sentences described in the exercises:

although

even though

though

while

Example: Create a sentence that supports one of Winn's eight points and makes a concession to those who don't agree with Winn.

• While it may be difficult at first to see television viewing as an addiction similar to alcoholism, I think Winn makes a strong case for labeling excessive viewing as an addiction.

Subordinators, Concessions, and Transitions

Notes

1. Create a sentence that supports one of Winn's eight points and makes a concession to those who don't agree with Winn.
2. Create a sentence that supports another one of Winn's eight points and makes a concession to those who don't agree with Winn.
3. Create a sentence that argues against one of Winn's eight points and makes a concession to those who do agree with Winn.
4. Create a sentence that argues against another one of Winn's eight points and makes a concession to those who do agree with Winn.

Transitions

Transitions are another valuable tool when building bridges between ideas. Consider how odd these sentences sound together:

> Mr. Beazer wasn't sure his wife would approve of the movie he rented for the children because it had some bad language in it. He loved the unpredictable plot line and the message at the end.

Now consider how these sentences sound when they have a transition acting as a bridge between them:

> Mr. Beazer wasn't sure his wife would approve of the movie he rented for the children because it had some bad language in it; however, he loved the unpredictable plot line and the message at the end.

The *however* warns the reader that an *opposite* idea is coming. The writer is acknowledging two opposing ideas.

Here's another example. Without a transition, the following sentences might appear to be a list of unrelated ideas:

> I think kids today spend too much time watching television. I think kids rely on high-tech toys instead of their own imaginations for fun.

In the following sentences, the relationship between the ideas is much clearer. The transition tells the reader that a *similar* idea is coming. Note that the transition comes at the beginning of a sentence.

> I think kids today spend too much time watching television. <u>Similarly</u>, I think kids rely on high-tech toys instead of their own imaginations for fun.

Subordinators, Concessions, and Transitions

Here is a list of transitions and their meanings: *Notes*

also, furthermore, next, similarly, in addition, likewise: express addition of similar ideas

consequently, therefore, thus, as a result: express cause-effect

however, otherwise, in contrast: express opposites

then, next, finally, now, first, second, third: express time

for example, such as, for instance: introduce an example

Practice #4   Identify the Transitions

In the following sentences, underline the transitions you find.

Example: I asked the question three times. Finally, she gave me an answer.

- I asked the question three times. <u>Finally</u>, she gave me an answer.

1. He didn't want to use television as a babysitter; however, he couldn't think of a better alternative.
2. The mother didn't limit the amount of television the children watched. Furthermore, she let them watch any programs they wanted.
3. My son's grades were dropping. Consequently, I took away his television privileges for a week.
4. I interviewed three children in my neighborhood; then, I interviewed their parents and day care providers.
5. I was surprised by what the preschool teacher said. For example, she said that she encourages parents to have their children watch *Sesame Street*.

Punctuating Correctly with Transitions

Unlike subordinators, transitions do not change independent clauses into dependent clauses. As a result, even if you add a transition to create a bridge between sentences, you still have to punctuate the sentences as two independent clauses. You have two options: You can use a period or a semicolon.

Option #1

Put a period between the two sentences and a comma after the transition word.

Subordinators, Concessions, and Transitions

Notes

I think we need clearer guidelines for how much television the children can watch. <u>Furthermore,</u> we need to set rules for using the computer.

Option #2
Put a semicolon between the two sentences and a comma after the transition word.

I think we need clearer guidelines for how much television the children can watch; <u>furthermore,</u> we need to set rules for using the computer.

Review these punctuation rules from Chapter 4.

Punctuation Rule #3 (Review)
You may use a semicolon to separate two complete sentences.

- The television broke; I turned to my dusty bookshelf to find a source of entertainment.

Punctuation Rule #4 (Review)
Follow an introductory word or phrase with a comma.

- Consequently, I watch only cable channels.

Punctuation Rules #3 and #4 (Combined)
Punctuation Rules #3 and #4 are both applied when you join two complete sentences with a semicolon and transition.

- I despise commercial interruptions; consequently, I watch only cable channels.

Practice #5   Using Transitions
On a separate piece of paper, rewrite the sentences, adding the transitions as directed.

Example: I used to think that I couldn't live without television. You can imagine my fear when I moved to a dorm room with no TV! (Use *thus* with a semicolon and a comma between the two sentences.)

- I used to think that I couldn't live without television; thus, you can imagine my fear when I moved to a dorm room with no TV!

1. Kyle thought Winn was right about the link between obesity and television. He felt that her theory about television being an addiction was a little nutty. (Use *however* with a semicolon and a comma between the two sentences.)

2. I did some further research into the effects of television on children. I created strict rules for television watching at my house. (Use *then* with a semicolon and a comma between the two sentences.)

3. I realized I was watching over 50 hours of television a week. I set a goal to spend at least five hours a week exercising and five more hours reading novels. (Use *consequently* with a semicolon and a comma between the two sentences.)

4. First, I did some research on the Internet. I went to the college library. (Use *next* and a comma to begin the second sentence.)

5. The researcher shared her notes with us. She loaned us some of her videotapes. (Use *furthermore* and a comma to begin the second sentence.)

6. The article came from a tabloid that is known for poor journalism. I don't think you should give it much attention. (Choose a transition from the following list that most clearly expresses the relationship between these two sentences: *however, therefore,* or *for instance.* Use the transition word with a semicolon and a comma to join the two sentences.)

7. I don't want my children watching television all day. I don't want them focused on video games or the computer. (Choose a transition from the following list that most clearly expresses the relationship between these two sentences: *otherwise, therefore,* or *likewise.* Use the transition word with a semicolon and a comma to join the two sentences.)

8. My grandkids were glued to the video screen in the minivan. They didn't even notice the amazing cliffs and waterfalls we drove by. (Choose a transition from the following list that most clearly expresses the relationship between these two sentences: *similarly, for instance,* or *as a result.* Use the transition word and a comma to begin the second sentence.)

Subordinators, Concessions, and Transitions

9. First, I made notes about the cartoons the kids were watching. I observed how they behaved immediately following the cartoons. (Choose a transition from the following list that most clearly expresses the relationship between these two sentences: *second, however,* or *consequently.* Use the transition word and a comma to begin the second sentence.)

10. My daughter used to drive me crazy by asking for everything she saw advertised on television. I told her she could only watch PBS. (Choose a transition that clearly expresses the relationship between these two sentences. Choose to join the sentences by using a semicolon and comma, or choose to keep the sentences separate.)

Transitions That Interrupt Sentences

Thus far you have learned that you can place transitions at the beginning of independent clauses to create a link between ideas. To add variety to your sentence structure, you can also *interrupt* a single sentence with a transition. Study the examples that follow.

> I always enjoyed reading. My brother, <u>however</u>, was hooked on television at an early age.
>
> The children were participating in a no-television week. Their afternoon playtime, <u>therefore</u>, changed.
>
> The kids discovered all sorts of old toys. Jason, <u>for example</u>, found his old Monopoly game.

Interrupting a sentence with a transition word can add variety to your style while also helping you to strengthen the coherence of your essay.

Punctuating Correctly with Interrupting Transitions

Punctuation Rule #7

If you interrupt a single sentence with a transition word, you must put a comma before and after the transition word.

- The kids were entranced by the documentary on volcanoes. I, therefore, extended their usual television time.
- Bob's classmates weren't persuaded by his arguments. Bob, consequently, decided to do a little more research.

Practice #6   Using Interrupting Transitions

- Read these sentence pairs carefully.
- Insert an appropriate transition word or phrase in the second sentence in each pair. Read each sentence aloud to make sure that you have made the best choice.
- Use each of these transitions once:

    similarly

    therefore

    however

    consequently

1. My spouse argues that a limited amount of television watching is

   okay.

   I, _____, want to throw out the set.

2. During the No-TV Week, the teachers saw that the students were

   doing better work on take-home assignments.

   The parents, _____, found that the kids com-

   pleted their chores more quickly.

3. I realized I hadn't played any sports with my kids in months.

   All of us decided, _____, to begin playing tennis at

   least one evening every week.

4. Sandy always had the television turned on.

   Her new roommate, _____, accused Sandy of being

   addicted to television.

Notes

In case you were wondering, placing an interrupting transition between the subject and verb does not violate Style Tip #1 (put the subject and verb close together). By putting a comma before and after the interrupting transition, you are telling your reader that the words in between the commas can be lifted out of the sentence, and the sentence will still function grammatically. Adding an interrupting word (with the necessary commas) actually improves the style of your writing because it adds a little variety—a little color.

Practice #7   More Practice with Interrupting Transitions

Interrupt the second sentence in each pair with a transition word. Write your new sentence on a separate piece of paper. Choose from the following list of transitions. (Use each transition once.)

furthermore
however
therefore
finally
for example
consequently
for instance

Example: Everyone in class had an opinion.
The class discussion was excellent.

• The class discussion, <u>consequently,</u> was excellent.

Hint: The interrupting transition word often fits most smoothly right after the subject and before the verb.

1. I wanted to paint a picture in my reader's mind. I focused on using my five senses to find details that would intrigue the reader.
2. My classmate said I used some great quotes. The quotes needed to be explained.
3. I think that if you involve your kids in fun after-school activities, they won't even think about turning on the television. My kids are so busy with soccer, piano, and homework that they don't even mention television during the week.
4. I knew one example wasn't enough to make readers take my side. I found two more examples to use in that paragraph.
5. Every student in the workshop group told Cassandra that she shouldn't try to argue against all of Winn's points. Cassandra selected two of the more complex points to argue.
6. I agree with McGinn that children do think while watching television. My son will talk to the television when watching *Blue's Clues.*

7. I watch television to learn about gardening, cooking, decorating, and even fixing my plumbing. Television offers me an easy mental escape at the end of a stressful day.

Practice #8   Creating Sentences with Transitions

Create original sentences according to the directions that follow. (Your sentences should connect to the topic of television or media multitasking. Some of these sentences might even end up in your essay.)

1. Write two original sentences. The second should start with *similarly.*
2. Write two original sentences. Connect the sentences using a semicolon, the transition *next,* and a comma.
3. Write two original sentences. The second should start with *also.*
4. Write two original sentences. Connect the sentences using a semicolon, the transition *then,* and a comma.
5. Write two original sentences. The second should start with *likewise.*

Practice #9   Creating Sentences with Interrupting Transitions

Create original sentences according to the directions that follow. (Your sentences should connect to the topic of television or media multitasking. Some of these sentences might even end up in your essay.)

1. Write two original sentences. Interrupt the second sentence with *however.*
2. Write two original sentences. Interrupt the second sentence with *therefore.*
3. Write two original sentences. Interrupt the second sentence with *for example.*

Subordinators, Concessions, and Transitions

Notes

4. Write two original sentences. Interrupt the second sentence with *consequently*.

5. Write two original sentences. Interrupt the second sentence with *furthermore*.

STYLE TIPS

Subordinators, concessions, and transitions can help you polish your sentences. Remember, your goal should be to move beyond achieving correct grammar. You can aim to have clear, interesting, engaging, informative, and varied sentences. Think of sentence style as you might think of fashion. You can come to class wearing a couple of potato sacks pinned together and you will be "dressed." Or you can spend a little more time and energy (and money) and walk through the door looking a bit more put together. (Fortunately, sentence style doesn't cost you any extra money.)

First, review the Style Tips below; then, apply them in the exercises that follow. You'll take plainly dressed paragraphs and turn up the volume on their style.

Style Tip #2 (Review)
Don't use more words than needed.

Style Tip #3 (Review)
Add variety to your sentence structure.

Style Tip #4 (Review)
Provide the necessary connections between ideas and show how ideas relate to one another.

Practice #10   To Multitask or Not to Multitask, That Is the Question
Read the following paragraphs aloud. Use subordinators, transitions, concessions, and Style Tips #2, #3, and #4 to help eliminate

unnecessary words, connect ideas, and add variety. Rewrite the newly edited paragraphs on a separate piece of paper.

Here are some subordinators and transitions to consider:

> *although, even though, though, while, whereas*
> *however, otherwise, in contrast*
> *then, next, finally, now, first, second, third*
> *for example, such as, for instance*

Remember to punctuate correctly!

Opinion #1

I think it is a waste of time to debate whether or not multitasking is healthy. Multitasking is inevitable in our modern world. We have so many technological tools at our fingertips. Life and work move much faster now. A person wants to be competitive in the job market. He better learn to do more than one task at a time. He will be left in the dust wondering why it takes him so much longer to get a project done. Employers will always promote the faster worker.

Opinion #2

I see the writer's point about speed and pleasing an employer. He forgets that employers also care about accuracy and thoroughness. David E. Meyer, of the University of Michigan, says, "When people try to perform two or more related tasks either at the same time or alternating rapidly between them, errors go way up." He goes on to say that "it takes far longer—often double the time or more—to get the jobs done than if they were done sequentially." Some employers will want people who can concentrate, be accurate, and think through complex problems. I definitely think we should debate the healthiness of multitasking. A debate will help us understand what we are doing, why we are doing it, and how we can do our jobs better.

Your Own Writing: Concessions and Transitions

Copy one paragraph from a journal entry or essay in which you are arguing a point. Look for places where a concession would help you maintain a reasonable tone while making your point stand out. Add the concession sentence.

Copy another paragraph from a journal entry or essay. Improve the coherence of your writing by building bridges with transition words:

Notes

- put a transition at the beginning of a sentence,
- use a transition and a semicolon to connect two sentences, or
- interrupt a sentence with a transition.

Using Connections *Online with* **mywritinglab**

For more practice with subordinators, concessions, and transitions, log onto www.mywritinglab.com to access the online resources for *Connections*, Third Edition.

Style Tips

Writing About Surveillance Technology

Main Topics

- Organizing your writing

- Communicating your ideas about surveillance technology

- Using adjectives, adjective phrases, adverbs, and prepositional phrases to make your sentences more expressive

Prickly City by Scott Stantis

Notes

At work and in college, you may find yourself swimming in data, facts, observations, and ideas. As a writer, reader, and critical thinker, you'll need strategies to organize this information so that you can make sense of it and use it. In this chapter, you'll concentrate on understanding and using different methods of *organizing* all the data, facts, observations, and ideas that you choose to communicate.

ORGANIZING YOUR WRITING

One way to think about organization is to remember that as a writer you are similar to a guide leading someone who temporarily doesn't see well. You want to make your reader's journey as smooth as possible (no bumps, cliffs, or wrong turns—unless carefully planned for dramatic effect), so you must *organize* what you say. Of course, you already organize ideas every day: When you explain to someone how to get to a specific file on your computer, when you summarize last night's great movie plot, or when you explain to your child why dishwashing detergent doesn't work in the clothes washer, you organize. In each case, you organize your thoughts to communicate clearly and quickly.

In this chapter, the organizing and communicating will not happen quite so quickly because you will be creating more formal responses to the complex topic of surveillance technology. Surveillance technology refers to the high-tech tools that can be used to watch people. Video cameras are the most common form of surveillance technology, but in this chapter, you will learn about a number of other surveillance tools, and you'll be exploring what happens to our way of life as we begin to watch and be watched more frequently. You will be using your critical thinking skills to carefully consider and sort through different ideas and opinions as you form your own opinions about surveillance technology. Then you'll focus, develop, and organize your ideas as you create a clearly written essay.

Organizing the Paragraph

In an organized paragraph, the writer states the main idea in the topic sentence. Then the writer offers detail and support that usually grow more specific and/or more important. A writer must also include an explanation of the details and supporting ideas. Paragraphs sometimes end with a wrap-up sentence that reminds the reader of the main point of the paragraph. Most paragraphs follow this general pattern:

- Main idea
- Increasingly specific and/or increasingly important details and support
- Wrap-up explanation

For example, consider the following body paragraph from an essay that appears later in this chapter. The essay, by Ivan Amato, focuses on surveillance technology—cameras and other types of technology that can watch people and provide information to the police and government. The body paragraph that follows has a topic sentence that announces the paragraph's main idea. Sentences 2 through 4 offer specific information, and the last sentence emphasizes that while the "clever" technology isn't perfected yet, it will be.

> There is no shortage of cleverness when it comes to building the surveillance state. At the Georgia Institute of Technology, scientists are developing sensor riddled "smart floors" that can identify people by the "force profiles" of their walking feet. Meanwhile, Princeton, NJ–based Sarnoff is working toward an antiterrorist technique that uses a special camera to identify individuals from a hundred meters off by the patterns of color, striation and speckles in their irises. This isn't easy, since the iris and its elements move so quickly relative to a distant camera that the technical task bears some resemblance to "tracking a ballistic missile," says Norman Winarsky, president of nVention, Sarnoff's venture technology company. Still, the technology is coming.

— main idea

— one example

a second example
— with detailed
explanation

— concluding sentence

However, some paragraphs have other, distinct patterns. Here are some other **patterns of organization** that you use every day for speaking, thinking, and writing:

- Least important ideas first, most important ideas last
- Least interesting ideas first, most interesting ideas last
- First idea or event that occurred, second, third, and so on

Occasionally these patterns overlap. That is, a writer might organize his ideas by a time pattern (telling what happened first, second, and so on), *and* he might have in mind that he is organizing his ideas according to importance. (The first event was least important to him, and the last event was most important to him.)

When revising a paragraph, a writer needs to think critically about organization and perhaps experiment with the order a bit. The writer

Notes

For additional information about transitions, see pages 300–308.

must also make sure that the reader can see the logical organization of ideas. The writer can help the reader by using transitions that show the relationships between ideas. For example, if the writer wants to show that the ideas in her paragraph go from the least important idea to the most important idea, she might use any of these transition phrases:

- significantly
- more importantly
- of most importance

If the writer wants to show that the ideas in her paragraph move from the first thing that happened to the second thing that happened and so on, she might use any of these transition words:

- first
- second
- next
- then
- last
- finally

There are many words and phrases writers can use to organize their thoughts and keep the reader on track. Consider how the following words help to explain the relationships between ideas.

To show that a similar idea follows

- also
- in addition
- similarly
- furthermore
- in fact (also adds emphasis)

To show that an example follows

- for example
- for instance

To show that an opposite idea follows

- in contrast
- otherwise
- however

To show that one idea has "caused" another

- consequently
- as a result

- therefore
- thus

Activities

Study an Organized Paragraph

Read the following well-developed paragraph. Then follow the directions beneath it.

> Is it a good idea to give up some of our privacy in exchange for greater protection against terrorists and other criminals? Some people will say, "Yes." In our volatile world, we need new "weapons" of information so that we can stop terrorist acts. Surveillance supporters will say, "If you're a good person, you have nothing to fear." Surveillance technology is only a problem for criminals and terrorists. However, others will say that watching people and invading their privacy won't actually prevent crime or terrorism. The opponents of surveillance technology point out that we can't really monitor all of these cameras all the time. More importantly, opponents argue that we may be creating a whole new group of problems (and crimes) if the recorded information is misused. How do we find the right balance between safety and freedom?

1. In the margins, mark the topic sentence (TS), the examples (Exam), explanations (Explan), and wrap up (W).

2. Highlight or circle any transitions you find, and think about what relationships these words are expressing.

3. What organizational pattern (or patterns) is the writer using?

Organize These Thoughts

Read the following topic sentence and list of supporting ideas for a single paragraph. The sentences have been mixed up and are in no rational order. Study the information and then decide what order the sentences should be in. (You may want to review the patterns of organization.) Referring to the earlier list of transitions, find transition words and phrases that would help build bridges between the ideas in the paragraph, and rewrite the sentences so that you have an organized paragraph with transition words that help the reader understand how all the ideas fit together. Write your version of the paragraph and compare it to the paragraphs your classmates create.

Hint: There may be more than one way to organize the sentences logically. There are many transitions to choose from.

Notes

Topic Sentence: I had a bad experience with surveillance technology at my last job.

He couldn't require us to take the test.

The manager had a good idea who was doing the stealing.

One of the employees was stealing money from the registers.

He decided to ask all of the employees to take a lie detector test.

We knew that if we didn't, we'd probably be fired.

I didn't want to work somewhere where I always felt like I was under suspicion for some crime.

Unfortunately, the test didn't tell him anything conclusively.

He couldn't prove it.

He added clear lockers in the break room so that he could see what we came in with and what we left with.

I felt like I was constantly under surveillance.

His next step was to install cameras over the registers.

I had enjoyed my first three years at that restaurant.

He told us that we could only bring our wallets, keys, and phones in clear bags into work.

I finally had to quit.

Organizing the Essay

The same principles for organizing a paragraph apply to organizing an essay. That is, the ideas in an essay, like the ideas in a paragraph, must be in a thoughtful, logical order. In addition, essays rely on transitions just as paragraphs do.

The organized essay has a clear thesis and topic sentences that relate to that thesis. Often the topic sentences will begin with transition words that explain to the reader why the paragraphs have been organized in a certain pattern. The patterns listed for paragraphs also work with essays. Here, again, are those patterns and some additional patterns:

- Least important ideas first, most important ideas last
- Least interesting ideas first, most interesting ideas last

- First idea or event that occurred, second, third, and so on
- One point about subject X, a related point about subject Y; another point about subject X, a related point about subject Y; and so on (comparison of two subjects)
- All points about subject X, divided into different paragraphs, and then all points about subject Y, divided into different paragraphs (comparison of two subjects)

Activity

Study an Organized Essay

Read the following essay carefully once, marking any unknown words.

The USA Patriot Act
by Megan Rainey

1   On September 11, 2001, America suffered an unprecedented tragedy. We lost nearly 3,000 lives that day, and we lost our precious sense of security. While Americans have been targeted by homegrown terrorists (Oklahoma City, for example), this is the first time that foreign terrorists have acted with such vengeance within our national boundaries. In an effort to boost security and calm national fear, the government quickly wrote and passed the USA Patriot Act—just six weeks after the World Trade Center disaster. As time passed and the cloud of panic dissipated, Americans have begun to question whether the Patriot Act is a danger to our personal privacy and the very fabric of our freedom or a necessary layer of protection in the modern world.

2   The Patriot Act (PA) is a long, complex piece of legislation, but its focus is to make it easier and faster for the government to gather information that might help protect us from future terrorist attacks. First, the PA allows the government to monitor a person's communications. The government can tap a telephone line and read e-mails without getting a warrant and without notifying the person being investigated. In addition, the PA allows government agents to open medical and financial records—again without warrants or notification. Even library and bookstore purchases can be monitored. The PA also makes it easier for the government to detain and deport immigrants. Of course, the government has always been able to do all of this surveillance, but the difference now is that agents do not need get a court order from a judge, and they do not have to notify the person being investigated. The goal

of the PA is to make it much easier and faster for investigators to get information, thus allowing us to get the terrorists before they get us.

3   The argument against the PA is that it goes too far. Opponents fear that the PA gives the government too much indiscriminate power and could lead to a situation where the American people fear our own government nearly as much as we fear foreign terrorists. For example, opponents are uncomfortable with the idea that a person who simply researches war and terrorism—checking out books at the library and making purchases at a bookstore—could suddenly be marked as a threat and investigated. Most recently, a judge struck down part of the Patriot Act that allowed the government to issue NSLs (National Security Letters). Government investigators have been sending these letters to Internet providers, telephone companies, and communication firms telling them to turn over not only all of the records of certain individuals but also the records of those individuals' associates. Consequently, simply exchanging an e-mail with a person being investigated could lead to *you* being investigated. The letters inform the recipients that they must not notify the individuals being investigated. Prior to the PA, an American could not be extensively investigated without also being notified. Opponents say this secrecy allows the government dangerous freedom and will, eventually, destroy every American's sense of personal privacy, security, and freedom.

4   In contrast, the proponents of the PA say that it is absolutely necessary to give our government more freedom and more ability to track, investigate, and arrest terrorists. The proponents point out that it is unfair and unrealistic to think that the U.S. government can eliminate sophisticated terrorist cells if we tie the government's hands with rules, restrictions, and time-consuming procedures. The proponents point out that while it might be uncomfortable to discover your phone and e-mail records have been investigated, it would be far worse to suffer another September 11th. They add that if you are innocent, you have nothing to fear. The modern world demands more powerful surveillance.

5   The Patriot Act has stirred some powerful debate. Are we endangering our Constitution, or are we protecting it? Can we exercise our right to life, liberty, and the pursuit of happiness while under a microscope? Should there be limits? What would those limits be? Can we openly debate the Patriot Act, or will being an opponent mark a person as a threat to the United States?

1. Reread the essay more carefully. Mark the thesis and topic sentences. Define any unknown terms.

2. Mark all transition words and phrases you find (at the beginning of paragraphs and within paragraphs). You may want to refer to the list

of transitions on pages 314–315, and keep an eye out for words that don't appear on that list but seem to be acting as transitions.

3. Note in the margins the organizational pattern the author has used to put her paragraphs in order. Note also how individual sentences relate to one another. For example, look for transitional words or phrases that tell you the author is connecting opposite ideas.

4. In your own words, what is the writer's purpose in writing this essay?

One Approach to Organization

Just as there are many ways that writers brainstorm, gather information, and draft essays, there are also many ways to organize information for an essay. In this chapter, you will practice one approach that uses index cards. When you reach the point in your writing process at which you are ready to outline the ideas of your essay, you'll write down one point per index card, label the card, and perhaps even color code the card. Then you'll be able to arrange the cards in different orders until you find an organizational pattern that fits with what you want to say. Here are some examples of how you can create the cards for an essay about the advantages and disadvantages of surveillance technology.

(front of card)

> *Advantage*
>
> Video cameras placed outside your home can protect your property.

Label the card as *Advantage* or *Disadvantage*. State one point on the front of the card. On the back of each card, explain where you got your idea.

(back of card)

> Personal experience. I caught a man trying to steal my car.

Notes   (front of card)

> *Disadvantage*
>
> We will always feel we are being watched, even in department stores.

(back of card)

> Amato, paragraph 14.

In this chapter, cards can be labeled as *Advantage, Disadvantage, 1984, the modern world,* or *the future,* depending on which writing assignment you're working on. Writing Assignment #1 will focus on advantages and disadvantages, whereas Writing Assignment #2 will focus on different time periods. You may even want to color code your cards—one color for advantage cards and another for disadvantage cards. (Or use one color for facts connecting to *1984,* another color for facts connecting to the modern world, and another for facts connecting to the future.) Use your own words when making these notes. On the front of each card, you'll have just one idea. On the back of the card, you'll write down where you got the information. If the information comes from a reading, you'll have to write down the author's name and the paragraph number. Then you'll be able to go back and read more about an idea if you need to, and you'll have your source information ready when you begin writing your essay.

You may find that some cards have ideas that will become topic sentences. Other cards will have ideas that belong in the bodies of paragraphs. The key is to write just one idea per card. Then you can easily move the ideas around until you have found the best way to group them and organize them.

At the outline stage of your writing process, feel free to make many cards because this way you'll have many ideas to choose from as you

prepare to write your essay, and it's easy to set aside a card that you decide doesn't fit. (Keep all the cards you make in this chapter. If you are
assigned both essays from this chapter, some of your cards may be
needed again.)

Points to Remember About Organization

- Although only five organizational patterns have been described so
  far, there are more than just five ways to organize ideas in an essay,
  and some of the patterns mentioned here can be combined. (You'll
  be introduced to more patterns later in the chapter.)
- Use a pattern that makes sense to you and that seems to fit with
  what you want to say.
- Stick to your pattern. Your reader will have an easier time understanding your ideas if you have a clear pattern of organization and
  if you stick to your pattern. Your reader will enjoy the smooth
  path you create.
- Use transitions to help guide your reader.

INVESTIGATING SURVEILLANCE TECHNOLOGY

Now that you have begun to think about the skill of organizing, you'll
begin your writing process. You'll discuss surveillance technology and
the many ways our lives have been affected by it. You'll have quite a bit
of information to consider and sort through. Later in this chapter, you
will find two writing assignments and step-by-step guidelines as you
complete your writing process.

Discuss and Engage

Surveillance technology is a broad term encompassing everything from
"nanny cameras" to satellites. As you begin thinking about this subject
area, consider these definitions. *Surveillance* means observation. *Technology*, in this case, refers to scientifically advanced equipment made
by humans. Put the terms together and we're talking about equipment
used to watch and observe people and events. Being watched can elicit
different reactions from people. Sometimes it can feel comforting, but
at other times it can feel intrusive.

Journal Assignment

Being Watched

Reread the comic strip on page 311. List a few of the feelings that the characters might be experiencing. When have you been watched? (You can consider being watched by cameras or by people you can actually see.) When have you felt good about being watched, and when have you felt uncomfortable?

Activity

Safety versus Privacy

Be sure to take notes during each step of this activity.

1. Working with a classmate or two, make a list of situations in which you have been watched by security cameras or security guards. Can you and your classmates think of any other forms of surveillance technology you have come in contact with? (You may want to think about airports, city streets, and government buildings as well as department stores.)

2. Discuss with your classmate(s) when and where high-tech surveillance seems appropriate.

3. Discuss how important privacy is to you. Do you mind being watched while in public? How do you feel about your telephone calls and e-mail being monitored? Is it okay to have your purchases monitored?

Journal Assignment

Advantages and Disadvantages of Surveillance Technology

Review your activity and journal notes on surveillance technology. What are the most positive aspects of surveillance technology? What worries you about the technology? Have your classmates said anything in class discussions that surprised you or that you disagreed with? Explain. (This journal is for your eyes only. Refer back to this journal when you are getting ready to write your essay.)

Writing Assignment #1: The Advantages and Disadvantages of Surveillance Technology

Here, in brief, is the writing assignment you are preparing for.

> *Do you see more advantages or disadvantages in the types of surveillance technology mentioned in "Big Brother Logs On"? Describe in detail the disadvantages and advantages that most intrigue you. (Note: It is possible to write an essay in which you say that you see an equal number of advantages and disadvantages.)*

Read, Discuss, Think Critically

This section of the chapter offers you a lengthy reading about the advantages and disadvantages of high-tech surveillance. You may find this reading to be challenging due to its length, terminology, and sophistication. Plan your reading time well, allowing yourself time to read it once just to get the general idea and then again to really understand the information.

Reading Assignment: "Big Brother Logs On"

Preview   Read the title, introductory material, subheadings, and the topic sentences. And review the following definitions and explanations to get a preview of some of the most important terms in the essay:

Ubiquitous (an adjective you will see many times in this essay) means widespread, constantly present.

Ubiquitous surveillance refers to cameras or other tools that other people can use to watch you all the time.

George Orwell's 1984 *and Big Brother:* George Orwell's book *1984* (published in 1949) is a novel that explores what it would be like if the government could watch us constantly, control our actions, and rewrite history. In the book, Big Brother was the name for the government or people who were always watching. Occasionally in this essay, you will see Orwell's name made into the adjective *Orwellian.* An Orwellian society would be a society that is very similar to the one described in *1984.*

Algorithm and *biometric* are also terms repeated many times in this essay. An algorithm is a step-by-step procedure that must be repeated again and again. This term is often used in connection to computers and mathematics. Biometric refers to a study of the body. For example, one biometric tool studies people's faces to see if they match any of the pictures of criminals in a computer database.

Notes

Anticipate   What do you think the article will be about? Use the "Notes" column to record your response.

Read and Reread   Read the entire essay quickly, marking unknown terms. Then reread more slowly and use the "Notes" column to interact with the essay. Mark important points and define unknown terms.

Big Brother Logs On*
by Ivan Amato

This article first appeared in *Technology Review*, September 2001.

Is privacy a right or a privilege? Recent developments in surveillance technology are calling the concept of privacy into question, as cameras invade our streets and software records our facial expressions while we shop. Is our loss of privacy inevitable?

1   The door to paranoia opens benignly—and early. Just think of Santa. He knows when you are sleeping. He knows when you're awake. He knows if you've been bad or good, for goodness' sake. And he knows these things all the time, even though you can't see him. Millions of kids all over the world happily and wholeheartedly believe in ubiquitous surveillance as a de facto piece of the annual Christmas present-getting machine. Parents just shake their heads in adoring wonder.

2   But those same parents might be shocked to learn how short the journey is from the pleasant surveillance fantasy of Santa to the freedom-squashing invasion of Big Brother. In the world detailed by George Orwell in the novel *1984,* surveillance cameras follow every move a person makes, and the slightest misstep, or apparent misstep, summons the authorities. Now, similarly, police departments, government agencies, banks, merchants, amusement parks, sports arenas, nanny-watching homeowners, swimming-pool operators, and employers are deploying cameras, pattern recognition algorithms, databases of information, and biometric tools that when taken as a whole can be combined into automated surveillance networks able to track just about anyone, just about anywhere.

3   While none of us is under 24-hour surveillance yet, the writing is on the wall. As Scott McNealy, CEO of Sun Microsystems, starkly told reporters in 1999, "You already have zero privacy. Get over it." The techno-entrepreneurs who are developing and marketing these tools

anticipate good things to come, such as reduced crime rates in urban environments, computer interfaces that will read eye movements and navigate the Web for you, and fingerprint or facial recognition systems and other biometric technologies that guarantee your identity and eliminate the need for passwords, PIN numbers and access cards—even identifying potential terrorists before they can strike.

4   But privacy advocates paint a far dimmer picture of this same future, accepting its reality while questioning whether it can be managed responsibly. "The technology is developing at the speed of light, but the privacy laws to protect us are back in the Stone Age," says Barry Steinhardt, associate director of the American Civil Liberties Union, which is among several groups that have tried, so far almost universally unsuccessfully, to introduce legislation aimed at protecting privacy. "We may not end up with an Orwellian society run by malevolent dictators, but it will be a surveillance society where none of the detail of our daily lives will escape notice and where much of that detail will be recorded."

The Fifth Utility

5   In many ways, the drama of pervasive surveillance is being played out first in Orwell's native land, the United Kingdom, which operates more closed-circuit cameras per capita than any other country in the world. This very public surveillance began in 1986 on an industrial estate near the town of King's Lynn, approximately 100 kilometers north of London. Prior to the installation of three video cameras, a total of 58 crimes had been reported on the estate. None was reported over the next two years. In 1995, buoyed by that success, the government made matching grants available to other cities and towns that wanted to install public surveillance cameras—and things took off from there.

6   Most of these closed-circuit TV systems are installed in business districts or shopping centers by British Telecommunications, the national phone network, and jointly operated and managed by law enforcement and private industry. In addition, some townships are using BT to hook up video telephony, a technology that allows transmission of video images via telephone lines—but in a monitor-friendly network that provides officials quick and easy remote access to the images. On another front, the U.K. Home Office, the government department responsible for internal affairs in England and Wales, is starting construction of what promises to be the world's biggest road and vehicle surveillance network, a comprehensive system of cameras, vehicle and driver databases, and microwave and phone-based communications links that will be able to identify and track the movements of vehicles nearly nationwide. All told, the country's electronic eyes are becoming so prevalent that

Notes

Stephen Graham of the Centre for Urban Technology at the University of Newcastle upon Tyne has dubbed them a "fifth utility," joining water, gas, electric and telephones.

7   The United States and many other parts of the developed world are not far behind in video surveillance. Just look at the cameras looking at you. They're in ATMs, banks, stores, casinos, lobbies, hallways, desktops, and along highways, main streets and even side streets. And those are the cameras you can see. Companies like All Security Systems of Miami, FL, advertise Clock Cameras, Exit Sign Cameras, Smoke Detector Cameras, and Covert Tie and Button Cams, as well as Nanny Cams and other easily hidden eyes, some of which send video signals wirelessly to a recorder located elsewhere.

8   But cameras seem relatively benign when compared to new technology being developed and deployed. Until recently, closed-circuit systems have fed video signals to monitors, which human beings had to watch in real time, or sent the images to recording media for storage. Now, however, the job of spotting suspicious people and behavior in this stream of electronic imagery is becoming automatic, with computers programmed with special algorithms for matching video pixel patterns to stored patterns associated with criminals or criminal actions—and the machines themselves passing initial judgment on whether a behavior is normal.

9   For example, last January at the Super Bowl in Tampa, FL, law enforcement agencies, without announcement, deployed a face recognition system from Viisage Technology of Littleton, MA. Cameras snapped face shots of fans entering the stadium. Computers instantly extracted a minimal set of features from each captured face, a so-called eigenface, and then compared the eigenfaces to those of criminals, stored in a database. The system purportedly found 19 possible matches, although no one was arrested as a result of the test. Less than six months later, in mid-July, Tampa police sparked public protests after deploying a face recognition system from Visionics, of Jersey City, NJ, to scan city sidewalks for suspected criminals and runaways.

10   And this is just the beginning of the technology being piloted and prototyped to watch you—and judge your behavior. Beginning in 1997, the U.S. Defense Advanced Research Projects Agency (DARPA) funded some 20 projects under a three-year program called Video Surveillance and Monitoring. That effort has just gathered new momentum under a $50 million follow-up program known as Human ID at a Distance. The aim is to determine if it's feasible to identify specific individuals at distances up to 150 meters.

11   Under the program, researchers at Carnegie Mellon University in Pittsburgh are investigating whether a remote sensing technique

Get Involved!

Rent the movie *Gattaca,* directed by Andrew Niccol, 1997. Explain to your class how this film connects to the topics in this essay.

known as "hyperspectral imaging"—a technology typically used by satellites to find minerals or peer through military camouflage—can be adapted for identifying specific human beings by measuring the color spectrum emitted by their skin. Skin absorbs, reflects and emits distinct patterns of color, and those patterns are specific enough to individual people to serve as spectral signatures. Such systems already work. But according to Robert Collins, a computer scientist at Carnegie Mellon's Robotics Institute, the process currently requires a person to sit stiffly in a chair as a sensor sweeps through hundreds of emitted wavelengths over a period of about five seconds. "Ideally, what will happen is we'll find some small group of wavelengths that we can use to distinguish people," explains Collins. That could reduce the scan time to a fraction of a second.

12   Another approach being developed involves a video-based network of sensors that would automatically measure such characteristics as leg length and waist width to provide, as Collins says, "the measurements you give to a tailor." The idea here, he says, is that those numbers should be able to serve as a kind of body fingerprint for identifying specific individuals.

13   There is no shortage of cleverness when it comes to building the surveillance state. At the Georgia Institute of Technology, scientists are developing sensor riddled "smart floors " that can identify people by the "force profiles" of their walking feet. Meanwhile, Princeton, NJ–based Sarnoff is working toward an antiterrorist technique that uses a special camera to identify individuals from a hundred meters off by the patterns of color, striation and speckles in their irises. This isn't easy, since the iris and its elements move so quickly relative to a distant camera that the technical task bears some resemblance to "tracking a ballistic missile," says Norman Winarsky, president of nVention, Sarnoff's venture technology company. Still, the technology is coming.

14   Beyond identity is intention—and there are technologies in the works for divining that as well. IBM has introduced a software product called BlueEyes *(see "Behind BlueEyes" TR May 2001)* that's currently in use at retail stores to record customers' facial expressions and eye movements, tracking the effectiveness of in-store promotions. And psychologist Jeffrey Cohn of Carnegie Mellon's Robotics Institute and colleagues have been trying to teach machines an even more precise way to detect facial expressions.

15   From video signals, the Carnegie Mellon system detects and tracks both invariant aspects of a face, such as the distance between the eyes, and transient ones, like skin furrows and smile wrinkles. This raw data is then reclassified as representing elemental actions of the face. Finally, a neural

Get Involved!

Rent the movie *Minority Report,* directed by Steven Spielberg, 2002. Take notes during the movie and then report to your class about the different types of high-tech surveillance you see in the movie and what you think their advantages and disadvantages are.

network correlates combinations of these measurable units to actual expressions. While this falls short of robotic detection of human intentions, many facial expressions reflect human emotions, such as fear, happiness or rage, which, in turn, often serve as visible signs of intentions.

16   Cohn points out that this particular work is just part of the team's more encompassing "goal of developing computer systems that can detect human activity, recognize the people involved, understand their behavior, and respond appropriately." In short, the effort could help lead to the kind of ubiquitous surveillance system that can automatically scan collective human activity for signs of anything from heart-attack-inducing Type-A behavior to sexual harassment to daydreaming at the wheel to homicidal rage.

The Good, the Bad and the Well-Intentioned

17   The list of emerging technological wonders goes on and on, which is why many observers argue it's no longer a question of whether ubiquitous surveillance will be applied, but under what guidelines it will operate—and to what end.

18   "Like most powerful technologies, total surveillance will almost certainly bring both good and bad things into life," says James Wayman, a former National Security Agency contractor who now directs human identification research at San Jose State University in California. Specifically, he notes, it will combine laudable benefits in convenience and public safety with a potentially lamentable erosion of privacy.

19   These contradictory values often trigger vigorous debate over whether it will all be worth it. The glass-half-full crowd contends that the very infrastructure of surveillance that conjures fears of Big Brother will actually make life easier and safer for most people. Consider the benefits of the "computer-aided drowning detection and prevention" system that Boulogne, France–based Poseidon Technologies has installed in nine swimming pools in France, England, the Netherlands and Canada. In these systems, a collection of overhead and in-pool cameras relentlessly monitors pool activity. The video signals feed into a central processor running a machine perception algorithm that can effectively spot when active nonwater objects, such as swimmers, become still for more than a few seconds. When that happens, a red alarm light flashes at a poolside laptop workstation and lifeguards are alerted via waterproof pagers. Last November, a Poseidon system at the Jean Blanchet Aquatic Center in Ancenis, Loire-Atlantique, France, alerted lifeguards in time to rescue a swimmer on the verge of drowning. Pulled from the water unconscious, the swimmer walked away from a hospital the next day.

20   Similarly, when cell phones and other mobile gadgetry start coming embedded with Global Positioning System transponders, it will be possible to pinpoint the carrier and quickly come to his or her aid, if necessary. Such transponders are already built into many new cars *(see "The Commuter Computer" TR June 2001).* A click of a button or the triggering of an air bag sends a call to a service center, where agents can then direct emergency personnel to the vehicle, even if the occupants are unconscious. A public ubiquitous surveillance system could also enhance safety by noticing, for example, if a car hits you or if large, unauthorized crowds start congregating around an accident or altercation. As with the car rescue systems, a person's plight could be recognized and help dispatched almost instantly, sort of how air bags are now immediately deployed on impact.

21   And not many argue about surveillance's ability to deter crime. Recent British government reports cite closed circuit TV as a major reason for declining crime rates. After these systems were put in place, the town of Berwick reported that burglaries fell by 69 percent; in Northampton overall crime decreased by 57 percent; and in Glasgow, Scotland, crime slumped by 68 percent. Public reaction in England has been mixed, but many embrace the technology. "I am prepared to exchange a small/negligible amount of privacy loss so I don't have to be caught up in yet another bomb blast/bomb scare," wrote one London computer programmer in an online discussion of the technology.

22   Do the developers of this controversial technology weigh the pros and cons of their creations? Robert Collins of Carnegie Mellon concedes that much of the work that might fall into the surveillance category conjures an Orwellian quease, but he joins a veritable chorus of colleagues who say it's not their station to be gatekeepers looking out for how the technology ultimately is used. "We who are working on this are not so interested in applying it to surveillance and Big Brother stuff," Collins says. "We're making computers that can interact with people better." Indeed, Collins notes that he and his colleagues are motivated by the notion of "pervasive computing," in which the technoenvironment becomes aware of its human occupants so that computers and other gadgets can adjust to human needs. The way it is now, he says, humans have to accommodate the limitations of machines.

23   Jonathon Philips, manager of DARPA's Human ID at a Distance program, puts it another way: "We develop the technology. The policy and how you implement them is not my province."

24   So who is watching the gate? Well, the courts are slowly getting involved. A U.S. Supreme Court decision last June determined that in the absence of a search warrant, the government's use of a thermal imaging

device to monitor heat coming off the walls of a suspected marijuana grower's private residence in Florence, OR, violated the Fourth Amendment prohibition against "unreasonable searches and seizures." The ruling could have far-reaching consequences for how new, more powerful surveillance technologies can be deployed. Overall, however, the responsibility of surveillance technology management and regulation is up for grabs in the United States, even as the technology proliferates. And so whether society goes Orwellian or not could well hinge on how responsibly the databases, biometric details and all the rest are managed and protected. After all, notes the ACLU's Steinhardt, it's a small step from a technological advance to a technology abuse.

25   Take the fact that the faces of a large portion of the driving population are becoming digitized by motor vehicles agencies and placed into databases, says Steinhardt. It isn't much of a stretch to extend the system to a Big Brother–like nationwide identification and tracking network. Or consider that the Electoral Commission of Uganda has retained Viisage Technology to implement a "turnkey face recognition system" capable of enrolling 10 million voter registrants within 60 days. By generating a database containing the faceprint of every one of the country's registered voters—and combining it with algorithms able to scour all 10 million images within six seconds to find a match—the commission hopes to reduce voter registration fraud. But once such a database is compiled, notes John Woodward, a former CIA operations officer who managed spies in several Asian countries and who's now an analyst with the Rand Corporation, it could be employed for tracking and apprehending known or suspected political foes. Woodward calls that "function creep."

26   Function creep is where things get really dicey for privacy advocates. Several grass-roots efforts now under way seek to rein in surveillance technology through more responsible privacy legislation. The Privacy Coalition, a nonpartisan collection of consumer, civil liberties, labor and family-based groups, is trying to get federal and state lawmakers to commit to its "Privacy Pledge," which contains, among other things, a vow to develop independent oversight of public surveillance technology and limit the collection of personal data. And several organizations, including the AFL-CIO, Communications Workers of America, 9to5, National Association of Working Women and the United Auto Workers, are supporting legislation to restrict electronic monitoring of employees. As Steinhardt declares, "We can't leave this to systems designers or the marketplace."

27   In spite of these broad efforts, a number of factors, not the least of which is disagreement in Washington about what form such legislation should take, are making it difficult to put words into action. Last year

Congress debated the Notice of Electronic Monitoring Act, which would have required companies to notify employees if they were being watched. Although that legislation died in committee, it will probably resurface again this year. As far as individual state laws are concerned, only Connecticut requires employers to tell employees if they are being monitored.

28   Which leads to the question of what exactly constitutes "private" activity. As former spymaster Woodward observes, a total-surveillance society will not actually expose individuals that much more than ordinary public circulation does now. "Once you leave your house and enter public spaces," he says, "just about everyone you can see can see you right back." In other words, you do not walk around most of the day with an expectation of privacy. Your face is not private, so if a camera sees you, it's no big deal. What's more, asks Woodward, even if rich and powerful entities, such as the government or mega-corporations, had sole access to a system capable of watching everyone all of the time, why would they bother? "The bottom line is that most of us are very boring. We flatter ourselves to think that someone is building a multibillion-dollar system to watch us," he says.

29   Even if public opinion does manage to slow down the deployment of surveillance infrastructure, no one involved in the debate thinks it will stop some form of Big Brother from arriving eventually. In his 1998 book *The Transparent Society,* which is well known in the privacy advocacy community, science fiction author and technology watcher David Brin argues that society inevitably will have to choose between two versions of ubiquitous surveillance: in one, only the rich and powerful use and control the system to their own advantage; in the second, more democratic future, the watchers can also be watched. Brin concedes that the latter version would mean everybody's laundry hung out in public view, but the transparency would at least be mutual. Rent a porn video and your wife knows it; but if she drives to your best buddy's house four times a week while you're at the office, you'll know that also.

30   Whether or not the coming era of total surveillance fits neatly into one of Brin's scenarios will be determined by a complex equation encompassing technological development and the decisions that local, state and federal governments choose to make. The question largely boils down to this: is privacy a right or a privilege? Most Americans assume it is a right, as in our "right to privacy." But the truth of the matter is that privacy isn't guaranteed by the Constitution. It is implied, certainly, but not assured. This subtle difference is being tested right now, within our own neighborhoods and workplaces.

Get Involved!

Find a copy of Brin's novel *The Transparent Society* in a library or bookstore. Read the first chapter and report to your class. What is the book about? Is it interesting or not? Why?

Get Involved!

Visit www.tecnology review.com and explore the site. Report back to your class about any new and interesting technology that you learn about.

Notes

Questions for Critical Thought

"Big Brother Logs On"

1. Amato has a strong vocabulary that helps make his writing both accurate and interesting. In your vocabulary notebook, define the following words (through context clues and by using the dictionary).

   deploying, paragraph 2
   malevolent, paragraph 4
   per capita, paragraph 5
   buoyed, paragraph 5
   benign, paragraph 8
   feasible, paragraph 10
   divining, paragraph 14
   invariant, paragraph 15
   transient, paragraph 15
   laudable, paragraph 18
   lamentable, paragraph 18
   conjures, paragraph 19
   proliferates, paragraph 24
   foes, paragraph 25
   rein in, paragraph 26

2. How does Amato's introduction draw you into the essay? Why is it effective?

3. Amato has quite a bit of information to give his readers. He carefully planned how he would group and organize his information, and his topic sentences are critical tools for showing the reader this organizational structure. Pick out four topic sentences that seem strong. Remember that a strong topic sentence will explain what the main point of the paragraph will be, and it may have a word or phrase that explains why the paragraph is located in that spot of the essay. (The word or phrase, called a *transition,* will point out how the paragraph connects directly to the paragraph before or the paragraph after.) Copy down these strong topic sentences and explain why you chose them.

4. What do the last two sentences in paragraph 8 mean?

5. In paragraph 6, surveillance cameras are called the "the fifth utility." What does this mean? (What are the other four utilities?) What is your reaction to surveillance cameras becoming the fifth utility?

6. In paragraph 20, the author notes that public cameras could alert police if "unauthorized crowds start congregating around an accident or altercation." Why would this be helpful? In what other situations might large crowds congregate? Would you always want police to be alerted? Explain.

7. Amato describes a number of advantages and disadvantages to high-tech surveillance. What are two advantages that interest you? What are two disadvantages that interest you?

8. In paragraph 25, Amato notes that Uganda has begun to use "faceprints." What problem does the author see with this technology in Uganda? Why might someone argue that the citizens of some third world countries have more to fear from high-tech surveillance?

9. How would you feel if all, or most, of your day was monitored by cameras and sensors? Explain.

10. Writers often use the title to give readers immediate hints about their main point. What is the main point of this reading and how does the title of this piece connect to the main point?

Journal Assignment

Big Brother: Friend or Foe?

Since September 11th, 2001, many people in the United States are fearful of terrorist attacks. In addition, some people are concerned about growing crime rates and bizarre, horrifying crimes like the Virginia Tech massacre. Do you fear for your safety on a regular basis? Do you think you would feel better if we had constant high-tech surveillance in public places? Do you think you would actually be safer? Do you worry about your privacy? After reading someone else's journal, just say, "Thank you," when you return it.

Explore the Writing Assignment

Here, again, is your writing assignment. Review it carefully before continuing. Underline the important terms in the assignment.

Do you see more advantages or disadvantages in the types of surveillance technology mentioned in "Big Brother Logs On"? Discuss in detail the disadvantages and advantages that most intrigue you. (Note: It is possible to write an essay in which you say that you see an equal number of advantages and disadvantages.)

Notes

Activities

Find Out Who Is Watching You

Choose one or both of the activities below. You may want to work in groups of two or three.

- Choose two or three public places to visit in your city. You could choose from any of these places: grocery store, bank, library, airport, mall, government building, a newly built school, or a clothing or record store. Observe how you are being observed. Are there cameras? (Are the cameras obvious or hidden or disguised?) Metal detectors? One-way mirrors? Do you have to show ID? Are there other methods of surveillance being used? Report your observations to your class.

- Interview a business owner or manager, or interview someone who is in charge of security at a business or office. Prepare some questions ahead of time. Sample questions: What are the security concerns of this business/office? What kinds of high-tech security do you currently use? What might you use in the future? (You might have to describe the types of high-tech surveillance you read about in Amato's essay.) You will want to prepare questions that are appropriate for the business/office and person you are visiting. Report your findings to your class.

Round-Table Discussion

Amato gave you many technical terms and many reasons why people both support and fear high-tech surveillance. As a way of becoming more familiar with the terminology, the different types of high-tech surveillance, and their advantages and disadvantages, you will have a round-table discussion with your classmates. A round-table discussion is an approach that many companies use to understand an issue, problem, or goal. Each participant must come with both information and questions. Follow the preparation steps carefully and you'll have a great discussion, and you'll find that writing the essay becomes much easier.

1. First, working as a class, make a list of all the types of high-tech surveillance tools mentioned in "Big Brother Logs On" and agree on a name for each type. For example, the surveillance technique in paragraph 12 could be called "body measure." Some of the high-tech tools already have names, like BlueEyes in paragraph 14.

2. Use the index card system described on pages 319–320 to record what you have learned about high-tech security. Begin by writing the name

of one type of high-tech security on a card. (Make a note next to the name telling which paragraph of Amato's essay you found it in.) On the back of the card, write one advantage or disadvantage with this type of high-tech security. You might repeat—in your own words—what you read in the essay, or you might jot down your own idea. (If you write about an advantage or disadvantage that you found in the essay, be sure to write down the source of the information. Did it come from Amato or someone else? If someone else, record his or her name and title or job. What paragraph?) You'll probably want to create more than one card for each type of high-tech security since most types of security have both advantages and disadvantages. Continue to create cards for each type of high-tech security mentioned in the essay.

3. On a separate piece of paper, make a list of questions you have about high-tech security and/or your writing assignment. Do you understand, basically, how each type of high-tech security works? (You do not have to be an expert, but you do need to have a reasonable understanding of how the technology works and in what places and why it might be used.)

4. During your round-table discussion, each student should have a chance to share a card and a question. You will need someone to keep track of ideas on a chalkboard or whiteboard. Each student, of course, will need to keep his or her own notes, copying down what is said, what is written on the board, and any comments or questions he or she has.

Brainstorm   Write freely about high-tech security. Review Amato's essay and your critical thinking answers. Think about what you observed in person. Review your round-table notes. Also, you may want to imagine yourself in an Orwellian world. What would it be like to be watched constantly? How would you feel? Would your behavior change? Is that okay? What are some of the advantages to high-tech security? What are some of the disadvantages?

When you are done writing, review your brainstorming notes and decide which advantages and disadvantages you want to focus on. Highlight the parts of your brainstorming that you think might be useful when writing your essay.

Consider Your Audience   Imagine a general audience for this essay— the citizens of the United States, or even an international audience. Write down what most people already know about high-tech security.

Notes

How do you think they feel about high-tech security? Now, consider what your audience probably doesn't know about high-tech surveillance. Make notes about the crucial types of information you will need to give your audience.

Create Your Thesis   In your own words, what must you do in your essay? Review the writing assignment. Experiment with thesis statements until you find one that clearly explains your focus.

Outline   Keeping your thesis in mind, carefully review your notes and readings. Although you completed some index cards in preparation for your round-table discussion, you will now need to create a complete set of cards that represents the ideas you will cover in your essay. You may want to review the section on index cards on pages 319–320. When you have all your cards filled out, review your cards and think about how to organize your ideas. Keep in mind that it is okay to discard some of the cards if the ideas on them don't seem to fit smoothly with your other ideas or if the ideas just don't interest you.

Experiment with different ways to organize your cards. (*Note:* One index card does not necessarily equal one paragraph. A paragraph can be built around one or more index cards.) Since the assignment asks you to state if you see more advantages or disadvantages, you may not have an equal number of paragraphs for disadvantages and advantages—unless you state in your thesis that you see an equal number of advantages and disadvantages. If you are saying there are more advantages than disadvantages, you may want to name and explain a few key disadvantages early in your essay and then focus on the most interesting advantages later in your essay. Obviously, this can work the other way around, too. (First discuss the few advantages and then discuss more disadvantages.)

It is also possible that you will want to organize your paragraphs by particular criteria. For example, if you want to focus on public versus private high-tech security, you could try this organizational approach:

- Advantages to having high-tech security on public streets (one or more paragraphs)
- Disadvantages to having high-tech security on public streets (one or more paragraphs)

- Advantages to having high-tech security in our homes (one or more paragraphs)
- Disadvantages to having high-tech security in our homes (one or more paragraphs)

To avoid creating an underdeveloped essay, it is important that you discuss only one advantage or disadvantage per paragraph. Also keep in mind what you learned in Chapter 6 about concessions (pages 297–300). You can't reasonably state that there are absolutely no advantages or state that there are absolutely no disadvantages. So, as you plan your outline, be sure to make room for each side.

When you have a pretty good idea of which index cards you'll use, how you'll group your ideas into paragraphs, and how you'll order your paragraphs, get together with a small group of classmates and show them what you've decided. Explain your choices. You may find that you need to make some changes, and you may get some new ideas from listening to how your classmates are organizing their cards.

Draft

Using your cards as a guide, begin drafting your essay. Your introduction should explain what your topic is and why it's important. (Remember that your audience includes people who may know very little about high-tech security.) In your body paragraphs, discuss the points you have selected. Give interesting examples that come from your imagination or personal experience. Description will work well in this essay, so consider how you might paint a picture in your reader's mind using adjectives, adverbs, and prepositional phrases. In your conclusion, tell your reader what you intended to accomplish in this essay.

Revise

Activity

Share Your Writing

Find a classmate to work with. Read each other's essays, and discuss the following questions as they relate to both essays.

- Have you discussed both advantages and disadvantages?

- Are you trying to cover more than one disadvantage or advantage in any of your paragraphs?

- Have you explained the terminology?

- Is there enough information and detail so that your reader will see your point of view? Have you used quotes from Amato's essay? Should you?

- Have you mentioned where you got your information? (See pages 489–494 for a review of how to cite sources.)

- Can your classmate understand and describe your organizational pattern? Can you make any improvements? Have you used transitions?

- What has your instructor been telling you to work on? Do you have any questions about this essay and the skills your instructor wants you to work on?

- What questions do you have about your essay? What are your greatest concerns?

After working with your classmate, make a list of improvements you want to make. Rank them from most important to least, and then tackle one task at a time.

Edit

Pay special attention to errors that you tend to repeat, and focus on one at a time. Also, does your instructor have a certain area he or she wants you to focus on?

Additional ideas for editing:

- Note that *Internet* is always capitalized. (*World Wide Web* is capitalized also.)

- Can you use any new vocabulary words in your essay?

You may also want to consider the following question after completing the sentence work at the end of the chapter (pages 350–363):

- Are you using adjectives, adverbs, and prepositional phrases to add detail and interest to your writing?

Writing Assignment #2: Orwell, the Modern World, and the Future

Here, in brief, is the writing assignment you are preparing for:

Compare the setting, mood, and role of surveillance technology in 1984 to the setting, mood, and role of surveillance technology in our modern world. Then make a forecast of your own and describe what the setting, mood, and role of surveillance technology might be like in 2050.

Read, Discuss, Think Critically

The first reading in this section is an excerpt from George Orwell's novel *1984*. As Orwell was writing this novel in 1948 and imagining a world of total video surveillance, most Americans were just getting their first television sets. Hence, many readers have noted that he was ahead of his time. The government he describes was modeled after the former USSR, and Orwell was exploring what the world would be like if a government had complete control over us, watching our every move and monitoring our thoughts.

In the second reading, a newspaper column, William Safire expresses his concerns about modern surveillance in Washington, D.C., and across the country. As you read these two pieces, think about how Orwell's imagined future is similar to and different from what is actually happening in our modern cities.

Reading Assignment: Excerpt from 1984

Preview   Read the introductory sentences and paragraphs 1 and 2.

Anticipate   What do you think this excerpt will be about? Write your response in the "Notes" column.

Read and Reread   Read the entire excerpt, marking unknown terms. Then reread more slowly and use the "Notes" column to respond to what you read. Mark important and interesting points and define unknown terms.

Excerpt from *1984*

by George Orwell

1   It was a bright cold day in April, and the clocks were striking thirteen. Winston Smith, his chin nuzzled into his breast in an effort to escape the vile wind, slipped quickly through the glass doors of Victory Mansions, though not quickly enough to prevent a swirl of gritty dust from entering along with him.

2   The hallway smelt of boiled cabbage and old rag mats. At one end of it a coloured poster, too large for indoor display, had been tacked to the wall. It depicted simply an enormous face, more than a metre wide: the face of a man of about forty-five, with a heavy black moustache and ruggedly handsome features. Winston made for the stairs. It was no use trying the lift. Even at the best of times it was seldom working, and at

present the electric current was cut off during daylight hours. It was part of the economy drive in preparation for Hate Week. The flat was seven flights up, and Winston, who was thirty-nine and had a varicose ulcer above his right ankle, went slowly, resting several times on the way. On each landing, opposite the lift-shaft, the poster with the enormous face gazed from the wall. It was one of those pictures which are so contrived that the eyes follow you about when you move. BIG BROTHER IS WATCHING YOU, the caption beneath it ran.

3   Inside the flat a fruity voice was reading out a list of figures which had something to do with the production of pig-iron. The voice came from an oblong metal plaque like a dulled mirror which formed part of the surface of the right-hand wall. Winston turned a switch and the voice sank somewhat, though the words were still distinguishable. The instrument (the telescreen, it was called) could be dimmed, but there was no way of shutting it off completely. He moved over to the window: a small-ish, frail figure, the meagreness of his body merely emphasized by the blue overalls which were the uniform of the party. His hair was very fair, his face naturally sanguine, his skin roughened by coarse soap and blunt razor blades and the cold of the winter that had just ended.

4   Outside, even through the shut window-pane, the world looked cold. Down in the street little eddies of wind were whirling dust and torn paper into spirals, and though the sun was shining and the sky a harsh blue, there seemed to be no colour in anything, except the posters that were plastered everywhere. The blackmoustachio'd face gazed down from every commanding corner. There was one on the house-front immediately opposite. BIG BROTHER IS WATCHING YOU, the caption said, while the dark eyes looked deep into Winston's own. Down at street level another poster, torn at one corner, flapped fitfully in the wind, alternately covering and uncovering the single word INGSOC. In the far distance a helicopter skimmed down between the roofs, hovered for an instant like a bluebottle, and darted away again with a curving flight. It was the police patrol, snooping into people's windows. The patrols did not matter, however. Only the Thought Police mattered.

5   Behind Winston's back the voice from the telescreen was still babbling away about pig-iron and the overfulfilment of the Ninth Three-Year Plan. The telescreen received and transmitted simultaneously. Any sound that Winston made, above the level of a very low whisper, would be picked up by it, moreover, so long as he remained within the field of vision which the metal plaque commanded, he could be seen as well as heard. There was of course no way of knowing whether you were being watched at any given moment. How often, or on what system, the Thought Police plugged in on any individual wire was guesswork. It was even conceivable that they

watched everybody all the time. But at any rate they could plug in your
wire whenever they wanted to. You had to live—did live, from habit that
became instinct—in the assumption that every sound you made was over-
heard, and, except in darkness, every movement scrutinized.

6   Winston kept his back turned to the telescreen. It was safer, though,
as he well knew, even a back can be revealing. A kilometre away the
Ministry of Truth, his place of work, towered vast and white above the
grimy landscape. This, he thought with a sort of vague distaste—this
was London, chief city of Airstrip One, itself the third most populous of
the provinces of Oceania. He tried to squeeze out some childhood
memory that should tell him whether London had always been quite
like this. Were there always these vistas of rotting nineteenth-century
houses, their sides shored up with baulks of timber, their windows
patched with cardboard and their roofs with corrugated iron, their crazy
garden walls sagging in all directions? And the bombed sites where the
plaster dust swirled in the air and the willow-herb straggled over the
heaps of rubble; and the places where the bombs had cleared a larger
patch and there had sprung up sordid colonies of wooden dwellings like
chicken-houses? But it was no use, he could not remember: nothing remained of his childhood except a series of bright-lit tableaux occurring
against no background and mostly unintelligible.

Questions for Critical Thought

Excerpt from 1984

1. George Orwell, a British writer, uses a few terms in ways that may
   be new to you. For example, in paragraph 2, Orwell uses *lift* and
   flat as nouns. Look these words up in the dictionary and find the
   noun definitions that come after the italicized words "chiefly Brit."
   ("Chiefly Brit" means that the meaning listed is most often used by
   people in Britain.) What does Orwell mean when he uses the words
   lift and *flat*? (*Note:* Some smaller dictionaries won't give the
   "chiefly Brit" definition. You may have to go to a larger dictionary.)

2. Review the reading and underline all the descriptive words and
   phrases that help paint a picture of the setting. Then write a paragraph describing the world in which Winston, the main character,
   lives. In a second paragraph, describe your reaction to his sur-
   roundings.

3. How is the word *party* being used in paragraph 3? What does this
   usage suggest to you about the society in which Winston lives?

4. What surveillance device is used to watch people like Winston? What is the device capable of seeing, hearing, or recording?

5. How would you feel about living under constant surveillance? How might such living conditions change your life and your view of society?

Reading Assignment: *"The Great Unwatched"*

Preview   Read the introduction and the topic sentences.

Anticipate   What do you think this article will be about? Write your response in the "Notes" column.

Read and Reread   Read the entire article, marking unknown terms. Then reread more slowly and use the "Notes" column to interact with the essay. Mark important and interesting points and define unknown terms.

The Great Unwatched
by William Safire

Stipulated: The protection of our capital, its monuments and centers of authority, is a vital national interest.

This article, dated February 18, 2002, appeared on the *New York Times* Web site, www.nytimes.com.

1   Early in our history, when faced with a potential rebellion of unpaid officers, one of our leaders employed an uncharacteristic emotional trick—pretending to be going blind—to appeal to the infuriated military men not to march on the capital. He soon had them in tears and in hand.

2   In another time, another leader risked all by turning the capital's defense over to the man most opposed to his political aims, gambling that he could later overcome the nation's gratitude to a man on horseback.

3   In our time, after the Pentagon was hit, the White House targeted and the Capitol anthraxed, D.C. again saw itself besieged. But now, in terror of an external threat, our leaders are protecting our capital at the cost of every American's personal freedom.

4   Surveillance is in the saddle. Responding to the latest Justice Department terror alert, Washington police opened the Joint Operation Command Center of the Synchronized Operations Command Complex

(S.O.C.C.). In it, 50 officials monitor a wall of 40 video screens showing images of travelers, drivers, residents and pedestrians.

5   These used to be the Great Unwatched, free people conducting their private lives; now they are under close surveillance by hundreds of hidden cameras. A zoom lens enables the watchers to focus on the face of a tourist walking toward the Washington Monument or Lincoln Memorial.

6   The monitoring system is already linked to 200 cameras in public schools. The watchers plan to expand soon with an equal number in the subways and parks. A private firm profits by photographing cars running red lights; those images will also join the surveillance network.

7   Private cameras in banks and the lobbies and elevators of apartment buildings and hotels will join the system, and residents of nursing homes and hospitals can look forward to an electronic eye in every room. A commercial camera atop a department store in Georgetown catches the faces of shoppers entering malls, to be plugged into omnipresent S.O.C.C.

8   Digital images of the captured faces can be flashed around the world in an instant on the Internet. Married to face-recognition technology and tied in to public and private agencies around the world, an electronic library of hundreds of millions of faces will be created. Terrorists and criminals—as well as unhappy spouses, runaway teens, hermits and other law-abiding people who want to drop out of society for a while—will have no way to get a fresh start.

9   Is this the kind of world we want? The promise is greater safety; the tradeoff is government control of individual lives. Personal security may or may not be enhanced by this all-seeing eye and ear, but personal freedom will surely be sharply curtailed. To be watched at all times, especially when doing nothing seriously wrong, is to be afflicted with a creepy feeling. That is what is felt by a convict in an always-lighted cell. It is the pervasive, inescapable feeling of being unfree.

10   As the law now stands, there is no privacy in public places; that's why sports stadiums are called "Snooper Bowls." A whisper to your spouse on your front porch is the public's business, say the courts; and on that intrusive analogy, long-range microphones may soon be allowed to pick up voice vibrations on windowpanes.

11   When your government, employer, landlord, merchant, banker and local sports team gang up to picture, digitize and permanently record your every activity, you are placed under unprecedented control. This is not some alarmist Orwellian scenario; it is here, now, financed by $20 billion last year and $15 billion more this year of federal money appropriated out of sheer fear.

12   By creating the means to monitor 300 million visits to the U.S. yearly, this administration and a supine opposition are building a system capable

Notes

of identifying, tracking and spying on 300 million Americans. So far, the reaction has been a most un-American docility.

13   It's Presidents' Day. To save the capital and thus the nation, the leader who manipulated his rebellious officers with an emotional pretense of incipient blindness was George Washington, and the one who risked creating a Caesar out of a necessary general was Abraham Lincoln. Neither would sacrifice our freedom to protect his monument.

Questions for Critical Thought

"The Great Unwatched"

1. The first three paragraphs in this essay work as the introduction. Explain Safire's approach to the introduction. What does he decide to talk about in order to pull us into his essay?

2. In your own words, restate Safire's thesis.

3. Look up the word *unwashed* in the dictionary to see what it means when used as an adjective. Safire is playing with words when he uses *unwatched* in the title and in paragraph 5 because he knows many readers will think of the word *unwashed*. He is drawing a connection between the *unwatched* and the *unwashed*. What is the connection? Explain why Safire chose the word *unwatched*.

4. List some of the specific kinds of surveillance mentioned in this newspaper column.

5. What are some of Safire's complaints and concerns about surveillance technology? Who will be affected? When? Where? According to Safire, how will it feel to be under so much surveillance?

6. In paragraph 12, what does the word *docility* mean? Explain Safire's point in that sentence.

7. How does Safire create a sense of completion in his conclusion?

Journal Assignment

Mood—Past, Present, and Future

In literature, writers can create a mood with their words. That is, authors can bring certain feelings out of us by choosing specific words to describe a setting, a person, or a situation. How would you describe the mood of *1984*? What feelings does the piece bring out? What words are most responsible for these feelings? Can you think of another reading or experience that brought out similar feelings in you? If you were to write a story about our modern world, government, and surveillance technology, what kind of mood would you try to create with your words? If you were to write about the future of the United States and the role of surveillance technology, what kind of mood would you want to create? After reading someone else's journal, just say, "Thank you," when you return it.

Explore the Writing Assignment

Here, again, is your writing assignment. Review it carefully before continuing. Underline the important terms in the assignment.

> *Compare the setting, mood, and role of surveillance technology in <u>1984</u> to the setting, mood, and role of surveillance technology in our modern world. Then make a forecast of your own and describe what the setting, mood, and role of surveillance technology might be like in 2050.*

Activity

Brainstorming Descriptions

Working with two or three classmates, complete the statements below. Each of you should record your own answers to refer back to later. Aim to be creative and detailed. You can go around in a circle more than once for each question because sometimes one person's response will inspire a new idea in someone else's mind. Some of the questions below ask for straight description or explanations. However, some encourage you to stretch your creativity as you think of similarities, differences, colors, and music. Have fun and be creative with this activity.

1. Orwell's Oceania is like

2. Oceania reminds me of

3. Being watched all of the time feels like

4. The opposite of Oceania would be

5. Privacy is important because

6. If I were to paint a picture of Oceania, I would use these colors:

7. If I were to choose music for a soundtrack for *1984*, I would use these songs:

8. I think surveillance technology in 2050 will include

9. I think the world in 2050 will look like

> 10. If I were to paint a picture of 2050, I would use these colors:
>
> 11. If I were to make a movie of 2050, I would use these songs in the soundtrack:

Brainstorm   Write freely about Orwell's Oceania, the modern world, and the future. Review the excerpt from *1984,* Safire's column, your journals, and your activity notes. This is a safe place to exercise your descriptive skills as you think about setting and mood. When you write about setting, think about addressing some of the same topics that Orwell does: buildings, streets, weather, apartments/homes, smells, colors, and so on. When you write about mood, you may want to stretch your vocabulary by using a thesaurus to look up common words like *sad* or *happy* to find other, more specific words. You may also want to refer back to Amato's essay from earlier in the chapter as you think about what our future world might look like.

When you are done writing, review your brainstorming notes and decide which ideas and descriptions you want to focus on. Highlight the parts of your brainstorming notes that you think might be useful when writing your essay.

Consider Your Audience   Imagine a general audience for this essay. Your readers might not be familiar with *1984* or surveillance technology. List the key background facts that you will need to include for your audience.

Create Your Thesis   Reflecting on the readings and your notes thus far, what will your main point be in this essay? Will you be emphasizing similarities between *1984,* the present, and the future? Will you be emphasizing differences? Will you create a balance between similarities and differences? Experiment with thesis statements until you find one that clearly explains your focus.

Outline   Complete one set of index cards for each time period: 1984 (as described by Orwell), the modern world, and our future world. You may want to color code each time period. Within each time period, you'll want *at least* one card for setting, one for mood, and one for surveillance.

You should move the cards around to find the best organizational pattern for your essay. It is possible to put all setting cards in one paragraph, all mood cards in another, and all surveillance cards in another.

Or you may find that it is better not to mix time periods within a paragraph. You may also decide to discuss mood, setting, and surveillance technology in any order that makes the most sense to you. Just be consistent once you decide on a logical pattern. For example, if you decide to cover first the mood, then the setting, and then the surveillance tools of *1984* in one paragraph, you'll want to follow the same order (mood then setting then surveillance tools) in the other paragraphs. Organization is important because you want to make it easy for your reader to follow your ideas, and the keys to good organization are logic and consistency.

You might also include some of your transition words on your cards after you've figured out the best order for your ideas.

Notes

Draft

Using your cards as a guide, begin drafting your essay. Your introduction should explain what your topic is and give your reader a brief background on the topic. Remember, save your specific details and examples for your body paragraphs. In your body paragraphs, begin with helpful topic sentences and offer interesting details, examples, and descriptions in the sentences that follow. In this essay, you may want a traditional conclusion paragraph or you may choose to make your paragraph about the future stand as the final paragraph. The goal for any conclusion paragraph is to help the reader feel that you have completed your discussion. If your paragraph on the future does this, it might be able to stand as your conclusion.

Revise

Activity

Share Your Writing

Find a classmate to work with. Read each other's essays, and discuss the following questions as they relate to both essays.

- Have you discussed *1984,* the modern world, and the future?

- Have you discussed the mood, setting, and the role of surveillance tools in *1984,* the modern world, and the future?

- Have you explained the terminology?

- Is there enough information and detail so that your reader will understand your main points? Should you add any more descriptions or explanations? Have you used any quotes from the readings? Should you?

- Have you mentioned where you got your information? (See pages 489–494 for a review of how to cite sources.)

- Can your classmate understand and describe your organizational pattern? Can you make any improvements? Have you used transitions?

- What has your instructor been telling you to work on? Do you have any questions about this essay and the skills your instructor wants you to work on?

- What questions do you have about your essay? What are your greatest concerns?

After working with your classmate, make a list of improvements you want to make. Rank them from most important to least, and then tackle one task at a time.

Edit

Pay special attention to errors that you tend to repeat, and focus on one at a time. Also, does your instructor have a certain area he or she wants you to focus on?

Additional ideas for editing:

- Note that *Internet* is always capitalized. (*World Wide Web* is capitalized also.)
- Can you use any new vocabulary words in your essay?

You may also want to consider the following question after completing the sentence work at the end of the chapter (pages 350–367):

- Are you using adjectives, adverbs, and prepositional phrases to add detail and interest to your writing?

TIME TO REFLECT

Journal Assignment

Your Progress as a Writer, Reader, and Critical Thinker

As you look back over the chapter, consider carefully what you have learned about organization.

- What should writers remember about organizing an essay well?
- What do you think you most benefited from in this chapter? And what did you do best in your essay(s)?

- As a reader, what skills did you sharpen in this chapter? Do these skills relate to organization?
- How is organizing an essay a critical thinking challenge?

SUMMARY OF CHAPTER 7

In Chapter 7, you have

- seen that organization is one key to keeping your readers interested and helping them understand and, perhaps, be persuaded by your ideas;
- learned that thinking critically about organizational patterns, choosing a logical pattern, and sticking to that pattern is important in creating a well-written essay; and
- learned to use transitions to build bridges between ideas to help your readers see your organizational structure.

Creating Expressive Sentences

CREATING EXPRESSIVE SENTENCES

Examining the Kernel Sentence
Creating More Meaningful Sentences
Using Adjectives to Improve Sentences
Using -ing Adjective Phrases to Improve Sentences
Using Have Form Adjectives to Improve Sentences
Using Adverbs to Improve Sentences
Using Prepositional Phrases to Improve Sentences

In this section, you will focus on making your sentences more descriptive and thereby more accurate and expressive. You will study adjectives, adverbs, and prepositional phrases and complete sentence combining exercises that will help you move from simple sentences to colorful, interesting, more sophisticated sentences.

Examining the Kernel Sentence

First, let's look at the *kernel sentence*. The **kernel sentence** is the subject and predicate of a simple sentence. In the following examples, subjects are underlined once and predicates are underlined twice.

   a. The camera is on.

   b. The officer watches people.

   c. The officer sees a crime.

   d. The storeowners review the videotape.

   e. On the tape, a clerk steals a watch.

Read sentences *a–e* aloud. Imagine that this is a paragraph from an essay. Most readers would find these sentences (and the essay) choppy and boring.

Creating More Meaningful Sentences

So how do writers make their sentences and essays more interesting? How do writers pack in more meaning? Experienced writers do a number of different things to make their writing come alive:

   • They use adjectives to describe the nouns in their sentences.

   • They use adverbs to describe the action in their sentences.

   • They use prepositional phrases to add more meaning to their sentences.

- They **embed** (or insert) phrases in their sentences to include more information.
- They combine short, simple sentences to create longer, more interesting sentences.

You'll begin practicing all these methods for creating interesting sentences in this chapter.

Using Adjectives to Improve Sentences

Adjectives are words that describe nouns. (Remember: *Nouns* are people, places, things, or ideas.) In the following examples, the adjectives are highlighted and the arrows point to the nouns they describe:

The new nanny sings a happy song about wheels on a bus.

The worried parents set up a secret camera to watch the nanny.

Practice #1   Class Discussion of Adjectives
As a class, list some adjectives on the chalkboard. If you are unsure if a word is an adjective, see if you can use it before a noun in a sentence. Be sure to list some adjectives that you might use in an essay about surveillance technology.

Practice #2   Revisiting the Kernel Sentences
Below, you are given kernel sentences *a–e* again. Complete the work described in questions 1–3.

a. The camera is on.

b. The officer watches people.

c. The officer sees a crime.

d. The storeowners review the videotape.

e. On the tape, a clerk steals a watch.

1. Highlight the nouns you see in the kernel sentences. These are the words that you will make more interesting by using adjectives.

2. In small groups, rewrite sentences *a–e*, adding adjectives that make the sentences more interesting. (Do not use adverbs or prepositional phrases yet. You'll work with those later.)

Here is one way to improve sentence *a*:

- The sophisticated, hidden camera is on.

Notes

Creating Expressive Sentences

Creating Expressive Sentences

Notes

Note: In the new version of sentence *a*, there are two adjectives that describe *camera*, so there must be a comma between the two adjectives. Review Punctuation Rule #1.

3. Share your sentences with your class.

Punctuation Rule #1 (Review)

Put commas between items in a series.

Examples:
• The hot, delicious food is on the table.
• He is tall, skinny, and handsome.

The last comma before *and* is optional.

Practice #3   **Reading Amato**

In the following exercises, the "K" sentence will be your kernel sentence. The sentences below this kernel sentence will have information (in this case, adjectives that are highlighted) that you should add into the kernel sentence. Combine the sentences and use correct punctuation. (The new sentences you write in exercises 1–14 can be written as three paragraphs: 1–6, 7–10, and 11–14.)

Examples:

> K: I installed a surveillance system in my home.
> The system is sophisticated.
> My home is new.

• I installed a sophisticated surveillance system in my new home.

> K: My brother says that the only protection he needs is his dog.
> His dog is loud.
> His dog is intimidating.

• My brother says that the only protection he needs is his loud, intimidating dog.

1. K: Ivan Amato wrote an essay called "Big Brother Logs On."
   The essay is lengthy.

When completing #1, remember the *a/an rule*. Use *a* before words that start with consonant sounds and *an* before words that start with vowel sounds.

2. K: With essays that have points, it is useful to first read just the introduction, subheadings, and conclusion.

   The essays are long.

   The points are many.

3. K: Then when the experienced reader has time, she can read through the essay quickly.

   The time is ample.

   The essay is complete.

4. K: While reading, she should underline words.

   The words are unfamiliar.

5. K: Some of the words in Amato's essay are "laudable," "lamentable," and "conjures."

   The words are difficult.

6. K: These are words to learn and use, but the reader doesn't have to look up their meanings when she first sees them.

   These words are important.

   The reader is efficient.

   [end of first paragraph]

7. K: After taking these steps, the reader might want to set goals for a rereading.

   The rereading should be careful.

8. K: For example, the reader might decide to reread and take notes on just the first points.

   The points are four.

9. K: This time, she could look up words and highlight points.

   The words are unfamiliar.

   The points are significant.

10. K: Then, the next day, the reader could tackle the points.

    The reader is smart.

    The points are remaining.

    [end of second paragraph]

11. K: Additionally, the reader might write a summary about the essay.

    The summary is short.

12. K: Also, she should find an opportunity to discuss and respond to the points in Amato's essay.

    The points are key.

Notes

13. K: She might do this in class, with a study group, or with a tutor.
    The tutor is helpful.
14. K: Breaking up tasks into pieces is a study strategy.
    The tasks are long.
    The pieces are manageable.
    The study strategy is good.

Using -ing Adjective Phrases to Improve Sentences

An *-ing* word (a present participle) cannot be a verb without a helper, and if the *-ing* word is not working as a verb, it could be acting as either a noun or an adjective. Let's review how *-ing* words function as adjectives.

Examples of *-ing words* (present participles) working as adjectives:

The ringing phone grates on my nerves.

The flashing light shows that the camera is on.

The laughing man dances for the so-called hidden camera.

Notice that in the sentences above, the single *-ing* word goes *before* the noun it describes.

Examples of *-ing phrases* (present participle phrases) working as adjectives:

The phone ringing in the next office grates on my nerves.

The children dancing the tango grew tired.

The light flashing in the upper corner shows that the camera is on.

The man laughing loudly dances for the so-called hidden camera.

Notice that in the sentences above, the *-ing* phrase has been placed after the noun it describes. An *-ing* phrase can also be placed at the front of the sentence if the noun it describes is the subject and the very next word. Placing the phrase in front allows you to keep your subject and verb directly next to one another. The *-ing* phrase acts as an introductory phrase. However, this arrangement may not sound good with every sentence. Which of the following sentences sound good to you?

Ringing in the next office, the phone grates on my nerves.

Dancing the tango, the children grew tired.

Flashing in the upper corner, the light shows that the camera is on.

Laughing loudly, the man dances for the so-called hidden camera.

The key point to remember is to place the *-ing* adjective phrase right next to (in front of or behind) the noun it describes. If the adjective phrase is separated from its noun, you might end up with a "dangling **modifier**" comment on your writing. (Later in your studies, you'll learn about "free modifiers" that can be placed pretty much anywhere in a sentence.)

Also remember to apply Punctuation Rule #4 when you use an *-ing* phrase to introduce a sentence.

Notes

A **modifier** is a word that describes another word.

Punctuation Rule #4 (Review)

Follow an introductory word or phrase with a comma.

- Reviewing the video footage, I saw the missing teenager get on a bus.

Practice #4   **Mall Security**

Combine the following choppy sentences to create descriptive, sophisticated sentences. (You'll be adding regular adjectives and *-ing* adjectives into the kernel sentences.) In the first four sentences, the adjectives that you should add into the kernel sentences are highlighted. Remember to punctuate your sentences correctly. (The new sentences you create in exercises 1–11 can be written as a paragraph.)

1. K: The teenagers are hurrying off to shop at the mall.
   The teenagers are laughing.
   The mall is busy.
2. K: The girls are the kids there.
   The girls are carrying gift lists.
   The kids are first.
3. K: Music plays in the background as the teenagers look for gifts.
   The music is cheerful.
   The gifts are special.
4. K: One young man named Juan walks through the electronics store.
   The young man is quiet.
   The young man is serious.
   The electronics store is chaotic.
5. K: Juan purchases a set of headphones and the MP3 player.
   The headphones are expensive.
   The MP3 player is the latest.

When completing items 4, 7, and 8, remember Punctuation Rule #1.

6. K: He drops his receipt.

He is walking through the aisles. (*Hint:* The *-ing* phrase here will work best if you put it in front of the pronoun it describes and start the sentence with it.)

The aisles are narrow.

7. K: As Juan exits the store, he sets off the alarm.

The alarm is loud.

The alarm is obnoxious.

8. K: A security guard rushes over to the young man.

The security guard is intimidating.

9. K: The guard pulls Juan into the security room at the back of the store.

The guard is doubting the boy's story about losing the receipt. (*Hint:* The *-ing* phrase here should go at the beginning of your new sentence because it is so long and will create too much separation between the subject and verb if you put it after the subject.)

The security room is dingy.

10. K: They see Juan paying for the items at the register.

They are looking at the security camera footage. (*Hint:* The *-ing* phrase here should go at the beginning of your new sentence because it will sound strange coming after the pronoun "they.")

11. K: The clerk who helped Juan returns from her break and vouches for his honesty, and Juan—a little angry and embarrassed—leaves the store.

The store is bustling.

Note: In your last sentence, an adjective phrase has been embedded in the sentence with a dash before it and after it. (This is another sentence structure you'll be working on as you continue your writing studies.)

Using Have *Form Adjectives to Improve Sentences*

There is another verb form that can act as an adjective: the *have form.* Usually the ***have*** **form** of a verb is the base form plus *-ed.* (The base form is the form you find listed first in the dictionary.) If the *have* form is used with a helping verb, then the *have* form is being used as a verb. However, without the helping verb, the *have* form can be an adjective.

Creating Expressive Sentences

base forms	*have* forms
experience	experienced
supervise	supervised
walk	walked
look	looked

Sometimes the *have* form is *irregular* (doesn't follow the normal pattern of adding *-ed*).

base forms	*have* forms
show	shown
see	seen
sing	sung
buy	bought

(For more examples, see the Chart of Irregular Verbs on pages 499–500.)

If you are ever unsure about verb forms, you can look up the base form in the dictionary. After the base form, you'll find the past-tense form, the *have* form, and finally, the *-ing* form. If the past-tense and *have* forms are the same, the dictionary will only list that form once.

(See "Using the Dictionary," page 465, for more information about how dictionaries are set up.)

In the following sentences, *have* form verbs are in phrases that are acting as adjective phrases. The *have* form verbs are underlined and the adjective phrases are highlighted.

This pressure-sensitive floor <u>developed</u> by the XYZ Corporation is the best on the market.

The security packages <u>purchased</u> today will cost 10 percent less.

As with the *-ing* phrases, a *have* form phrase can often be placed at the front of the sentence if the noun it describes comes immediately after it. Punctuation Rule #4 will apply to such sentences.

<u>Developed</u> by the XYZ Corporation, this pressure-sensitive floor is the best on the market.

<u>Purchased</u> today, the security packages will cost 10 percent less.

Notes

Practice #5   **My Space**

Now try some more sentence combining that uses all the types of adjectives we have discussed (regular adjectives, *-ing* adjectives, and *have* form adjectives.) (The new sentences you write in exercises 1–14 can be written as a paragraph.)

1. K: A girl put her opinions on her My Space page.

   The girl is teenage.

   The girl was thinking about the Iraq war.

2. K: She expressed her dislike for the president with words.

   Her dislike is strong.

   Her words are violent.

3. K: Later, in her government class, she learned that it is against the law to make such statements about the president.

   The statements are harsh.

4. K: She took the statements off of her page.

   The statements were inflammatory.

5. K: However, it was too late, and one day the Secret Service showed up at her high school.

   Her high school was quiet.

   Her high school was suburban.

6. K: The agents frightened the woman.

   The agents were questioning her in private.

   The woman was young.

7. K: The story about the Secret Service made the news.

   The Secret Service was showing up on a high school campus.

   The news was national.

8. K: The family received responses from people all over the country.

   The responses were mixed.

9. K: Some people criticized the girl and her parents.

   The people were calling the family unpatriotic.

   The girl was outspoken.

10. K: Others supported the family and questioned the agents' actions.

    Others were surprised that the Secret Service reads teenage My Space pages.

11. K: The father wrote a letter to the local newspaper.

    The father was concerned about our right to free speech and our ability to discuss differences peacefully.

12. K: He apologized for his daughter's choice of words, but pointed out that our own leaders use the same terms regularly in their speeches.

    The choice of words was inappropriate.

    The terms are violent.

13. K: The entire episode raises questions about free speech, its limits, and the government's ability to monitor our communication.

    The questions are interesting.

14. It also raises questions about our abilities to debate in a manner and tolerate viewpoints.

    The manner is civilized.

    The viewpoints are different.

Practice #6   Creating Sentences with Adjectives

Create three sentences that might show up in an essay about surveillance technology. Make sure that each sentence uses adjectives that help add vivid detail and meaning. Underline the adjectives in your sentences.

Using Adverbs to Improve Sentences

Adverbs are words that describe verbs, adjectives, other adverbs, and whole groups of words. Often (but not always), adverbs end in *-ly*. Adverbs usually explain *where, when, how, why,* or *to what extent.* In the following sentences, the adverbs are highlighted and the arrows show which words the adverbs describe:

The man spoke *angrily* about the money spent on surveillance.

Another woman argued *eloquently* in favor of more cameras.

The city council thoroughly *studied* the issue.

Practice #7   Class Discussion of Adverbs

List some adverbs on the board. If you are unsure if a word can be used as an adverb, try putting it into a sentence and discussing it with your classmates. Be sure to put some adverbs on the board that you might use in an essay on surveillance technology.

Notes

Practice #8   Making Security Safe

In the following exercises, combine sentences using adverbs to add meaning. The words that are (or will become) adverbs are highlighted.

1. K: My government class discussed surveillance in America.

   The discussion was recent.

   We discussed the topic thoroughly.

   (*Hint:* Change *recent* into an adverb by adding -*ly* and place it at the beginning of the sentence.)

2. K: We studied how our security needs might conflict with the checks and balances system.

   We studied carefully.

3. K: We think the watchers will have to be observed.

   We will need to observe them constantly.

4. K: In addition, we must develop a system for reviewing and deleting personal information gathered through surveillance.

   We must review and delete the information regularly.

Practice #9   Thinking About High-Tech Security

In the following exercises, combine sentences using adjectives and adverbs to add meaning. (You may have to change an adjective into an adverb when combining sentences.)

1. K: Ivan Amato doesn't believe that Americans should try to stop advances.

   Amato's beliefs are clear.

   The advances are technological.

   (*Hint:* Change *clear* into an adverb by adding an -*ly*.)

2. K: ACLU's Steinhardt says an advance can change into an abuse.

   The advance is technological.

   The change can be easy.

   The abuse is technological.

   (*Hint:* Change *easy* into an adverb by changing the *y* to *i* and adding -*ly* and put it before *change*.)

3. K: In 1999, Scott McNealy, CEO of Sun Microsystems, told reporters, "You already have zero privacy. Get over it."

   His statement was blunt.

   (*Hint:* Change *blunt* into an adverb.)

Remember the *a/an rule*. Use *a* before words that start with a consonant sound. Use *an* before words that start with a vowel sound.

4. K: John Woodward, employed by the CIA, argues that no one wants to watch each of us.

Woodward is a former employee of the CIA.

The watching is constant.

(*Hint:* Change *former* into an adverb and place it before *employed*. Change *constant* into an adverb and place it at the end of the sentence.)

5. K: I am a person, but I am also a person who doesn't want Big Brother peering at me.

I am a person who abides by the law.

I enjoy my privacy.

Big Brother seems suspicious.

(*Hint:* Change *abides by the law* into the adjective *law-abiding*. Change *privacy* into an adjective and place before the second *person*. Change *suspicious* into an adverb and place after *peering*.)

6. K: The man argues that we should support the city's plan to install cameras on streets.

The man is leading the neighborhood watch meeting.

The argument is persuasive.

The plan is new.

The streets are public.

(*Hint:* Change *persuasive* into an adverb.)

7. K: My classmate explained the similarities between Orwell's novel and the movie.

The similarities were interesting.

The similarities were frightening.

The movie was released.

The release was recent.

(*Hint:* Change *recent* into an adverb.)

8. K: I make faces into the ATM camera.

I am hoping to make some security person laugh.

I make the faces on purpose.

The faces are strange.

(*Hint:* Place the *-ing* adjective phrase that begins with *hoping* at the beginning of your new sentence. Put a comma after the phrase. Change *purpose* into an adverb.)

9. K: If we spend amounts of time and money on security, will we ignore the causes of crime and terrorism?

The amounts are excessive.

The causes are root.

10. K: In an effort to keep her safe, the parents made their daughter wear the device.

The parents were reluctant to take this action.

The device was for tracking.

(*Hint:* Change *reluctant* into an adverb.)

Practice #10   Creating Sentences with Adverbs

Create three sentences that might show up in an essay about surveillance technology. Use adverbs to create more meaning and detail. Underline the adverbs you have added.

Using Prepositional Phrases to Improve Sentences

A prepositional phrase, as you studied in Chapter 4, is a phrase made up of a preposition and its object. These phrases can add significant information to sentences, making the sentences far more compelling and precise. In the following sentences, the prepositional phrases are bracketed:

[In his essay "Big Brother Logs On,"] Ivan Amato discusses his concerns [about high-tech surveillance].

He writes [about face recognition, iris scanning, and hidden cameras] and how we will all be affected [by these tools].

Practice #11   Class Discussion of Prepositional Phrases

List some prepositional phrases on the chalkboard that might show up in an essay about surveillance technology.

Practice #12   Adding Prepositional Phrases

Combine the following sentences, using prepositional phrases to create more interesting sentences. The prepositional phrases that should be added to the kernel sentences are bracketed.

1. K: When I write, I always research the topic.

I write [about a controversial issue].

I research [at the library].

2. K: I go to find articles.

I go [to the computers].

The articles are [from magazines and newspapers].

3. K: Last week, the librarian helped me find information.

The information was [for my essay].

My essay is [about security] [at airports].

Practice #13   On Camera

Combine the following sentences, using prepositional phrases, adjectives, and adverbs to add greater detail and meaning. (The new sentences you write in exercises 1–7 can be written as one paragraph.)

1. K: From the moment I leave the house, I'm on camera.

I leave in the morning.

2. K: First, the bus has a camera to discourage and record crime.

It is a security camera.

3. K: When I get off the bus downtown and walk three blocks, I pass cameras that hang.

I walk to work.

There are six cameras.

The cameras are on traffic signal poles.

4. K: When I enter my building, I must pass, show an identification card, and smile.

I pass through the metal detector.

I smile at the cameras.

The cameras are outside and inside the elevators.

5. K: It's all practice.

The practice is good.

The practice is for me.

6. K: I'm preparing and must deal.

The preparation is for the day that I am a star.

I will be rich and famous.

I will have to deal with the paparazzi.

7. K: I think I'll be great and smile.

I'll smile easily.

I'll smile for the cameras.

Notes

> **Practice #14   Creating Sentences with Prepositional Phrases**
> Write three sentences that you might use in an essay about surveillance technology. Use some prepositional phrases in these practice sentences. Underline the prepositional phrases you use.

STYLE TIPS

This entire chapter has focused on creating expressive sentences. You've practiced adding adjectives, adjective phrases, adverbs, and prepositional phrases. Adding these elements to your writing not only adds interest, but also clarifies your meaning. You are able to be more specific and precise in what you have to say.

Of course, it is always possible to have too much of a good thing. Too much description—especially for the wrong audience or in the wrong piece—could be negative. For example, if your supervisor asks for a quick summary of how the training went, she might not want any detailed description.

When you've come to the editing stage of your writing process, and you're looking at the style of your sentences, think about who your audience is and what your purpose in writing is. Adjust your style accordingly. Also, read your work aloud and listen carefully. How does it sound? If English isn't your first language or if you've never been a serious reader, your "ear" for language may not be strong yet. In that case, you want to read—both silently and aloud—many pieces of good writing. Your brain will soak up the sentence patterns and style, and you'll develop an "ear" for writing that you can rely on.

The following exercises ask you to work with a paragraph and sentences that would be appropriate for a college class. You'll be applying Style Tip #5.

> *Style Tip #5*
> *Look for opportunities to add details, descriptions, and information to your sentences.*

Practice #15 Warming Up Your Style Muscles

Read the following paragraph aloud. The paragraph is grammatically correct, but it isn't as informative, precise, or interesting as it could be.

> I think our children will grow up expecting to be watched, and their demands and desires will be far different than what many adults ask. I, for example, don't like the idea that the government may have a file. I feel bad to think that my phone calls, e-mails, and purchases may be recorded. What if I become friends with a person the government is investigating? I have political views. If the government began to investigate me, I'm afraid of what some agent might conclude. I don't want to stop attending protests or writing letters out of fear. I believe the thing about this country is our right to express ourselves and question the government. But if we become too afraid to speak out, what might happen to us?

Now, using words from the lists below, rewrite the paragraph and fill in the blanks with adjectives, an adverb, and prepositional phrases. When you are finished, read the edited paragraph aloud.

Adjectives	**Adverbs**	**Prepositional Phrases**
uncomfortable	freely	for privacy
close		for today
strong		on me
inexperienced		to my representatives
vindictive		
political		
greatest		

> I think our children will grow up expecting to be watched, and their demands and desires _____ will be far different than what many adults ask _____. I, for example, don't like the idea that the government may have a file _____. I feel _____ to think that my phone calls, e-mails, and purchases may be recorded. What if I become _____ friends with a person the government is investigating? I have _____ political views. If the

Notes

government began to investigate me, I'm afraid of what some _____,

_____ agent might conclude. I don't want to stop attending _____

protests or writing letters _____ out of fear. I believe the _____ thing

about this country is our right to express ourselves _____ and question

the government. But if we become too afraid to speak out, what might

happen to us?

Practice #16   An Editing Challenge

Add adjectives, adverbs, and prepositions to the sentences below to make them more precise and more interesting. In some sentences, you may choose to add just one word. In other sentences, you might choose to add two or more words. Here are a few suggestions and questions to consider as you improve the sentences.

- When you look at the nouns, ask what adjectives might describe these nouns. (Examples: *great, clever, frightening*)
- With verbs, ask how the action is performed. (Examples: *quickly, suddenly, slowly*)
- To add prepositions, ask questions like these: Where did this happen? (Examples: *in school, at the intersection downtown, on the hill*) Who is involved and how? (Examples: *to me, by my instructor, for my kids*) When did this happen? (Examples: *in the future, on my day off, in my old age*) You may want to think about this list of common prepositions as you create prepositional phrases: *about, at, by, for, in, on.*

    1. I wrote an essay.
    2. I researched the topic.
    3. My introduction explains my position.
    4. I used facts, metaphors, and experience.
    5. I asked the tutor.
    6. I like the conclusion.
    7. I shared my essay.

Your Own Writing: Creating Expressive Sentences   Notes

Study a piece of your writing (a journal entry or a paragraph from an essay). Underline any adjectives, adverbs, and prepositional phrases you find. Revise the piece adding adjectives, adverbs, and prepositional phrases to make your sentences more descriptive and expressive. Underline all adjectives, adverbs, and prepositional phrases in your revised work.

Using Connections *Online with* PEARSON **mywritinglab**

For more practice with creating expressive sentences, log onto www.mywritinglab.com to access the online resources for *Connections*, Third Edition.

Style Tips

8

Writing About Music and Poetry

Main Topics

- Inferring and analyzing in your essays

- Communicating your interpretations of song lyrics and poems

- Combining sentences with coordinators and subordinators

Mutts

MUTTS © Patrick McDonnell. King Features Syndicate.

On the job and in college, you'll frequently use your analysis and inference skills. These critical thinking skills require you to break down something complex into smaller pieces (**analyze**) and figure out meaning by studying these pieces (**infer**). You analyze and infer frequently throughout your day. For instance, if you ask a friend to drive you to the library, and your friend heaves a big sigh and says, "Oh, I guess I could if I have to," you automatically *analyze* the sigh and the words "guess" and "have to," and you *infer* that even though your friend said he would drive you, he doesn't really want to.

In other situations, analyzing and inferring can be more challenging. In a laboratory, for example, a scientist might analyze large bodies of data and infer information about how a particular cancer is caused, or a businessperson might study a product or market and infer information about how to best sell the product. In college, a history student might analyze the events leading to World War I and infer information about the cause of the war, or a literature student might analyze a novel and infer meaning from the text as part of the coursework. In this chapter, you'll strengthen your analytical and inferential skills as you think about music lyrics and poetry, two forms of communication that often need to be studied in depth in order to be fully understood and appreciated.

ANALYSIS AND INFERENCE IN YOUR WRITING

As you may have guessed, all the essays you've been writing have required you to analyze and infer. You may have studied advertisements and inferred information about the types of audiences the ads were targeting. You may have analyzed information about people and determined whether or not they qualified as heroes. You may have also analyzed the advantages and disadvantages of media and surveillance technology. Academic writing assignments generally require this kind of critical thinking since studying information and discovering relationships (causes, effects, advantages, and disadvantages) are at the core of college work. In this chapter, you'll take a closer look at what you've been doing in your essays and further sharpen your analytical skills.

Analyzing and Inferring in Your Essays

When you wrote your earlier essays, you took large topics (advertising, heroes, television, media, and surveillance technology), broke them down into smaller pieces (one ad, one heroic person, a few advantages or disadvantages of television, media, or surveillance technology), analyzed key facts, and inferred information. For example, if you wrote about advertising, you selected one ad to study closely and broke that down into smaller pieces to look at colors, words, people, and props. In fact, if there were people in the ad, you looked even more closely and studied their age, ethnicity, expressions, clothing, posture, and so on. From this information, you inferred the advertiser's message and who the advertiser was trying to attract with the ad.

Breaking down large topics into smaller pieces is what analytical and inferential thinking is all about. The structure of an academic essay is perfect for this kind of work. The thesis allows you to state a main idea, and the paragraphs allow you to discuss pieces of that main idea one at a time. To do this well, you must use an effective writing process that allows you to explore, learn, divide things into smaller pieces, and think critically. Brainstorming, discussing, reading, outlining, drafting, revising, and editing make such exploration and learning possible.

Analyzing and Inferring in Your Paragraphs

As you've read, academic essays are structured perfectly for analytical writing. The paragraph, in particular, offers an effective structure for analysis and inference. In the topic sentence of the paragraph, the writer states one specific point that supports the thesis of the essay. Then in the body of the paragraph, the writer offers evidence gathered from readings and discussion. Finally, the writer analyzes the evidence and makes inferences about that evidence.

Activity

Study These Data and This Analytical Paragraph

Here are some statistics that were published on the Recording Industry Association Web site.

Recording Industry Association of America, 2006 Consumer Profile

	1997	1998	1999	2000	2001	2002	2003	2004	2005	2006
Genre										
Rock	32.5	25.7	25.2	24.8	24.4	24.7	25.2	23.9	31.5	34.0 %
Rap/Hip-hop[1]	10.1	9.7	10.8	12.9	11.4	13.8	13.3	12.1	13.3	11.4
R&B/Urban[2]	11.2	12.8	10.5	9.7	10.6	11.2	10.6	11.3	10.2	11.0
Country	14.4	14.1	10.8	10.7	10.5	10.7	10.4	13.0	12.5	13.0
Pop	9.4	10.0	10.3	11.0	12.1	9.0	8.9	10.0	8.1	7.1
Religious[3]	4.5	6.3	5.1	4.8	6.7	6.7	5.8	6.0	5.3	5.5
Classical	2.8	3.3	3.5	2.7	3.2	3.1	3.0	2.0	2.4	1.9
Jazz	2.8	1.9	3.0	2.9	3.4	3.2	2.9	2.7	1.8	2.0
Soundtracks	1.2	1.7	0.8	0.7	1.4	1.1	1.4	1.1	0.9	0.8
Oldies	0.8	0.7	0.7	0.9	0.8	0.9	1.3	1.4	1.1	1.1
New Age	0.8	0.6	0.5	0.5	1.0	0.5	0.5	1.0	0.4	0.3
Children's	0.9	0.4	0.4	0.6	0.5	0.4	0.6	2.8	2.3	2.9
Other[4]	5.7	7.9	9.1	8.3	7.9	8.1	7.6	8.9	8.5	7.3
Format										
Full-length CDs	70.2	74.8	83.2	89.3	89.2	90.5	87.8	90.3	87.0	85.6 %
Full-length cassettes	18.2	14.8	8.0	4.9	3.4	2.4	2.2	1.7	1.1	0.8
Singles (all types)	9.3	6.8	5.4	2.5	2.4	1.9	2.4	2.4	2.7	3.4
Music videos/Video DVDs	0.6	1.0	0.9	0.8	1.1	0.7	0.6	1.0	0.7	1.1
DVD audio	NA	NA	NA	NA	1.1	1.3	2.7	1.7	0.8	1.3
Digital Download	NA	NA	NA	NA	0.2	0.5	1.3	0.9	5.7	6.7
SACD	NA	NA	NA	NA	NA	NA	0.5	0.8	1.2	0.0
Vinyl LPs	0.7	0.7	0.5	0.5	0.6	0.7	0.5	0.9	0.7	0.6

[1]Rap: Includes Rap and Hip-Hop.

[2]R&B: Includes R&B, Blues, Dance, Disco, Funk, Fusion, Motown, Reggae, Soul.

[3]Religious: Includes Christian, Gospel, Inspirational, Religious, and Spiritual.

[4]Other: Includes Big Band, Broadway Shows, Comedy, Contemporary, Electronic, EMO, Ethnic, Exercise, Folk, Gothic, Grunge, Holiday Music, House Music, Humor, Instrumental, Language, Latin, Love Songs, Mix, Mellow, Modern, Ska, Spoken word, Standards, Swing, Top-40, Trip-hop.

The following paragraph was written after careful analytical study of those statistics.

      After studying the data available, I have concluded that in addition to selling CDs online, we must also begin to sell digital downloads. Statistics on recorded music and music videos reveal a reduction in the number of cassette sales (4.9 percent to 1.1 percent) and CD sales (89.3 percent to 87 percent) from 2000 to 2005. This amounts to an overall 5.8 percent decrease in sales. However, this decrease may be accounted for in the sale of digital downloads, which have increased steadily from 0.2 percent of music sales in 2001 to 5.7 percent in 2005. These

Notes

statistics suggest we should begin selling digital downloads on our Web site as well as CDs.

1. Which statistics on the Web site did this writer pay closest attention to? Highlight the statistics he used.

2. Highlight the topic sentence of this paragraph. What is this writer promising to write about? Explain his purpose in your own words.

3. Put a box around the part of the paragraph that contains the specific support for the main idea.

4. After offering specific support, this writer explains the support and then wraps up the paragraph by making a recommendation. Put "E" next to the lines of the paragraph that *explain* the support, and put "R" next to the lines that express this writer's *recommendation*.

5. Describe in your own words the different parts of this analytical paragraph.

Analyzing Music Lyrics and Poetry

Music and poetry are both covered in this chapter because they are similar in many ways. They are both creative expressions that have the ability to go beyond the boundaries of gender, ethnicity, and class to appeal to just about everyone. Although most people have favorite songs or poems, people won't always agree on how to interpret these songs or poems—which leads to interesting discussions and excellent analytical brain work.

The key difference between a song lyric and a poem is, of course, that one is set to music and the other isn't. However, many poems do have a rhythm of their own, and some poems end up being put to music. If you have never enjoyed studying poetry, but love music, you might find that many of the things you love about music—its ability to paint pictures in your mind, its ability to make you feel certain emotions, and its ability to help you escape everyday life—are also true of poems.

This section of the text will offer you some basic information about lyrics and poems. You'll learn a few terms that will help you when you begin to analyze specific pieces.

Form   The words in lyrics and poems sometimes rhyme, but often they do not. Sometimes poems will follow a specific, formal rhythmic pattern called **meter.** Other times, poems, like lyrics without their musical notes, will have an inconsistent rhythm or no rhythm.

Paragraphs in music lyrics and poems are called stanzas. Stanzas can be long or short, and, much like the paragraphs in journalistic writing, they generally don't have topic sentences.

Language Because lyricists (people who write music lyrics) and poets are interested in creating images and feelings, and because they generally don't insist on only one interpretation of their work, they don't write in complete, detailed sentences. (You'll find that capital letters and periods aren't used like they are in academic writing.) Lyricists and poets choose their language very carefully, finding words that will create the message, image, or feeling they are aiming for. When analyzing lyrics and poems, you'll want to pay attention to the vocabulary. Is the writer using slang? Is the language formal? Is it the language of a child? Of a parent? Of a lover? Of a sister? What types of words are being used?

Lyricists and poets also use **figurative language** to compare things—helping to paint an image in the reader's mind. "She cried like a baby" is an example of figurative language. The person, "she," is not really a baby, but the writer is saying she cried like one—painting the image of loud, constant crying in our minds. Sometimes the word "like" is left out: "The moon, a silver platter in the sky, lit our way." The moon isn't really a silver serving dish. The writer is simply saying it's similar in appearance to a "platter."

Effect By choosing to use certain words and figurative language, the writer is sending a message to her audience. She is creating a specific image in the reader's mind and a certain mood. For example, if a writer uses words like *unrippled water, glassy reflection, grass warm and still,* she may be trying to create images of summer at a lake. She may also be creating a quiet, calm, peaceful mood. If she adds that "the lake was a lonely child waiting for summer visitors to return," she is continuing these images by using figurative language and suggesting that the lake sits still and quiet—like a lonely child might, waiting for the excitement and commotion of friends. The writer's message in these lines might be that there is beauty and peace in anticipating the summer. Both the quiet and the excitement can be admired.

Notes   *Responding and Interpreting*   Because lyricists and poets don't fully explain and develop their ideas the way essayists do, it's often difficult to be absolutely certain what a song or poem means. Many people find this uncertainty to be the magical part of lyrics and poetry. Each person hearing or reading the lyric or poem will create images in his own mind based on his own experiences. However, although there is usually room for more than one interpretation, your formal analytical essay must be based on a careful study of the vocabulary and the figurative language. The interpretation you offer in your essay must be something you can carefully and thoughtfully defend by offering specific support from the song or poem itself.

Discussing   Discussing the lyrics and poems with classmates will help you increase your understanding of the pieces because other people will see things and make connections that you may miss. You and your classmates can help one another by listening to each other's responses and respectfully challenging each other to provide proof and support for each interpretation.

How One Reader Analyzed and Responded to a Poem   The handwritten notes here represent one student's personal and class notes about a poem written by Langston Hughes, a poet who lived from 1902 to 1967. A major African American voice in the field of literature, Hughes frequently wrote using vocabulary that represented southern speech and a rhythm similar to blues or jazz music. This poem, like many of his, explores the southern African American experience of migrating north. It was also put to music and can be considered both a poem and a song. Look at how one reader studied and responded to the poem by listening to the class discussion and analyzing the language carefully.

Evenin' Air Blues

Notes from class
southern style
vocab.

Langston Hughes

suggests he used to live in the South.

My notes

(Folks,) I come up North
Cause they told me
(de) North was fine.
I come up North
Cause they told me de North was fine.
Been up here six months—
I'm about to lose my mind.

Repeats, creates a rhythm.

Things have not gone well.

southern style vocab.

This mornin' for breakfast
I chawed de mornin' air. ——————— *Is he hungry? No money? No job?*
This mornin' for breakfast
Chawed de mornin' air.
But this evenin' for supper, ——————— *He has spirit and humor.*
I got evenin' air to spare.

He has spirit.

Believe I'll do a little dancin'
Just to drive my blues away,— ——————— *Yes. He's suffering. Things are not going well.*
A little dancin'
To drive my blues away,
Cause when I'm dancin'
De blues forgets to stay.

southern vocab.

But if you was to ask me
How de blues they come to be,
Says if you was to ask me
How de blues they come to be— ——————— *Is he saying he's feeling sad because he faces the same discrimination in the North as he did in the South?*
You wouldn't need to ask me:
Just look at me and see. ———————

Notes

My Informal Response to "Evenin' Air Blues"

I think this is a beautiful "song" about an African American man's struggle to make a life for himself after he has moved from the South to the North. It seems to me that he had high hopes when he moved: "I come up North/Cause they told me de North was fine." But now he says, "I'm about to lose my mind." I don't think he has any money or a job because he doesn't have anything to eat: "I chawed de mornin' air." (My instructor said that line referred to eating and was written in a southern dialect.) Oh, and one of my classmates pointed out the beauty of this poem: the speaker's spirit. Instead of crying and complaining, the speaker dances! Wow. This poem is both painful and beautiful.

How One Reader Analyzed a Song in an Essay

The following essay is a student analysis of "Silent Legacy" by Melissa Etheridge from the CD *Yes I Am*. (The song appears on pages 386–387.) As you read the student paper, note how the student has examined what she terms "clues" that reveal the speaker's struggle between resigning herself to her parents' expectations and accepting who she is.

A Silent Legacy

The song "Silent Legacy" appearing on Melissa Etheridge's CD *Yes I Am* caught my attention because of the title as well as the deep lyrics. The title "Silent Legacy" is part of the refrain, which is repeated through the song. "Silent Legacy" in this song refers to a secret inheritance. After reading the lyrics, I feel the speaker is uncovering her true feelings about her hidden sexuality.

My first clue was found in stanza 3. This stanza focused on a teen dealing with feelings pertaining to her sexuality that she cannot control. I understand this when I read that she is "craving for affection." But to come back into her parent's home, she has to deny her sexual feelings: "Deny all that you feel / And they will bring you home again." Because most parents talk to their children about sex, I feel that the song must deal with something other than a heterosexual relationship. And since some groups condemn homosexuality, I thought this song was about homosexuality.

My second clue was found in stanza 5. It talks about the teen entering puberty and not knowing how she would feel. I got this from the lines, "Your body is alive / But no one told you what you'd feel." The parents have had a hard time dealing with the fact that their daughter is having homosexual feelings. I get this from the line, "they cover it with shame." Because her parents cannot understand what their daughter is going through, she feels nothing but anger toward them. This became clear to me when the speaker suggests that the more the parents try to cover her feelings with shame, these feelings turn to rage.

My last clue comes from stanza 6. This teen is depressed and caught up in emotions about her sexuality. To her, there is no way out. I got this from the refrain, "as you pray in your darkness / For wings to set you free / You are bound to your silent legacy." She is desperately searching for help to find a solution; this is from the lines, "You are digging for the answers / Until your fingers bleed." Also, the parents are trying to use religion to make her feel bad enough to deny her feelings and to make her feel ashamed about what she feels. I got that from the lines, "They feed you guilt / To keep you humble keep you low / Some man and myth they made up / A thousand years ago." I truly feel that the speaker's parents were probably quoting scripture to her because of the last line.

The song deals with a teenage girl stuck in her emotions about her sexuality. It is a song directed at parents so that they'll listen and not be so close-minded about sexuality. It's also a song to fellow sufferers who may not feel accepted because of their sexuality.

I believe this song was important for Melissa Etheridge to write because at one time she went through what she is singing about. According to barnes&noble. com, Etheridge recently wrote a book titled *The Truth Is . . .* , which is a biography of her life in which she discusses openly her own "coming out." Her "coming out" has enabled her to become an advocate for gays and lesbians.

Whether Etheridge was talking about herself or someone else, this song shares deep emotion and hope and sends a message to parents about teens caught between the love of their parents and the love of their own lives.

—*Melody Bruley, student writer*

Activity

Analyze the Student Sample

1. Highlight the main idea or thesis in Bruley's essay.

2. How does Bruley organize her ideas in this essay? Would you organize anything differently?

3. Bruley includes quotations from the song, but she doesn't stop there. She explains what she sees in the quotations. Pick one instance where she does this particularly well. Explain your choice.

Points to Remember About Analyzing Lyrics and Poems

- Respond honestly. Discuss lyrics and poems with others.
- Divide the lyric or poem into small pieces (lines and words), and study these pieces. Use your critical thinking skills and look carefully at vocabulary and figurative language.
- When writing an essay, have clear topic sentences that connect to the thesis and that cover one piece of the lyric or poem at a time.
- Use examples from the lyric or poem to support the points you make. Include particular vocabulary words and figurative language.
- Explain your support.

Notes

Writing Assignment #1: *Analyzing Music Lyrics*

In this assignment, you'll strengthen your ability to analyze and infer as you study music lyrics. This analysis requires you to study the details of the lyrics so that you can draw conclusions about what the songs mean.

Here, in brief, is the writing assignment you are preparing for:

Write an essay about one of the songs in this book or a song you have chosen and reviewed with your instructor. In your essay, summarize what you think the song is about. Then choose a couple of the most interesting parts to support your point and show that you have read the lyrics carefully and have good reasons for your interpretation.

Keep this assignment in mind as you begin to analyze music lyrics.

Discuss and Engage

Activities

Analyze the Mutts *Cartoon*

Analyze the cartoon on page 368 and answer the following questions:

1. Describe what is happening in the first frame of the cartoon. (What does the musical note represent? What does "SQUAWK KRAW EEEEE" represent?)

2. In the second frame, why didn't the cartoonist write any words? What is going on between the two birds?

3. Why did the cartoonist choose the words "Man" and "digs"? What do these words mean to you?

4. Can you infer anything about the birds by the way they look?

5. What is the cartoonist's message?

Your Experiences with Music

Discuss with your classmates the types of music you like. Which songs do you like the most, and why? Are there people in your class who listen carefully to lyrics in songs? What do they look for in good lyrics? Are you always sure what a song means?

Get Involved!

Go online to www.lyrics.com and find lyrics that would be interesting and challenging to analyze. Bring the lyrics to two or three songs to class and share them with your classmates.

> ### Journal Assignment
>
> #### Thoughts About Song Lyrics
>
> Write about song lyrics and how you and your classmates react to them. Write down some of your favorite lyrics and explain why they are important to you. Also, write about some lyrics that you have heard or read, but haven't enjoyed. Why didn't you like these lyrics? (This is for your eyes only. Refer back to this journal when you are getting ready to write your essay on music.)

Read, Discuss, Think Critically

This section of the chapter offers you the lyrics to four songs, in a variety of styles: classic rock (John Lennon), country (Randy Travis and The Dixie Chicks), and mellow rock (Melissa Etheridge). Notice that the title of the song is given first, then the name of the performer and album.

Reading Assignment: "Imagine"

> Preview   Read the title and the first two stanzas.
>
> Anticipate   What do you think this song will be about? What kind of mood or message do you think it has? Use the "Notes" column to record your thoughts.
>
> Read and Reread   Quickly read the lyrics one time, marking unknown terms. Then reread more slowly and use the "Notes" column to record images and meanings that come to mind. Also write down any questions you have. Define unknown terms. Finally, listen to the song or read it aloud.

Imagine
John Lennon

Imagine

1   Imagine there's no heaven
It's easy if you try
No hell below us

Notes

Above us only sky
Imagine all the people
living for today. . . .

2   Imagine there's no countries
It isn't hard to do
Nothing to kill or die for
And no religion too
Imagine all the people
living life in peace. . . .

3   You may say I'm a dreamer
But I'm not the only one
I hope someday you'll join us
And the world will be as one.

4   Imagine no possessions
I wonder if you can
No need for greed or hunger
A brotherhood of man
Imagine all the people
Sharing all the world. . . .

5   You may say I'm a dreamer
but I'm not the only one
I hope some day you'll join us
And the world will live as one.

Questions for Critical Thought
"Imagine"

1. What is your general reaction to this song? How does it make you feel? What words and images in the lyrics support your reaction?

2. Summarize what you think each stanza is about.

3. Lennon uses the term "imagine" frequently. Why is the repetition of this word necessary?

4. What do you think is the general message of this song?

5. Does any particular line or image in the song make you reconsider the way you or others live their lives? Explain.

Reading Assignment: *"Old 8 x 10"*

Preview   Read the title and the first two stanzas.

Anticipate   What do you think this song will be about? What kind of mood or message do you think it has? Write down your thoughts in the "Notes" column.

Read and Reread   Quickly read the lyrics one time, marking unknown terms. Then reread more slowly and use the "Notes" column to record images and meanings that come to mind. Also write down any questions you have. Define unknown terms. Finally, listen to the song or read it aloud.

Old 8 x 10

Randy Travis

Old 8 x 10

1   Well I know it ain't much
But it's all that I have since she's gone
One black and white memory of the only love I've ever known
One moment in time when we were together
A page from the past to haunt me forever
A constant reminder that hearts heal much slower than bones

2   Now my whole world's in one 8 x 10
With four metal walls holding it in
Through one plate-glass window
'Neath the blanket of dust
Stands an 8 x 10 picture of us
I wish I'd have told her
What I felt inside
Back when her sweet love was flowing like wine
I wish she would come back and love me again
The way that she loved me
In that old 8 x 10

3   Now the silence is deafening
As the day turns to dark
Her presence gets stronger with each beat of my heart
I pretend that she's here and we've made a new start

Notes

And for a moment
She's back in my arms

4   Now my whole world's in one 8 x 10
With four metal walls holding it in
Through one plate-glass window
'Neath the blanket of dust
Stands an 8 x 10 picture of us
There's an 8 x 10 picture of us

Questions for Critical Thought

"Old 8 x 10"

1. What does the title tell you about the song? What does it make you think of?

2. What do the following lines refer to?

    "One black and white memory of the only love I've ever known"

    "One moment in time when we were together"

    "Now my whole world's in one 8 x 10"

    What is he singing about? (What is "black and white"? What "moment in time" is he referring to? What is the 8 x 10?) (He is using figurative language here.)

3. He also sings about "four metal walls holding it in" and "one plate-glass window." What are these walls? What is this window? (He is using figurative language here.)

4. What is the general feeling of the song? What image do you have of the speaker in the lyrics? What can you say about him, his life, and his home? What details in the lyrics support your reactions?

5. Do any of the lines or images in these lyrics remind you of yourself or your life? Explain.

Reading Assignment: "Silent House"

Preview   Read the title and the first two stanzas of the song.

Anticipate   What do you think this song will be about? In the "Notes" column describe the mood and message you're anticipating based on the opening stanzas of the song.

Read and Reread   Read the lyrics through once, marking unknown terms. Then reread the lyrics again. Use the "Notes"
column to record images and ideas that come to mind. Define
any terms you marked during your first reading. Also, write
down any questions you have. Finally, listen to the song or read it
aloud.

Silent House

The Dixie Chicks

*Words and Music by Emily Robison, Martie Maguire, Natalie Maines,
and Neil Finn*

Taking the Long Way

1   These walls
    Have eyes
    Rows of photographs
    And faces like mine
    Who do
    We become
    Without knowing where
    We started from

2   It's true
    I'm missing you
    As I stand alone
    In your room

3   Every day that will pass you by
    Every name that you won't recall
    Everything that you made by hand
    Everything that you know by heart

4   And I will try to connect
    All the pieces you left
    I will carry it on
    And let you forget
    And I'll remember the years
    When your mind was clear

Notes

How the laughter and life
Filled up this silent house

5   One room
Two single beds
In the closet hangs
Your favorite dress
The books
That you read
Are in scattered piles
Of paper shreds

6   Everything that you made by hand
Everything that you know by heart

7   And I will try to connect
All the pieces you left
I will carry it on
And let you forget
And I'll remember the years
When your mind was clear
How the laughter and life
Filled up this silent house
Silent house

8   In the garden
Off the living room
A chill fills the air
And the lilies bloom

9   And I will try to connect
All the pieces you left
I will carry it on
And let you forget
And I'll remember the years
When your mind was clear
How the laughter and life
Filled up this

10 And I will try to connect
All the pieces you left

I will carry it on   *Notes*
And let you forget
And I'll remember the years
When your mind was clear
How the laughter and life
Filled up this silent house

11   Silent house

Questions for Critical Thought

"Silent House"

1. Describe your general reaction to the song. How does it make you feel? Which of the words or images contribute to this feeling?

2. What relationship do you think the speaker had with the person who is gone? What words or images lead you to infer this?

3. What was the speaker's home life like in earlier years? How has it changed?

4. What might have happened to the person who left? What clues lead you to this conclusion?

5. What's life like for the speaker now? What does the speaker try to do? Why?

6. Could you relate to the speaker's experience? If so, how? If not, why not?

Reading Assignment: "Silent Legacy"

Preview   Read the title and the first two stanzas.

Anticipate   What do you think this song will be about? What kind of mood or message do you think it might have? Respond in the "Notes" column.

Read and Reread   Quickly read the lyrics one time, marking unknown terms. Then reread more slowly and use the "Notes" column to record images and meanings that come to mind. Also write down any questions you have. Define unknown terms. Finally, listen to the song or read it aloud.

Silent Legacy

Melissa Etheridge

Yes I Am

1   Why did you steal the matches
From the one room motel
Once they gave you answers
Now they give you hell
They will never understand
They wonder where did they go wrong
How could you be so selfish
Why can't you get along

2   And as you pray in your darkness
For wings to set you free
You are bound to your silent legacy

3   You've seen it in the movies
And you've heard it on the street
Craving the affection
Your blood is full of heat
They don't listen to your reasons
As original as sin
Deny all that you feel
And they will bring you home again

4   And as you pray in your darkness
For wings to set you free
You are bound to your silent legacy

5   Your body is alive
But no one told you what you'd feel
The empty aching hours
Trying to conceal
The natural progression
Is the coming of your age
But they cover it with shame
And turn it into rage

6   And as you pray in your darkness
For wings to set you free

You are bound to your silent legacy
You are digging for the answers
Until your fingers bleed
To satisfy the hunger
To satiate the need
They feed you on the guilt
To keep you humble keep you low
Some man and myth they made up
A thousand years ago

7   And as you pray in your darkness
For wings to set you free
You are bound to your silent legacy

8   Mothers tell your children
Be quick you must be strong
Life is full of wonder
Love is never wrong
Remember how they taught you
How much of it was fear
Refuse to hand it down
The legacy stops here

9   Oh my child

Questions for Critical Thought

"Silent Legacy"

1. What does the title "Silent Legacy" suggest to you?

2. What is your general reaction to the music lyrics? How do they make you feel?

3. The following lines appear in stanza 1: "They wonder where did they go wrong / How could you be so selfish / Why can't you get along." Who might ask "Where did we go wrong?" or "How could you be so selfish?" or "Why can't you get along?" Look at the other times "they" is used. Who do you think "they" refers to in this song?

4. Read through the song and note where the words "sin," "shame," and "guilt" show up. What do you think the person in this song is struggling with?

5. The last stanza in this song is distinctly different in tone and message. Explain.

6. What do you think the "silent legacy" is?

7. Do any of the lines or images in these lyrics remind you of yourself or your life? Explain.

Journal Assignment

An Informal Response to the Songs

Write out your thoughts about two or three of the songs in this book. What do they mean? What clues do you have for the meaning? During class discussion, did any of your classmates point out things you hadn't seen in the songs? After reading someone else's journal, just say, "Thank you," when you return it.

Explore the Writing Assignment

Here, again, is your writing assignment. Review it carefully before continuing. Underline the important terms in the assignment.

Write an essay about one of the songs in this book or a song you have chosen and reviewed with your instructor. In your essay, summarize what you think the song is about. Then choose a couple of the most interesting parts to support your point and show that you have read the lyrics carefully and have good reasons for your interpretation.

Brainstorm   Review your work so far in this chapter. What song do you want to write an essay about? Write freely in response to the writing assignment and explore your reasons for choosing your selected song. What message(s), images, and emotions in this song interest you? What clues in the song support your interpretation of the song?

Activity

Analyzing a Song

A chart like the one that follows may be used to help you move from stanza to stanza in order to analyze the lines and better understand the song you've chosen to write about. "Silent Legacy" is used as an example here, but you can use a similar chart to analyze any song.

On a separate piece of paper, create a chart like the one below. Moving stanza by stanza, or even line by line, list images or language that suggest the meaning of the song:

	Image/Language	Possible Meaning
Stanzas 1–2	"hell"	place of torment
	"bound to silent legacy"	tied to something passed down but unspoken
Stanzas 3–4		
Stanzas 5–7		
Stanzas 8–9		

In a sentence or two, sum up what these images suggest:

Describe the speaker in the song. Which lines reveal something about the speaker's mood or concerns?

Who is the speaker addressing? What clues suggest this?

Who is the audience? What clues reveal the audience?

Consider Your Audience   You should not assume that your audience knows the song you'll be writing about. Write a brief summary of the song that lets your audience know what the song is basically about. You may find that all or part of this summary fits into the introduction of your essay.

Create Your Thesis   Review your writing assignment, notes, and summary. Your thesis should tell the reader the general message of the song you've chosen. Experiment with several thesis statements until you find one that clearly states your conclusions about the song.

Outline   Consider now how you'll support your thesis statement. Remember that in an analytical essay, you must break the larger topic down into smaller pieces that can be studied. One approach to song lyrics is to study one stanza per paragraph. However, you may not want to cover all the stanzas. Perhaps you feel there are three or four key stanzas you want to focus on. Another approach might be to cover any or all of the following in separate paragraphs: mood, message, audience, speaker, or images.

Take time now to think critically about what your major supporting points will be, and write topic sentences that express these supporting points.

Next, think about the order of your main points. Experiment with your outline until you have found a method of organization that makes sense to you. Show your outline to a classmate, tutor, or your instructor, and ask if that reader can see a focused, organized essay plan.

Draft

Remember that you should direct your thoughts to a reader who is unfamiliar with the song you are writing about. In your introduction, you'll need to "introduce" the song and the songwriter and tell why you decided to write about this song. Then state what you intend to explain through analysis. In the body of your paper, you'll go into more detail about a few parts of the song. Be sure to discuss the writer's vocabulary choices and any figurative language. As you write multiple drafts, your explanation will become clearer. In your conclusion, explain what you hope the reader learned from your essay.

Revise

Activity

Share Your Writing

Find a classmate to work with. Read each other's essays and apply the following questions to each:

- Have you explained the overall message of the song?

- Have you then offered smaller pieces of the song that you have studied in detail?

- Does each paragraph have a clear topic sentence?

- Are your paragraphs in a logical order? Have you used transitions where you need them?

- Have you offered the reader specific information from the song to support your major points?

- Have you explained that specific information fully? (What is obvious to you may not be obvious to the reader.)

> • What areas of writing has your instructor suggested you work on?
>
> After working with your classmate, make a list of improvements you want to make. Rank them from most important to least, and then tackle one task at a time.

Edit

Read your essay aloud and look for (and listen for) awkward spots and typographical errors.

Review your essay again slowly and consider the following:

- Look for errors you tend to repeat, focusing on one type of error at a time.
- Does your instructor have a certain area he or she wants you to focus on?
- Put song titles in quotation marks.
- When you quote lines from a song lyric, put a slash between lines. For example, if you quoted these lines from "Imagine," you would use the slash like this: "Imagine there's no countries / It isn't hard to do."

After completing the work on pages 406–422, consider the following question:

- Have you combined sentences with coordinators and subordinators to better express your ideas?

Writing Assignment #2: Analyzing Poetry

> In this assignment, you'll sharpen your analytical and inferential skills as you study poetry. This analysis requires you to study the details of the poems so that you can draw conclusions about what they mean.
>
> Here, in brief, is the writing assignment you are preparing for:
>
> *Choose one of the poems in this book, or a poem you and your instructor have agreed on, and write an essay in which you reveal the meaning of the poem to your reader. In your essay, you'll need to summarize the poem and then take the reader through the poem, stanza by stanza or line by line, in order to explain the poem's meaning.*
>
> Keep this assignment in mind as you proceed to analyze the poems presented in this chapter.

Notes

Discuss and Engage

Activity

Discuss Poetry

Discuss the term *poetry* with your classmates and develop a group definition of poetry. Think about what a poem should contain or do in order to
be called a poem. Also talk about the kind(s) of poetry you enjoy reading or writing. Discuss any poems you remember having learned in the
past.

Get Involved!

Go online to
www.poems.com or
www.emule.com/poetry
and find two or three
poems that would be
interesting and
challenging to analyze.
Bring the poems to
class and share them
with your classmates.

Journal Assignment

Thinking About Poetry

Write out your own definition of a what a poem is. Be sure to include
what you believe to be the essential elements of a good poem. Are there
similarities between music lyrics and poems? (This is for your eyes only.
Refer back to this journal when you are getting ready to write your essay
on poetry.)

It may help you to know one of the official definitions of *poetry:*

> A term applied to the many forms in which human beings have given rhyth-
> mic expression to their most imaginative and intense perceptions [or views] of
> the world, themselves, and the relation of the two.

> —*C. Hugh Holman and William Harmon,*
> A Handbook to Literature, *5th ed.*

As Holman and Harmon point out, poetry expresses humans' most
creative views of themselves and the world.

Before moving on, check your definition with Holman and Harmon's.
How does it compare? What are the differences? You may wish to revise
your definition to include new information.

Read, Discuss, Think Critically

This section of the chapter contains five poems. The poems were all
written by well-known poets and represent a variety of concerns that
you'll explore as you discuss and analyze the poems in class.

Reading Assignment:

"Sympathy"

Preview   Read the title, information following the title, and the first stanza.

Anticipate   What do you think this poem will be about? In the "Notes" column, describe the mood and message you're anticipating based on the opening stanza.

Read and Reread   Read the poem through once, marking unknown terms. Then reread the poem again. Use the "Notes" column to record images and ideas that come to mind. Define any terms you marked during your first reading. Also, write down any questions you have. Finally, read the poem aloud.

Sympathy
Paul Laurence Dunbar (1872–1906)

Paul Laurence Dunbar was the first African American poet to gain national attention before his death at the age of 33. His poem "Sympathy" appeared in *Lyrics of the Hearthside*, which was published in 1899. The poem would later serve as inspiration for Maya Angelou's autobiography *I Know Why the Caged Bird Sings*.

1   I know what the caged bird feels.
Ah me, when the sun is bright on the upland slopes,
when the wind blows soft through the springing grass
and the river floats like a sheet of glass,
when the first bird sings and the first bud ops,
and the faint perfume from its chalice steals.
I know what the caged bird feels.

2   I know why the caged bird beats his wing
till its blood is red on the cruel bars,
for he must fly back to his perch and cling
when he fain would be on the bow aswing.
And the blood still throbs in the old, old scars
and they pulse again with a keener sting.
I know why he beats his wing.

3   I know why the caged bird sings.
Ah, me, when its wings are bruised and its bosom sore.
It beats its bars and would be free.

Notes

It's not a carol of joy or glee,
but a prayer that it sends from its heart's deep core,
a plea that upward to heaven it flings.
I know why the caged bird sings.

Questions for Critical Thought

"Sympathy"

1. Why do you think Dunbar titled this poem "Sympathy"?

2. Read the first stanza. Describe the scene as the speaker does. What does the caged bird feel?

3. Read the second stanza. Describe what happens when the caged bird beats his wings inside the cage. Why would the caged bird continue to beat his wings against the bars of the cage?

4. Read the third stanza. Describe the song of the caged bird. What song does the caged bird sing?

5. Dunbar uses the image of the caged bird to make an important statement in 1899. What do you think Dunbar is saying in this poem?

Reading Assignment: "A Work of Artifice"

Preview   Read the title and the first seven lines of the poem.

Anticipate   What do you think this poem will be about? What kind of mood or message do you think it has? Record your thoughts in the "Notes" column.

Read and Reread   Quickly read the poem one time, marking unknown terms. Then reread more slowly and use the "Notes" column to record images and meanings that come to mind. Also write down any questions you have. Define unknown terms. Finally, read the poem aloud.

A Work of Artifice

Marge Piercy (b. 1936)

American poet and novelist

1   The bonsai tree
in the attractive pot
could have grown eighty feet tall
on the side of a mountain
till split by lightning

6   But a gardener
   carefully pruned it.
   It is nine inches high.
   Every day as he
   whittles back the branches
11   the gardener croons,
   It is your nature
   to be small and cozy,
   domestic and weak;
   how lucky, little tree,
16   to have a pot to grow in.
   With living creatures
   one must begin very early
   to dwarf their growth:
   the bound feet,
21   the crippled brain,
   the hair in curlers,
   the hands you
   love to touch.

Questions for Critical Thought

"A Work of Artifice"

1. Carefully consider the title. What does the word *artifice* mean?

2. Read the first five lines aloud. What picture do you see in your mind?

3. Read lines 6 through 8 aloud. What picture do you see now?

4. Read lines 9 through 16 aloud. What do you think of the gardener? Do you agree that the tree is lucky "to have a pot to grow in"? Explain.

5. Toward the end of the poem, the image changes, and we are no longer focusing on a tree. What do you see? What do you think Piercy is saying in this poem?

Reading Assignment: "The Road Not Taken"

Preview   Read the title and the first two stanzas.

Anticipate   What do you think this poem is about? What kind of mood or message do you think it has? Record your thoughts in the "Notes" column.

Notes

Read and Reread   Quickly read the poem one time, marking unknown terms. Then reread more slowly and use the "Notes" column to record images and meanings that come to mind. Also write down any questions you have. Define unknown terms. Finally, read the poem aloud.

The Road Not Taken
Robert Frost (1874–1963)

American poet

1   Two roads diverged in a yellow wood,
And sorry I could not travel both
And be one traveler, long I stood
And looked down one as far as I could
to where it bent in the undergrowth.

2   Then took the other, as just as fair,
And having perhaps the better claim,
Because it was grassy and wanted wear;
Though as for that the passing there
Had worn them really about the same,

3   And both that morning equally lay
In leaves no step had trodden black,
Oh, I kept the first for another day!
Yet knowing how way leads on to way,
I doubted if I should ever come back.

4   I shall be telling this with a sigh
Somewhere ages and ages hence:
Two roads diverged in a wood, and I—
I took the one less traveled by,
And that has made all the difference.

Questions for Critical Thought
"The Road Not Taken"

1. What is your general reaction to this poem? How does it make you feel? What words or images in the poem promote this feeling?

2. Describe the movements of this traveler (the speaker) in the poem. Describe what the speaker sees and then does in response.

3. It is possible that this "road" that the speaker did not take is an example of figurative language. Perhaps the speaker is not thinking of an actual road. What could he or she be speaking of? Do any other lines in the poem suggest that this interpretation might be right?

4. What is significant about the fact that he or she took the road "less traveled by"? If this is another example of figurative language, what does this road "less traveled by" represent?

5. Can you relate to what Frost is saying in his poem? Have you had a similar experience?

Notes

Reading Assignment: *"Wild Nights"*

Preview   Read the title and the first two stanzas.

Anticipate   What do you think this poem will be about? What kind of mood or message do you think it has? Respond in the "Notes" column.

Read and Reread   Quickly read the poem one time, marking unknown terms. Then reread more slowly and use the "Notes" column to record images and meanings that come to mind. Also write down any questions you have. Define unknown terms. Finally, read the poem aloud.

Wild Nights
Emily Dickinson (1830–1886)

Considered one of America's greatest poets, Dickinson did not follow conventional poetic forms but constructed her own special form of verse. The dashes included are hers.

1 Wild Nights—Wild Nights
   Were I with thee
   Wild Nights should be
   Our luxury!

2 Futile—the Winds—
   To a Heart in port—

Notes

> Done with the Compass—
> Done with the Chart!
>
> 3   Rowing in Eden—
> Ah, the Sea!
> Might I but moor—Tonight—
> In Thee!

Questions for Critical Thought

"Wild Nights"

1. What is your general reaction to the poem? How does it make you feel? What words create this feeling?

2. What is happening to the speaker in this poem? How do the words and sea imagery help to describe the speaker's feelings?

3. What are your favorite lines in this poem? Why?

4. Have the images or words made you think about your own life or experiences? If so, explain.

Reading Assignment: "Annabel Lee"

Preview   Skim the poem once. Notice that the lines are numbered (every fifth line) and an extra space appears between stanzas.

Anticipate   What does the poem appear to be about? Write your response in the "Notes" column.

Read and Reread   Read the poem again, marking unknown terms. Then reread more slowly and use the "Notes" column to write down your impressions. Define unknown terms.

Annabel Lee
by Edgar Allan Poe

This poem, dating from 1849–1850, is believed to focus on the past practice of arranged marriage and the treatment of disobedient daughters.

> It was many and many a year ago,
> In a kingdom by the sea,
> That a maiden there lived whom you may know
> By the name of ANNABEL LEE;

Notes

5   And this maiden she lived with no other thought
        Than to love and be loved by me.

    I was a child and *she* was a child,
        In this kingdom by the sea,
    But we loved with a love that was more than love—
10   I and my ANNABEL LEE—
    With a love that the winged seraphs of heaven
        Coveted her and me.

    And this was the reason that, long ago,
        In this kingdom by the sea,
15 A wind blew out of a cloud, chilling
        My beautiful ANNABEL LEE;
    So that her highborn kinsman came
        And bore her away from me,
    To shut her up in a sepulchre
20   In this kingdom by the sea.

    The angels, not half so happy in heaven,
        Went envying her and me;
    Yes! that was the reason (as all men know,
        In this kingdom by the sea)
25 That the wind came out of the cloud by night,
        Chilling and killing my ANNABEL LEE.

    But our love it was stronger by far than the love
        Of those who were older than we—
        Of many far wiser than we—
30 And neither the angels in heaven above,
        Nor the demons down under the sea,
    Can ever dissever my soul from the soul
        Of the beautiful ANNABEL LEE:

    For the moon never beams without bringing me dreams
35   Of the beautiful ANNABEL LEE;
    And the stars never rise, but I feel the bright eyes
        Of the beautiful ANNABEL LEE;
    And so, all the night-tide, I lie down by the side
    Of my darling—my darling—my life and my bride,
40   In the sepulchre there by the sea—
        In her tomb by the sounding sea.

Notes

Questions for Critical Thought

"Annabel Lee"

1. If you were going to argue that this poem is about the old practice of arranged marriage and the punishment of disobedient daughters, what evidence from the poem would you use to support this position? What images contribute to this idea?

2. Do you see any other possible meanings? If so, what evidence from the poem would you use to support this meaning? What images, words, or themes contribute to this idea?

3. Explore the images of life and death in the poem. Which images suggest life or living to the fullest? Which suggest death or the end of life as once known?

4. What do you believe the poem says about love? Using evidence from the poem, explain.

Journal Assignment

Thinking About the Poems

Write out your thoughts about two or three of the poems in this book. What does each poem reveal? What clues do you have to unlock the meaning in each poem? During class discussion, did any classmates reveal an unusual interpretation of one of the poems? Which poem do you like the best? Why? After reading someone else's journal, just say, "Thank you," when you return it.

Explore the Writing Assignment

Here, again, is your writing assignment. Review it carefully before continuing. Underline the important terms in the assignment.

Choose one of the poems in this book, or a poem you and your instructor have agreed on, and write an essay in which you reveal the meaning of the poem to your reader. In your essay, you'll need to summarize the poem and then take the reader through the poem, stanza by stanza or line by line, in order to explain the poem's meaning.

Brainstorm   Review your work so far for this assignment. What poem do you want to write an essay about? Write freely in response to the

writing assignment and explore your reasons for choosing your selected poem. What message(s), images, or emotions in this poem interest you? What clues in the poem support your interpretation?

Activity

Analyzing a Poem

A chart like the one that follows may be used to help you move from stanza
to stanza in order to analyze the lines and better understand the poem
you've chosen to write about.

    Create your own chart. Then, moving stanza by stanza or even line by
line, list images or language that suggests the meaning of the poem:

	Image/Language	Possible Meaning
Stanza 1		
Stanza 2		
Stanza 3		
Stanza 4		
Stanza 5		

    In a sentence or two, sum up what these images suggest:

    Describe the speaker in the poem. Which lines reveal something about
the speaker's mood or concerns?

    Who is the speaker addressing? What clues suggest this?

    Who is the audience? What clues reveal the audience?

Consider Your Audience You should not assume that your audience
knows the poem you are writing about. Write a brief summary of the
poem that lets your audience know what the poem is about. You may find
that all or part of this summary fits into the introduction of your essay.

Create Your Thesis Review your writing assignment, notes, and summary. Your thesis should tell the reader what the general message of the
poem is. Experiment with several thesis statements until you find one
that clearly states your analytical conclusions about the poem you have
chosen.

Outline   Now think about how you'll support your thesis statement. Remember that in an analytical essay, a writer must break the larger topic down into smaller pieces that can be studied. One approach to poems is to study one stanza per paragraph. However, you may not want to cover all the stanzas. Perhaps you feel there are three or four key stanzas you want to focus on. (If you analyze "A Work of Artifice," which only has one stanza, you could select particular lines that work together to create an image or message and cover these groups of lines, each in a different paragraph.) Another approach might be to cover any or all of the following in separate paragraphs: mood, message, audience, speaker, or images.

Take time now to think critically about what your major supporting points will be and write topic sentences that express these supporting points.

Next, think about the order of your main points. Experiment with your outline until you have found a method of organization that makes sense to you. Show your outline to a classmate, tutor, or your instructor and ask if that reader can see a focused, organized essay plan.

Draft

Remember that you should direct your thoughts to a reader who is unfamiliar with the poem you are writing about. In your introduction, you'll need to "introduce" the poem and poet and tell why you decided to write about this poem. Also, mention what you intend to explain through analysis. In the body of your paper, you'll go into more detail about a few parts of the poem. Be sure to discuss the writer's vocabulary choices and any figurative language. As you write multiple drafts, your explanation will become clearer. In your conclusion, explain what you hope the reader learned from your essay.

Activity

Study a Student Sample

Review the following introduction and conclusion from one student's essay. Mark what you like in each paragraph. Then respond to the questions and statements that follow. (The title of the essay is "The Art of Deception.")

(Introduction)

   My personal interpretation of the poem "A Work of Artifice" by Marge Piercy is that the poem is about stunting growth and the deceitfulness used to accomplish it. Basically, some people often stunt other people's growth for their own personal gains. The reason I chose this poem is because I can relate from my own personal experience. My ex-husband used the same type of deception toward me to fulfill his own idea of the person I should be. Just as the gardener stunts the growth of the bonsai tree, he determines the shape and size of the tree. The gardener even selects the tree's pot, all to his liking.

(Conclusion)

   This poem in my opinion is clearly not about the tree's or creature's wants, desires, or capabilities. Therefore it is about what the gardener and the person who is crippling the brain want. These people are doing the deceiving and stunting of growth, creating their own expectations of their ideals. I feel this is an injustice that happens all too often in life, far too many times, all in the name of love. I can say I have been that bonsai/creature. I speak from my own horrible experience; I have been left scarred by the treachery and deceit of such an act of love. I fell prey to the crooning and whittling until it almost cost me my life. I believed and trusted this individual, that he had my best interest at heart, only to learn that it was purely a selfish motive that drove him. Yet with every branch they whittle and prune, they still croon.

—*Ruth, student writer*

1. The writing assignment asks that you summarize the poem and your reasons for writing in the introduction. Highlight Ruth's summary and reasons for writing.

2. A conclusion should connect back to the introduction without repeating it. Underline the sentences in the conclusion that connect most closely to the introduction.

3. Note in Ruth's conclusion where she borrows words from the poem. Why is this effective?

Revise

Activity

> **Share Your Writing**
>
> Find a classmate to work with. Read each other's essays and consider the following questions in relation to each essay:
>
> - Have you explained the overall message of the poem?
>
> - Have you then offered smaller pieces of the poem that you have studied in detail?
>
> - Does each paragraph have a clear topic sentence?
>
> - Are your paragraphs in a logical order? Have you used transitions where you need them?
>
> - Have you offered the reader specific information from the poem to support your major points?
>
> - Have you explained that specific information fully? (What is obvious to you may not be obvious to the reader.)
>
> - What areas of writing has your instructor suggested you work on?
>
> After working with your classmate, make a list of improvements you want to make. Rank them from most important to least, and then tackle one task at a time.

Edit

Read your essay aloud and look for (and listen for) awkward spots and typographical errors.

Review your essay again, slowly, and consider the following:

- Look for errors you tend to repeat, focusing on one type of error at a time.

- Does your instructor have a certain area he or she wants you to focus on?

- Put poem titles in quotation marks.

- Put a slash between lines of the poem. (For example, if you were to quote these lines from "The Road Not Taken," you would use a slash like this: "Two roads diverged in a yellow wood, / And sorry I could not travel both / And be one traveler, long I stood.")

After completing the work on pages 406–422, consider the following question:

- Have you used coordinators and subordinators to shape your sentences?

TIME TO REFLECT

> ### *Journal Assignment*
>
> ### *Your Progress as a Writer, Reader, and Critical Thinker*
>
> As you look back over the chapter, consider what you have learned about analysis and inference. You may want to consider these questions before you write:
>
> - What does it mean to analyze something?
> - Which parts of the chapter were particularly helpful in sharpening your analysis and inference skills? Explain.
>   - the activity, pages 370–372
>   - the sample analysis, pages 374–375
>   - the charts, pages 389 and 401
>   - the student samples, pages 375–377 and 402–403
> - In your own essay, where have you demonstrated your analysis skills? (Be specific.)
> - How can you use your analysis skills as a reader?

SUMMARY OF CHAPTER 8

In this chapter, you have

- strengthened your analysis and inference skills as you studied song lyrics and poetry;
- learned that analysis and inference require you to break larger subjects down into smaller pieces;
- learned that after careful study of the smaller pieces, you can infer information; and
- learned that when writing analytical essays, you must present your major point or conclusion, the pieces of proof that support the conclusion, and explanations of each piece of proof.

Notes

COMBINING SENTENCES WITH COORDINATORS AND SUBORDINATORS

Reviewing Coordinators
Sentence Combining
Reviewing Subordinators

In this chapter, you'll review some of what you learned in Chapter 4 about clauses, coordinators, and subordinators. Then you'll take that knowledge one step further by completing a number of sentence combining exercises. You'll find that soon you are using more coordinators and subordinators in your writing without even having to think about them.

Reviewing Coordinators

Coordinators, as you may remember, are special words that you can use to join independent sentences. These words help you show how the idea in one sentence relates to the idea in another sentence. So to use these words effectively, you must choose them carefully.

There are seven coordinators:

for	and	nor	but	or	yet	so
f	a	n	b	o	y	s

One way to remember these seven words is to remember the acronym *FANBOYS*.

Here are a few points to remember about coordinators.

- The *co* in *coordinators* is a prefix that tells you they create *equal* relationships between the ideas that they join. Think about the equal relationships expressed by these words: *coworkers, coauthors, coexist.* All these words suggest equality. (Neither coworker is more important. Coauthors are equal partners, and to coexist is to live together without one dominating.) When you join sentences with coordinators, you will be showing how they relate to another, but you will *not* be emphasizing one idea over the other, nor will you be making either sentence a dependent clause.

- Each of the FANBOYS expresses a different relationship.

  for: expresses a relationship of *effect-cause*. The idea in the first sentence is the effect. The idea in the second sentence is the cause.

  She chose this song, <u>for</u> it makes her feel happy.

and: expresses a relationship of *addition.* The idea in the first sentence is added to the idea in the second sentence.

> She enjoys this song, <u>and</u> she wants others to enjoy it.

nor: expresses a relationship of *negative addition.* The idea in the first sentence is negative, and another negative idea is added in the second sentence.

> I do not like her guitar playing, <u>nor</u> does he like her guitar playing. (*Note:* When you use *nor,* the subject and verb in the second sentence switch positions. Also, the *nor* in the second half expresses "not," so you don't need another "not.")

but: expresses a relationship of *opposition.* The idea in the first sentence is the opposite of the idea in the second sentence (or the first idea *contrasts* with the second idea).

> I told her I didn't like her guitar playing, <u>but</u> she played anyway.

or: expresses a relationship of *alternatives.* The idea in the first sentence is one option. The idea in the second sentence is another option.

> She should stop playing, <u>or</u> she should go where I can't hear her.

yet: expresses a relationship of *opposition.* The idea in the first sentence is the opposite of the idea in the second sentence (or the first idea *contrasts* with the second idea).

> She heard my opinion, <u>yet</u> she didn't stop playing.

so: expresses a relationship of *cause-effect.* The idea in the first sentence causes the idea in the second sentence.

> She said I hurt her feelings, <u>so</u> she stopped talking to me.

- You may use coordinators to begin sentences. Writers do this occasionally to add a little emphasis to the second sentence.

> She should stop playing. <u>Or</u> she should go where I can't hear her.

- You must apply Punctuation Rule #2 when joining sentences with coordinators.

Notes

> ### Punctuation Rule #2 (Review)
>
> *When you join two independent clauses with a coordinating conjunction, you need to put a comma after the first independent clause.*
>
> • She said I hurt her feelings, so she stopped talking to me.

Sentence Combining

As you work through the sentence combining exercises in this chapter, keep the following points in mind:

- You'll benefit the most when doing these exercises if you write out your complete sentences. (Don't just draw arrows or insert words.) By practicing these sentence patterns and paying attention to the punctuation rules, these sophisticated patterns will eventually become second nature to you.

- Often the sentences in these exercises can be joined in more than one way. Follow the directions. (If the exercise asks you to use coordinators to join sentences, do that—even if you can think of other ways to join the ideas.)

- You and your classmates may sometimes disagree on precisely which joining word should be used. That's okay as long as you can each defend your choice.

Practice #1   Music Tastes

Using carefully selected coordinators, join the sentences that follow and express the relationships given to you. (Make sure that you combine two *complete* sentences.) Use each of the coordinators once.

Example:

(Express a relationship of addition.)
Music is a wonderful way for people to communicate their ideas.
They can express their feelings.

- Music is a wonderful way for people to communicate their ideas, and they can express their feelings.

1. (Express a relationship of alternatives.)
   I might open the show with my new song.
   Stephen might perform his favorite song.

2. (Express a relationship of opposition.)
   My favorite music sounds energetic.
   Occasionally I like to listen to mellow tunes.
3. (Express a relationship of effect-cause.)
   My dad is dancing.
   He hears his favorite country song.
4. (Express a relationship of cause-effect.)
   My sister is blaring her rap music.
   The dog hides under the rug.
5. (Express a relationship of negative addition.)
   I didn't understand Mike's new song.
   I didn't like the rhythm.
6. (Express a relationship of opposition.)
   My mother loves rock and roll.
   My father enjoys country and jazz.

Practice #2   Mozart

Using carefully chosen coordinating conjunctions (or coordinators), join the sentences that follow.

(Austrian composer Wolfgang Amadeus Mozart lived from 1756 to 1791.)

1. He was unusual.
   He began to compose music at the age of 5.
2. He wrote music for the piano, violin, French horn, and string quartets.
   He wrote wonderful symphonies, operas, serenades, sonatas, and religious music.
3. He was famous during his lifetime.
   He was quite poor.

Practice #3   Louis Armstrong, a.k.a. Satchmo

Using carefully selected coordinators, join the sentences that follow. Sentences 1–11 will create three paragraphs. The italicized sentences add extra information. You do not have to change (or join) the italicized sentences in any way. When you write your completed paragraphs, include the italicized sentences.

Combining Sentences with Coordinators and Subordinators

Combining Sentences with Coordinators and Subordinators

Notes

1. Louis Armstrong was born in 1901.
   He lived in New Orleans, Louisiana.
   When he was 7 years old, his parents separated.

2. He and his mother needed money.
   He began singing.

3. He sang on the streets of New Orleans.
   He earned only pennies.

4. At age 13 he was arrested.
   He was sent to a home for street children.
   While living there, he learned to play the cornet (an instrument similar to the trumpet).

5. Two kind teachers helped him learn to play the cornet.
   They were not professional musicians.
   They accidentally taught him some bad habits.
   One of those habits was puffing up his cheeks when he played the cornet.

6. Later in life when he visited London as a well-known musician, the people called him Satchelmouth.
   He blew his cheeks as large as a "satchel" (a bag for carrying books or clothing).
   That name later turned into his nickname "Satchmo."
   [end of first paragraph]
   As one of the most famous jazz trumpet players, Armstrong was a true creative artist.

7. He was known for his ability to improvise on stage.
   He created "scat" singing where the human voice is used like an instrument.

8. Most singing relies on words.
   Instruments produce musical notes.
   Scat singing requires the singer to pronounce nonsense syllables.
   [end of second paragraph]
   Finally, some remember Armstrong as a pioneer in music.

9. He was part of the Creole Jazz Band.
   They were the first black jazz ensemble band to record an album.

10. Later, he had his own band.

They performed as Louis Armstrong and His Hot Five.

Even though he accomplished so much in his lifetime, one private dream was left unfulfilled.

11. He wanted to sing the national anthem at Shea Stadium where his favorite team, the New York Mets, played.

He practiced all his life.

He was never invited to sing.

He died in 1971.

Practice #4   Selena

Using carefully selected coordinators, join the sentences that follow. Use a variety of coordinators. Sentences 1–5 will create one paragraph. The italicized sentences add extra information. You do not have to change (or join) the italicized sentences in any way. When you write your completed paragraph, include the italicized sentences.

1. Selena Quintanilla-Perez was born in 1971 in South Texas.

She began performing professionally when she was only 10 years old.

2. She sang Tejano music.

She was extremely popular in the Tejano culture of the South.

3. She sang in Spanish.

She couldn't actually read Spanish.

She grew up speaking English in a school system that discouraged speaking Spanish.

When she began singing Tejano music, she had to learn the Spanish lyrics phonetically.

4. Her band, Los Dinos, was a family band.

Her sister Suzette played the drums.

Her brother A. B. played bass and wrote songs.

Her father Abraham was the manager.

Critics say she had a strong jubilant voice that was intoxicating in its joy and liveliness. Tragically, in 1994 she was shot and killed in a Corpus Christi motel by the president of her fan club.

Notes

5. She did not reach her goal of breaking into the "mainstream" music scene.

She did not see an album reach number one.

However, in July 1995 her posthumous album Dreaming of You *reached number one on* Billboard's *album chart. She is greatly missed by her family and fans.*

Practice #5   Create Sentences with Coordinators

Create three sentences that might show up in an essay about one of the lyrics or poems you analyzed. (You might use sentences you wrote in response to "Questions for Critical Thought.") These sentences must each have two independent clauses joined by a coordinator.

Reviewing Subordinators

You may remember that a *subordinator* is a word that can attach to an independent sentence and make that sentence a dependent clause. A dependent clause cannot stand on its own but can be joined to an independent clause, making a longer, more expressive sentence. Consider the prefix *sub*. *Sub* means under or lower. Think of the words *submarine, subconscious, subfreezing, subhuman, submerge*. All these words suggest the idea of being under or lower: a *submarine* travels underwater. *Subfreezing* is below freezing. *Subhuman* means being beneath the human race in development, and to *submerge* means to place underwater. So, when you use a *subordinator,* you will be lowering one idea, making it dependent.

To review the subordinators that allow you to make concessions in your writing, see pages 297–300.

There are many subordinators, and you don't need to memorize them. As you work through the exercises in this section you'll learn the important points about how to use them to combine sentences and how to punctuate these new sentences correctly.

Here is a list of subordinators:

although	*since*
after	*though*
because	*unless*
even though	*when*
if	*while*

Like the coordinators you just studied, these subordinators help you express specific relationships between ideas. You must choose them carefully when joining sentences. Refer to the following explanations when completing the subordinator exercises.

- Subordinators expressing *opposition and concession*: although, even though, though, while
- Subordinators expressing *time* relationships: after, since, when, while
- Subordinators expressing *effect-cause* relationships: because, since
- Subordinators expressing *conditions*: if, unless

Punctuation Rule #5 (Review)

When you begin a sentence with a subordinated or dependent clause, you must put a comma after the subordinated (or dependent) clause.

- <u>Although the poem began with an interesting image,</u> the rest of the poem was really quite boring.

Punctuation Rule #6 (Review)

If the subordinated clause comes after the independent clause, you do not need a comma.

- The poem began with an interesting image <u>although the rest of the poem was quite boring.</u>

Practice #6   Edgar Allan Poe

- Join the sentences that follow using subordinators that express the relationship given to you.
- Use as many different subordinators as possible.
- In some instances, the subordinator will fit best at the beginning of the first sentence. In other instances, the subordinator will fit best at the beginning of the second sentence.
- Your final product will be one paragraph. (Include the italicized sentences when you write out your paragraph.)

   Edgar Allan Poe was born in 1809.

1. (Express a relationship of time.)
   He was very young.
   He became an orphan.

Notes

2. (Express a relationship of effect-cause.)

He had nowhere to go.

His godfather took him in, and they lived in England from 1815 to 1820.

3. (Express a relationship of opposition.)

He had the opportunity to attend a number of different schools during the years 1820–1831.

He left these schools before completing his education.

4. (Express a relationship of opposition.)

He also joined the army.

He left that too.

5. (Express a relationship of opposition.)

In 1836 he married his cousin.

She was only 13 years old.

6. (Express a relationship of time.)

His wife died at age 24.

He wrote his famous poem "Annabel Lee."

His other famous works include "The Raven," "The Tell-Tale Heart," and "Pit and the Pendulum." Poe had a drinking problem that seriously affected his health, and in 1849 he died at the age of 40.

Practice #7   Reading Poe's Poetry and Short Stories

- Join the sentences that follow using subordinators that express the relationship given to you.
- Use as many different subordinators as possible.
- In some instances, the subordinator will fit best at the beginning of the first sentence. In other instances, the subordinator will fit best at the beginning of the second sentence.
- Your final product will be one paragraph.

1. (Express a relationship of opposition.)

I enjoy reading his poems and short stories.

They scare me a little.

2. (Express a condition.)

   I won't read them.

   The lights are on.

3. (Express a condition.)

   My brother likes to read them.

   The electricity goes out.

4. (Express a relationship of effect-cause.)

   I think my brother enjoys this.

   He likes to scare me.

Practice #8   Emily Dickinson

- Join the sentences that follow using carefully chosen subordinators.

- Use as many different subordinators as possible.

- In some instances, the subordinator will fit best at the beginning of the first sentence. In other instances, the subordinator will fit best at the beginning of the second sentence.

- Your final product will be one paragraph. Include the italicized sentences when you write your paragraph.

   Emily Dickinson was born in 1830.

1. Growing up, she was exposed to a large, powerful social circle.

   She grew up in a politically active family concerned with civic issues.

   In fact, her family had a role in founding the Amherst Academy and the Amherst College.

2. She was ready for school.

   She attended Amherst Institute and Mount Holyoke Female Seminary.

3. She completed only one year at the seminary.

   She spent most of her time in her room in the family home.

4. She did not enjoy visiting in person.

   She kept up a constant correspondence with a number of friends.

Notes

5. She wrote poems throughout her life.

No one realized how many until after her death.

Her sister found 1,147 poems in a dresser in Dickinson's room.

6. She wrote almost 2,000 poems as an adult.

Only two poems were published during her lifetime.

Practice #9   Reading Dickinson

- Join the sentences that follow using carefully chosen subordinators.
- Use as many different subordinators as possible.
- In some instances, the subordinator will fit best at the beginning of the first sentence. In other instances, the subordinator will fit best at the beginning of the second sentence.
- Your final product will be one paragraph.

1. I love reading Dickinson's short, intriguing poems.

They are very challenging.

2. I can't understand them.

I read them several times.

3. I read them aloud.

I get a clearer idea of what she is saying.

4. I'd like to take a class on Dickinson.

There's so much to learn about her and her poems.

Practice #10   Creating Sentences with Subordinated Clauses

Create three sentences that you might use in an essay about music or poetry. These sentences must each contain a subordinated clause and an independent clause.

Practice #11   Maya Angelou

This is a coordinator and subordinator review exercise.

- Carefully choose the best coordinators and subordinators and combine the sentences below.

Combining Sentences with Coordinators and Subordinators

- Use a variety of coordinators and subordinators and be sure to punctuate your sentences correctly.
- In some instances, the subordinator will fit best at the beginning of the first sentence. In other instances, the subordinator will fit best at the beginning of the second sentence.
- Your final product will be two paragraphs. Be sure to include the italicized sentences in your final paragraphs.

1. Maya Angelou was born in 1928.
   Her name was Marguerite Johnson.
2. She was very young.
   Her parents divorced.
   She moved to Arkansas with her brother Bailey.
3. She was 7 years old.
   She was sexually assaulted.
4. She told who assaulted her.
   He was killed.
5. She felt guilty for what she thought her words had done.
   She quit talking for 6 years.
   [end of first paragraph]
   When she was older, she lived with her mother in San Francisco.
6. Angelou ran away.
   She lived with other homeless children in a junkyard.
   Later she became the city's first black streetcar conductor.
7. She was 16.
   She had a son.
   However, a difficult childhood, trauma, and poverty haven't stopped her from enjoying life and trying new things.
8. She has worked as a Creole cook, singer, songwriter, dancer, and actress.
   She has been an educator, social activist, and writer.
   She read her poem "On the Pulse of the Morning" at President Clinton's inauguration.

Combining Sentences with Coordinators and Subordinators

Notes

Practice #12   **Listening to Maya Angelou**

This is a coordinator and subordinator review exercise.

- Carefully choose the best coordinators and subordinators, and combine the sentences below.
- Use a variety of coordinators and subordinators, and be sure to punctuate your sentences correctly.
- In some instances, the subordinator will fit best at the beginning of the first sentence. In other instances, the subordinator will fit best at the beginning of the second sentence.

1. I have read Angelou's *I Know Why the Caged Bird Sings.*
   I enjoyed it.
   I enjoy her poetry even more.
2. I could listen to her read aloud.
   That is the ultimate in enjoying her words.
   She has a stunning, deep, rich voice.
3. I heard her speak once.
   I was in college.
   I have never heard a voice that magical since.
4. I heard her in person.
   I bought some audio recordings of her telling stories about her life.
5. She will always be a person I admire greatly.
   She has strength, compassion, humor, a sense of joy, and a beautiful voice to tell us about life.

STYLE TIPS

Thus far in *Connections*, the style tips have focused on moving, deleting, and adding words or phrases and on combining sentences. In this chapter, you'll find the last style tip. It focuses on the last task before publishing (or turning in) a piece of writing.

Style Tip #6

Enhance clarity by avoiding spelling, punctuation, capitalization, and usage errors.

Nothing will hurt your professional reputation faster, perhaps, than misspelled words. While many people can't identify what might be wrong with a poorly shaped sentence or a poorly written document, many can point out a spelling error. Punctuation, capitalization, and usage errors also detract from your message and damage your professional image. So, while the work may seem tedious, it is crucial that you take this last step and check your work for spelling, punctuation, capitalization, and usage errors.

Proofreading in General

Proofreading takes time and patience. You may want to read your work aloud. Or you may want to cover your page with a blank piece of paper and reveal one line of text at a time so that you can concentrate better. If you work with a tutor, try to identify your errors on your own and fix them. If you're unsure how to fix something, circle it and ask the tutor. Don't use the tutor as an editing crutch because you won't always have a tutor by your side.

Spelling

Our best advice for spelling is *when in doubt, look it up*. You should use spell check programs when working on the computer, but don't rely on them to do all of your work. They will not, for instance, alert you when you have used the wrong word but spelled it correctly (using *their* instead of *there*). In addition, you need to make an effort to memorize the correct spellings of words because there will be situations when you must write without a computer.

Pay attention to the words that you tend to misspell. Keep a list of words that you can refer to easily. Also, use the list to memorize a couple of words a week. Tape these words to your bathroom mirror or some other spot that you look at frequently.

Practice #13

You may want to refer to "Spelling Matters" on pages 474–484 to help you find the spelling errors in the sentences below.

1. I read a newspaper article that said that woman are better at interpreting literature.
2. However, the man in my college class seem to be really good at analysing the songs in our book.

3. I think the scientists quoted in that artical need to take another look at their findings.

Punctuation

If you memorize the seven punctuation rules in this book, you'll have 90 percent of your punctuation needs covered. As you continue to study writing, you'll cover a few more rules. Use the list on pages 538–539 in this text as you check the punctuation in your sentences.

Practice #14   Punctuation

Refer to the list on pages 538–539 to help you find and fix the punctuation errors in the following sentences.

1. When I heard the song I changed my mind about the meaning of the lyrics.
2. I thought studying poetry would be boring but I actually enjoyed that assignment.
3. I thought Steven's interpretation was clever he saw the symbolism in the poem.

Capitalization and Usage

On pages 534–538, you'll also find information about capitalization and using the right word (usage). As with spelling and punctuation, you will need to be patient as you carefully check your capitalization and word choices. Practice—through exercises and writing assignments—will help your mind absorb the rules and guidelines, but most writers keep some reference books handy to double-check their work.

Practice #15   Capitals and the Right Words

Review the rules on pages 534–538 as you check these sentences for capitalization and usage errors.

1. Maya Angelou's book *I Know why the caged Bird Sings* is won of my favorites.
2. My classmates shared there opinions about the book.
3. If my teacher doesn't except my essay late, I don't know what I'll do.

Getting Extra Editing Help   Notes

If you're having trouble identifying errors in your own writing, don't despair. As with all of the other writing skills you've practiced this year, editing and polishing take practice to master. At first you could have a tutor label and explain all of your editing errors. The tutor might need to guide you through the corrections, too. Soon, though, you can ask your tutor just to mark errors, without naming them or explaining them. After gaining a bit more experience, you can ask your tutor just to put a check mark in the margin next to sentences that have errors. (Four checks next to a line would indicate four errors in that line.) Then find and fix them on your own. Pretty soon, you'll be editing independently.

Practice #16

The paragraph below has many editing errors. You may want to refer to the spelling advice on pages 474–484 and the usage, capitalization, and punctuation rules on pages 534–539. Find the errors, correct them, and write a polished version of the paragraph on a separate piece of paper.

> The end of the term is near and I am relieved. My chemistry class was especially tough we had to memorize to many formulas. In history, I had to read 14 chapters in the textbook in addition to a long book about world war II. My math teacher was pretty easy on the homework but he did'nt explain new concepts very well. My best class was my english class because I got to select a naval to read. I chose To kill a mockingbird. I love that book. If I could do this semester over again I'd take fewer units. My advise to students is to take the minimum number of units. I wish I had, I wouldn't be so tired now.

Your Own Writing: Coordinators, Subordinators, and Editing

Study a piece of your writing (a journal entry or a paragraph from an essay) that you have not shown to a tutor or your instructor. Have you used coordinators and subordinators to help clarify the ideas in your writing? Did you follow Punctuation Rules #2, #5, and/or #6 when using coordinators and subordinators? Underline any of these joining words that you used. Can you add any additional coordinators or subordinators? Then comb through this piece of writing and check the spelling, punctuation, capitalization, and usage.

Style Tips

Style Tips

Notes

Using** Connections **Online with mywritinglab

For more practice with coordinators, subordinators, and editing, log onto www.mywritinglab.com to access the online resources for *Connections,* Third Edition.

CHAPTER

Writing the In-Class Essay

Main Topics

- Preparing to write the in-class essay

- Employing the writing and reading processes
  in timed writing situations

- Writing the timed essay

- Writing the argumentative essay in class

Copyright United Feature Syndicate Inc.

So far in this text, you have been using the writing process to develop your writing skills in out-of-class writing assignments. But there may be times when you will be required to write essays in class within a specified period of time such as an hour or two. Keep in mind that timed essays are a key component of many college courses and may be used

- to determine entrance into a particular field of study,
- to determine entrance into or exit from a writing class,
- to determine basic writing proficiency for graduation,
- to gauge students' development as writers at various points of the term, or
- to measure students' knowledge in a subject area.

By studying and applying the strategies you learn in this chapter, you'll continue to improve your skills and increase your ability to write effectively in timed situations.

THE WRITING PROCESS IN TIMED SITUATIONS

Although the thought of writing an entire essay in an hour or two may make you feel uneasy, you should know that the very same strategies you have learned and practiced this term in your out-of-class writing assignments will serve you in your in-class writings as well. In this section, you'll study strategies for writing in class, learn how to analyze and respond to the in-class writing prompt, and practice writing the timed essay.

Preparing to Write

In order to write well in timed situations, you must be mentally and physically prepared for the task. You must be as well rested and relaxed as possible. It's a good idea to arrive early to class on these days. Then you'll have a few minutes to get out paper and pen, think about the task, and envision yourself writing. It may help to do a quick five-minute freewrite. Any topic will do. You could freewrite on how you're feeling about writing in class. Or if you have an idea about what the topic might be, you could get the juices flowing by listing ideas or by writing on the topic in general.

Using the Writing Process in In-Class Writings

When writing an out-of-class essay, you have ample opportunity to rethink ideas, revise, and make your essay better. However, with an in-class essay, you are required to complete your essay in a set amount of time. Because of this time limit, writers sometimes panic and make a serious mistake—they just start writing. Writing without a plan is like traveling in unknown territory without a map.

In order to write a successful in-class essay, you must read and understand the prompt, brainstorm ideas, decide what main idea to present, and list supporting points—all before writing the essay. Experienced writers have learned to set aside a portion of class for these activities. (Be careful, however, not to spend so much time on these activities that there's no time left for writing. You should spend no more than 20 to 25 percent of the allotted time on these planning activities.)

The bulk of writing time, which is anywhere from 60 to 75 percent, should be devoted to proving the main idea set up in the first few minutes of class. At this time, you jot down the introduction and thesis, and then begin addressing the supporting points one by one. (When a reading has been assigned, you should bring it to class with important points and interesting quotations highlighted for easy reference.)

The final portion of class should be devoted to revision and then to editing. Although you don't necessarily need to rewrite your entire essays (though some students do), you should go back and revise words, phrases, and sentences. If you've written on every other line, you can easily revise by drawing a line through a sentence that doesn't work and rewriting that sentence in the blank line above. If you are working on a computer, the revision process is much easier. You need only return to certain spots to insert new text and delete what doesn't work.

Editing is the very last stage of the process. Be sure to leave the final few minutes of time to read for errors in spelling, capitalization, sentence boundaries, and verb tense. You should also look carefully for your own common grammar errors. If using a computer, run spell check before printing your essay.

Tips for Writing the In-Class Essay

- Ask your instructor for a sample of a previous essay exam to study and practice.
- Try to anticipate the kinds of questions that might be asked.
- If you know the topic beforehand, discuss it with classmates or friends.
- Arrive early so you can mentally prepare.

Notes
- Think positive thoughts—envision yourself writing a strong essay.
- Outline, list, or freewrite on potential topics.
- Neatness counts, but don't worry too much about penmanship.
- Write on every other line to allow for changes and revision.
- If writing on a computer, use spell check (if permitted) before printing your essay.

Anticipating the Writing Prompt

Even if you have no idea what the writing prompt will be, you can still prepare to write. If you are taking a content course like sociology, for instance, you could review sections of your textbook and any lecture notes you have taken. Then you would be in a better position to *anticipate* the kind of essay question your instructor might assign. If your instructor has been lecturing on dating and how technology has entered into courtship, and if she has recently assigned the class an article to read entitled, "Love Online," you might anticipate that your instructor would be assigning an essay on contemporary dating trends.

You might even complete a cluster to see what area of the topic you would be most interested in writing on.

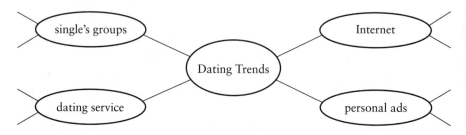

If you're in a class in which controversial issues are being discussed, you could complete a pro/con list on a topic from class:

Should High Schools Provide Students with Condoms?	
Pro (For) —Yes, this would help ensure that teenagers would practice safe sex.	*Con (Against)* —No, this is the equivalent of giving teenagers permission to have sex.

It's important to do as much preparatory work as possible before an in-class essay. If you have read and done some brainstorming ahead of time, you'll feel much more confident about the in-class writing experience. And even if you haven't been given a reading and don't have an idea of what the writing topic will be, remember that you can still "warm up" by brainstorming, summarizing chapters, studying your notes, and anticipating essay questions.

Activity

Warm-Up Topics

If you have no idea what the writing prompt will be, you can still practice your brainstorming and writing skills before the day of the in-class writing. Here are a few topics to practice on:

- Your favorite or most interesting class

- Your hero

- The best or worst job you ever had

- Your view on gun control

- Your first love

- Your view on living together before marriage

- Your favorite hobby

- Your view on censoring music lyrics

- The best or worst lesson you learned

- Your view on children's TV

- Your view on whether or not the United States should reinstate the draft

- Your view on whether or not grade school children should have Internet access at home (or at school)

- Your view on metal detectors in grade schools

- Your view on a current controversial issue

Understanding the Writing Prompt

Once you're in class and the writing prompt has been handed out, your most important task begins. In the first few minutes of class, you must read and break down the prompt to make sure that you understand it so that you can address its parts.

This first prompt has not been connected to an outside reading, so students would receive this topic "cold" on the day they write.

Write about what you see as one of the most serious problems in your city or state today. First, explain the problem. Then, discuss what you think can and should be done to try to solve it.

Breaking it down:

• Note the opening general statement. Students are being asked to write about "one of the most serious problems in your city or state today." (Notice *one*, not two or three; *today*, not yesterday; and *your city or state*, not the entire country.)

• That general statement is followed by two steps. The first asks students to *explain* or define one of the most serious problems.

• Students are then asked to *discuss* what they think *can* and *should* be done to solve the problem. In other words, they are being asked for a solution to the problem.

In the next prompt, students have been given a cartoon to consider and then analyze in an essay.

Doug Marlette

Prompt: Write an essay in response to the comic strip, "Why Johnny Can't Read."

For this prompt, students haven't been given much in the way of direction. What they have been told is to "write an essay in *response* to the comic strip," which means that students are expected to offer their opinions (agreeing or disagreeing with the comic strip's message).

- Before beginning to write, students should carefully consider the title of the piece, the picture, and the artist's message.

- They should also brainstorm (listing ideas or writing down their reactions to the cartoon), focus on the most important issue or idea they see, and then develop a thesis *before* writing.

- In developing the body of the essay, students should draw support from their own observations or experiences with television. Students should also refer to any articles about television they might have read.

Activity

Writing the In-Class Essay

Review the *Grand Avenue* comic strip on the opening page of this chapter. Then set aside two hours to write a practice essay on the following prompt:

> *Write an essay in response to the comic strip, Grand Avenue, explaining the advantages and/or disadvantages of personal technology (such as the iPod).*

Consider these steps as you address the writing prompt:

- Before beginning to write, think about the title, the images, and the message that's being conveyed.

- Spend a few minutes brainstorming ideas.

- Form your thesis.

- Draft your essay.

- Support your thesis with examples from your own experiences or observations.

- Review what you've written and revise and edit as necessary.

USING THE READING PROCESS IN IN-CLASS WRITINGS

Sometimes your instructor will give out a reading ahead of time and will expect you to come to the next class prepared to write about an issue raised in the reading. If this is the case, then you would read the

Notes

piece as soon as possible so that you would have time to reread, think, and talk about the reading. You would be wise to practice your reading process and summary skills in preparation for writing.

Let's say that your instructor announces that you'll be writing an in-class essay during your next class period. She then assigns "The Shameful Secret of Illiteracy in America" by Penni Wild, which appears on pages 430–432, and tells you to be prepared to write about the ideas expressed in the article. Here is a plan of attack for this type of writing task.

Follow the PARTS of the reading process (pages 83–84) to make sure that you understand the article. Begin by previewing the article, looking at the title, publication information, and main ideas. Then, as you read, anticipate what the article is about. Highlight key terms and ideas as you read, but don't look up the words yet. Next, reread the article, but this time more slowly, looking up those unfamiliar terms you highlighted earlier and making notes in the "Notes" column so that you'll remember main ideas. Respond to any reading questions that follow the reading. Answering questions will give you a bit of practice writing about the various aspects of the article. Think about and discuss the article and the ideas in the article with classmates, friends, or family members. And, finally, summarize the article, restating the most important points in your own words. By now, you'll know the article very well, so well in fact that you'll probably have some strong opinions to express on the topic.

Activity

Preparing to Write In-Class Essay #1: Illiteracy in America

You're preparing to write an essay in your next class on a topic taken from "The Shameful Secret of Illiteracy in America" by Penni Wild, which follows.

1. Follow the reading process as you read the article.

2. Answer the Questions for Critical Thought.

The Shameful Secret of Illiteracy in America
by Penni Wild

The word is not just a sound or a written symbol. The word is a force; it is the power you have to express and communicate, to think, and thereby to create the events in your life.
—Don Miguel Ruiz

1   One New Jersey woman, "Maria," read at a third grade level. She held a job and fudged her way through everyday tasks without reading. When she would go to a restaurant, she would order what she knew was on the menu—a hamburger, salad or grilled chicken—or point to someone else's plate at the next table and ask for "what he's having." Maria even went so far as to keep her illiteracy a secret even from her husband of ten years. Because she could not read the mail, she would pretend that she forgot her glasses at work or say that she had been too busy to open the mail and ask her husband to do it. One day, they were walking past a shop window with a sign in it. As they looked at the display, the husband suddenly realized that his wife could not read. Maria was embarrassed and humiliated. But she sought help and now reads, works on a computer and teaches others to read.

2   In 2002, before the Subcommittee on Education Reform Committee on Education and the Workforce, United States House of Representatives, actor James Earl Jones testified: "92 million Americans have low or very low literacy skills—they cannot read above the 6th grade level. To be illiterate in America—or anywhere for that matter—is to be unsafe, uncomfortable and unprotected. For the illiterate, despair and defeat serve as daily fare. Can any of us who do know how to read really understand the sadness that is associated with the inability to read? Can we truly relate to the silent humiliation, the quiet desperation that can't be expressed, the hundreds of ways that those who cannot read struggle in shame to keep their secret? The struggle out of illiteracy . . . is still a part of the story of America."

3   Today, our nation faces an epidemic that is destructive to our future. The disease is functional illiteracy. According to the most recent National Assessment of Educational Progress (NAEP), it has overtaken one-third of America's children by the fourth grade—including two-thirds of African-American students and almost half of all children in the inner cities.

4   The basic definition of literacy is the ability to read and write. So the basic definition of illiteracy is the inability to read and write.

5   Beyond the basic definitions, there is significance in the shocking statistics about the functionally illiterate. What illiteracy means is that millions may not be able to understand the directions on a medicine bottle, or be able to read their telephone bill, make correct change at a store, find and keep a job, or read to a child.

6   Illiteracy has long been viewed as a social and educational issue—someone else's problem. However, more recently we have come to understand the economic consequences of the lack of literacy skills for America and American business.

7   Illiteracy has a significant impact on the economy. According to *Nation's Business* magazine, 15 million adults holding jobs today are functionally illiterate. The American Council of Life Insurance reports that three-quarters of the Fortune 500 companies provide some level of remedial training for their workers. And, a study done by the Northeast Midwest Institute and The Center for Regional Policy found that business losses attributed to basic skill deficiencies run into the hundreds of millions of dollars because of low productivity, errors and accidents.

8   In addition, as reported in the 1986 publication entitled *Making Literacy Programs Work: A Practical Guide for Correctional Educators* (for the U.S. Department of Justice, National Institute of Corrections), one-half of all adults in federal and state correctional institutions cannot read or write at all. Only about one-third of those in prison have completed high school.

9   Evidence indicates that the problem begins at home. A National Governors' Association Task Force on Adult Literacy reported that illiteracy is an inter-generational problem, following a parent-child pattern. Poor school achievement and dropping out before completing school are commonplace among children of illiterate parents.

10   The reasons for illiteracy are as varied as the number of non-readers. The adult non-reader may have left school early, may have had a physical or emotional disability, may have had ineffectual teachers or simply may have been unready to learn at the time reading instruction began.

11   Because they are unable to help their children learn, parents who can't read often perpetuate the inter-generational cycle of illiteracy. Without books, newspapers or magazines in the home and a parent who reads to serve as a role model, many children grow up with severe literacy deficiencies. Clearly, there is no single cause of illiteracy.

12   Adults have many reasons for requesting reading help. Many are prompted by the need for increased levels of literacy in their jobs. Others may wish to read to a child, read the Bible or write to a family member for the first time. All express a hope for a better quality of life through higher levels of literacy.

13   According to Barbara Bush, "It suddenly occurred to me that every single thing I worry about—the breakup of families, drugs, AIDS, the homeless—everything would be better if more people could read, write and understand."

14   Let us all do what we can to make illiteracy not a part of the story of America today but a part of America's past.

Questions for Critical Thought

Illiteracy in America

1. How many Americans have low to very low literacy skills? How do low literacy skills affect people's ability to function in society?

2. What impact does illiteracy have on our economy?

3. Where does illiteracy appear to begin and why?

4. What can be done to address the problem of illiteracy in America?

5. Summarize the article.

6. Finally, take time to anticipate what the essay prompt might be about. Brainstorm ideas for possible prompts.

Once you've completed the reading process, you're ready to analyze the writing prompt and plan your essay. When reading a prompt, look for *key words* that indicate a certain kind of approach:

• If you see *take a position, take a stand,* or *argue for or against,* then you can be sure you're supposed to be persuading an audience to believe as you do about an issue.

• If you see *examine the sides* or *discuss,* you're being asked to provide a more balanced view of both sides of the issue.

• If you see *explain, describe,* or *define,* you're being asked to help your reader see and understand through your explanation.

Activity

Analyzing the Prompt

Here is an in-class prompt for "The Shameful Secret of Illiteracy in America."

Write an essay examining the effects of illiteracy in America today and explain how we might address this national epidemic. Support your discussion with evidence from the reading and from your own experiences and/or observations.

1. Underline the key terms in the prompt.

2. Paraphrase (rewrite in your own words) the essay prompt. You may even want to rewrite the prompt as a question (or two).

Notes   ### *In-Class Writing Assignment #1: Illiteracy in America*

> Set aside a two-hour period to write an essay on the prompt for "The Shameful Secret of Illiteracy in America." Be sure to divide your time wisely so that you have time for prewriting, writing, revising, and editing.

In some situations, you may not be given the reading ahead of time. You may be expected to read an article in class and then write on a theme or issue raised in that piece. In this case, you would still follow the first few steps of the reading process to make sure that you understood the reading. Rather than summarizing the article as you would if you had been given the option to take it home, you would simply list main ideas in the margins as you read and reread the article in class.

WRITING THE ARGUMENTATIVE ESSAY IN CLASS

Argument is an important part of many of the discussions you'll engage in as college students. When you argue, you try to persuade an audience to believe as you do about a cause, an issue, or an idea. Handling an argument in an essay can be tricky. On the one hand, you need to get your point of view across. On the other hand, you need to represent the opposition fairly without canceling out your own arguments. So how do you accomplish such a feat in a timed writing situation? In this section, you'll learn the strategies for writing an effective argument in class. But first you'll examine the essential elements of an argument.

In the Argumentative Essay

- The writer establishes a clear position on the issue.
- The writer presents the opposing view fairly. The writer doesn't ignore the opposing view but presents it, then tries to refute it (argue against it). (The writer who doesn't mention the opposing view has written a one-sided argument.)
- The writer supports his or her own position with evidence in the form of facts, examples, or experience.

The Writer Takes a Stand   When you've been given a writing prompt that asks you to argue an issue, you've been given a very specific task—take a position and prove your point. Consider the following writing prompts:

- Argue for or against testing college athletes for drug use.
- Argue for or against raising the national smoking age to 21.
- Argue for or against condoms being distributed to students at local middle schools and high schools.
- Argue for or against stricter handgun regulations.
- Argue for or against spanking as an effective method of discipline for children.
- Argue for or against children being required to wear uniforms at public schools.
- Argue for or against censorship of pornography on the Internet.
- Argue for or against mandatory military service for both males and females.
- Argue for or against continuing the NASA space program.
- Argue for or against legalization of marijuana for medical use.
- Argue for or against [add your own issue].

Before you could take a position on any of these topics, you would need to spend some time brainstorming. The pro/con list is an excellent tool for brainstorming argumentative topics.

Should College Athletes Be Drug Tested?	
Pro (For) —Yes, college athletes should be tested because they represent the school.	*Con (Against)* –No, it's a violation of privacy.

Notes

Once you've listed as many pros and cons as you can think of, you'll be in a better position to decide where you stand on the issue. Have you come up with more pros than cons? Are some arguments more important than others? (Draw a line through less important ones.) At this point, ask yourself which side you agree with most. This will be the side to take in your argument.

The Writer Organizes the Arguments   Once you've established your position, you'll identify and highlight the top two or three arguments on each side of the issue. These are the arguments you'll address as you write your essay.

Consider organizing your arguments in one of the following ways:

- Listing the least important ideas first, most important ideas last
- Alternating pro/con arguments: pro argument, con argument, pro argument, con argument, and so on
- Presenting all pro arguments (divided into different paragraphs) and then all con arguments (divided into different paragraphs)

To avoid a one-sided argument and to show your audience that you are fair and well educated, you should present your opponents' view as well as your own. You may even admit that your opponents have some legitimate points. However, you will want to point out that your points are more important, more persuasive, and probably more in number. How do you address the opposition without weakening your own argument?

Here are a few methods:

- Mention fewer of your opponents' ideas compared to the number of your ideas.
- Mention your opponents' ideas early and then focus the rest of your essay on your ideas.
- Mention your opponents' ideas and then explain why these ideas are not as strong as yours or why your ideas are better.

Strategies for Writing the Argument in Class

As discussed earlier in this chapter, sometimes you will be given a writing prompt at the start of class and will be expected to write an essay on the topic from your general knowledge. Such is the case with the argument prompt that follows.

Write an essay in which you argue for or against middle school children having computers and Internet access in their bedrooms.

Action Strategies

- Read and analyze the prompt.
- Develop a pro/con list on the topic.
- Establish your position.
- Highlight the most important points on both sides of the issue.
- Decide on an organizational pattern to follow.
- Draft the essay, presenting pros and cons, but make sure your position is clear and well supported.
- Revise your essay.
- Edit your essay.

Activity

Writing the In-Class Argument

Using the action strategies mentioned, respond to this prompt:

> *Write an essay in which you argue for or against middle school children having computers and Internet access in their bedrooms.*

Set a time limit of two hours to complete the essay.

In other situations, you will be given an essay to read, think about, and discuss before writing an argument in class. Two such in-class writing assignments follow.

In-Class Writing Assignment #2: *Arguing For or Against Hands-Free Laws*

1. In preparation for writing an in-class essay, read "Mixed Signals in Hands-Free Phone Debate" by Judy Lin, which follows. Be sure to use the reading process as you read the article.

2. Using the action strategies for writing in-class arguments, respond to the following prompt:

> *Write an essay in which you argue for or against requiring all drivers to use hands-free devices when talking on their phones while driving. Be sure to support your position with evidence, examples, or observations.*

Set a time limit of two hours to complete your essay.

Notes

Mixed Signals in Hands-Free Phone Debate*

A bill seeks to ban hand-helds while driving, but some experts say more study is needed.

by Judy Lin

This article appeared in the *Sacramento Bee* on June 19, 2006.

1   Americans spent 1.7 trillion minutes on their cell phones last year. Although no one knows how many minutes were spent talking while driving, one state senator wants to make sure Californians keep both hands on the steering wheel.

2   "We know you're distracted. We know the risk has risen dramatically. Now the question is one of control," Sen. Joe Simitian, D-Palo Alto, told fellow lawmakers on the Senate floor in making his fifth attempt to ban the use of hand-held phones while driving.

3   His proposal, Senate Bill 1613, cleared the Senate last month and is expected to be vetted by the Assembly Transportation Committee in the coming weeks. If passed, drivers would face initial fines of $20, going up to $50 for subsequent offenses beginning in July 2008.

4   As California considers joining a growing number of states and cities imposing cell phone restrictions, there are conflicting reports on whether hands-free is safer than hand-held. New York, which was the first state to implement a ban back in 2001, has yet to complete a review of the law's impact.

5   While many studies have shown cell phone use is a common form of driver distraction, experts say there has been relatively little direct research comparing hands-free with hand-held devices.

6   And some wonder if talking on a cell phone isn't more distracting than the manner in which it is done.

7   There's no denying that more Americans than ever are using cell phones—207 million estimated subscribers at last count. And when they talk and drive, they are increasing their chances of getting into accidents.

8   In April, the National Highway Transportation Safety Administration and the Virginia Tech Transportation Institute released findings that nearly 80 percent of crashes involved some form of driver inattention. The most common distraction reported was the use of cell phones, followed by drowsiness.

---

*Judy Lin, "Mixed Signals in Hands-Free Phone Debate," *The Sacramento Bee,* June 19, 2006, pp. A1, A15. © The Sacramento Bee, 2006. Reprinted with permission.

9   For now, some consider the restrictions an imperfect solution to the dangers posed by today's high-tech gadgets.

10   "Hands-free alone isn't necessarily the answer because the distraction can be the act of talking. Any soccer mom probably knows that," said Candysse Miller, executive director of the Insurance Information Network of California, a nonprofit consumer education group funded by the insurance industry.

11   "But it's certainly an improvement from holding a phone to your face." The NHTSA study found that dialing on cell phones and similar devices increased the risk of a crash or near-crash by three times.

12   Meanwhile, talking or listening on the phone increased the driver's risk by only 1.3 times.

13   University of Utah psychologist David Strayer and his colleagues were among those to question the notion that hands-free cell phones are safer than hand-helds.

14   Their 2003 study showed that motorists suffer from "inattention blindness" because they are distracted by a cell phone conversation.

15   Such findings have prompted Sprint/Nextel to oppose SB 1613. Caroline Semerdjian, a spokeswoman for the company, said the bill doesn't consider features like Nextel's walkie-talkie feature known as "push-to-talk," which can't be used hands-free.

16   "Such laws are ineffective because they are difficult to enforce," wrote Semerdjian in an email.

17   "(They are) unfair because they single out one distraction when many different distractions can lead to traffic accidents."

18   Simitian doesn't dispute that. However, he believes given the choice between using a hand-held and hands-free device, it's better to choose the latter.

19   Citing findings in a simulated driving study by the NHTSA, Simitian said drivers are less prone to weave back and forth, maintain more consistent speed and react faster to brake lights when they are on hands-free sets.

20   "You have almost three times as much time to react to an accident when you have your hands free at the wheel than you do clutching a foreign object to your ear," the senator said. "That's the difference between 2.1 seconds and 5.9 seconds."

21   He said Japan witnessed a 52 percent drop in the number of traffic accidents involving cell phones after imposing a hand-held ban.

22   The electronics industry, too, has grown sensitive to safety concerns, creating new tools from wireless headsets and speaker-phone functions to voice-activated or one-touch dialing. These features and accessories are aimed at keeping a driver's hands on the wheel and eyes on the road.

Notes

23   "When used properly, these products are great tools that help drivers focus on the road," said Gary Shapiro, president and CEO of the Consumers Electronics Association.

24   But Miller, of the insurance network, considers technology a double-edged sword. "While it helps you out, it's another button to push," she said.

In-Class Writing Assignment #3: Arguing For or Against Electronic Badges for Children

1. In preparation for writing an in-class essay, read "Electronic Badges for Students Put Parents, Privacy Groups on Edge" by Marjie Lundstrom, which appears below. Be sure to use the reading process as you read.

2. Using the action strategies for writing in-class arguments (page 437), respond to the following prompt:

   Write an essay in which you argue for or against children being required to wear electronic badges at school. Be sure to support your position with evidence, examples, or observations.

   Set a time limit of two hours to complete your essay.

Electronic Badges for Students Put Parents, Privacy Groups on Edge*
by Marjie Lundstrom

This article appeared in the *Sacramento Bee* on February 10, 2005.

1   Earnie Graham says he was just thinking about student safety and teacher convenience when he ordered his 590 elementary and junior high kids to be the first in California to wear electronic security badges.

2   The badges, which have a radio-frequency antenna that is electronically read when students pass through monitored doorways, seemed like a promising tool for keeping attendance, said Graham, superintendent/

---

*Marjie Lundstrom, "Electronic Badges for Students Put Parents, Privacy Groups on Edge," *The Sacramento Bee*, February 10, 2005, p. A3. © The Sacramento Bee, 2005. Reprinted with permission.

principal of the Brittan Elementary School District in Sutter, 51 miles northwest of Sacramento near Yuba City.

3   Sort of a bar code for kids.

4   "It's exciting. I thought we could be on the cutting edge of something," Graham said. "I just thought it was kind of Star Trekkie."

5   What Graham's voyage to the new frontier got him was a whole galaxy of trouble.

6   For three weeks, the 52-year-old educator has contended with angry parents, ambivalent kids, cranky email, multiple public meetings, bad press—and, now, a letter of rebuke from the American Civil Liberties Union.

7   The ACLU of Northern California, along with two national privacy rights groups, objected to the mandatory badges in a Feb. 7 letter, saying that their use "is more than offset by the danger posed in implementing this intrusive new technology." The groups, joined by some parents, contend that the Radio Frequency Identification tags jeopardize students' safety and their privacy.

8   Each badge includes the child's picture, name, grade and the chip with an identifying number that is recognized by the reader.

9   "It is our goal that no child in the United States be tagged or tracked," the parents of a 13-year-old student said in a statement issued by the ACLU. "We want it to be stopped here, in Sutter, Calif., and we don't want any child to be tracked anywhere. Our children are not pieces of inventory."

10   In this town of 2,885, parental concern—Graham calls some of it paranoia—has spread like a summer wildfire.

11   "I don't accept this; I'm really disappointed," said 38-year-old Rebecca Cagle, whose eighth-grade son was sporting his badge this week with a red lanyard. "If my kid comes up missing, there's going to be hell freezing up."

12   Her son, 14-year-old Michael Hughes, shrugged off the new policy as no big deal, though he admits to having stepped on his badge.

13   "If I have to take this to court," his mom said, "I will."

14   This wasn't what Graham had bargained for when he embarked on the plan, which began as an experiment last year for kids attending summer school. Graham said he'd been approached by a local businessman, whose company wanted to partner with the school in testing the new technology, at no cost to the school.

15   Graham agreed, and about 100 students carried the badges this summer.

16   "There were no complaints, no problems, no costs, no issues. Nothing. Nada. Zero," Graham said.

Notes

17   So he took the plan before the school board in October, asking that the program be extended to the 160 junior high students. Board members agreed.

18   By January, all seemed ready. Graham, who hates the word "tracking," thought he could extend the badges to the entire student population, kindergarten through eighth grade. He sent a brief note home to parents Jan. 12, about a week before the ID badges were issued.

19   The rumblings soon began.

20   By this week, Graham was attending his third public meeting on the subject, with parents and students expressing both concern and support for this new world. Over and over, the administrator has said the data are secure, the technology is safe, likening it to passing by a motion detector.

21   A special school board meeting has been called for Tuesday to formally review the matter.

22   "They're very concerned about becoming buried in legal fees," Graham said.

23   This much is obvious: Monitoring people is a lot different in many people's minds than tracking packaged produce. Add in children and it's new territory. Last year, the new director of the Department of Motor Vehicles was publicly flayed for her idea that the state consider putting satellite tracking devices in cars and taxing motorists for how much they drive.

24   Some frontiers, it would seem, are not ready to be crossed.

SUMMARY OF CHAPTER 9

In this chapter, you have

- studied and applied strategies for writing in class;
- learned how to analyze and respond to different kinds of writing prompts and assignments;
- continued to develop your writing, reading, and critical thinking skills;
- practiced writing essays in a set amount of time; and
- focused on writing the argumentative essay in timed situations.

EDITING AND STYLE TIPS

When completing a piece of timed writing, it might seem impossible to bother with style. Certainly your priorities are to understand the question, formulate a main idea, and then support it in an organized fashion. However, instructors and employers will be looking at your sentences, too. You want to allow yourself time to polish your piece. Here is a list of things to check for, listed from most important to least:

- Verb errors (verb tense and verb form, subject-verb agreement; see pages 496–516 for more information)

- Sentence boundary errors (fragments, comma splices, and run-ons; see pages 516–532 for more information)

- Spelling (see pages 474–484 for more information)

- Usage (see pages 534–537 for more information)

- Punctuation (see pages 538–539 for a list of punctuation rules)

- Sentence structure (see pages 539–540 for a list of style tips)
    - having strong clear subjects and verbs
    - placing subjects and verbs next to one another
    - eliminating unnecessary words
    - using transitions, FANBOYS, subordinators, adjectives, adverbs, and prepositional phrases

You may not be able to methodically check for each item listed above during a timed writing. Be strategic in the way you spend your final minutes; move from the top of this list toward the bottom, and think about the types of errors you tend to make. What have your instructors asked you to work on? Finally, keep in mind that instructors know that timed writings simply can't be as polished as take-home pieces. Focus on doing your best and using your time wisely. Good luck!

END-OF-TERM PROGRESS JOURNAL

Completing a college writing course is an admirable accomplishment. Take time in this final journal to reflect on your growth as a writer, reader, and critical thinker. (Draw comparisons between your skills and processes at the beginning of the term to your skills and processes now at the end of the term. Be specific.)

- How has your reading process changed? Explain.
- How has your writing process changed? Explain.
- How have your critical thinking skills improved? Explain.

Notes
- Have your attitudes toward reading, writing, and critical thinking changed? Explain.
- Which specific writing skills have improved the most? (Think about your ability to focus, organize, and develop ideas.)
- How have your sentence skills changed?
- What skills and processes do you still need to work on?
- What writing assignment from this term are you most proud of? Why?

We recommend that you share this journal with your classmates. We hope that your class has become a community of writers who are interested in each other's progress.

Good luck in your future writing, reading, and critical thinking endeavors!

Using Connections *Online with* **mywritinglab**

For more practice with writing in-class essays, log onto www.mywritinglab.com to access the online resources for *Connections*, Third Edition.

Mastering Your Study Skills

This section of Connections *provides information and exercises to help you master your study skills.*

- Taking notes
- Keeping a notebook
- Making the most of a good tutor
- Using computers
- Using the Glossary and Index
- Discovering your learning style
- Using the dictionary
- Building your vocabulary
- Spelling matters
- Reading aloud: a trick of the trade
- Using outside sources

TAKING NOTES

You'll get much more out of your reading and lectures if you learn to take notes well since taking notes is one way to be an active participant in the reading, writing, and critical thinking processes. When taking notes, you're involved in the process of actively listening and identifying the most important points, then transcribing those points into writing that makes sense to you so that you can review the information later.

Sometimes taking notes is as simple as leaving a check next to an interesting idea in your reading. In other cases, taking notes involves writing out the speaker's main points while listening to a lecture. In this section, you'll learn how to take notes when reading and while listening.

Writing in the Margins: Becoming a More Active Reader

One simple way to become a more active reader is to make notes in book margins as you read. Does this suggestion surprise you? If so, you were probably taught *not* to write in your textbooks in elementary or secondary school. Since textbooks were usually passed down from one class to the next, or sold at the end of the school year, you may have been told to keep the margins clean. However, effective readers usually write in the margins of their textbooks. You should feel free to use the margins of your own books for restating main ideas, responding to what you've read, or making connections to other books or articles you've read.

In the following excerpt from his essay, "How to Mark a Book," Mortimer Adler, the founder of the Great Books Program, explains why marking up books is important.

> Why is marking a book indispensable to reading? First, it keeps you awake. (And I don't mean merely conscious; I mean wide awake.) In the second place, reading, if it is active, is thinking, and thinking tends to express itself in words, spoken or written. The marked book is usually the thought-through book. Finally, writing helps you remember the thoughts you had, or the thoughts the author expressed.
>
> —*Saturday Review, 1940*

Adler suggests, as do other reading experts, that the act of writing in response to reading helps you think through and retain ideas. And if you've made notes next to important ideas in the text, you can easily refer back to these ideas when you review. For study purposes, marking your book makes sense. If you get into the habit of noting important points or ideas in your text, then you'll be a step ahead when it's time to study for an exam.

Using the "Notes" Column in This Text   Because we understand the importance of being an active reader, this text provides an ongoing "Notes" column in the margins. This column gives you a place to record your immediate reactions to a reading, jot down questions that come to mind as you read, identify main points, or brainstorm ideas for your writing. In short, the "Notes" column is meant to encourage you to become a more active reader.

To give you an idea of how you might use the "Notes" column, we've included the first three paragraphs of an essay that appears in the textbook *America and Its People*. Note the reader's comments in the margin of the text.

Notes

The Modern Family
by James Kirby Martin et al.

This selection appeared in the American history book, *America and Its People*.

1   Does a father have the right to give his children his last name even if his wife objects? Can an expectant mother obtain an abortion without her husband's permission? Should a teenager, unhappy with her parents' restrictions on her smoking, dating, and choice of friends, be allowed to have herself placed in a foster home? Should a childless couple be permitted to hire a "surrogate mother" to be artificially inseminated and carry a child to delivery? These are among the questions that the nation's courts have had to wrestle with as the nature of American family life has, in the course of a generation, been revolutionized.

These are interesting questions. I wonder if all of them will be answered in the body of the essay. The essay appears to be about the American family.

2   During the 1950s, the Cleavers on the television show *Leave It to Beaver* epitomized the American family. In 1960, over 70 percent of all American households were like the Cleavers: made up of a breadwinner father, a homemaker mother, and their kids. Today, "traditional" families with a working husband, [a homemaker], and one or more children make up less than 15 percent of the nation's households. And as America's families have changed, the image of the family portrayed on television has changed accordingly. . . .

"Epitomize": to be a typical example. Were the Cleavers really a typical American family? Maybe the writers mean simply that most families then had a father, mother, and children.

3   Profound changes have reshaped American family life in recent years. In a decade, divorce rates doubled. The number of divorces today is twice as high as in 1966 and three times higher than in 1950. The

True, the family has changed: divorce rate, single-parent households, couples living together are all higher now than in the '50s or '60s.

rapid upsurge in the divorce rates contributed to a dramatic increase in the number of single-parent households. . . . The number of households consisting of a single woman and her children has tripled since 1960. A sharp increase in female-headed homes has been accompanied by a startling increase in the number of couples cohabitating outside of marriage. The number of unmarried couples living together has quadrupled since 1970.

It's clear from the reader's margin notes that she engaged in her reading. She speculated about what the reading would cover, she looked up an unfamiliar term and put the definition where she will see it when she reviews, and she asked questions and made comments that show she had thought about the reading.

Although this reader made extensive comments in the "Notes" column, this isn't always necessary. Let's look at another brief selection marked in a different way.

Topic sentence

Support: facts and statistics

Creative wrap-up

Television is the most popular of the popular media. Indeed, if Nielsen research and other studies are correct, there are few things that Americans do more than they watch television. On average, each household has a TV on almost fifty hours a week. Forty percent of households eat dinner with the set on. Individually, Americans watch an average of thirty hours a week. We begin peering at TV through the bars of cribs and continue looking at it through the cataracts of old age.

—*Joshua Meyrowitz, from "Television: The Shared Arena"*

In this case, the reader used the "Notes" column for labeling the parts of the paragraph as opposed to making comments on the reading. The point is to use the "Notes" column as needed. *You* are the one who decides how to use the margins.

Additional Ideas for Engaging with Your Reading

Not every book comes equipped with a "Notes" column. However, most books have enough of a margin or some blank pages at the ends of chapters that you can use for notetaking. Here are some of Adler's pointers for marking not just your textbooks, but any book you may read.

1. *Underlining:* of major points, of important or forceful statements.

2. *Vertical lines at the margin:* to emphasize a statement already underlined.

3. *Star, asterisk, or other doo-dad at the margin:* to be used sparingly, to emphasize the . . . most important statements. . . .

                                                           *   *Notes*

4. *Numbers in the margin:* to indicate the sequence of points the author makes in developing a single argument.

                                                         1, 2, 3

5. *Numbers of other pages in the margin:* to indicate where else in the book the author made points relevant to the point marked; to tie up the ideas in a book, which, though they may be separated by many pages, belong together.

                                                     see page 67

6. *Circling key words or phrases.*

                                                     critical thinking

7. *Writing in the margin, or at the top or bottom of the page, for the sake of:* recording questions (and perhaps answers) that a passage raised in your mind; reducing a complicated discussion to a simple statement; or recording the sequence of major points right through the book.

As you actively engage in your reading, you should freely adapt Adler's suggestions to fit your needs as a reader. You can also consider using Post-its™ to record notes and mark important pages.

Becoming a More Active Listener

From the moment you walk into a classroom, you're expected to listen to and remember what the instructor says. But remembering everything the instructor says is quite a task. You've probably been told how important it is to take notes. But taking notes effectively is easier said than done. To take useful notes, you must first learn how to listen.

In his article "Learning to Listen," William H. Armstrong (who has taught history for over fifty years) briefly explains the history of the lecture and the difficulties people have in listening.

> Before books and printing, the primary element in acquiring knowledge was listening. A "lecture" originally meant a "reading" from some precious manuscript. The reader read slowly and stopped to explain difficult passages to his listeners. The process has changed; reading is no doubt the primary element in acquiring knowledge, but listening remains the second most important element.
>
> Why is listening . . . the most difficult of the learning processes? The practices of seeing (reading), writing, and thinking are exercised within the person. But listening takes on the complexity of the listener having to coordinate their mental powers with an outside force—the person or thing to which the listener is listening. This demands the discipline of subjecting the mind of the listener to that of the speaker.

The second problem in learning to listen arises from lack of associated control. When you learn to read, your eyes control the speed with which you read. When you write there is actual physical control in your hand. In thinking, the analysis of thought travels at exactly the speed capacity of your mind. But when you begin to train yourself to be a good listener, you are faced with a difficulty not unlike that of trying to drive a car without brakes. You can think four times as fast as the average teacher can speak.

Only by demanding of yourself the most unswerving concentration and discipline can you hold your mind on the track of the speaker. This can be accomplished if the listener uses the free time to think around the topic—"listening between the lines" as it is sometimes called. It consists of anticipating the teacher's next point, summarizing what has been said, questioning in silence the accuracy or importance of what is being taught, putting the teacher's thoughts into one's own words, and trying to discern the test or examination questions that will be formed from this material.

If you find your mind wandering after only a few minutes of class, you need to work on developing your concentration. Armstrong suggests that you begin by concentrating for the first ten minutes of every class period. As you focus on the instructor or task at hand, block out other sounds that might keep you from listening. Then, as your ability to listen develops, extend your period of concentration. Eventually, you'll be able to stay focused for the entire class period. Taking notes will help you stay focused.

Taking Lecture Notes   This is the scenario in many classrooms: The instructor begins speaking when the class period starts, and students write down the most important points. Later, they will review their notes when it's time to take the midterm or final. Sounds easy enough, doesn't it? But taking effective notes (as you may have discovered) can be quite challenging.

Here are some tips (from Armstrong and other instructors) for taking lecture notes:

- *Be a good listener.* If you aren't listening, you can't possibly take good notes.
- *Be prepared.* You need the tools with you, ready, in order to take lecture notes. This means blank paper, pencil or pen, or laptop in hand when class starts.
- *Listen for clues* in the lecture that suggest an important point is being made. Remember, you can't write down everything the instructor says. Trying to do so will only frustrate you. Listen for the repeated

phrases "the important point" or "we must remember." When you
hear such clues, be ready to write.

- *Watch the overhead or board.* If the instructor displays or lists
  points, write those down. The instructor wouldn't write them
  down if they weren't important.
- *Don't break your concentration* to worry about spelling or grammar.
- *Ask the instructor to repeat or clarify points* as necessary.
- *Review and fill in your notes* after a lecture so that you don't
  forget what you've heard.
- *File your notes* in an organized manner (in your notebook) so that
  they're in place when you need to study them.

Journal Assignment

Taking Effective Lecture Notes

Taking effective lecture notes can help you get better grades. Reflect on
how you've taken notes in the past. Then consider what you've learned
about listening and taking notes in this chapter. Which strategies do you
intend to use in your next class? How will you use these strategies to improve your reading, writing, and critical thinking skills?

KEEPING A NOTEBOOK

Being well organized is another key to success. The well-organized person carefully files away important papers and assignments so that
they're easily found when needed. By learning to organize a notebook,
you'll not only develop your organization and study skills, you'll simplify your life. The idea is to make your own life easier by keeping
journal entries, reading questions, class activities, writing assignments,
and other work handy.

To begin, you'll need a three-ring binder (1½- to 2-inch width), a
package of dividers, and loose-leaf paper.

Two Basic Methods of Organization

There are many ways to organize a notebook, but we'll focus on two
specific ways—organizing by process and organizing by assignment.

No matter which method you use, your course syllabus should appear first in your notebook.

When one assignment builds on another, it helps to *organize your work by process.* The idea is to organize assignments as you complete them so that you can see your writing develop through a chapter. Begin by filling out a divider for each chapter. Then, under each chapter divider, keep every assignment you complete—from activities to reading questions to journal entries to drafts—filed in order of completion. Also include any pages of your own: questions about the assignment, brainstorming activities, outlines, or any articles you discover and want to add to your body of research. Include your early rough drafts, developing drafts, and later drafts in order of completion. Also include a copy of your final drafts as well as the graded drafts returned by your instructor. As you complete each chapter, you'll be able to flip through the assignments and easily see how your essays developed.

Another approach is to *organize your work by assignment.* In this case, you store journal entries under one divider, reading questions under another, sentence work under another, and so on. If you choose this approach, consider using the following headings:

a. Journal Assignments

b. Reading Questions

c. Class Activities

d. Lecture Notes

e. Writing Assignments

f. Sentence Work

g. Vocabulary

(other sections as needed)

If you use this approach, the "Writing Assignments" section should still store—from beginning to end—all the drafts of your essays. As you store these drafts, you'll begin to understand and develop your own process for writing. Also in this writing assignments section, jot down any thoughts or reactions you have to the assignments or any questions you have about the assignments so that you can ask your instructor. Feel free to include your brainstorming notes, idea clusters, lists, and freewriting. Also include early outlines, rough drafts, developing drafts, and later drafts. Finally, store a copy of your final draft as well as the graded draft returned by your instructor. As the semester progresses, this section of your notebook will become the largest. At a glance, you'll be able to see how your essays developed.

MAKING THE MOST OF A GOOD TUTOR

As a supplement to your assigned work, we recommend that you see a tutor. Your reading and writing skills will improve much more quickly if you can discuss your work frequently outside of class. And although study groups made up of students from your class are an excellent idea, too, it is important to discuss your work with a more experienced writer. This is where tutors come in.

Whether you are feeling secure or insecure about your reading and writing skills, you can benefit from tutorial assistance. (Even professional writers hire editors to help them rethink and revise portions of their writing.) However, it's extremely important that you have a clear idea about what you can expect from a tutoring session. A tutor who does too much for you can actually slow down your growth as a reader, writer, and thinker. You'll want to find a tutor who offers guidance and tools for success while encouraging you to do the work yourself. Here are things to look for in a good tutor.

A Good Tutor Should

- be on time and ready to help you;
- listen carefully to you and your concerns about writing;
- ask you questions about your assignment, your deadlines, and your concerns;
- probably comment first on the global aspects of your writing: your focus, development, and organization;
- respond honestly to your writing;
- discuss some possible ways to improve weak spots, but let you do the actual improvements;
- explain a grammatical error to you and different ways to correct it, but have you identify and fix it in your own writing; and
- tell you how many spelling errors he or she sees, but let you find the errors and fix them yourself.

A Good Tutor Should Not

- waste your time by being consistently late or by talking about things unrelated to the writing task;
- rewrite sections of your paper or give you the "right words" to say (yours are the right words and ideas); or
- proofread your paper by marking and correcting your grammar, punctuation, and spelling mistakes.

Finding a Good Tutor

To find a good tutor, go to the writing center, the computer lab, your English instructor, or your college counselor to ask for a referral. Most colleges have some kind of tutorial service available at little to no cost. It's up to you, however, to use your college's system to your advantage. If you begin working with a tutor and discover that he or she isn't listening to or understanding your needs, then don't waste your time. Arrange to work with another tutor.

Making the Most of a Tutoring Session

The more enthusiasm and interest you put into your tutoring sessions, the more you'll get out of them. Think about it from the tutor's perspective for a moment. A tutor often works one-on-one with students for several hours in a single day. If you were a tutor, wouldn't you feel energized by those students who arrived at their sessions prepared to work? Here are some tips on how you can be a good tutee:

- *See the tutor on a regular basis.* Have a set appointment time, if possible, for once or twice a week. Be on time.
- *Set goals with the tutor.* Discuss and write down your strengths and weaknesses as a reader and writer. Prioritize your writing goals. Review this list with your instructor after your instructor has had time to evaluate some of your writing. Revise your goal list as your instructor suggests. (Review this list at midterm with your instructor.)
- *Bring in and discuss readings.* Discuss vocabulary words, main ideas, and interesting points.
- *Bring in and discuss the actual writing assignment.* Make sure you understand the requirements of the writing assignment.

- *Brainstorm ideas for your writing assignments.*
- *Show drafts to your tutor.* Ask what is the strongest part of the draft and what is the weakest. (Consider your list of goals for improvement.)
- *Write a short to-do list each week* before you leave the tutoring session. Make an agreement about what you will bring with you next time.

Because your time with a tutor is limited, be *on time*—with materials organized—and ready to work. Plan to ask questions and share concerns about your writing.

USING COMPUTERS

In college and on the job, you'll be expected to type most of what you write. You'll become a more efficient writer if you begin the practice of writing your essays on a computer. You don't need to know any fancy computer tricks to benefit from using a computer. You only need to know a few basic commands, which you can learn in the computer lab on your campus. You'll also need to know how to type or be willing to learn. (Most college computer labs have computers equipped with typing tutorials.)

Here are a number of tasks that you can complete easily on the computer:

- Freely pour out ideas to discover what you're thinking.
- Move paragraphs and sentences with ease.
- Add and delete information without having to retype your entire essay.
- Check word definitions with the computer's dictionary.
- Check spelling with the computer's spell-check program.

If you're unsure about where the computer lab is on your campus, ask your instructor or counselor. Both should be able to direct you to this important resource.

USING THE GLOSSARY AND INDEX

This book provides two additional resources for writers that you should know about. The first one is the *glossary*. Whenever an important term

Get Involved!
Investigate one of the resources available to students on your campus. For example, look into day care, counseling, tutoring, or financial aid services. Or visit the library or a computer lab. Report back to your classmates, telling them important features of the service: hours, location, eligibility requirements, and so on.

Notes is mentioned for the first time, it will appear in boldface. The definitions of these boldfaced terms are listed alphabetically in the glossary (page 541). Take a moment to look up the meaning of two of these terms in the glossary: **audience** and **purpose**.

You can also find out information and the location of other terms or general subjects by looking in the *index* (page 549). Terms in the index, as in the glossary, are listed in alphabetical order. Look up *audience* and *purpose* in the index to see where these terms appear in the text.

DISCOVERING YOUR LEARNING STYLE

Each person has his or her own **learning style**—a method that makes learning easier. Researchers have found that there are basically four styles: **visual, auditory, tactile,** or **kinesthetic.**

- **Visual learners** learn best when they see the material.
- **Auditory learners** learn best when they hear the material.
- **Tactile learners** learn best when they can write down the material.
- **Kinesthetic learners** learn best when they can involve their bodies in the learning process.

If you know what your learning style is, you will have an advantage in college because then you can study in the way that is best for you. For example, if you are a visual learner, you will want to use charts and to review cards and pictures when you are studying. However, if you know that you are an auditory learner, you know that lecture classes will be easier for you, and you might even tape record information to play back to yourself. If you are a tactile learner, you will want to find ways to learn information that involves taking notes or tracing letters. And if you're a kinesthetic learner, you will want to learn through physical movement: building models, organizing note cards, and so on. (You'll notice in this textbook that we offer activities and approaches that work for all kinds of learners: charts to express and organize ideas, reading aloud to help you edit your essays, note cards to organize your thoughts in an essay, and many more.)

No one learns *only* one way. You may learn best with visual materials, second best with auditory materials, third best with tactile materials, and so on. The key is knowing how you learn best, making the most of that method, and strengthening your other styles as you go along.

Discovering Your Learning Style

Take the test that follows and find out what your strongest learning style is. Then carefully review the study tips for each learning style.

Barsch Learning Style Inventory
by Jeffrey Barsch, Ed.D.

To gain a better understanding of yourself as a learner you need to evaluate the way you prefer to learn. We all should develop a style which will enhance our learning potential. The following evaluation is a short, quick way of assessing your learning style.

This is not a timed test. Try to do as much as you can by yourself. You surely may, however, ask for assistance when and where you feel you need it. Answer each question as honestly as you can. There are thirty-two questions.

When you are finished, transfer each number to its proper place on page 460. Then, total each of the four columns on that page. You will then see, very quickly, what your best method of learning is, i.e., whether you are a **visual, auditory, tactile** or **kinesthetic** learner. By this we mean, whether you as an individual learn best through seeing things, hearing them, through the sense of touch, or through actually performing the task.

For example:

- If you are a visual learner, that is, you have a high visual score, then by all means be sure you see all study materials. Use charts, maps, filmstrips, notes, and flashcards. Practice visualizing or picturing spelling words, for example, in your head. Use brightly colored markers to highlight your reading assignments. Write out everything for frequent and quick visual review.
- If you are an auditory learner, that is, have a high auditory score, then be sure to use tapes. Sit in the lecture hall or classroom where you can hear lectures clearly. Tape your class or lecture notes so that you can review them frequently. After you have read something, summarize it on tape. Verbally review spelling words and lectures with a friend.
- If you are a tactile learner, that is, if you have a high tactile score, you might trace words, for example, as you are saying them. Facts that

Notes

must be learned should be written several times. Keep a supply of scratch paper just for this purpose. Taking and keeping lecture notes will be very important.

- If you are a kinesthetic learner, that is, if you have a high kinesthetic score, it means you need to involve your body in the process of learning. Take a walk and study your notes on flashcards at the same time. It is easier for you to memorize school work if you involve some movement in your memory task.

If several of your scores are within 4 or 5 points of each other, it means that you can use any of those senses for learning tasks. *When you are in a hurry, use your best learning styles. When you have extra time, improve your weak sensory areas.* Discuss the results of this test with your teacher or counselor. You will develop through conversation other helpful ways to study more efficiently. Good luck in your efforts to identify and use a more effective study pattern.

Place a check on the appropriate line after each statement.

	Often	Sometimes	Seldom
1. I can remember more about a subject through listening than reading.	_____	_____	_____
2. I follow written directions better than oral directions.	_____	_____	_____
3. Once shown a new physical movement, I perform it quickly with few errors.	_____	_____	_____
4. I bear down extremely hard with pen or pencil when writing.	_____	_____	_____
5. I require explanations of diagrams, graphs, or visual directions.	_____	_____	_____
6. I enjoy working with tools.	_____	_____	_____
7. I am skillful with and enjoy developing and making graphs and charts.	_____	_____	_____
8. I can tell if sounds match when presented with pairs of sounds.	_____	_____	_____
9. I can watch someone do a dance step and easily copy it myself.	_____	_____	_____
10. I can understand and follow directions on maps.	_____	_____	_____
11. I do better at academic subjects by listening to lectures or tapes.	_____	_____	_____

	Often	Sometimes	Seldom	Notes
12. I frequently play with coins or keys in my pockets.	_____	_____	_____	
13. I enjoy perfecting a movement in sports or dancing.	_____	_____	_____	
14. I can better understand a news article by reading about it in the paper than by listening to the radio.	_____	_____	_____	
15. I can chew gum, smoke, or snack during studies.	_____	_____	_____	
16. I feel the best way to remember is to picture it in my head.	_____	_____	_____	
17. I enjoy activities that make me aware of my body's movement.	_____	_____	_____	
18. I would rather listen to a good lecture or speech than read about the same material in a textbook.	_____	_____	_____	
19. I consider myself an athletic person.	_____	_____	_____	
20. I grip objects in my hands during learning.	_____	_____	_____	
21. I would prefer listening to the news on the radio rather than reading it in a newspaper.	_____	_____	_____	
22. I like to obtain information on an interesting subject by reading relevant materials.	_____	_____	_____	
23. I am highly aware of sensations and feelings in my hips and shoulders after learning a new movement or exercise.	_____	_____	_____	
24. I follow oral directions better than written ones.	_____	_____	_____	
25. It would be easy for me to memorize something if I could just use body movements at the same time.	_____	_____	_____	
26. I like to write things down or take notes for visual review.	_____	_____	_____	
27. I remember best when writing things down several times.	_____	_____	_____	
28. I learn to spell better by repeating the letters out loud than by writing the word on paper.	_____	_____	_____	

	Often	Sometimes	Seldom

29. I frequently have the ability to visualize body movements to perform a task, e.g., correction of a golf swing, batting stance, dance position, etc. _____ _____ _____

30. I can learn spelling well by tracing over the letters. _____ _____ _____

31. I feel comfortable touching, hugging, shaking hands, etc. _____ _____ _____

32. I am good at working and solving jigsaw puzzles and mazes. _____ _____ _____

Scoring Tips:

Try moving down one column at a time. Begin with the VISUAL column where the #2 is listed. Look back at your answer for #2 of the survey. If you answered OFTEN, you would put 5 points next to #2 in the Pts. column. If you answered SOMETIMES, you would put 3 points next to #2. And if you answered SELDOM for #2, you would list 1 point in the Pts. column. Work your way down the VISUAL column until you've recorded your scores for numbers 7, 10, 14, 16, 22, 26, and 32 of the survey. After recording the scores in this column, add up the points in the VISUAL column and record the total at the bottom next to VPS=. Move next to the AUDITORY column and insert the appropriate number of points for each survey statement. Total the points at the bottom next to APS=. Then complete the TACTILE column and finally the KINESTHETIC column. Your highest score will tell you what your preferred learning style is.

Scoring Procedures:

OFTEN = 5 points
SOMETIMES = 3 points
SELDOM = 1 point

Place the point value on the line next to its corresponding item number. Next, add the points to obtain the preference scores under each heading.

Visual		**Auditory**		**Tactile**		**Kinesthetic**	
No.	Pts.	No.	Pts.	No.	Pts.	No.	Pts.
2	_____	1	_____	4	_____	3	_____
7	_____	5	_____	6	_____	9	_____
10	_____	8	_____	12	_____	13	_____
14	_____	11	_____	15	_____	17	_____
16	_____	18	_____	20	_____	19	_____
22	_____	21	_____	27	_____	23	_____
26	_____	24	_____	30	_____	25	_____
32	_____	28	_____	31	_____	29	_____
VPS =		APS =		TPS =		KPS =	

VPS = Visual Preference Score
APS = Auditory Preference Score
TPS = Tactile Preference Score
KPS = Kinesthetic Preference Score

Study Tips for Different Learning Styles

Directions: Use the study tips outline for your first learning preference and then reinforce what you are learning with tips from your second preference. When you have extra time, work on strengthening your weaker sensory areas. Remember that if several of your scores are within 4 or 5 points of each other, then you can use any of those senses for learning.

I. Tips for Visual Learners (those who learn by seeing/visualizing)

1. Write down anything you want to remember, such as a list of things to do, facts to learn for a test, etc.

2. Try to write down information in your own words. If you don't have to think about the material and restate it in your own words, you won't really learn it.

3. Underline or highlight important words you need to learn as you read.

4. When learning a new vocabulary word, visualize the word.

5. When you have a list of things to remember, keep the list in a place where you will be sure to see it several times a day. Suggestions: bulletin board by your desk at home, in your notebook, on the mirror in the bathroom, etc.

6. Try drawing a picture of any information you want to learn. Try making a diagram, a chart, or actually drawing people, things, etc.

7. Always read any material in the textbook before going to class so you have a chance to visually connect with the information before hearing it.

II. Tips for Auditory Learners (those who learn through hearing/listening)

1. Use a tape recorder to record notes when reading instead of writing facts down. Play it back while you are riding in the car, doing dishes, washing the car, jogging, etc.

2. Subvocalize—that is, talk to yourself about any information you want to remember. Try to recite it without looking at your notes or the book.

3. Discuss with others from your class and then quiz each other on the material. Really listen to yourself as you talk.

4. When learning a new vocabulary word, say it out loud. Then spell it out loud several times. See if it rhymes with a word you know. You could even try singing the word in a song.

5. To learn facts, say them out loud, put the facts to music or read them into a tape recorder. Then listen often to what you have recorded.

6. When writing, talk to yourself. First, tell yourself what you will write, say it out loud as you write it, and then read aloud what you have written or tape record it.

7. Always read material in your textbook to be learned after hearing the information first in the class lecture (unless the instructor assigns the reading first before class so you can participate in class discussions).

III. Tips for Tactile Learners (those who learn through touch/tracing)

1. Try to study through practical experiences, such as making models or doing lab work.

2. Trace words and letters to learn spelling and to remember facts.

3. Use the computer to reinforce learning through the sense of touch.

4. Recopy your notes as you study for an exam.

5. Write facts to be learned on 3" x 5" cards, with a question on one side and the answer on the other.

6. When working with a study group, think of T.V. quiz games (*Jeopardy*, etc.) as ways to review information.

IV. Tips for Kinesthetic Learners (those who learn through physical activity)

1. Take frequent, short breaks (5–10 minutes) in study periods.

2. Memorize or drill while walking, jogging, or exercising.

3. Try expressing your abilities through dance, drama, or sports.

4. Try standing up when you are reading or writing.

5. Write facts to be learned on 3" x 5" cards, with a question on one side and the answer on the other. Lay out the cards, quiz yourself, shuffle them, lay them out again, and quiz yourself again.

6. When working with a study group, think of T.V. quiz games (*Jeopardy*, etc.) as ways to review information.

7. Study through role playing.

V. Tips for Multisensory Learners (Any Combination of the Above Styles)

Use any combination of the above study tips. It may take some experimentation before you find the best techniques for you.

Activity

Making the Most of Your Learning Style

Find other classmates who share your learning style. (If you don't get the chance to do this with classmates, work individually or with a tutor.) Review the study tips for your learning style and try to rewrite each tip so that it applies specifically to the work you do in this class. Then choose another class you are taking and rewrite the tips so that they specifically work for that class. You may also want to do this for your second learning style.

USING THE DICTIONARY

The following section on using the dictionary will help you see what an important tool the dictionary is to the writer, the student, and the person in the work world.

Every college student should own (and carry, if possible) a good dictionary, because the dictionary can help you

- spell,
- define words,
- find the right verb forms, and
- find other forms of a word.

The next four subsections will help you understand how the dictionary works and how you can use the dictionary for the purposes listed above.

Using the Dictionary to Spell

Imagine that you are working on an essay about Anne Frank's diary. You have typed the following quote into your essay and returned Frank's diary to the library. You're editing your essay, and you want to make sure you've spelled *recapture* correctly.

> I can shake off everything if I write; my sorrows disappear, my courage is reborn. But, and that is the great question, will I ever be able to write anything great, will I ever become a journalist or a writer? I hope so, oh, I hope so very much, for I can recapture everything when I write, my thoughts, my ideals, and my fantasies.

> —Anne Frank (1929–1945)
> *diary entry 4/4/44,* Diary of a Young Girl

A word like *recapture* is fairly easy to look up in a dictionary. By sounding out the word, you know to begin by looking up words beginning with *re*. Then you can narrow your search to words beginning with *reca* or *reka*, and by scanning the entries on the page, you will find *recapture*.

Other words might be more difficult to find when you are unsure of the spelling. Do your best to sound them out and then scan the dictionary pages. Other options include asking a tutor, instructor, or friend to help you get started. You can also try using an electronic dictionary or a computer dictionary. The advantages to these two kinds of dictionaries are that you can type in a word by the way it sounds to you, and often, but not always, the electronic or computer dictionary can figure out what you are looking for.

Be aware, too, that sometimes you may look up a word in the dictionary and not find it because it is in a form that is not listed. For example, if you looked up *recapturing,* you would not find it listed in bold print in its own entry in the dictionary. With *recapturing,* you would simply look for a form of the word that is listed in bold print, then check that entry to see if the form you want is listed. In other words, you'd look up *recapture* and find *-turing* toward the front of the entry. This tells you the word is spelled *recap + turing.* In other situations, you may find the form you want listed at the end of an entry.

Finally, if you are using a computer to complete your essays, you can use spell check. This is a program that will check your writing for you. But be careful not to rely on it too much. A spell-check program cannot catch wrong word errors. (For example, if you typed in *recapturing* instead of *recaptures,* spell check would see nothing wrong with your work. A more common problem is when a writer mixes up words like *their/there* or *to/too* or *its/it's.* Spell check does not help in these situations, either.)

Activity

Using the Dictionary to Correct Misspellings

Look up the following misspelled words in a dictionary to find the correct spellings. If you can, use an electronic or computer dictionary for three of them. Write down the correct spelling next to each word and where you found it (book, computer, or electronic dictionary).

assend (to climb upwards)

bankrupped (having no money)

filanthropist (someone who gives to charities)

rationnaly (reasonably)

gord (like a squash or pumpkin)

cresent (shape of a partial moon)

seperate (to keep apart)

perpatrator (someone who commits a crime)

Using the Dictionary to Find Word Meanings

Imagine that you're unsure just what *recapture* means in the Frank quote. You want to find the meaning in the dictionary.

> I can shake off everything if I write; my sorrows disappear, my courage is reborn. But, and that is the great question, will I ever be able to write anything great, will I ever become a journalist or a writer? I hope so, oh, I hope so very much, for I can recapture everything when I write, my thoughts, my ideals, and my fantasies.
>
> —*Anne Frank (1929–1945)*
> *diary entry 4/4/44*, Diary of a Young Girl

The dictionary says,

¹**re•cap•ture** \(ˌ)rē-ˈkap-chər\ *n* (1752) **1 a:** the act of retaking **b:** an instance of being retaken **2:** the retaking of a prize or goods under international law **3:** a government seizure under law of earnings or profits beyond a fixed amount
²**recapture** *vt* (1799) **1 a:** to capture again **b:** to experience again <by no effort of the imagination could she ∼ the ecstasy—Ellen Glasgow> **2:** to take (as a portion of earnings or profits above a fixed amount) by law or through negotiations under law*

When you look at a dictionary entry, you can't just pick any part of the entry and apply that information to the word and sentence you are interested in. *Recapture*, for example, can be a transitive verb or a noun. The *n* and *vt* tell us that. You have to figure out how the word you want to define is being used. In the quote above, *recapture* is being used as a verb, so you should pay attention to the second entry ²**recapture** *vt*. The dictionary gives two verb definitions. The first definition has two parts. Part *a* might fit what Frank is saying. Part *b* seems even closer, especially when you consider the example from Ellen Glasgow. The second definition doesn't seem to fit at all. Using the first definition, you can figure out that writing helps Frank to experience again her thoughts, ideals, and fantasies.

So, remember that when you are looking up a word for meaning, look carefully at the other words in the sentence and surrounding sentences. These other words are the context that you must study so that you can choose the right definition in the dictionary.

---

*By permission. From *Merriam-Webster's Collegiate® Dictionary*, Eleventh Edition © 2007 by Merriam-Webster, Incorporated (www.Merriam-Webster.com).

Activity

Finding Meanings in the Dictionary

Find definitions for the eight words in italics in the following reading. This is part of the introductory section to Marie Winn's essay "The Trouble with Television." Make sure that the definitions you write down fit how the words are used in this context.

1   Of all the wonders of modern technology that have *transformed* family life during the last century, television stands alone as a universal source of parental *anxiety*. Few parents worry about how the electric light or the automobile or the telephone might *alter* their children's development. But most parents do worry about TV.

2   Parents worry most of all about the programs their children watch. If only these weren't so violent, so sexually *explicit*, so *cynical*, so unsuitable, if only they were more innocent, more educational, more worthwhile.

3   Imagine what would happen if suddenly, by some miracle, the only programs available on all channels at all hours of day and night were delightful, worthwhile shows that children love and parents wholeheartedly approve. Would this eliminate the nagging anxiety about television that troubles so many parents today?

4   For most families, the answer is no. After all, if programs were the only problem, there would be an obvious solution: turn the set off. The fact that parents leave the sets on even when they are *distressed* about programs reveals that television serves a number of purposes that have nothing to do with the programs on the screen.

5   Great numbers of parents today see television as a way to make child-rearing less *burdensome*. In the absence of Mother's Helper (a widely used nineteenth-century patent medicine that contained a hefty dose of the *narcotic* laudanum), there is nothing that keeps children out of trouble as reliably as "plugging them in."

Using the Dictionary to Find Verb Forms

I can shake off everything if I write; my sorrows disappear, my courage is reborn. But, and that is the great question, will I ever be able to write anything great, will I ever become a journalist or a writer? I hope so, oh, I hope so very much, for I can recapture everything when I write, my thoughts, my ideals, and my fantasies.

—Anne Frank (1929–1945)
diary entry 4/4/44, Diary of a Young Girl

Assume that you are writing an essay, and you want to relate your own experiences to what Anne Frank says in her diary entry. You like the way she says, "I can shake off everything if I write." You want to say, "I too have shaked (?) off troubles when writing." The problem is that you're not sure if *shaked* is the right form of the verb. Dictionary entries list verb forms so that you can easily find information like this.

If you go to www.Merriam-Webster.com and type in *shake,* you'll see a screen that says **shake** *9 entries found.* Shake [1, verb] will be highlighted in a boxed list of words. Below the box you'll see the word, the pronunciation, the function (in this case, *verb*), and the inflected forms (meaning other forms of the word).*

Notes

shook ◄))\\'shu̇k\\; **shak•en** ◄))\\'shā-kən\\; **shak•ing**

Dictionaries generally follow the same format. With an irregular verb like *shake*, a dictionary will first give its *base form* (shake), then its *past tense form* (shook), then its *have form* or *past participle form* (shaken), then (sometimes) its *present participle form* (shaking).

You can now see that the sentence is incorrect: "I too have shaked(?) off troubles when writing." The dictionary says that after the helping verb *have* you should use *shaken*. The correct sentence would read: "I too have shaken off troubles when writing."

Activity

Verb Forms in the Dictionary

Look up the following irregular verbs in the dictionary and make a chart that shows their base form, past tense form, and *have* form.

(*Note:* With some irregular verbs, the past tense and the *have* form are the same. For example, *lose*—base form, *lost*—past tense form, and *lost*—have form.)

For a discussion of irregular verbs and a list of the most common irregular verbs, see pages 498–503.

1. arise	6. hold
2. bid	7. keep
3. burst	8. leave
4. forget	9. prove
5. hide	10. slide

---

*By permission. From *Merriam-Webster's Collegiate® Dictionary*, Eleventh Edition © 2007 by Merriam-Webster, Incorporated (www.Merriam-Webster.com).

Using the Dictionary to Find Other Forms of a Word

> I can shake off everything if I write; my sorrows disappear, my courage is re-born. But, and that is the great question, will I ever be able to write anything great, will I ever become a journalist or a writer? I hope so, oh, I hope so very much, for I can recapture everything when I write, my thoughts, my ideals, and my fantasies.
>
> —*Anne Frank (1929–1945)*
> *diary entry 4/4/44,* Diary of a Young Girl

One effective way to improve your vocabulary is to pay attention to the different forms a word can take. If, for example, you added the word *ideal* (from the Frank quote) to your vocabulary notebook, you might notice in the dictionary all the words listed before and after *ideal: idea, idealism, idealist, idealistic, ideality,* and *ideally.* Being aware of and studying word forms is key to communicating clearly, and your dictionary can help you.

Consider the following sentences in which writers have used the wrong form of a word:

1. He is headed down a *destructional* way.
2. People are judged by what they *product* on the job.
3. He works without *supervise.*

   (*from* Errors and Expectations, *Mina Shaughnessy*)

In sentence 1, the writer needs an adjective to describe *way.* In sentence 2, the writer needs a verb for the subject *they.* In sentence 3, the writer needs a noun to follow *without.*

These writers may have sensed that they weren't using the correct form of the word they wanted. When a writer knows or thinks that she has used the wrong form of a word, the dictionary is a perfect resource.

Activities

Correcting Word Forms

In the dictionary, look up the misused words in examples 1–3 (*destructional, product, supervise*) and list the different forms you find. Choose the correct forms for sentences 1–3 and rewrite the sentences.

Studying Word Forms

Write down the definitions of words 1–5 that follow and the different forms you find in the dictionary. Write down what part of speech each form represents: *n.* (noun), *v.* (verb), *adj.* (adjective), or *adv.* (adverb). Make sure that the new words you write down connect at least loosely in meaning to the word you look up.

 Example:
a. organize:

- *organize (verb) to put together in an orderly fashion*

- *organizer (noun)* [found at the end of the entry defining *organize*]

- *organization (noun)*

(But don't include *organist.* It looks similar, but doesn't connect in meaning.)

 1. illusive:

 2. glorify:

 3. simplify:

 4. violent:

 5. empathy:

BUILDING YOUR VOCABULARY

Writing, reading, and critical thinking grow more interesting, more complex, and more rewarding as your vocabulary grows. With a larger vocabulary, you'll do all of the following:
- understand your readings more easily and more completely,
- express your own thoughts more clearly and accurately, and
- think through complex concepts defined with difficult vocabulary more easily.

 In this subsection, you'll study the steps to building a better vocabulary.

Read and Recognize Vocabulary Choices

The first step in working on your vocabulary is to read as much as you can. This is the most natural (and painless) way to improve your vocabulary. If you don't currently read much, begin by reading materials that seem easy and interesting to you. Make reading a regular part of your day. Periodically, push yourself to read something different or something that seems more difficult. This way you'll be exposed to a larger variety of words.

Enjoying what you read is key to improving your vocabulary because if you don't relax and enjoy, you probably won't read much. You should also get into the habit of recognizing the choices writers make when selecting their words. Writers want their writing to be clear and compelling, and, fortunately, the English language offers many word choices.

Consider what it would be like if we only had "good" and "bad" as our adjectives. ("Dinner was good. The band was bad. The dancing was bad. The dessert was good.") Not only would our language be repetitive, but we also would be incredibly limited in the feelings and information that we could communicate to others.

John Krakauer, author of *Into Thin Air*, demonstrates in the following paragraph the powerful results of making good vocabulary choices. He is describing how exhausted he was when he reached the top of Mount Everest and, consequently, how he couldn't quite appreciate the moment.

> Straddling the top of the world, one foot in China and the other in Nepal, I cleared the ice from my oxygen mask, hunched a shoulder against the wind, and stared absently down at the vastness of Tibet. I understood on some dim, detached level that the sweep of the earth beneath my feet was a spectacular sight. I'd been fantasizing about this moment, and the release of emotion that would accompany it, for many months. But now that I was finally here, actually standing on the summit of Mount Everest, I just couldn't summon the energy to care.

Instead of saying "standing at the summit," he says, "Straddling the top of the world, one foot in China and the other in Nepal." The image he paints with these words is clearer and more interesting. Instead of saying he "looked down into Tibet," he says he "stared absently down at the vastness of Tibet." With these words, we get a better sense of the incredible sight in front of him and, importantly, his inability at that time to really appreciate the view.

By noticing other writers' choices, you will deepen your understanding of how certain words are used, and you will become more aware of the choices you make in your own writing. You will begin to see opportunities to clarify your thoughts through your choice of vocabulary words.

Defining Words Through Context Clues

Of course, recognizing and admiring the choices other writers make is just the first step in building your vocabulary. The next step is for you to learn new words as you read, and contrary to what you might think, going to the dictionary is not the first step to understanding unfamiliar words.

It is important to be able to figure out the meanings of unfamiliar words by considering the *context* in which they appear. This means that you should consider the entire sentence and nearby sentences when trying to figure out the meaning of a word. Other words and other sentences will often give you clues as to what the unfamiliar word means. Doing this well will save you time—since you won't have to reach for the dictionary so often—and you are more likely to develop a deeper understanding of the word in question by studying how it is used.

For example, the word *banal* in the following paragraph might be unfamiliar to you. Read the entire paragraph, highlight the word *banal*, and study the rest of the paragraph for clues to the meaning of *banal*.

> [Krakauer has just reached the summit of Everest and has realized he is out of bottled oxygen; he is worried about how he will make it down the mountain with no extra oxygen.] I removed my now useless [oxygen] mask, planted my ice ax into the mountain's frozen hide, and hunkered on the ridge. As I exchanged banal congratulations with the climbers filing past, inwardly I was frantic: "Hurry it up, hurry it up!" I silently pleaded. "While you guys are [goofing around] here, I'm losing brain cells by the millions!"

Krakauer tells us clearly that he is frightened about what will happen to him. He is "frantic," "pleading," yelling at people in his mind. What kind of congratulations would he offer other people when he is feeling this way? Well, he wouldn't be offering sincere, joyful congratulations. He would probably be saying what was expected without really feeling the happy emotions. *Banal* is an adjective you can use to describe something unoriginal, worn out, and flat.

Activity

Context Clues in Textbooks

Find a reading in this textbook that you have not read yet that has at least three words you are unfamiliar with. Read the entire paragraph(s) in which

> the words appear. Write down the words that are unfamiliar to you, the context clues you find for each word, and the meanings you figure out on your own. (Also, write down the name of the reading, page numbers, and paragraph numbers.) Then compare your definitions to the dictionary definitions.

Keeping a Vocabulary Notebook

Whether you are confident that you have figured out what a word means through context clues or whether you have used a dictionary, the next step is to record the new word and information about the new word. Simply writing down information helps you remember it. Then referring back to and studying what you have written brings you even closer to the point at which these new words will become a part of your everyday vocabulary. (Be sure to enter in your notebook all unfamiliar words you come across in *all* of your classes—not just your English class.)

An entry in your vocabulary notebook should look like this:

Vocabulary word	*demure* (from *Into Thin Air*)
Sentence it showed up in	"Demure and reserved, the forty-seven-year-old Namba was forty minutes away from becoming the oldest woman to climb Everest . . . "
Meaning in context	I think it means quiet.
Information from dictionary	It is an adjective. Pronunciation: di•myoor' Other forms of the word: demurely (adverb), demureness (noun) Definition: Sedate in manner or behavior; reserved, shy

Activity

> **Vocabulary Notebook**
>
> Return to the words you defined in the activity, "Context Clues in Textbooks," on pages 471–472. Add these new words and their definitions to your vocabulary notebook. Be prepared to share them with your instructor and classmates.

Writing out all this information will help you learn new words, but don't stop there. You must actually *use your notebook*. Study the words you enter in your notebook. Study words while brushing your teeth, riding the bus, ironing clothes, and so on. Quiz classmates.

Also, take a chance now and then and *use your new words* when you speak and write. The words might feel a little awkward at first, but you must use them to make them a permanent part of your vocabulary.

Special ESL Vocabulary Concerns

If English is not your first language, then you may have special vocabulary concerns. Consider the following suggestions:

A. Read and write in English as often as possible. Of course, you'll have required work in college, but you should also read for pleasure in English. Find a magazine or novel that interests you and read. Begin keeping a journal in English. You can write about what happens during your days; you could focus on your school experiences; you could write about what you're reading for pleasure. A journal simply gives you another opportunity to use your English.

B. Speak English as often as possible. Join study groups at your college. Work with an English-speaking tutor.

C. Listen to English. Television is helpful for this, but an even better choice is to listen to books on CD. You can check these out from libraries or purchase them at bookstores. Sometimes you can find unabridged novels on CD, and you can then read while also listening to the CD.

Here are some suggestions for audio books:

- *Into Thin Air: A Personal Account of the Mount Everest Disaster* by Jon Krakauer

- *To Kill a Mockingbird* by Harper Lee (story about race relations in the South, a young girl growing up, and the trial of a black man)

- *A Night to Remember* by Walter Lord (sinking of the *Titanic*)

- *Wouldn't Take Nothing for My Journey Now* by Maya Angelou (reflections on some of the lessons Angelou has learned in her life)

Note: Most contemporary best-sellers are on CD. (See books by Stephen King, John Grisham, and so on.)

D. Keep an idiom notebook. There are many English idioms, and the only way to learn them is by memorization since rules don't apply.

An **idiom** is an expression that may not make sense if you translate it directly word by word. Here are some sample idiom notebook entries.

kicked the bucket: died

got up on the wrong side of the bed: woke up in a bad mood

caught a movie: watched a movie

caught a bus or *took a bus:* rode a bus

dumped that class or *dumped that girl (or boy):* stopped attending that class or stopped dating that girl (or boy)

tie the knot: marry

SPELLING MATTERS

Developing spelling skills is an important part of your progress as a student, writer, and employee because often your writing meets people before you do.

- You may send a résumé or letter of inquiry about a job.
- You may fill out an application for college admission.
- You may communicate through letters or e-mail.

First impressions are important. Whether you think it's fair or not, you may be judged in the business world and in college by the number of spelling errors appearing in your writing because many see the ability to spell as an indication of intelligence and literacy.

In the age of computers and spell check, employers and professors consider spelling errors avoidable and unacceptable. In the business world, misspellings detract from the overall quality of an employee's work and could cost the company a client or business opportunity. In college, misspellings could result in a student receiving a lower score on an essay or project.

The fact is that many people struggle with spelling and dread the thought of memorizing endless lists of spelling words in order to improve. However, there are some strategies that you can learn and practice to improve your skills and reduce the number of spelling errors.

This section offers a combination of explanation and action strategies to help you strengthen your spelling skills:

- You'll discover why spelling errors occur.
- You'll learn some practical strategies for overcoming individual spelling issues.
- You'll review the spelling of plurals, verbs, and homophones.
- You'll learn when to use the apostrophe.

As you begin this section, it's important to recognize that spelling difficulties are unique to the individual. There is no one-size-fits-all solution, but there are some basic things that you can do to help yourself become a more accurate speller.

Understanding Spelling

English is a language that has been evolving over centuries. As written English developed, people were fairly relaxed when it came to spelling and simply spelled words according to sound. However, spelling according to pronunciation posed a communication problem, since the pronunciation of words varied from region to region. As the language evolved, some people began to fear that words would lose their connection to sounds.

By the late eighteenth century, Benjamin Franklin and others had begun to lobby for a standardized and more simplified system of spelling. Today, many still believe that spelling should be simplified. But for now, here are some basic facts that help explain why spelling can be difficult:

- In English, a single sound may be spelled in several different ways. For example, examine the different spellings of the sound *sh* in *shell, sugar, ration, anxious, occasion, pressure,* and *champagne.*
- Some letters in English are silent in certain situations. Think about the silent *k* in *k*nife as opposed to the spoken *k* in *k*ite, or the *p* in *p*neumonia as opposed to *p*arty.
- Spelling in English is less consistent than in some other languages, such as Spanish, in which letters and sounds are often matched.

Notes

- English contains many words that sound alike but have different spellings and meanings. Consider the difference in meaning between *here* and *hear,* or *to, too,* and *two.*
- English is a blend of many languages, which helps explain why our spelling system is inexact.

Even though English contains some irregular spellings, you should also know that most English spellings follow basic, rational patterns or "rules." Only a few vary completely from the patterns and must therefore be memorized.

Why Spelling Errors Occur

As you've seen, there are some reasons why spelling can be difficult in general. However, there are also reasons why spelling may be difficult for the individual.

- Those with less reading experience may have trouble recognizing misspellings in their own writing.
- Those with less writing experience may sometimes scramble letters within a word.
- Those with less experience speaking English or those who do not fully pronounce words may find it difficult to spell by sound.
- Those who don't know how to break words into syllables or form word variations (such as plurals or verb tenses) may make spelling errors that otherwise could be avoided.

Overcoming Spelling Problems

Although it may seem too easy to suggest that by writing, reading, and speaking more, your spelling will improve, the fact is that it will. Just as reading skills improve as you read more and writing skills improve as you write more, your spelling will improve as you read and write. But there are many other things you can also do to develop your spelling skills.

The Spelling Log   Perhaps one of the easiest ways to help yourself become a better speller is to carry a small 3" x 5" spiral notebook with you. In it, you would keep a list of problem words—words that cause *you* trouble—spelled correctly. When faced with a situation in which you must write, you would have your personal spelling list with you. Of course, you would add to this list as you begin to be more aware of your spelling and the kinds of spelling errors you're making consistently.

- While editing essays in a workshop, a classmate finds a misspelling (not a typo) in your essay. You would add it to your list.

- When you receive your essay back from your instructor, you would check for any misspellings your instructor found and then add them to your list.

- As you're reading, you notice a word that you realize you've been misspelling. You would add it to your list.

Keeping a personal spelling list means that you're taking responsibility for your spelling and becoming more aware of your own repeated spelling errors.

Spell Check   Most computer writing programs today come with spell check, a program that identifies possible misspellings in papers and documents. Basically, spell check works by searching the computer's dictionary and highlighting any words that don't appear in the dictionary. In most cases, when spell check highlights a word, it will offer a list of suggested spellings. It's likely that the correctly spelled word is in that list. If so, you only need to select the correct spelling, and the program will replace the incorrect spelling in the paper. Spell check also identifies possible capitalization errors and repeated words errors. You should use spell check whenever you write on a computer, especially during the editing stage of the writing process. If your spelling skills are particularly weak, you should type out all of your homework on a computer (in addition to your essays) and then use spell check before turning it in. (There are many variations of spell check. If you're working in a computer lab, ask the computer technician to show you how to use it the first time.)

Spell check does have a few drawbacks, however. When a misspelling is highlighted, and you've been given a list of suggested spellings, don't assume the correct spelling for the word will always be on the list. It may not be. If it isn't, you'll need to go to the dictionary to find that word. Also, spell check will not catch words that sound alike but have different meanings (such as *to, too,* and *two*). If you're trying to decide between using *hear* or *here,* for instance, go to the dictionary or to

Notes   "The Right Word" in Section V of this text and look up the meanings of the words. Finally, spell check might not identify errors in proper names and places, so when editing your paper, be sure to check these spellings yourself.

The Dictionary   The dictionary is an invaluable spelling tool. Not only does the dictionary give you the spelling of a word, but it also offers the plural of nouns, and, for verbs, the basic tenses. When in doubt about how to spell a word, you can always look it up in the dictionary.

But how do you look up a word if you don't know how to spell it? Usually you do so through trial and error, looking up the word by pronunciation and then trying slightly different variations of spelling until you find the word. If you find looking up words in the dictionary nearly impossible, however, you might benefit from a misspeller's dictionary.

The Misspeller's Dictionary   A misspeller's dictionary contains two columns of words: one column lists words as they are typically misspelled and a corresponding column lists the same words spelled correctly. For instance, in such a dictionary, you might see the following entries:

Incorrect	Correct
eco	echo
eightteen	eighteen

Often this type of dictionary also contains a section on **homophones** (words that sound alike but have different meanings) and their meanings, such as *find* (locate) and *fined* (given a penalty).

The Spelling List   Another speller's tool is a pocket-size spelling list. In it, words have been broken into syllables so that they're easier to look up according to pronunciation:

bi•og•ra•phy   re•cant   ty•po

Such spelling lists include the correct spellings for the most commonly misspelled words.

Both the misspeller's dictionary and the spelling list are light and small enough to carry with you everywhere.

A Review

The spelling log, spell check, dictionary, and misspeller's dictionary will certainly help you cut down on the number of spelling errors in your writing. But there are a few areas of spelling that students find particularly troublesome. In this subsection, we'll review the spellings of plurals, the past-tense form and *have* form of verbs, homophones, contractions, and possessives.

Plurals   Change a noun from singular to plural according to the following rules:

- To form the plural of most nouns, add *s* to the word: *tree* to *trees, action* to *actions.*
- To form the plural for nouns ending in *s, ss, sh, ch, x,* and *z* (a hissing sound called a **sibilant** sound), add *es* to the word: *church* to *churches, hush* to *hushes, box* to *boxes, kiss* to *kisses.*
- To form the plural for nouns ending in *o,* add *s* or *es* to the word, depending on the word: *hero* to *heroes, stereo* to *stereos.* (*Note:* Since some of the words ending in *o* are followed by *s* and some are followed by *es,* you should look them up in the dictionary when you're uncertain.)
- To form the plural of a noun that ends in *y* when preceded by a vowel, add *s: toy* to *toys, monkey* to *monkeys.*
- To form the plural of a noun that ends in *y* when preceded by a consonant, change the *y* to *i* and add *es: party* to *parties, rally* to *rallies.*

Not all plurals are formed by adding *s* or *es.* Some words are adopted from other languages and keep their original plural spellings. Others are simply irregular plurals, exceptions to the rules mentioned above. Here are a few examples:

Singular	Plural
analysis	analyses
child	children
criterion	criteria
datum	data
foot	feet
goose	geese

Notes

Singular	Plural
man	men
medium	media
moose	moose
mouse	mice
tooth	teeth
woman	women

When in doubt about forming a plural, look up the singular form of the word in the dictionary. You'll find the plural form of the word listed after the singular form.

Verb Tense   The past-tense form and the *have* form of verbs pose spelling problems for students only when these forms are irregular. In most cases, the past-tense form and *have* form are easy to spell. Simply add *ed* to the end of the base form or add just *d* if the base form ends in *e*.

Examples of regular verbs:

Base	**Past**	*Have*
generate	generate*d*	generate*d*
talk	talk*ed*	talk*ed*

Examples of irregular verbs:

Base	**Past**	*Have*
drive	dr*o*ve	driv*en*
sing	s*a*ng	s*u*ng

When you have questions about verb forms, you can look up the base form in the dictionary. After the base form, you'll find the past-tense form, the *have* form, and finally the *-ing* form. (If the past-tense form and *have* form are the same, the dictionary will list that form once.) Or you can check the "Common Irregular Verbs" chart on pages 499–500 of the text for spellings of the most common irregular verbs.

Homophones   Homophones are words that sound alike but are spelled differently and have different meanings. Homophones cause problems for students who may believe they're spelling words correctly when, in fact, they're spelling the *wrong* words correctly. This is another instance in which your dictionary is an invaluable tool. When in doubt about which spelling to use, look it up. Another resource in this text is "The Right Word" on pages 534–537, which contains a listing of words that are often confused such as *to, too,* and *two. (To* means *toward a particular direction: I traveled to Paris to see the Mona Lisa. Too* means *also: My husband went, too. Two* is the number: *We discovered two can travel for the price of one.)*

Apostrophe   The **apostrophe** is used in two very different ways in English. It's used to form possessives—my *daughter's* new car—and contractions—she *can't* drive yet. Because the apostrophe is used in such different ways, students are often confused about when and how to use the apostrophe. We'll examine both uses.

Contractions   A **contraction** is a word with an apostrophe in it. The apostrophe indicates where letters have been left out.

- *it + is = it's*
- *had + not = hadn't*
- *she + would = she'd*

Notice that *it's* is a contraction of the words *it* and *is.* Also note that the apostrophe shows where a letter has been left out. In the second example, *hadn't* is a contraction of the words *had* and *not.* In this case, too, the apostrophe shows where a letter is missing. And the apostrophe in *she'd* is a contraction of *she* and *would.* The apostrophe shows where several letters have been left out. *In a contraction, the apostrophe indicates where a letter or letters have been left out.*

Activity

Practice in Forming and Using Contractions

Change the following word combinations into contractions. Look up any you're unsure of in your dictionary.

1. he + would = _____

2. what + is = _____

3. can + not = _____

4. will + not =_____

5. should + have =_____

6. I + have =_____

7. you + are =_____

8. do + not =_____

9. it + will =_____

10. we + are =_____

Now write four or five sentences that use all of the contractions you've just formed. (You can use more than one contraction in each sentence.)

Possessives   A **possessive** is a word that shows ownership. In this subsection, you'll learn to form the possessives of nouns and pronouns. In addition, you'll learn the special rules that apply when forming the possessive of proper nouns.

Forming the Possessive of Nouns

To form the possessive of a singular noun, use an apostrophe + *s*.

- The student's goal is to become a doctor.
- My puppy's tail wags whenever I pet her.

To form the possessive of a plural noun, just add an apostrophe.

- The students' desks are arranged in a circle.
- The ladies' lunches were delivered late.

Note: Irregular plurals (those not ending in *s*) require an apostrophe + *s*.

- The children's toys were scattered across the day care floor.
- The men's volleyball team challenged the women's volleyball team to a game.

Forming the Possessive of Proper Nouns

To form the possessive of a **proper noun** (a specific name or title), use an apostrophe + *s*.

- Justin Timberlake's new hit reached the top of the charts.
- President Bush's State of the Union Address was telecast on all major networks.

- Jennifer Lopez's new film will be out next week.
- Ed Harris's Oscar nomination brought him lots of attention.

Activity

Practice Forming Possessives

Change the following nouns into possessives:

1. lady to _____

2. ladies to _____

3. man to _____

4. men to _____

5. child to _____

6. children to _____

7. actress to _____

8. actor to _____

9. twins to _____

10. instructors to _____

Change the following proper nouns into possessives:

11. Joie to _____

12. Hopkins to _____

13. Miles to _____

14. Inez to _____

15. Cruiz to _____

16. Lewis to _____

17. Olts to _____

18. Jones to _____

19. Thomas to _____

Once you've formed the possessive of each noun, use five of the newly formed possessives in two or three sentences.

Notes

Forming Possessive Pronouns

There are two basic types of pronouns: personal and indefinite. **Personal pronouns** (which refer to specific persons, places, or things) *do not need* apostrophes to show ownership, but **indefinite pronouns** (which refer to nonspecific persons or things) *do need* apostrophes to indicate ownership.

- Personal pronouns *do not need* apostrophes to show possession. They include *hers, his, its, mine, ours, theirs,* and *yours.* Consider this sentence: Samantha earned *her* degree. Because *her* is a personal pronoun, no apostrophe is necessary.

- Indefinite pronouns *do need* apostrophes to show possession. Add *'s* to indefinite pronouns when showing possession: *anybody's, anyone's, everybody's, nobody's,* and *somebody's.* Study this sentence: *It was anybody's game.* Because *anybody* is an indefinite pronoun, an *'s* must be added to show possession.

Activity

Practice Using Personal and Indefinite Pronouns

Write five sentences that include personal pronouns (no apostrophes) and five that include indefinite pronouns (with apostrophes) that show possession.

READING ALOUD: A TRICK OF THE TRADE

Most professional writers routinely read their own writing aloud. They know that reading aloud will help them identify weaknesses in their writing.

Here is a writing scenario that might be familiar to you:

> A student works hard on her essay. She follows all the process steps. The student is proud of the final version of her essay: it is interesting, thoughtful, carefully created. The student takes the time to proofread and is sure that the essay is nearly perfect.
>
> The instructor reads the essay and appreciates the thoughtful meaning in the essay. The instructor responds to the ideas and offers suggestions about how to keep improving writing skills. The instructor sees places where the student needs more information and needs to delete or move information. The instructor also notes <u>many</u> spelling, grammatical, and typographical errors.

The student appreciates the instructor's writing suggestions, and wonders why she didn't see those spots that clearly need some improvement. And the student is shocked at the number of minor errors in what she thought was a perfect paper. How did the student miss all those spelling, grammar, and typing errors?! The student feels discouraged.

This scenario is fairly common. Sometimes writers are surprised that they didn't see the weak spots in their papers. Mostly, this is a normal part of acquiring good writing skills, but it can also be a sign that the writer hasn't been able to see her paper objectively.

Now, the mechanical errors (spelling, typing, and grammar errors) may seem minor, but they can confuse the reader, and they certainly ruin a professional image.

Being a good reviser and proofreader takes time and practice. The more you read and write, the better you will get, provided you don't rely on a tutor or friend to do your revising or proofreading work for you. However, there are a few ways to acquire good revising and proofreading skills *more quickly*. One method is to *read aloud*.

Reading Aloud Helps When You Revise

Students at California State University, Sacramento, were required one semester to read all of their essays aloud into tape recorders. Students were amazed at all the problems and errors they found in their essays. On the tapes they would say things like, "American students don't study enough. That's why they score lower than students in other countries. Hmm . . . I bet I need some proof here." Or, "The woman murdered her husband. She is against capital punishment. Oh, that sounds funny. That doesn't flow." Reading aloud helped these students see their writing more clearly, more objectively.

There are, in fact, many benefits to reading aloud. If you read your essays aloud frequently, you will find places

- to add information,
- to delete unnecessary information, and
- to add transitions or move information.

And reading aloud while writing your essay will help you get going again if you lose focus or run out of things to say. Reading aloud is a tool professional writers rely on:

Notes

We spoke before we wrote, historically and individually. Writing is not quite speech written down but it is speech transformed so that it may be heard. The voice lies silent within the page, ready to be turned on by a reader.

We know our language best by hearing it and speaking it. Writing is an oral/aural act and we do well to edit out loud, hearing the text as we revise and polish it. Should we add this, slow that down, speed it up here, take time to define this term, use this word, this construction? What is traditional and expected by the reader? What best supports and communicates the meaning of the draft? These questions can often be answered by reading the line out loud, taking something out and reading it out loud, putting something in and reading it out loud. Hand, eye, and ear, a constant interplay.

—Donald Murray, American novelist, poet,
Pulitzer Prize–winning journalist, and writing instructor

Reading Aloud Helps When You Edit

Finally, when you are proofreading (editing) your essay, read aloud frequently. Don't leave this to the last minute because you may find areas where you left out a whole sentence, or you may find minor errors that you want to fix on the computer or typewriter before handing in your work. Look for these kinds of errors:

- Misspelled words
- Missing words/sentences
- Wrong words
- Words repeated or used too often
- Punctuation errors
- Subject-verb agreement errors
- Verb tense errors
- Run-ons, comma splices, and fragments

Activity

Reading Your Own Writing Aloud

Read aloud a piece of your writing that has not yet been seen by anyone else. (Ideally, you should read a draft of an essay, but a journal entry or even answers to reading questions will do.) Read your writing several times. Mark any errors or problems that you see now that you hadn't seen before.

Reading Aloud Helps You Develop a Writer's "Ear"

Experienced writers, like Donald Murray, who was quoted earlier in this section, have what we call an "ear" for language. They know what *sounds* good. By reading material aloud, they can easily hear punctuation errors, awkward sentences, and weak spots in focus, development, or organization. You can improve your "ear" for language by reading good pieces of writing aloud. Here are some recommendations:

- Choose an essay out of this textbook each week and read it aloud at home.
- Participate in class when your instructor wants to read an essay aloud.
- Choose something you really like to read (a newspaper, magazine, novel, or poem) and read aloud to your spouse, significant other, or children.
- Listen to books on CD (available at bookstores and libraries).

If you do some or all of these activities, you will improve your

- vocabulary,
- sense of how sentences should flow, and
- sense of how writers can focus, develop, and organize writing.

Some Final Notes About Reading Aloud

- When a piece of reading is very difficult to understand, try reading it aloud. (Students find it especially helpful to read aloud such things as famous speeches, poetry, and works by Shakespeare because these were meant to be heard.)
- Read to your children. Your "ear" for language will improve and, besides, study after study shows that reading aloud to children helps children build their vocabularies, their "ear" for language, their problem-solving skills, and so on.
- When you read aloud in private, you will be preparing yourself for those situations at school and work when you must present oral reports.
- When you read aloud, note words that you are unsure about pronouncing. Look in a dictionary and study the pronunciation information. Ask a tutor or instructor how to pronounce these words.

They are bound to show up again (perhaps when you need to make an oral report).

Activity

Reading Angelou Aloud

The following reading is a chapter from Maya Angelou's *Wouldn't Take Nothing for My Journey Now*. Angelou, a poet and writer, is well-known for the "voice" in her writing. Her vocabulary and sentence structure make her meaning nearly sing off the page. Read this aloud and enjoy the power of Angelou's voice. (Her book is available on CD.)

Complaining

When my grandmother was raising me in Stamps, Arkansas, she had a particular routine when people who were known to be whiners entered her store. Whenever she saw a known complainer coming, she would call me from whatever I was doing and say conspiratorially, "Sister, come inside. Come." Of course I would obey.

My grandmother would ask the customer, "How are you doing today, Brother Thomas?" And the person would reply, "Not so good." There would be a distinct whine in the voice. "Not so good today, Sister Henderson. You see, it's this summer. It's this summer heat. I just hate it. Oh, I hate it so much. It just frazzles me up and frazzles me down. I just hate the heat. It's almost killing me." Then my grandmother would stand stoically, her arms folded, and mumble, "Uh-huh, uh-huh." And she would cut her eyes at me to make certain that I had heard the lamentation.

At another time a whiner would mewl, "I hate plowing. That packed-down dirt ain't got no reasoning, and mules ain't got good sense. . . . Sure ain't. It's killing me. I can't ever seem to get done. My feet and my hands stay sore, and I get dirt in my eyes and up my nose. I just can't stand it." And my grandmother, again stoically with her arms folded, would say, "Uh-huh, uh-huh," and then look at me and nod.

As soon as the complainer was out of the store, my grandmother would call me to stand in front of her. And then she would say the same thing she had said at least a thousand times, it seemed to me. "Sister, did you hear what

Brother So-and-So or Sister Much-to-Do complained about? You heard that?"
And I would nod. Mamma would continue, "Sister, there are people who went
to sleep all over the world last night, poor and rich and white and black, but
they will never wake again. Sister, those who expected to rise did not, their
beds became their cooling boards and their blankets became their winding
sheets. And those dead folks would give anything, anything at all for just five
minutes of this weather or ten minutes of that plowing that person was grumbling
about. So you watch yourself about complaining, Sister. What you're supposed
to do when you don't like a thing is change it. If you can't change it, change the
way you think about it. Don't complain."

It is said that persons have few teachable moments in their lives. Mamma
seemed to have caught me at each one I had between the ages of three and
thirteen. Whining is not only graceless, but can be dangerous. It can alert a
brute that a victim is in the neighborhood.

USING OUTSIDE SOURCES

Citing sources can get very complicated and must be done with precision. The guidelines here will help you use outside information for the assignments in this book. Other classes may require you to learn more about citing sources, so be sure to ask your instructor about the appropriate handbook for you to use in other classes.

Introduction to Outside Sources

An **outside source** is a person or publication that supplies you with information.

Outside information is any fact or idea that someone other than you came up with.

A writer often uses information from other sources when writing her own essay, book, or article. Sometimes a writer will use something she heard on television or in a speech. Sometimes a writer will use something she read in an encyclopedia, a newspaper, a textbook, or a magazine. There are many places to get useful information.

Guidelines A–E will help you get started on using outside sources.

Notes

A. Why Writers Use Outside Sources

- A writer may hear or read something interesting and want to discuss it in more detail.
- A writer may come across an idea she disagrees with and want to argue against it.
- A writer may find information that supports something she already wants to discuss.

B. Selecting Outside Sources

Of course, a writer can't use information from just anywhere. The source of the information must be one that readers will respect. For example, a writer should use information from a reputable publication or a recognized expert. Readers might not believe information that comes from a gossip magazine, and they might not be too interested in what your neighbor down the street once dreamt about aliens from outer space. Choose your sources carefully. When doing research, keep careful notes on where you get your information. Write down the following source information whenever possible:

> author
>
> title (of book, or title of essay or article with the title of the magazine or newspaper it appeared in)
>
> date
>
> page number
>
> volume number (when the source is a journal or encyclopedia)

C. Quantity of Outside Sources

You can use a little outside information or a lot of outside information, depending on what you are writing. In a cover letter for your résumé, you probably wouldn't use many (if any) outside sources. In a scientific report, you'd probably use many outside sources. Most of the college essays you write will call for *some* outside information. Here's a good general rule: Outside information should play a supporting role to what you have to say. That is, your ideas should come first and take center stage. If you are ever worried about having too many pieces of outside information in your writing, highlight all information that you borrowed from an outside source. If you highlight more than a third of your essay, you probably have too much outside information and too few of your own original ideas.

D. Where to Use Your Outside Sources

Generally, you want to use the quotes and borrowed information in the body of a paragraph. Sometimes you can start a paragraph with a quote, but usually you need to begin with a topic sentence. Rarely, you can put outside information at the end of a paragraph. Usually, you, as the writer, must interpret outside information. You must explain it and analyze it for the reader. Otherwise, your reader might interpret the information in ways you don't expect.

E. The Most Important Thing to Remember About Outside Sources

Interpret, explain, and analyze your outside information. Readers don't want a bunch of quotes. They want your well-supported ideas.

Read the following paragraph.

I think most people believe that only "super" humans doing incredible acts bring about significant, positive change in our world. I know I used to think that way. It wasn't until I read Paul Rogat Loeb's essay "Civil Rights Movement Was the Sum of Many People" that I began to reshape my thinking. Loeb, author of *Soul of a Citizen: Living with Conviction in a Cynical Time*, says that "change is the product of deliberate, incremental action, whereby we join together to try to shape a better world." The key terms here are "deliberate" and "incremental." Change could happen by accident, but more often it is planned, and it is the result of many smaller steps, not just a single media-attracting event. I find this comforting because change seems more attainable if average people can take small steps toward it.

—*Terry Mason*

Activity

Following the Guidelines for Citing Sources

Review guidelines A–E. Explain whether or not Mason follows each of these guidelines. Discuss each guideline and how it is or is not followed.

Using Outside Information

When you use ideas and information that belong to someone else, you must give that person credit. If you do not do this, you'll be guilty of **plagiarism.** In some cultures, it is common practice to copy the words of an expert without mentioning the expert. Such a practice stems from the idea that copying these words is the writer's way of saying,

Notes

"These are better words and ideas than I could ever come up with." However, in American colleges and businesses, writers are expected to give credit to the person who first came up with the idea or information. Plagiarism can be grounds for being dismissed from a college or job, so it is important that you know how to use outside information and give credit to the person who first stated the information. Giving credit to the original sources is called **citing your sources.** (The information that follows focuses mainly on how to use quotations. However, even if you put someone else's ideas into your own words and you don't use quotation marks, you must still say where you got these ideas.)

First, you should know that information that is considered "general knowledge" doesn't have to be cited. For example, if you are writing an essay about George Washington, and you find his birthdate in an encyclopedia, you do not have to cite this encyclopedia. Washington's birthdate can be found in many different sources: It is considered general knowledge.

However, if you want to use a piece of information that cannot be found in many different places, you must say where you got the information.

There are many ways of incorporating a quotation into your essay. Here are five of the most common patterns. The sample quotation comes from the essay "Civil Rights Movement Was the Sum of Many People" by Paul Rogat Loeb which appears on pages 204–206. (When you introduce a quotation, put a comma after the introductory phrase and capitalize the first word in the quotation. Pattern #5 is different because of the word *that*.)

According to the introductory material on page 204, Loeb is the author of a book called *Soul of a Citizen: Living with Conviction in a Cynical Time.* This information helps establish Loeb's credibility as a source worth quoting.

Pattern #1: *Paul Rogat Loeb, author of* Soul of a Citizen: Living with Conviction in a Cynical Time, *states: "Parks' journey suggests that change is the product of deliberate, incremental action, whereby we join together to try to shape a better world."*

[Author's name], [author information], states:

Pattern #2: *In "Civil Rights Movement Was the Sum of Many People" Paul Rogat Loeb, author of* Soul of a Citizen: Living with Conviction in a Cynical Time, *states: "Parks' journey suggests that change . . . ."*

In [name of the article] [author's name], [author's info.], states:

Pattern #3: *According to Paul Rogat Loeb, author of* Soul of a Citizen: Living with Conviction in a Cynical Time, *"Parks' journey suggests that change . . . ."*

According to [author's name], [author's info.],

or

According to [name of article],

If the writer had already introduced Paul Rogat Loeb and explained his status as an expert, the writer could have just said the following:

Pattern #4: *Loeb states, "Parks' journey suggests that change . . . ."*

[Author's last name] states,

Pattern #5: *Loeb states that "Parks' journey suggests that change . . . ." or Loeb states that "change is the product of deliberate, incremental action . . . ."*

[Author's name] states that [no capital letter at the beginning of the quote unless the quote begins with a proper noun]

You can introduce quotes with a variety of words and phrases. Here are some examples:

Loeb states,

Loeb explains,

Loeb observes,

Loeb suggests,

Loeb notes,

Note: The first time you use a source, it is a good idea to explain who or what your source is. If your source is a person and the person is an expert, what is this person's job title? Where does he or she work? If the source is a journalist, for what magazine or newspaper does the journalist write? If you are using statistics, from what government agency or private company did you get the statistics? Your reader is more likely to trust your information if you include these kinds of details.

Activity

Practice in Citing Sources

1. Choose some interesting quotes from "Civil Rights Movement Was the Sum of Many People," pages 204–206. Write five sentences

Notes

showing that you can use each of the five different quoting patterns. Be very careful that you punctuate correctly and use capital letters when necessary.

2. Review other readings and find some other patterns for using quotes. (Look in the newspaper, textbooks, magazines, and so on.) Write down three quotes you find that have slightly different patterns than the five mentioned here.

Using Connections *Online with* PEARSON **mywritinglab**

For more practice with mastering your study skills, log onto www .mywritinglab.com to access the online resources for *Connections*, Third Edition.

Understanding, Correcting, and Avoiding Sentence Errors

This section of Connections *reviews six kinds of sentence errors that can do the most damage to clear communication. The information and exercises in this section will help you understand why writers sometimes make these errors, how to correct each kind of error, and how to avoid making these errors in the future.*

- Understanding, correcting, and avoiding verb form errors
- Understanding, correcting, and avoiding verb tense errors
- Understanding, correcting, and avoiding subject-verb agreement errors
- Understanding, correcting, and avoiding fragments
- Understanding, correcting, and avoiding run-ons
- Understanding, correcting, and avoiding comma splices

Notes

UNDERSTANDING, CORRECTING, AND AVOIDING VERB FORM ERRORS

In this section, you'll study verb form errors. In particular, you'll work on

- understanding verb form errors,
- correcting verb form errors, and
- avoiding verb form errors.

Understanding Verb Form Errors

A verb form error occurs when a writer uses the wrong form of a verb. Here are examples of verb form errors:

> Yesterday, I <u>beginned</u> my assignment.
>
> The cook <u>freezed</u> the leftover meat.
>
> Simone <u>choosed</u> the most challenging task.

Here are those same sentences using correct verb forms:

> Yesterday, I <u>began</u> my assignment.
>
> The cook <u>froze</u> the leftover meat.
>
> Simone <u>chose</u> the most challenging task.

This subsection reviews verb tenses and then focuses on two verb forms that can be a little tricky for writers.

As you may remember, verbs can come in a number of different forms depending on what tense they are in. In Chapter 2, you reviewed the simple tenses: the present, past, and future. Here are sentences using those tenses and a few other tenses you may not have studied yet (although you already use them when you speak and write).

> Today, I <u>walk</u> to the river. (present tense)
>
> Yesterday, I <u>walked</u> to the river. (past tense)
>
> Tomorrow, I <u>will walk</u> to the river. (future tense)
>
> I <u>have walked</u> to the river every day since I was fifteen. (present perfect tense)
>
> (The *present perfect tense* helps you show that an action took place in the past and continues to take place.)
>
> After I <u>had walked</u> to the river, I decided to call the game warden. (past perfect tense)

(The *past perfect tense* shows that an action took place at a nonspecific time in the past or that the action took place before another time or action.)

I <u>am walking</u> to the river. (present progressive tense)

(The *present progressive tense* shows that an action is continuing.)

I <u>was walking</u> to the river. (past progressive tense)

(The *past progressive tense* shows that an action started and continued in the past.)

There are even a few more tense variations not listed here!

Don't worry; you don't need to memorize all of these different tenses. To avoid the most common verb form errors, you really only need to study and be aware of three verb forms: the *base form,* the *past tense form,* and the *have form* (also called the *past participle form*) which is used with the perfect tenses.

The base form of a verb is the form you would look up in the dictionary. It is in the present tense and has no special endings.

work

I <u>work</u> for the school district.

print

I <u>print</u> my name neatly.

save

The firefighters <u>save</u> the child.

The **past tense form** is the form you use when writing in the past tense. Verbs in the past tense usually end in *-ed*.

worked

Last year, I <u>worked</u> for the school district.

printed

Yesterday, I <u>printed</u> my name neatly.

saved

Yesterday, the firefighters <u>saved</u> the child.

The *have* form (or the **past participle form**) is the form you would use when writing in one of the perfect tenses mentioned earlier. The **present perfect tense** is formed by using *has* or *have* plus the verb in the *have* form. This tense will tell the reader one of two things: the action took place in the past and continues to take place in the present, or the action took place at a nonspecific time in the past.

worked

> He <u>has worked</u> for the school district for the last four years. (The action in this sentence took place in the past and continues to take place in the present so the present perfect tense fits.)

printed

> I <u>have printed</u> my name neatly. (The action in this sentence occurred at a nonspecific time in the past so the present perfect tense fits.)

The **past perfect tense** is formed by using *had* plus the verb in the *have* form. This tense tells the reader that the action took place before another time or action in the past. Most often, you will use this tense with words like *before* and *after*. Don't use the past perfect form unless you are comparing two past times. (It is a common mistake for students to use *had* unnecessarily.)

saved

> After the firefighters <u>had saved</u> the child, the parents were arrested for child neglect. (The "saving" takes place in the past before the arresting.)

For a review of past participles (*have* form verbs) working as adjectives, see pages 175–179.

The *have* form of a verb can also be transformed into an adjective to describe nouns. When acting as an adjective, the *have* form will not have *has*, *have*, or *had* in front of it. In the next two examples, the verb is underlined twice. In the second sentence, you'll see a highlighted *have* form verb that has been transformed into an adjective.

> I <u>have printed</u> three copies of the letter.
> The printed word <u>is</u> not always true. (*Printed* is now an adjective describing *word*.)

The next two sentences also include *have* form verbs that have been transformed into adjectives. The verbs are underlined twice. The *have* form verbs that are working as adjectives are highlighted.

> The watched pot never <u>boils.</u>
> The disciplined student <u>studied</u> for hours.

So far we have focused on regular verbs. **Regular verbs** are verbs that change tense in a predictable way: add *-ed* to create the past tense or the *have* form (past participle form). The tricky part—which sometimes leads to a verb form error—comes when irregular verbs are used. **Irregular verbs** change form in unpredictable ways when they change tenses. The sentences at the beginning of this chapter all had irregular verbs: *begin*, *freeze*, and *choose*. You can look up these words in the chart that follows. (The chart does not name *all* irregular verbs, but it does name quite a few.) Notice how the past tense is not created by simply adding *-ed,* and notice that the *have* form is often different from the past tense (unlike with regular verbs).

Notes

Common Irregular Verbs

Base	Past	*Have* Form
awake	awoke, awaked	awakened, awaked
be	was	been
become	became	become
begin	began	begun
bite	bit	bitten, bit
blow	blew	blown
break	broke	broken
bring	brought	brought
build	built	built
buy	bought	bought
catch	caught	caught
choose	chose	chosen
come	came	come
cost	cost	cost
cut	cut	cut
dive	dived, dove	dived, dove
do	did	done
draw	drew	drawn
dream	dreamed, dreamt	dreamed, dreamt
drink	drank	drunk
drive	drove	driven
eat	ate	eaten
fall	fell	fallen
feel	felt	felt
find	found	found
fit	fit, fitted	fit, fitted
fly	flew	flown
freeze	froze	frozen
get	got	got, gotten
give	gave	given
go	went	gone
grow	grew	grown
hear	heard	heard
hit	hit	hit
know	knew	known

The first column shows the base form, which is the form you'd look up in the dictionary. The second column shows the past tense of the verb. The third column shows the *have* form (also called the past participle form). You can use this chart as a reference tool. You can also find the correct form of any irregular verb by looking in the dictionary. The dictionary lists irregular verbs in this same order—base form, past form, and *have* form. See "Using the Dictionary" on pages 463–469 for more information.

Notes

Base	Past	*Have* Form
lay [to put or place]	laid	laid
lead	led	led
let	let	let
lie [to recline]	lay	lain
pay	paid	paid
put	put	put
ride	rode	ridden
ring	rang	rung
rise	rose	risen
run	ran	run
say	said	said
see	saw	seen
set [to place]	set	set
shake	shook	shaken
shine	shone, shined	shone, shined
shrink	shrank	shrunk
sing	sang	sung
sit [to be seated]	sat	sat
speak	spoke	spoken
spring	sprang	sprung
steal	stole	stolen
swim	swam	swum
take	took	taken
teach	taught	taught
tear	tore	torn
throw	threw	thrown
wake	woke, waked	waked, woken
wear	wore	worn
win	won	won
write	wrote	written

There are no rules to explain irregular verbs. You have to memorize them or look them up in a dictionary. (Or you can refer to the chart provided here.)

Practice #1 Using the Correct Verb Form
In the following exercises, fill in the blanks with the correct verb forms.

• Read your answers aloud when you are done. (Reading these sentences aloud will help you check your work and will help you develop an "ear" for correct verb forms.)

Examples: Today I go to the farmer's market and buy all the vegetables for the week.

Using past tense verbs: Yesterday, I _____ to the farmer's market and _____ all the vegetables for the week.

- Yesterday, I _went_ to the farmer's market and _bought_ all the vegetables for the week.

Sharon catches a beautiful trout.

Using the _have_ form to create the present perfect tense: Sharon _____ a beautiful trout.

- Sharon _has caught_ a beautiful trout.

Felix dives into the water.

Using the _have_ form to create the past perfect tense: Before Felix _____ into the water, I sensed that this was not going to turn out well.

- Before Felix _had dived_ into the water, I sensed that this was not going to turn out well.

1. My neighbor's dog bites the mailman. Using a past tense verb: My neighbor's dog _____ the mailman.

2. The judge speaks to the media. Using a past tense verb: The judge _____ to the media.

3. The sun rises and wakes the campers. Using past tense verbs: The sun _____ and _____ the campers.

4. I feel that we need to rethink donating money to that cause. Using the _have_ form to create the present perfect tense: For some time now, I _____ that we need to rethink donating money to that cause.

5. Kenny's act draws a huge crowd. Using the _have_ form to create the past perfect tense: Before his trouble with the law, Kenny's act _____ a huge crowd.

6. My kids grow into responsible adults. Using the _have_ form to create the present perfect tense: My kids _____ into responsible adults.

Notes

7. I am happy to volunteer on Saturday. Using a past tense verb: I _____ happy to volunteer on Saturday. (*Hint: Am* is a form of *be*.)

8. The father becomes worried about the kids. Using a past tense verb: (write the whole sentence)

_____

_____

9. He steals the last cookie from the plate. Using the *have* form to create the present perfect tense: (write the whole sentence)

_____

_____

10. Martin Luther King Jr. speaks his mind. Using a past tense verb: (write the whole sentence)

_____

_____

Practice #2   Creating Sentences with *Have* Form Verbs as Adjectives

Part One

Write the *have* form of each irregular verb in the blank.

break   _____

- break   *broken*

1. freeze   _____
2. choose   _____
3. drive   _____
4. steal   _____
5. write   _____

Part Two

For a review of *have* form adjectives, see pages 356–357.

Referring to the list of *have* form verbs in Part One, use a *have* form verb as an adjective modifying the subject in each sentence.

Example: The bicycle was worthless.

- The *broken* bicycle was worthless.

1. Her confession was a surprise to everyone.
2. The scientist dedicated his life to finding a cure.
3. The smile on her face didn't seem genuine.
4. The jewelry would be hard to sell.
5. Only a few would be allowed to visit the laboratory.

Practice #3   Creating Sentences Using Irregular Verbs

Create the sentences described in the following exercises.

1. Create a sentence that is in the past tense. Use an irregular verb.
2. Create a sentence that is in the present perfect tense. Use an irregular verb.
3. Create a sentence that is in the past perfect tense. Use an irregular verb.

Correcting Verb Form Errors

Practice #4   Correcting Verb Form Errors

In the following exercises, find the verb form errors and rewrite the sentences on another piece of paper, correcting the errors. Read the correct sentence aloud to check your work and further develop your "ear" for correct verb forms.

1. Last year, I builded an outdoor fireplace in my backyard.
2. Before I had drawed the final plans, my brother gave me some suggestions for making the fireplace more energy efficient.
3. After much consideration, I choosed the gray bricks.
4. The gray bricks costed a bit more than the standard red bricks.
5. After I had layed the last brick, I decided we should have a party to celebrate.
6. My project payed off nicely.
7. When we refinanced, the appraiser sayed that the fireplace added $15,000 to the price of our home.

Avoiding Verb Form Errors

If you tend to make verb form errors, you should check all of your verbs at the editing stage of your writing process. Keep a list of irregular verbs

Notes that you have misused before, perhaps with your spelling words, so that you can easily check your work.

UNDERSTANDING, CORRECTING, AND AVOIDING VERB TENSE ERRORS

In this section, you'll study verb tense errors. In particular, you'll work on

* understanding verb tense errors,
* correcting verb tense errors, and
* avoiding verb tense errors.

Understanding and Correcting Verb Tense Errors

For a further review of verb tense, go to Chapter 2, pages 74–76.

As you may remember from Chapter 2, verbs can change tense. In fact, they are the only types of words that can change tense. There are quite a few different tenses in English. Review the different verb tenses in the following sentences:

Present tense: I talk with my friends.

Past tense: Yesterday, I talked with my friends.

Future tense: Tomorrow, I will talk with my friends.

Present progressive tense: I am talking with my friends.

Past progressive tense: I was talking with my friends.

Future progressive tense: I will be talking with my friends.

See pages 496–498 to review the perfect tenses.

There are also the perfect tenses and the future progressive tenses, but for the purposes of this section, we will focus on just the simple tenses to help you understand, correct, and avoid unnecessary verb tense shifts.

Shifting between verb tenses unnecessarily can ruin clear communication. Your readers expect you to be consistent with your verb tenses. Shifting between verb tenses is like jumping around in time. Readers find this confusing. These sentences, for example, are confusing because they use different tenses:

Years ago, young women rarely <u>went</u> to college. They <u>expect</u> to be housewives.

The first verb, *went,* is in the past tense, which seems appropriate since the writer is looking back in history. The second verb, *expect,* is in the present tense. This is confusing. Is the writer now talking about modern society? Here are the sentences with consistent verb tenses:

Years ago, young women rarely <u><u>went</u></u> to college. They <u><u>expected</u></u> to be housewives.

Now both verbs are in the past tense, and the idea in the sentence is clearer.

These two sentences suffer from unnecessary shifts in verb tense:

I <u><u>volunteer</u></u> at the local soup kitchen. (present tense)

I <u><u>met</u></u> interesting people. (past tense)

The sentences are clearer when they are both written in the same tense:

I <u><u>volunteer</u></u> at the local soup kitchen. (present tense)

I <u><u>meet</u></u> interesting people. (present tense)

Occasionally, you may need to shift tenses within a paragraph or even a single sentence:

If I <u><u>am</u></u> late today, I <u><u>will lose</u></u> my job.

In this case, the first verb is in the present tense, and the second verb is in the future tense. However, this shift makes sense because the writer is thinking about being late now and what will happen in the future. The general rule, however, is to consistently use the same tense throughout a piece of writing.

Practice #1   Correcting Shifts in Verb Tense

- Underline the verbs twice.
- Find the verb tense errors.
- On a separate piece of paper, correct the sentences so that the verbs in each pair of sentences are in the same tense.
- Underline the verbs twice in your sentences.

For a review of verbs, see pages 28–37 and pages 74–81 in Chapters 1 and 2.

Example: The woman updates her résumé. She sent it with a cover letter to two prospective employers.

- The woman <u><u>updates</u></u> her résumé. She <u><u>sent</u></u> it with a cover letter to two prospective employers.
- The woman <u><u>updates</u></u> her résumé. She <u><u>sends</u></u> it with a cover letter to two prospective employers.

1. Kevin cuts the article out of the newspaper. He wanted to show it to his roommate, Hal.

Notes

2. The article compares the salaries of college graduates to non-college graduates. Kevin wanted to encourage Hal to keep trying.

3. Recently, Hal failed a class. The bad grade surprises Hal.

4. He thought that he was doing okay in the class. However, he rushes through his final assignment.

5. Now, Hal wonders if he belongs in college. He thought about taking some time off.

6. Once, I thought about dropping out. My dad says okay—on one condition.

7. He said that I needed to have a good alternative plan. I do not have a better plan than finishing school.

8. I stayed in school, and I earn my degree.

9. Now, I am relieved to have my degree because the job I had required a degree.

10. Besides helping me to get a good job, earning my degree turned out to be a great experience. Last week, I apply to the graduate program at the university in town.

Practice #2 **Reviewing Verb Tense**

Read the following paragraph and decide what tense it should be in.

- Then rewrite the paragraph on a separate piece of paper.
- Underline the verbs.
- Change the tense of any verbs that are incorrect.

My last essay was about technology and required some research. I enjoy doing the research. In fact, I learn a lot about hidden surveillance cameras in stores and even schools. One store I visited had cameras hidden in plants. I share my findings with my classmates. One of my classmates interviews the security officer at an insurance firm. She learns about their fingerprint scanner and their voice recognition system. Another student described the high-tech security tools that she saw at the airport. Yesterday, the instructor handed back the essays. She said they were very interesting because we spend so much time researching and discussing the reading in the book.

Practice #3   **Manipulating Verb Tense**
Write a paragraph on any topic of your choice. Use the present tense. Then rewrite the paragraph using the past tense. Underline all verbs in both paragraphs.

Practice #4   **Applying Your Verb Tense Knowledge**
Select a piece of your writing—a journal entry or essay—that has verb tense errors in it. Rewrite the piece, correcting all verb tense errors.

Avoiding Verb Tense Errors

If you frequently make verb tense errors, you should check all your verbs at the editing stage of your writing process. You may want to place a piece of paper over your essay and reveal one sentence at a time. Find the verb in each sentence and see if it is in the right tense. With time and practice, you will find that you make fewer verb tense errors.

UNDERSTANDING, CORRECTING, AND AVOIDING SUBJECT-VERB AGREEMENT ERRORS

In this section, you'll learn about subject-verb agreement errors. In particular, you'll work on

- understanding subject-verb agreement errors,
- correcting subject-verb agreement errors, and
- avoiding subject-verb agreement errors.

Understanding and Correcting Subject-Verb Agreement Errors

Subject-verb agreement errors can be very distracting to your reader. A **subject-verb agreement error** means you have used a plural subject with a singular verb or that you have used a singular subject with a plural verb. Both of these sentences have subject-verb agreement errors.

She ask a question. (singular subject with a plural verb)

They votes for the new program. (plural subject with a singular verb)

To insure clear communication, subjects and verbs must agree in number. If you have a singular subject, you must have a singular verb. If you have a plural subject, you must have a plural verb. **Plural** means more than one. For example, *they* and *we* are both plural.

This sentence has a singular subject and a singular verb:

She asks a question.

Now this sentence has a plural subject and a plural verb:

They ask a question.

Notice how the subject and verb change when you move from the singular to the plural:

She votes for the new program. (singular subject and verb)
We vote for the new program. (plural subject and verb)

Writers make subject-verb agreement errors for a couple of different reasons:

- When we speak, we may not hear how some verbs end in *s* and some don't. Therefore, when we write, we might forget to pay attention to how verbs should end.
- If you speak in a dialect that has different rules for verb endings, you might not use the verb endings that standard American English requires. In academic writing, subjects and verbs must agree in number.

Third Person Singular, Present Tense

The most common time for people to make a subject-verb agreement error is when they are using third person singular, present tense. For example, these sentences have subject-verb agreement errors:

Instructor Smith work with students after class.
She enjoy getting to know her students.

Here are the sentences with no subject-verb agreement errors:

Instructor Smith works with students after class.
She enjoys getting to know her students.

The following chart demonstrates the rule to remember: When you use *he, she,* or *it* (or another third person singular word) in the present tense, put an *s* or *es* on the verb.

	Singular	Plural

First Person (the person speaking)	I
	    work
	    kiss
	    write
		we
		    work
		    kiss
		    write

Second Person (the person or people being spoken to)	you
	    work
	    kiss
	    write
		you
		    work
		    kiss
		    write

Third Person (the person or people being spoken about)	he, she, it
	
	Or any word that can be used instead of *he, she,* or *it* (examples: Mr. Smith, the police officer, the child)
	    work*s*
	    kiss*es*
	    write*s*
		they
		    work
		    kiss
		    write

The following chart shows some irregular verbs. (There are present tense *and* past tense verbs listed here.)

	Singular	Plural

First Person (the person speaking)	I
	    do
	    am
	    was
		we
		    do
		    are
		    were

Second Person (the person or people being spoken to)	you
	    do
	    are
	    were
		you
		    do
		    are
		    were

Third Person (the person or people being spoken about)	he, she, it
	
	Or any word that can be used instead of *he, she,* or *it* (examples: Mr. Smith, the police officer, the child)
	    does
	    is
	    was
		they
		    do
		    are
		    were

Notes

Practice #1   Practicing Subject-Verb Agreement

• On a separate piece of paper, rewrite these sentences in the third person singular. (Your subject in each new sentence will be *he, she, it,* or another word that can be used instead of *he, she,* or *it.*)

• Use the present tense.

• Underline the verbs twice.

Example: I write an essay about television.

• He <u>writes</u> an essay about television. (It would be acceptable to use a name like *Steven* or a phrase like *my classmate* instead of *he.*)

1. Analyzing the song, I decide to listen to it a couple more times.
2. I ask the tutor to respond to my analysis. (*Hint:* Remember to change *my* when you revise the sentence.)
3. We listen to George's explanation.
4. They are anxious to hear our response.
5. I enjoy analyzing songs and poems.
6. I am now interested in taking a film analysis class.
7. I begin my essay with a comparison of two different songs.
8. They recite the poem.
9. I go to the poetry reading.
10. I do an excellent job.

Practice #2   Creating Sentences with Subjects and Verbs That Agree

Create the sentences described below. Use the present tense only.

1. Create a sentence that uses *I* as the subject. Then write the sentence again and change the subject to *he.* Make sure your subjects and verbs agree in number.
2. Create a sentence that uses *we* as the subject. Then write the sentence again and change the subject to a proper name (like *Frank* or *Mrs. Carlisle*). Make sure your subjects and verbs agree in number.

Indefinite Pronouns

Writers often make mistakes with subject-verb agreement when using indefinite pronouns as subjects. For example, this sentence has a subject-verb agreement error:

<u>Everyone</u> <u>decide</u> to go to the theater.

Here is the same sentence written correctly:

<u>Everyone</u> <u>decides</u> to go to the theater.

This is the rule to remember: Generally, indefinite pronouns are considered to be third person singular and require singular verbs.

The following list provides examples of indefinite pronouns.

any	*everybody*	*no one*
anybody	*everyone*	*someone*
anyone	*nobody*	*something*
anything	*nothing*	*somebody*

These sentences are written correctly:

<u>Everybody</u> <u>agrees</u> to turn off the television for a week.

<u>Somebody</u> <u>takes</u> notes.

Practice #3   Subject-Verb Agreement at the Movies

In the following sentences, the subjects are indefinite pronouns, and they do not agree in number with the verbs.

- Underline the subjects once.
- Underline the verbs twice.
- On another sheet of paper, rewrite these sentences, correcting the subject-verb agreement errors. Use *only* the present tense. Underline the verb twice.

Example: No one want to ask the first question.

- <u>No one</u> <u>want</u> to ask the first question.
- No one <u>wants</u> to ask the first question.

1. Nobody want to miss the movie.
2. Nothing scare him like a movie about spiders.
3. Everybody agree to meet after the movie.

4. No one like the movie.

5. Somebody suggest a comedy for the next film.

6. Something in this film remind me of an old Hitchcock film.

7. Someone in our group send a reminder to each of us.

8. Everyone gather for the next movie.

Practice #4   Using Indefinite Pronouns and Maintaining Subject-Verb Agreement

Create the sentences described below. Use the present tense.

1. Create a sentence that uses *everyone* as the subject.

2. Create a sentence that uses *no one* as the subject.

3. Create a sentence that uses *nothing* as the subject.

Phrases Can Create Confusion

If a subject and verb are separated by a long phrase, it can be easy to make a subject-verb agreement error. For example, this sentence has a subject-verb agreement error:

A tutor from one of the learning centers <u>help</u> dedicated students.

Here is the sentence correctly written (with a singular subject and verb):

A <u>tutor</u> from one of the learning centers <u>helps</u> dedicated students.

Remember that you won't find your subject or verb in a prepositional phrase, so you can bracket the prepositional phrases and see your subject more clearly. You can then make sure that the subject and verb agree. (See pages 78–79 for a review of prepositional phrases.)

A <u>tutor</u> [from one of the learning centers] <u>helps</u> dedicated students.

This sentence has a subject-verb agreement error:

Computers in the classroom is an asset to writing students.

Bracketing the prepositional phrase makes it easier to see and correct the error. Here is the sentence correctly written.

<u>Computers</u> [in the classroom] <u>are</u> an asset [to writing students].

Also, remember that *-ing* words are not verbs unless they have a helping verb in front of them. Sometimes descriptive *-ing* phrases can

If you follow Style Tip #1 (page 120), you would also move the prepositional phrase so that it doesn't come between the subject and verb. *In the classroom, computers are an asset to writing students.*

cause confusion with subject-verb agreement. You may want to cross out descriptive *-ing* phrases to help you see the subject and verb more clearly. This sentence, for example, has a subject-verb agreement error:

> The students listening to music in the pub is taking a break from studying.

Here is the sentence again. The descriptive *-ing* phrase has been crossed out, the prepositional phrase has been bracketed, and the subject-verb agreement error has been corrected:

> The students ~~listening to music in the pub~~ <u>are taking</u> a break [from studying].

Practice #5   Watching Out for Phrases

There are subject-verb agreement errors in these sentences.

- Bracket prepositional phrases and cross out descriptive *-ing* phrases.
- Underline the verbs twice and the subjects once.
- On a separate piece of paper, rewrite these sentences (including the prepositional and *-ing* phrases) so that there are no subject-verb agreement errors.
- Underline the verbs twice.
- Use the present tense.

Example: The advertisement, representing the downtown stores, are printed in black and white.

- The <u>advertisement,</u> ~~representing the downtown stores,~~ <u>are</u> printed [in black and white].
- The <u>advertisement,</u> representing the downtown stores, <u>is</u> printed in black and white.

  1. The words at the top of the ad encourages people to come shopping for a special gift for Valentine's Day.
  2. The pictures of chocolates and lingerie is at the top of the ad.
  3. The words, describing a decline in romantic feelings over many years of marriage, brings your eye down to the last image—a vacuum.
  4. The final sentences of the advertisement encourages people of all ages to come to the mall.

5. My mom, having been married for 35 years, think the ad is offensive.

6. My dad, laughing at the not-so-hidden messages, decide to go to the mall for a vacuum.

7. One of my classmates in my psychology class bring me two advertisements.

8. The ad advertising milk and its high content of calcium show a little girl standing next to an enormous dinosaur skeleton.

9. The colors and facial expressions in the ad about Cartier diamonds makes me think of romance.

10. The women in the commercial wearing the jewelry looks very happy.

Practice #6   Create Sentences with Phrases

Create the sentences described in the following exercises. Use only the present tense. Make sure your subjects and verbs agree.

1. Create a sentence that begins with these words: *The man explaining the rules to the children and their parents*

2. Create a sentence that begins with these words: *The children next to the fountain by the trees*

3. Create a sentence that has a descriptive *-ing* phrase (participial phrase) in the middle.

4. Create a sentence that has two prepositional phrases that come right after the subject and before the verb.

There *and* Here *Sentences*

Sentences that begin with *there* or *here* don't have clear subjects; neither *there* nor *here* will be the subject, so subject-verb agreement errors are easy to make. This sentence, for example, has a subject-verb agreement error:

There <u>is</u> two people in the advertisement.

Here is the sentence correctly written:

There <u>are</u> two people in the advertisement.

With *there* and *here* sentences, the subject will come after the verb in the sentence. Find the subject and make sure that your subject and verb agree in number. For example, this sentence has a subject-verb agreement error:

Notes

Here is the marketing information and the product description.

With the verb and subject identified, the error is clear:

Here <u>is</u> the <u>marketing information</u> and the <u>product description.</u>

Here is the sentence correctly written:

Here <u>are</u> the <u>marketing information</u> and the <u>product description.</u>

You may also want to revise the sentence and get rid of the *there* or *here* since *there* and *here* sentences aren't always effective. This sentence, for example, can be revised and made stronger:

There <u>are</u> four people employed in this office.

The sentence can be revised and given a stronger, clearer verb and subject.

<u>We</u> <u>employ</u> four people in this office.

Four <u>people</u> <u>work</u> in this office.

Practice #7   Correcting Subject-Verb Agreement Errors in *There* and *Here* Sentences

These sentences have subject-verb agreement errors.

- Underline the verbs twice.
- Underline the subjects once.
- Then, on a separate piece of paper, rewrite the sentences so that they do not begin with *there* or *here* <u>and</u> so that they have no subject-verb agreement errors. You may add information to the sentences as you revise.
- Use the present tense.

Example: According to my analysis, there is two evil people in this story.

- According to my analysis, there <u>is</u> two evil <u>people</u> in this story.
- According to my analysis, two people are evil in this story.

1. There is different ways of looking at this story.
2. There is two ways for him to respond.
3. Here is the opinions of my classmates.
4. There are one very good reason for choosing this character as the most evil.
5. Here is two of my classmates' essays to read.

Notes

> 6. There are an Internet Web site offering essays for sale.
> 7. There is three ways of organizing these arguments.
> 8. Here is the draft and the revision.
> 9. There is a sample introduction and conclusion on page 32.
> 10. Here is the instructor's comments and my tutor's suggestions.

Practice #8   Creating and Revising *There* and *Here* Sentences

Create the sentences described in the following exercises. Use the present tense. Make sure your subjects and verbs agree.

1. Create a sentence that begins with *here*.
2. Revise the sentence you created in #1 so that it does not begin with *here*.
3. Create a sentence that begins with *there*.
4. Revise the sentence you created in #3 so that it does not begin with *there*.

Avoiding Subject-Verb Agreement Errors

If you frequently make subject-verb agreement errors, you should check all your verbs at the editing stage of your writing process. You may find it easier to see specific sentence errors if you place a piece of paper over your essay and reveal one sentence at a time. Find the verb in each sentence and see if it agrees in number with the subject. After you have checked your own work, you might want to ask a tutor to check your essay and then tell you how many (if any) subject-verb agreement errors he or she sees. Then see if you can find them and fix them on your own. With time and practice, you will find that you make fewer subject-verb agreement errors.

UNDERSTANDING, CORRECTING, AND AVOIDING FRAGMENTS

This section focuses on sentence fragments. You'll work on

- understanding fragments,
- correcting fragments, and
- avoiding fragments.

Understanding Fragments

A fragment is an incomplete sentence. It may be a phrase (a group of words missing a subject, a verb, or both). Or it may be a dependent clause (a group of words with a subject and verb that cannot stand on its own).

The following examples show fragments that are phrases. Following each fragment is a complete sentence. (The verbs are underlined twice and the subjects are underlined once in the complete sentences.)

After her divorce. (This fragment is a prepositional phrase.)

After her divorce, <u>she</u> <u>was</u> unsure about marrying again. (The prepositional phrase now introduces a complete sentence.)

The young, single man hoping to meet someone special. (This fragment is a noun phrase with an adjective phrase attached.)

The young, single <u>man</u> <u>was hoping</u> to meet someone special. (In this revision, the verb is now complete; *was hoping* is the verb. The fragment is now a complete sentence.)

Planning a singles dance party. (This fragment is a participial phrase.)

<u>Planning</u> a singles dance party <u>is</u> a lot of work. (*Planning* is now working as the subject in the complete sentence.)

These fragments are dependent clauses:

When I asked my grandparents about their courtship.
Since he plans on marrying later in life.
Although I hadn't yet met his family.

A dependent clause, as you may remember, has a subject and verb, but it cannot stand by itself because of the subordinator attached to it. Here is a list of subordinators that can create dependent clauses:

For a review of dependent and independent clauses, see pages 163–173 in Chapter 4 and pages 294–300 in Chapter 6.

although	*since*
because	*though*
even though	*when*
if	*while*

The dependent clauses listed above can be joined to independent clauses to create complete sentences, or the subordinators can be removed to change the dependent clauses into independent clauses.

Notes

When I asked my grandparents about their courtship, they were happy to share their memories. (The dependent clause has been joined to an independent clause.)

I asked my grandparents about their courtship. (The subordinator has been removed to create an independent clause.)

Since he plans on marrying later in life, he wants to buy his house in a family-oriented neighborhood. (The dependent clause has been joined to an independent clause.)

He plans on marrying later in life. (The subordinator has been removed to create an independent clause.)

Although I hadn't yet met his family, I was sure I would enjoy spending Christmas at his family's home. (The dependent clause has been joined to an independent clause.)

I hadn't yet met his family. (The subordinator has been removed to create an independent clause.)

Practice #1   Identifying Fragments

Place an "F" next to each sentence that is actually a fragment. Put a "C" next to complete sentences.

Example: If I want to research different marriage ceremonies.

• If I want to research different marriage ceremonies. *F*

1. When I think about the high divorce rate in this country.
2. Because her parents divorced when she was young.
3. Interviewing four recently married couples.
4. Jason will explain the history behind wedding rings.
5. By beginning the essay with historical information.
6. If I were writing that advice column.
7. She wonders about our society's insistence on monogamy.
8. Even though I thought he had a valid point.
9. Since my reading audience may not agree with me.
10. Discussing my essay with my tutor.

Correcting Fragments

There are a number of ways to correct fragments.

A. If you have a fragment that is missing a subject, a verb, or both, you can add the missing element. This fragment has no subject or verb:

>   Speaking to the senior class.

Here the fragment has been revised by adding a verb and allowing the initial fragment to work as the subject.

>   Speaking to the senior class was frightening.

In this revision, a subject and verb have been added and the initial fragment becomes the completing idea.

>   I enjoyed speaking to the senior class.

B. If you have a fragment that is really a dependent (or subordinated) clause, you can get rid of the subordinator. This fragment is really a dependent clause because of the *when*.

>   When the students asked questions.

To correct this fragment, remove the subordinator.

>   The students asked questions.

C. Or if you have a fragment that is really a dependent (or subordinated) clause, you can finish the sentence by adding an independent clause. Here is the fragment again.

>   When the students asked questions.

The fragment becomes a sentence when an independent clause is added.

>   When the students asked questions, I realized that they had been listening closely to my speech.

Practice #2   Correcting Fragments
Correct each fragment below using one of these three different methods.

- Add the missing element(s).
- Get rid of the subordinator.
- Keep the subordinator and complete the idea. (You can add information before or after the subordinated clause.)

Write your new sentences on a separate piece of paper and *use each method at least once.*

Notes

Example: If you are concerned that your ideas don't flow.

• If you are concerned that your ideas don't flow, you should think about using transition words or phrases.

1. When we discussed good dating practices.
2. Because our modern lifestyle has changed.
3. Although my mom and dad were both pretty modern in their views.
4. Reviewing the next reading on advertisements.
5. Since I am not a good artist.
6. One of my friends who draws really well.
7. After three hours of scouring magazines.
8. If you want to work together on the advertisement.
9. Carefully choosing the words.
10. When my classmates reviewed my work.
11. Because I was nervous.
12. Professor Minturn from the history department.

Practice #3   Correcting Fragments in Your Own Writing

Select one of your paragraphs or essays that has fragments. Rewrite the paragraph or essay, correcting your fragments.

Avoiding Fragments

If you are writing fragments in your essays, see if there is a pattern.

• Do you create a fragment when you begin a sentence with an *-ing* word?

• Do you end up with a fragment when you use *because* or other subordinators?

Don't stop using *-ing* words or subordinators. Just begin watching out for them and making sure that you complete your sentences.

When you reach the editing stage of your writing process, review your essay sentence by sentence, keeping an eye out for *-ing* words or subordinators that might create fragments. It is important for you to be able to find and fix your own fragments, but if you need help at first, ask a tutor to check for fragments. Find out how many you have—but not where they are—then find them and fix them on your own. Check your work with your tutor.

UNDERSTANDING, CORRECTING, AND AVOIDING RUN-ONS

This subsection focuses on run-on sentences. You'll work on

- understanding run-ons,
- correcting run-ons, and
- avoiding run-ons.

Understanding Run-Ons

A **run-on sentence** is really two sentences that run together with no punctuation between them. A run-on sentence is sometimes called a **fused sentence.** A writer may accidentally create a run-on when ideas in two sentences are closely related. In this situation, the writer may make the mistake of presenting two sentences as one. The following sentences are actually run-ons:

> I enjoyed Bobryk's essay he included interesting detail and humor. (The first sentence ends after the word *essay.*)

> Wong explains how she felt as a child then she expresses her feelings as an adult. (The first sentence ends after the word *child.* Remember that *then* cannot join sentences. It's a transition.)

> I was surprised to read that women still earn less than men I thought that wasn't true anymore. (The first sentence ends after the word *men.*)

Practice #1   Identifying Run-Ons

Identify which of the following sentences are actually run-ons. When you find a run-on, put an "R" next to the sentences, and use a slash to mark where one sentence ends and the other begins. Mark correct sentences with a "C."

Example: I need to develop a better writing process then my final essays might be stronger.

- I need to develop a better writing process / then my final essays might be stronger. *R*

  1. I should take the first few steps of the writing process slower I misunderstood the last essay assignment.

  2. During the Superbowl, they show the funniest advertisements.

  3. I hate watching network television there are too many commercial interruptions.

Notes

4. My classmates and I got together to study the advertisements.

5. I'm going to take my outline to my tutor my last essay had some organizational problems because I didn't do an outline.

6. He did some great analysis he explained how a modern ad had hidden racist messages.

7. Until our class discussion, I hadn't realized how pervasive cheating is in college.

8. My classmate told everyone to watch a PBS special that is on tonight.

9. The program will show that many college students cheat regularly they say that cheating is the only way they can get into good graduate school programs.

10. If that television program is accurate, Jack isn't the only cheater out there.

Correcting Run-Ons

Consider this run-on:

The man was considered a hero he had stood up to the office bully.

There are four ways to correct run-on sentences.

A. Put a period after the first sentence and capitalize the first letter of the second sentence.

The man was considered a hero. He had stood up to the office bully.

B. Separate the two sentences with a semicolon. (A semicolon is just as strong as a period.)

The man was considered a hero; he had stood up to the office bully.

See pages 163–166 and 406–412 for more information on using coordinators.

C. Join the two sentences with a comma and a coordinating conjunction, or coordinator. (The seven coordinating conjunctions are *for, and, nor, but, or, yet,* and *so.*)

The man was considered a hero, for he had stood up to the office bully.

See pages 169–173, 294–300, and 412–418 for more information on using subordinators.

D. Add a subordinator and change one of the complete sentences to a subordinated clause. (Some subordinators are *if, when, because,*

although, and *since.* If the new subordinated clause comes first, put
a comma after it.)

The man was considered a hero since he had stood up to the
office bully.

Practice #2 Correcting Run-Ons

Correct each run-on two different ways. Write your new sentences
on a separate piece of paper.

Example: I haven't yet picked a hero to write about I'm really interested in three different people.

  a. Correct this run-on using method B.

  b. Correct this run-on using method D.

- a. I haven't yet picked a hero to write about; I'm really interested
  in three different people.
- b. I haven't yet picked a hero to write about since I'm really interested in three different people.

1. Perhaps I should check the resources at the library there might
   be more information available on one of my prospective heroes
   than on the others.

   a. Correct this run-on using method A.
   b. Correct this run-on using method C.

2. The personal hero assignment was cool I learned a lot about my
   dad.

   a. Correct this run-on using method B.
   b. Correct this run-on using method D.

3. Analyzing films can be tough I think I did a good job.

   a. Correct this run-on using method A.
   b. Correct this run-on using method C.

4. Bernie LaPlante is not your typical hero he doesn't look, talk, or
   even act like you expect.

   a. Correct this run-on using method A.
   b. Correct this run-on using method C.

Notes

5. I'm going to interview my uncle for my essay he's a fire investigator.

a. Correct this run-on using method B.

b. Correct this run-on using method D.

6. I saw another movie that deals with heroism I found some more information for my essay.

a. Correct this run-on using method B.

b. Correct this run-on using method D.

See pages 300–308 for more information on using transitions.

Using Transitions to Correct Run-Ons

A *transition* is a word or phrase that creates a meaningful bridge between ideas and sentences. Transitions can be very useful when correcting run-ons. Here are some common transitions:

consequently

however

then

therefore

This sentence is actually a run-on:

Winn's article made me see how television can be harmful to children I plan on making some new restrictions at our house.

The run-on can be corrected using a semicolon and a transition:

Winn's article made me see how television can be harmful to children; therefore, I plan on making some new restrictions at our house.

When using transitions, keep in mind that they are different from coordinating conjunctions or subordinators, which can join sentences with commas. Transitions do not join sentences. You must keep the two sentences separate by using a period or a semicolon.

These sentences show how to use transitions correctly. Notice that each transition is followed by a comma.

I don't have any day care on Mondays. Consequently, I have to let the television baby-sit the kids so I can get my homework done.

I don't have any day care on Mondays; consequently, I have to let the television baby-sit the kids so I can get my homework done.

I realize that television can be an unhealthy influence. However, I don't think that I need to throw the television set away.

I realize that television can be an unhealthy influence; however, I don't think that I need to throw the television set away.

Practice #3   Correcting Run-Ons with Transitions

Correct the following run-ons by using transitions and appropriate punctuation.

- Use each of the following transitions at least once.
  consequently

  however

  then

  therefore
- Use semicolons in some sentences.
- Use periods to separate other sentences.

Example: Obesity runs in my family I'm careful about making sure that my kids get exercise every day.

- Obesity runs in my family; therefore, I'm careful about making sure that my kids get exercise every day.

1. We wanted more time to read, do homework, talk, and play games we stopped watching television during the week.

2. I was impressed by all the research *Sesame Street* does I don't feel so bad about letting my kids watch it.

3. The kids have to do their chores and their homework first they can watch television or play on the computer.

4. I don't like my kids to watch anything other than G-rated movies they really like action movies that have the PG or PG-13 ratings.

5. Stacey has fond memories of watching sitcoms in the evenings with her parents she doesn't want to eliminate television from her children's lives.

6. Each of my kids made a list of their favorite programs we made a schedule so that each child gets to watch two programs a week.

7. Most of the videos on VH1 are too sexy I don't let the kids watch them.

8. My neighbors don't own a television their kids come to our house every afternoon to watch cartoons.

9. I know reality shows are the latest thing I just can't stand them.

10. My kids have to earn B averages at school I'll let them play video games.

> ### Practice #4   Correcting Run-Ons in Your Own Writing
> Select one of your paragraphs or essays that has run-ons. Rewrite the paragraph or essay, correcting your run-ons.

Avoiding Run-Ons

If run-ons are showing up regularly in your essays, look to see if there is a pattern.

- Do you create a run-on when you use transitions?
- Do you create a run-on when ideas seem closely related?

When you reach the editing stage of your writing process, review your essay sentence by sentence, keeping an eye out for transition words and closely related sentences that might be written as run-ons. It is important for you to be able to find and fix your own run-ons, but if you need help at first, ask a tutor to check for run-ons. Find out how many you have— but not where they are. Then find them and fix them on your own. Check your work with your tutor.

UNDERSTANDING, CORRECTING, AND AVOIDING COMMA SPLICES

This section focuses on comma splice errors. You'll work on

- understanding comma splices,
- correcting comma splices, and
- avoiding sentence comma splices.

Understanding Comma Splices

A **comma splice** is two sentences incorrectly joined with a comma. A writer may create a comma splice because the ideas in two sentences are closely related and the writer feels the need to pause. The writer might then insert a comma between the two sentences. However, a comma cannot do the job of a period, and the result is a comma splice error.

These sentences have comma splice errors. The comma in each example is separating complete sentences.

I am grateful for technology, I don't know what I'd do without my computer and cell phone.

My dad is really uncomfortable with high-tech stuff, he hasn't learned how to send or receive e-mail.

You may have heard that every time you "hear" a pause in your writing you should use a comma. This is *not* a good rule to follow. Where you hear a pause and where your reader hears a pause may be quite different, and scattering commas throughout your paper will cause confusion. There are specific reasons for using commas, and you shouldn't use a comma unless you can name a specific comma rule. Here is a brief list of comma rules.

Notes

Punctuation Rule #1 (see pages 115 and 352)
Put commas between items in a series.
• I rely on my cell phone, pager, and e-mail.

Punctuation Rule #2 (see pages 165 and 408)
When you join two independent clauses with a coordinating conjunction, you need to put a comma after the first independent clause.
• I turned off my pager, for I didn't want to be interrupted.

Punctuation Rule #4 (see pages 167, 177, 302, and 355)
Follow an introductory word or phrase with a comma.
• Wanting to save time, Felicia grabbed fast food on the way home.

Punctuation Rule #5 (see pages 170, 296, and 413)
When you begin a sentence with a subordinated or dependent clause, you must put a comma after the subordinated (or dependent) clause.
• When she got her cell phone bill, she nearly fainted.

Punctuation Rule #6 (see pages 171, 296, and 413)
If the subordinated clause comes after the independent clause, you do **not** *need a comma.*
• She nearly fainted when she got her cell phone bill.

Punctuation Rule #7 (see page 304)
If you interrupt a single sentence with a transition word, you must put a comma before and after the transition word.
• Her brother, however, was not surprised.

Practice #1   Identifying Comma Splices

Identify which of the following sentences have comma splice errors.

• When you find a comma splice, put "CS" next to the sentence, put a period where the comma is, and begin the second sentence with a capital letter.

• If the sentence is correct, put a "C" next to the sentence.

Notes

> *Note:* A few of the following sentences use commas correctly. Refer to the comma rules listed earlier to check how the commas are used.
>
> Example: I was surprised by the Macionis article, I hadn't thought about the negative sides to modernization.
>
> • I was surprised by the Macionis article. I hadn't thought about the negative sides to modernization. *CS*
>
> 1. The technology inventory assignment was interesting, we came up with a long list of high-tech gadgets.
> 2. Sharon hadn't ever been on the Internet, so she asked the librarian for help.
> 3. My roommate lives on frozen dinners, she doesn't ever eat fresh food.
> 4. Frozen dinners are convenient, but they cost a lot more than fresh ingredients.
> 5. Worried that the babysitter might be mistreating their child, the parents installed a hidden camera.
> 6. The company told its employees that they were being watched, the state law required the company to do so.
> 7. The character in the movie burned his own fingers on purpose, he wanted to eliminate his fingerprints.
> 8. Because his DNA revealed certain physical defects, the character in the book assumed another person's identity.
> 9. I don't like having surveillance cameras on our streets, I feel my privacy has been invaded.
> 10. Security is a priority at all airports, the government is trying to prevent terrorist attacks.

Correcting Comma Splices

There are four ways to correct comma splice errors. (Notice that these are the same methods you can use to correct run-ons.) Study this comma splice and methods A–D for correcting the comma splice:

> George Orwell's book *1984* was interesting to read, many of the surveillance tools Orwell mentions are now being used.

A. Put a period after the first sentence and capitalize the first letter of the second sentence.

> George Orwell's book *1984* was interesting to read. Many of the surveillance tools Orwell mentions are now being used.

B. Separate the two sentences with a semicolon. (A semicolon is just as strong as a period.)

> George Orwell's book *1984* was interesting to read; many of the surveillance tools Orwell mentions are now being used.

C. Join the two sentences with a comma and a coordinating conjunction, or coordinator. (The seven coordinating conjunctions are *for, and, nor, but, or, yet,* and *so*.)

See pages 163–166 and 406–412 for more information on using coordinators.

> George Orwell's book *1984* was interesting to read, for many of the surveillance tools Orwell mentions are now being used.

D. Add a subordinator and change one of the complete sentences to a subordinated clause. (Some subordinators are *if, when, because, although,* and *since.* If the new subordinated clause comes first, put a comma after it.)

See pages 169–173, 294–300, and 412–418 for more information on using subordinators.

> George Orwell's book *1984* was interesting to read because many of the surveillance tools Orwell mentions are now being used.

Practice #2   Correcting Comma Splices

Correct each comma splice two different ways. Write your new sentences on a separate piece of paper.

Example: I enjoy writing songs, I express my feelings and comment on current political issues.

  a. Correct this comma splice using method B.

  b. Correct this comma splice using method D.

- a. I enjoy writing songs; I express my feelings and comment on current political issues.

- b. I enjoy writing songs because I express my feelings and comment on current political issues.

  1. I was surprised that her lyrics were so complex, I still didn't like the CD.

      a. Correct this comma splice using method A.
      b. Correct this comma splice using method C.

2. The lyrics were perfect for this assignment, their complexity would make the analysis interesting.

   a. Correct this comma splice using method B.
   b. Correct this comma splice using method D.

3. Steven's introduction wasn't clear, he didn't have enough detail.

   a. Correct this comma splice using method A.
   b. Correct this comma splice using method C.

4. I wanted to hear the song before writing my draft, I thought listening to it might help me understand it better.

   a. Correct this comma splice using method B.
   b. Correct this comma splice using method D.

5. I had always thought that I hated poetry, I found Frost's poem interesting.

   a. Correct this comma splice using method A.
   b. Correct this comma splice using method C.

6. I was surprised, my classmates thought I did a great job summarizing the lyrics.

   a. Correct this comma splice using method B.
   b. Correct this comma splice using method D.

Using Transitions to Correct Comma Splices

If you use method A or B to correct a comma splice, you must use a period or a semicolon to separate complete sentences. Occasionally, you may want to use a transition with these methods. (You cannot use these transitions with just a comma to join complete sentences.)

Here are some common transitions:

consequently	*then*
however	*therefore*

The first sentence in this group has a comma splice error. The second and third sentences show how a transition can be used to correct the comma splice error.

I needed evidence to back up my point, I carefully chose some quotes from the song lyric.

I needed evidence to back up my point; consequently, I carefully chose some quotes from the song lyric.

I needed evidence to back up my point. Consequently, I carefully chose some quotes from the song lyric.

As with the previous group of sentences, the first one here has a comma splice error. The second and third sentences show how a transition can be used to correct the comma splice error.

I don't think I'll ever be a professional writer, I feel confident that I can write better reports at work now.

I don't think I'll ever be a professional writer; however, I feel confident that I can write better reports at work now.

I don't think I'll ever be a professional writer. However, I feel confident that I can write better reports at work now.

Practice #3   Correcting Comma Splices with Transitions

The following sentences have comma splice errors. On a separate piece of paper, correct them using transitions.

- Choose transitions from this list:
  consequently   *then*
  however   *therefore*
- Use semicolons in some sentences.
- Use periods to separate other sentences.

Example: Ms. Stanley was pleased with Michael's improved writing skills, she offered him the promotion.

- Ms. Stanley was pleased with Michael's improved writing skills; therefore, she offered him the promotion.

1. I feel more confident about my speaking skills, I'm still not crazy about public speaking.
2. Jordan worked in the manufacturing department, he moved over to marketing.
3. Jenny knew that she could get her essays done faster if she had a computer, she used her Christmas bonus to buy one.
4. The new software is complicated, I need to take a training class.
5. I need to finish this book about Jesse Ventura, I want to start this novel called *Winter Prey*.

Notes

6. My classmate said the essay "The Great Unwatched" was good, I decided to read it.

7. I knew she had a wonderful personal library, I asked if I could borrow a couple of books.

8. My grandmother and I had a great time discussing her heroic uncle, we've decided to write some more stories about family members.

9. Caleb didn't have much faith in himself, he bought an essay on the Internet.

10. The editor at the school paper offered me a job, I already have two jobs!

Practice #4   Correcting Comma Splices in Your Own Writing

Select one of your paragraphs or essays that has comma splices. Rewrite the paragraph or essay, correcting your comma splices.

Avoiding Comma Splices

If comma splices are showing up regularly in your essays, look to see if there is a pattern.

• Do you create a comma splice when you use transitions?

• Do you create a comma splice when ideas seem closely related?

When you reach the editing stage of your writing process, review your essay sentence by sentence, keeping an eye out for transition words and closely related sentences that might lead you to create comma splices. Remember that there are specific rules for using commas. See page 527 and pages 538–539 for a review of those rules.

It is important for you to be able to find and fix your own comma splices, but if you need help at first, ask a tutor to check for comma splices. Find out how many you have—but not where they are. Then find them and fix them on your own. Check your work with your tutor.

Using Connections *Online with* **mywritinglab**

For more practice with understanding, correcting, and avoiding sentence errors, log onto www.mywritinglab.com to access the online resources for *Connections,* Third Edition.

Easy Reference Rules and Style Tips

This section of Connections *offers rules that you can easily and quickly refer to when necessary.*

- The right word
- Capitalization
- Punctuation rules
- Style tips

THE RIGHT WORD

Sometimes words that are close in sound or meaning can be confusing. Yet using the right word in an essay or report can mean the difference between being understood or misunderstood. This section includes a list of commonly confused words (like *to, too,* and *two*) and their basic meanings. For additional information on these words, consult your dictionary.

a, an   Use **a** before words beginning with any consonant sound even if the word actually starts with a vowel: *a horse, a unicorn, a Cadillac.* Use **an** before words beginning with any vowel sound even if the word actually starts with a consonant: *an honor, an act, an evergreen tree.*

accept, except   **Accept** is a verb meaning to receive. *Hal accepted the invitation.* **Except** means but. *Everyone ate ice cream except Cheshire.*

advice, advise   **Advice,** a noun, is an opinion about a problem or issue. *His advice helped me make a decision about which car to buy.* **Advise** is a verb meaning to suggest. *He advised me to wait until interest rates are lower.*

advise, advice   See **advice, advise.**

affect, effect   **Affect,** a verb, means to have an influence on. *Studies suggest that TV violence affects behavior.* **Effect,** as a noun, means a result. *The negative effects of cigarette smoking have been documented.*

are, hour, our   **Are,** a verb, is the plural form of *to be. We are a team.* **Hour** refers to time. *The clock struck on the hour.* **Our** is the possessive form of *we. Our team won the tournament.*

effect, affect   See **affect, effect.**

except, accept   See **accept, except.**

hear, here   **Hear** means to be able to listen. *I hear knocking at the door.* **Here** means present at this time or location. *I arrived here this morning.*

here, hear   See **hear, here.**

hour, our, are   See **are, hour, our.**

its, it's   Its is the possessive form of *it*. *The canary chirped its song.* **It's** is a contraction meaning it is. *It's time to go.*

know, no   **Know,** a verb, means to understand. *I know how to study well.* **No** means not so. *No, I'm not eating now.*

no, know   See **know, no.**

one, own, won   **One** means a single thing. **Own,** a verb, means to possess. *Chandra owned one cat.* **Won** is the past tense of the verb *win. We won the tennis tournament.*

our, are, hour   See **are, hour, our.**

own, won, one   See **one, own, won.**

peace, piece   **Peace,** a noun, means the absence of disagreement. *In times of peace, the people live in harmony.* **Piece** refers to a portion of something. *I'll order a piece of pie.*

piece, peace   See **peace, piece.**

than, then   **Than** is used to indicate an unequal comparison between two things. *The A's maintained a better record than the Giants.* **Then** refers to a time in the past. *Back then, most people grew their own vegetables.* **Then** also means the next thing. *First is the polo competition; then, the gymnasts will perform.*

their, there, they're   **Their** is the possessive form of *they. Their faces turned in unison.* **There** refers to location. *The lid is there on the counter.* **There** can also introduce a sentence. *There are 10,000 employees in that company.* **They're** is a contraction for *they are. They're our favorite guests.*

then, than   See **than, then.**

there, they're, their   See **their, there, they're.**

they're, their, there   See **their, there, they're.**

threw, through   **Threw** is the past tense form of the verb *throw*. *He threw the baseball.* **Through** refers to something passing from one side to the other. *The baseball crashed through the window.*

through, threw   See **threw, through.**

to, too, two   **To** means toward. *I traveled to Paris to see the Mona Lisa.* It is also part of an infinitive. *They want to eat, then to sleep.* **Too** means also. *My husband went, too.* **Too** also means excessive. *There was too much noise for me to hear well.* **Two** is the number. *We discovered that travel for two is cheaper than travel for one.*

too, two, to   See **to, too, two.**

two, to, too   See **to, too, two.**

your, you're   **Your** is the possessive form of *you*. *Your heroism is inspiring.* **You're** is a contraction of *you are*. *You're going to receive a promotion.*

you're, your   See **your, you're.**

wear, where   **Wear** is a verb meaning to put on something. *Sandra wears her baseball cap.* **Where** means at or in what place. *Where is the morning newspaper?*

weather, whether   **Weather,** a noun, refers to atmospheric conditions. *The weather changed from rain to snow.* **Whether** suggests that a decision will be made between two alternatives. *Soleil had to decide whether or not to attend the conference.*

whether, weather   See **weather, whether.**

which, witch   **Which** refers to choice. *Which of these would you prefer?* A **witch** is a female sorcerer. *The witch cast a spell.*

when, win   **When** refers to time. *When will we take our vacation?* **Win,** as a verb, means to achieve victory. *We win every year.* As a noun, **win** is the victory. *Andre enjoyed a spectacular win.*

win, when   See **when, win.**

where, wear   See **wear, where.**

witch, which   See **which, witch.**

won, one, own   See **one, own, won.**

CAPITALIZATION

Capitalize proper nouns (naming *specific* people, places, or things).

San Francisco	Texas
Whitney Houston	*New York Times*

(But not **common nouns,** naming nonspecific people, places, things, or ideas: songwriter, newspaper, book, state, class.)

Capitalize the days of the week, months, and holidays.

Monday   November   Thanksgiving

Capitalize the first word in a sentence.

She traveled to Philadelphia by train.

Capitalize the first word of a quoted sentence.

The instructor said, "Essays are due Thursday."

Capitalize *specific* courses

Art 101   Biology 1A

(But not subject areas: history, geography.)

Capitalize *I* when used as a personal pronoun.

My writing improved as I learned to revise.

Capitalize a specific language, nationality, and ethnicity.

Native American	Asian American	Swiss
French	Hispanic	African American

Capitalize the names of celestial bodies.

Mars   Milky Way

Capitalize the first and last words and other significant words in titles of books, films, movies, television series, compact discs, magazines, and journals.

The Color Purple	*South Park*	*A Short History of the World*
GQ	*Vogue*	*The Bridges of Madison County*

(Don't capitalize *a, an, the,* or prepositions unless they are the first or last word in a title.)

Notes **Capitalize names of wars and historical events.**

the Vietnam War the American Revolution

Capitalize names of government agencies, corporations, and institutions.

Bank of America Microsoft

Department of Defense Stanford University

Do not capitalize the seasons: summer, fall, winter, spring.

Do not capitalize centuries: the twenty-first century.

PUNCTUATION RULES

Punctuation Rule #1 (See pages 115 and 352.)

Put commas between items in a series.

Example:

The exhausted, confused, and frustrated writer leaned back in his chair.
(The comma before the *and* is optional with a list like this.)

Punctuation Rule #2 (See pages 165 and 408.)

When you join two independent clauses with a coordinating conjunction, you need to put a comma after the first independent clause.

Example:

*At midnight he finally remembered his thrilling opening line, **and** he began to type.*

Punctuation Rule #3 (See pages 167 and 302.)

You may use a semicolon to separate two complete sentences.

Example:

He needed to find the words now; his editor was waiting for his work.

Punctuation Rule #4 (See pages 167, 177, 302, and 355.)

Follow an introductory word or phrase with a comma.

Example:

Sitting at his computer, he brainstormed ideas.

Note: Punctuation Rules 3 and 4 are both applied when you join two complete sentences with a semicolon and transition.

He came up with three promising topics; **then,** *he focused on a single idea.*

Punctuation Rule #5 (See pages 170, 296, and 413.)

When you begin a sentence with a subordinated or dependent clause, you must put a comma after the subordinated (or dependent) clause.

Example:
If he could just remember that great opening line, the rest would flow.

Punctuation Rule #6 (See pages 171, 296, and 413.)

If the subordinated clause comes after the independent clause, you do not *need a comma.*

Example:
The rest would flow **if he could just remember that great opening line.**

Punctuation Rule #7 (See page 304.)

If you interrupt a single sentence with a transition word, you must put a comma before and after the transition word.

Example:
For two long hours, ***however,*** *no words came to his mind.*

STYLE TIPS

Style Tip #1 (See page 120.)

Use strong subjects and verbs whenever possible and place them carefully in your sentences.

Style Tip #2 (See pages 122, 234, and 308.)

Don't use more words than needed.

Notes

Style Tip #3 (See pages 179, 234, and 308.)

Add variety to your sentence structure.

Style Tip #4 (See pages 179, 234, and 308.)

Provide the necessary connections between ideas and show how ideas relate to one another.

Style Tip #5 (See page 364.)

Look for opportunities to add details, descriptions, and information to your sentences.

Style Tip #6 (See page 418.)

Enhance clarity by avoiding spelling, punctuation, capitalization, and usage errors.

Using Connections *Online with* **mywritinglab**

For more practice with easy reference rules and style tips, log onto www.mywritinglab.com to access the online resources for *Connections,* Third Edition.

Glossary

action verb: a word that expresses activity or movement (31).

activities: work that puts into practice new writing concepts or ideas (xxxiv).

adjectives: words that describe nouns (451).

adverbs: words that describe verbs, adjectives, other adverbs, and whole groups of words (359).

analyze: to break down a complex concept into smaller, less complex pieces and then study the pieces (369).

antecedent: the noun that a pronoun refers to (220).

anticipate: a step in the reading process when the reader guesses what the reading will be about based on his or her preview of the reading material. Readers also anticipate (or guess what will come next) while reading the entire piece for the first time (83).

apostrophe: a punctuation mark used to show possession. An apostrophe can also be used in a contraction (two words joined as one) (481).

audience: any person or persons a writer is communicating to (12).

auditory learner: a person who learns best when listening to the material (456).

base form: the most basic form of the verb, it is in the present tense and has no special endings. This is the form you would look up in the dictionary (75).

body: the middle section of an essay or paragraph that supports the claim established in the introduction or topic sentence (40).

body paragraphs: paragraphs that appear after the introduction of an essay and before the conclusion. They contain information that helps support the claim established in the introduction (43).

brainstorming: exploring ideas by writing freely on a topic without concern for grammatical correctness or form (141).

citing your sources: giving credit to the original source of information (492).

clause: a group of words with a subject and verb (163).

coherence: the quality of being clear and connected. In a coherent essay, all the ideas clearly connect to each other and to the main point (151).

cohesion: unity; in a cohesive essay, ideas are unified (265).

comma splice: an error that is created when two complete sentences are joined as one with only a comma to separate them (526).

command sentence: a sentence that gives someone work to do. This type of sentence has the implied subject *you* (116).

common noun: a nonspecific person, place, thing, or idea (537).

complete sentence: a group of words containing a subject and a verb and expressing a complete idea; also known as an independent clause (28).

con argument: an argument against something (263).

concession: an instance in which the writer acknowledges the opponent's position (297).

conclusion: the final paragraph in a piece of writing. It sums up the most important points, restates the writer's claim, and draws the piece to an end (40).

context: the surrounding words, sentences, and ideas in which another word/idea appears (91).

contraction: a word with an apostrophe indicating where letters have been left out (481).

coordinating conjunction: a word that can be used to join independent sentences: *for, and, nor, but, or, yet, so* (164).

dependent clause: a group of words with a subject and verb that cannot stand alone. Also known as a subordinated clause (169).

development: the process of moving from a basic idea to a fully expressive, well-supported main idea that communicates to a specific audience for a specific purpose (238).

drafting: the stage of the writing process in which the writer produces a rough, but complete, version of an essay (14).

editing: the stage of the writing process in which the writer works on improving sentence structure, usage, punctuation, and spelling. Editing usually occurs toward the end of the writing process and is also known as the "polishing" stage (14).

embed: to insert phrases into sentences to add meaning (351).

essay: an organized, multiparagraph piece of writing in which the writer focuses on and develops a particular issue or theme for a specific audience and purpose (40).

essay assignment: the writing assignment instructions; also known as the essay or writing prompt (142).

essay prompt: the essay assignment instructions (142).

excerpt: a piece of a longer reading (46).

FANBOYS: an acronym for the seven coordinating conjunctions (164).

figurative language: language that compares two things, helping to paint an image in the reader's mind (373).

focused essay: an essay with a clear thesis and body paragraphs that directly support the thesis (187).

focused paragraph: a paragraph with a clear topic sentence and information that connects directly to the topic sentence (186).

fragment: an incomplete sentence (169).

freewriting: a form of brainstorming in which writers allow their thoughts about the writing assignment or topic to flow freely onto the page (141).

fused sentence: two sentences incorrectly joined as one with no punctuation separating them; also known as a run-on sentence (521).

gerund: an *-ing* word that is working as a noun (112).

***have* form:** a verb form that often ends in *-ed*, but not always. This verb form is also called the past participle form (356).

helping verbs: verbs that work with other words to create complete verbs (35).

homophones: words that sound alike but have different spellings and meanings (478).

idiom: an expression that may not make sense if it is read literally or translated word for word (474).

implied subject: a subject that is not stated. Command sentences have the implied subject *you* (116).

imposters: words that look like verbs but really aren't (76).

indefinite pronouns: pronouns that refer to non-specific people, places, or things (219).

independent clause: a group of words that can stand alone as a sentence (163).

infer: to draw a conclusion based on evidence (369).

infinitive: a phrase consisting of *to* + a verb. An infinitive is not a verb (77).

introduction: the opening paragraph(s) of a piece of writing. It explains what the piece will be about and may suggest the order and direction of the body paragraphs that follow (39).

irregular verbs: verbs that change form in unpredictable ways (498).

journals: "freewriting zones." They are an opportunity to explore ideas on paper without fear of judgment (xxxiii).

kernel sentence: the subject and predicate of a simple sentence (350).

kinesthetic learner: a person who learns best when involving the body in the learning process (456).

learning style: a method by which an individual learns best (456).

linking verb: a verb that connects or links the subject to information in the sentence (32).

making a concession: acknowledging the opponent's position (297).

meter: a specific, formal rhythmic pattern used in poetry (373).

modifier: a word that describes another word (355).

noun: a word that names a person, place, thing, or idea (111).

outline: a formal and thorough list of all major points and supporting points in an essay, or a quick list of just the major points (142).

outside information: any fact or idea that someone else came up with (489).

outside source: a person or publication that supplies you with information (489).

paragraph: a single unit of writing that makes a specific point (14).

parallel structure: having two or more items in a sentence arranged in a similar grammatical form (227).

paraphrase: to restate someone else's writing or speech in your own words (10).

participial phrase: a group of words consisting of a present or past participle and the words attached to that participle. A participial phrase can include prepositional phrases (175).

PARTS: the five stages of the reading process—preview, anticipate, read and reread, think critically, summarize (83).

passive voice: a term that describes a sentence structure in which the intended subject receives rather than performs the action (125).

past participle form: a verb form that often ends in *-ed,* but not always. This verb form is also called the *have* form (497).

past perfect tense: a verb tense formed by using *had* plus the verb in the *have* form. This tense tells the reader that the action took place before another time or action in the past (498).

past tense form: a verb tense indicating past action or being; it usually ends in *-ed* (497).

patterns of organization: methods for arranging ideas in a paragraph or essay (313).

personal narrative: a piece of writing in which an individual recounts an event or series of events from his or her life, usually to make a point or to help the reader better understand an issue (94).

personal pronouns: pronouns that refer to specific people, places, things, or ideas (484).

phrase: a group of words that is missing a subject, a verb, or both (173).

plagiarism: using information that belongs to someone else without giving that person credit (491).

plural: more than one (508).

possessive: a word that shows ownership (482).

predicate: in a sentence, the verb and all the words that come after the verb (28).

predrafting: the part of the writing process in which the writer discusses, reads, thinks critically, plans, and organizes (14).

prepositional phrase: a group of words consisting of a preposition and its object (78).

present participles: words ending in -*ing* (76).

present perfect tense: a verb tense formed by using *has* or *have* plus the verb in the *have* form. This tense tells the reader one of two things: the action took place in the past and continues to take place in the present, or the action took place at a nonspecific time in the past (497).

pro argument: an argument in favor of something (263).

process package: a collection of work—including class notes, all brainstorming, an outline, a draft, and more (130).

pronoun: a word that can be used instead of a noun in a sentence (111).

proper noun: a specific name, title, or organization (482).

purpose: the author's reason for writing (12).

questions for development: a set of questions used by writers and journalists to "flesh out" ideas (242).

quotation: an exact, word-for-word passage or statement taken from another speaker or writer (23).

reading assignments: assignments that help you engage in the steps of the reading process (xxxiv).

reading process: a series of stages readers go through to help them comprehend (understand) and retain (remember) what they have read. There are five stages in this process: preview, anticipate, read and reread, think critically about, summarize (83).

regular verbs: verbs that change tense in predictable ways (498).

response: a written, thoughtful reaction to what you have read; a commentary on the most important or intriguing ideas presented in a piece (89).

revising: the part of the writing process in which the writer evaluates his or her essay and then rewrites portions to strengthen focus, organization, or development (14).

rough draft: an early, imperfect version of a piece of writing (14).

run-on sentence: two sentences incorrectly joined as one with no punctuation separating them; also known as a fused sentence (521).

sentence work: practice in developing and refining sentences (27).

sibilant sound: a hissing sound (479).

stanzas: paragraphs in music lyrics and poems (99).

subject: the person, place, thing, or idea that is performing the action expressed by the verb or that is being described by the verb (28).

subject-verb agreement error: a sentence error that occurs when the subject and verb in a sentence do not "agree" in number (507).

subordinated clause: a group of words with a subject and verb that cannot stand alone; also known as a dependent clause (169).

subordinators: words that can attach to independent clauses and make them dependent (or subordinated) clauses (169).

summarize: restate the main ideas of a piece of writing in your own words; also the last stage of the reading process (84).

summary: a concise retelling of the main points of a longer piece of writing (59).

synonyms: words that have similar meanings (219).

tactile learner: a person who learns best when taking notes (456).

test of time: the act of placing *yesterday, today,* or *tomorrow* at the beginning of a sentence to see which word (or words) must change tense. The word that changes is the verb (75).

thesis statement: the main idea of an essay, chapter, or article (42).

think critically: to look beyond the surface of an issue or action and examine the purpose or motivation behind it; also, the fourth stage of the reading process, in which readers discuss important points with classmates or answer questions as they "make sense" out of their reading (11).

topic sentence: general statement that introduces the main idea of a paragraph (14).

transitions: words or phrases that help show relationships between ideas and add coherence to paragraphs or essays (151).

verb: the word that expresses the action in the sentence or links the subject to descriptive information. It tells when the action (or connecting) is taking place (28).

verb tense: tells the reader when the action (or linking) takes place (74).

visual learner: a person who learns best by seeing the material (456).

writing process: the steps a writer takes when completing a writing assignment (14).

writing-reading-critical thinking connection: the act of using your writing, reading, and critical thinking skills to understand an issue and communicate your ideas about the issue (3).

Credits

TEXT CREDITS

CHAPTER 1

Pages 7–10: From Kenneth W. Davis, *The McGraw-Hill 36-Hour Course in Business Writing and Communication,* pp. 6–8. Copyright © 2005 by Kenneth W. Davis. Reproduced with permission of The McGraw-Hill Companies.

Pages 19–22: From Kenneth W. Davis, *The McGraw-Hill 36-Hour Course in Business Writing and Communication,* pp. 2–5. Copyright © 2005 by Kenneth W. Davis. Reproduced with permission of The McGraw-Hill Companies.

CHAPTER 2

Pages 41–42: Maggie Bandur, "Women Play the Roles Men Want to See," *The Daily Northwestern,* January 23, 1996. By permission of The Daily Northwestern at Northwestern University, Evanston, IL.

Pages 46–48: Alex Thio, "Preparing for Marriage" from *Sociology: A Brief Introduction,* 3rd ed. Copyright © 1997 by Longman Publishers. Reprinted by permission of Addison-Wesley Educational Publishers, Inc.

Pages 52–55: Jeffrey Marx, "He Turns Boys Into Men." © 2004 Jeffrey Marx. Initially published in *Parade Magazine,* August 29, 2004. All rights reserved.

Pages 60–61: From James M. Henslin, *Essentials of Sociology: A Down-to-Earth Approach,* 7th edition. Published by Allyn and Bacon, Boston, MA. Copyright © 2007 by Pearson Education. Reprinted by permission of the publisher.

Page 64: James Kirby Martin, Randy Roberts, Steven Mintz, Linda O. McMurry, and James H. Jones, from "The Modern Family" from *America and Its People,* 2nd ed. Copyright © 1993 by HarperCollins College Publishers. Reprinted by permission of Addison-Wesley Educational Publishers, Inc.

CHAPTER 3

Pages 85–87: Elizabeth Wong, "The Struggle to Be an All-American Girl," *Los Angeles Times,* September 7, 1980. By permission of the author, www.elizabethwong.net.

Page 90: Copyright © 2006 by Houghton Mifflin Company. Reproduced by permission from *The American Heritage Dictionary of the English Language,* Fourth Edition.

Page 91: William E. Thompson and Joseph V. Hickey, "Feminism: The Struggle for Gender Equality" from *Society in Focus: The Essentials.* New York: Harper-Collins College Publishers, 1996.

Pages 92–93: Kavita Menon, "In India, Men Challenge a Matrilineal Society," *Ms.* Magazine, September/October 1998.

Pages 95–97: Jim Bobryk, "Navigating My Eerie Landscape Alone." From *Newsweek,* March 18, 1999. © 1999 Newsweek, Inc. All rights reserved. Used by permission and protected by the Copyright Laws of the United States. The printing, copying, redistribution, or retransmission of the Material without express written permission is prohibited.

Page 100: Lorna Dee Cervantes, "Refugee Ship." Reprinted with permission from the publisher of *A Decade of Hispanic Literature: An Anniversary Anthology.* (Houston: Arte Público Press–University of Houston, 1982).

Pages 102–103: James Kirby Martin, Randy Roberts, Steven Mintz, Linda O. McMurry, and James H. Jones, from *America and Its People,* 2nd ed. Copyright © 1993 by HarperCollins College Publishers. Reprinted by permission of Addison-Wesley Educational Publishers, Inc.

CHAPTER 4

Pages 149–150: John J. Macionis, from *Sociology,* 5th ed., p. 140. Copyright © 1995 by Prentice-Hall, Inc. Reprinted by permission of Pearson Education, Inc., Upper Saddle River, NJ.

Pages 155–156: "The Most Evil Character," author unknown. Every attempt has been made to identify an author or original source. If the author/source can be identified, please contact the publisher listed on the title page of this text.

CHAPTER 5

Pages 204–206: Paul Rogat Loeb, "Civil Rights Movement Was the Sum of Many People," *Sacramento Bee,* January 16, 2000. Reprinted by permission of the author.

Pages 207–211: Carol Einstein, from *Einstein's Who, What, and Where,* Book 3. Cambridge, MA: Educators Publishing Service, 2005. Copyright © 2005 by Carol Einstein. Reprinted by permission of the author.

CHAPTER 6

Page 239: Joshua Meyrowitz, from "Television: The Shared Arena," *The World & I,* July 1990, pp. 465–481. © 1990 by Joshua Meyrowitz. Reprinted with permission of the author.

Page 240: Peter Christenson and Maria Ivancin, *The "Reality" of Health: Reality Television and the Public Health* (#7567), The Henry J. Kaiser Family Foundation, October 2006, pp. 10–11. This information was reprinted with permission from the Henry J. Kaiser Family Foundation. The Kaiser Family Foundation, based in Menlo Park, California, is a nonprofit, private operating foundation focusing on the major health care issues facing the nation and is not associated with Kaiser Permanente or Kaiser Industries.

Pages 240–241: David R. Croteau and William Hoynes, *Media/Society: Industries, Images, and Audiences,* 3rd ed. Thousand Oaks, CA: Pine Forge Press, 2003, p. 5.

Pages 244–246: Ulla G. Foehr, *Media Multitasking Among American Youth: Prevalence, Predictors and Pairings* (#7592), The Henry J. Kaiser Family Foundation, December 2006, pp. 9–10. This information was reprinted with permission from the Henry J. Kaiser Family Foundation. The Kaiser Family Foundation, based in Menlo Park, California, is a nonprofit, private operating foundation focusing on the major health care issues facing the nation and is not associated with Kaiser Permanente or Kaiser Industries.

Pages 249–258: Marie Winn, "The Trouble with Television," from *Unplugging the Plug-In Drug* by Marie Winn, copyright © 1987 by Marie Winn. Used by permission of Viking Penguin, a division of Penguin Group (USA) Inc.

Pages 269–275: Daniel McGinn, "Guilt Free TV." From *Newsweek,* November 11, 2002. © 2002 Newsweek, Inc. All rights reserved. Used by permission and protected by the Copyright Laws of the United States. The printing, copying, redistribution, or retransmission of the Material without express written permission is prohibited.

Pages 276–278: Karen Springen, "Why We Tuned Out." From *Newsweek,* November 11, 2002. © 2002 Newsweek, Inc. All rights reserved. Used by permission and protected by the Copyright Laws of the United States. The printing, copying, redistribution, or retransmission of the Material without express written permission is prohibited.

Pages 286–288: Amy Sara Clark, "This Is Your Brain Online," CBSNews.com, June 14, 2006. © MMVI, CBS Broadcasting Inc. All rights reserved. Reprinted with permission. CBS News Archives.

CHAPTER 7

Pages 317–318: Megan Rainey, "The USA Patriot Act." Reprinted by permission of the author.

Pages 324–331: Ivan Amato, "Big Brother Logs On," *Technology Review,* September 2001, pp. 58–63. Copyright 2001 by MIT Technology Review. Reproduced with permission of MIT Technology Review in the format Textbook via Copyright Clearance Center.

Pages 339–341: George Orwell, excerpt from *Nineteen Eighty-Four* by George Orwell, copyright 1949 by Harcourt, Inc. and renewed 1977 by Sonia Brownell Orwell, reprinted by permission of the publisher.

Pages 342–344: William Safire, "The Great Unwatched," *The New York Times,* February 18, 2002, Op-ed. Copyright

© 2002 by The New York Times Co. Reprinted with permission.

CHAPTER 8

Page 371: Recording Industry Association of America. From 2006 Consumer Profile, www.riaa.com.

Pages 374–375: Langston Hughes, "Evenin' Air Blues," from *The Collected Poems of Langston Hughes* by Langston Hughes, edited by Arnold Rampersad with David Roessel, Associate Editor, copyright © 1994 by The Estate of Langston Hughes. Used by permission of Alfred A. Knopf, a division of Random House, Inc.

Pages 379–380: John Lennon, "Imagine." Words and Music by John Lennon. © 1971 (Renewed 1999) LENONO.MUSIC. All Rights Controlled and Administered by EMI BLACKWOOD MUSIC INC. All Rights Reserved. International Copyright Secured. Used by Permission.

Pages 381–382: "Old 8 × 10." Words and music by Joe Chambers and Larry Jenkins. Copyright © 1988 Universal-MCA Music Publishing, Inc., a division of Universal Studios, Inc. (ASCAP) International copyright secured. All rights reserved. By permission of Universal Music Publishing Group.

Pages 383–385: Emily Robison, Martie Maguire, Natalie Maines, and Neil Finn, "Silent House." Words and Music by Neil Finn, Emily Robison, Martie Maguire, and Natalie Maines. Copyright © 2006 Roundhead Music and Woolly Puddin' Music. All Rights for Roundhead Music Administered by Chrysalis Songs. All Rights Reserved. Used by Permission.

Pages 386–387: Melissa Etheridge, "Silent Legacy." Words and Music by Melissa Etheridge. Copyright © 1993 MLE Music (ASCAP). All Rights Reserved. Used by Permission.

Page 392: C. Hugh Holman and William Harmon, *A Handbook to Literature,* 5th ed. New York: Macmillan, 1986.

Pages 393–394: Paul Laurence Dunbar, "Sympathy" from *Lyrics of the Hearthside.* New York: Dodd, Mead, and Co., 1899.

Pages 394–395: Marge Piercy, "A Work of Artifice," copyright © 1970 by Marge Piercy, from *Circles on the Water* by Marge Piercy. Used by permission of Alfred A. Knopf, a division of Random House, Inc.

Page 396: Robert Frost, "The Road Not Taken" from *Mountain Interval.* New York: Henry Holt, 1916.

Pages 397–398: Emily Dickinson, "Wild Nights—Wild Nights!" Reprinted by permission of the publishers and the Trustees of Amherst College from *The Poems of Emily Dickinson,* Thomas H. Johnson, ed., Cambridge, Mass.: The Belknap Press of Harvard University Press, Copyright © 1951, 1955, 1979, 1983 by the President and Fellows of Harvard College.

Pages 398–399: Edgar Allan Poe, "Annabel Lee." First published in 1849.

Index